Keeping Salvation Ethical

Studies in
Anabaptist and Mennonite History
No. 35

Keeping Salvation Ethical

J. Denny Weaver

Studies in Anabaptist and Mennonite History

Edited by Cornelius J. Dyck, Leonard Gross, Beulah Stauffer Hostetler, Albert N. Keim, Walter Klaassen, John S. Oyer, John D. Roth, Steve Reschly, and Editor-in-Chief Theron F. Schlabach.

Published by Herald Press, Scottdale, Pennsylvania, and Waterloo, Ontario, in cooperation with Mennonite Historical Society, Goshen, Indiana. The Society is primarily responsible for the content of the studies, and Herald Press for their publication.

°Out of print but available in microfilm, photocopies, or remainders.

Keeping Salvation Ethical

Mennonite and Amish
Atonement Theology
in the Late Nineteenth Century

J. Denny Weaver
Foreword by C. Norman Kraus

HERALD PRESS
Scottdale, Pennsylvania
Waterloo, Ontario

Library of Congress Cataloging-in-Publication Data
Weaver, J. Denny, 1941-
    Keeping salvation ethical : Mennonite and Amish atonement theology
in the late nineteenth century / J. Denny Weaver ; foreword by
C. Norman Kraus.
        p. cm. — (Studies in Anabaptist and Mennonite history ; no. 35)
    Includes bibliographical references and index.
    ISBN 0-8361-3118-5 (alk. paper)
    1. Atonement—History of doctrines—19th century. 2. Christian
ethics—History—19th century. 3. Mennonites—Doctrines—History—
19th century. 4. Amish—Doctrines—History—19th century.
I. Title. II. Series.
BT263.W43 1996
230'.97'09034—dc20   96-32281
                                                                       CIP

The paper used in this publication is recycled and meets the minimum requirements of American National Standard for Information Sciences—Permanence
of Paper for Printed Library Materials, ANSI Z39.48-1984.

Bible quotations are used by permission, all rights reserved; those by the author
are from the *New Revised Standard Version Bible,* copyright 1989, by the
Division of Christian Education of the National Council of the Churches of
Christ in the USA. Other quotations in the sources are taken from Luther's
Bibel, translated from German, or modeled on the King James Version of *The
Holy Bible.*

KEEPING SALVATION ETHICAL
Copyright © 1997 by Herald Press, Scottdale, Pa. 15683
    Published simultaneously in Canada by Herald Press,
        Waterloo, Ont. N2L 6H7. All rights reserved
Library of Congress Catalog Number: 96-32281
International Standard Book Number: 0-8361-3118-5
Printed in the United States of America
Book design by Gwen M. Stamm/Cover photo by Marilyn Nolt

06 05 04 03 02 01 00 99 98 97 10 9 8 7 6 5 4 3 2 1

In memory of Alvin and Velma,
who passed on the tradition

Contents

Foreword

This book is long overdue, and J. Denny Weaver has done all of us a service by sifting through a large body of material and sorting out what is theologically significant. As is well known, systematic theology was not a priority for most nineteenth-century Mennonite leaders in North America! So in order to uncover the theological substance and to present a theological picture, Weaver had to catch clues where he could and read the implicit as well as the explicit.

Already in the 1970s, Theron F. Schlabach called our attention to the shifting language patterns of North American Mennonite leaders in the late 1800s as they began to absorb influences from revivalism and the Sunday school and mission movements. He noted that Mennonites' emphasis on peace and nonresistance was "beginning to move away from the center and a bit nearer the periphery" of their language about salvation (*The Mennonite Quarterly Review*, July 1977, 224). Then in his *Gospel Versus Gospel* (1980), Schlabach briefly documented what he described as a "shift away from references to the nonresistant gospel" (49). Now Weaver gives us a full-length study of this theological shift.

While the focus of his work is on atonement, Weaver has provided a context and documented his thesis with a broader survey of doctrinal teaching. He has also included a valuable chapter on the evangelical developments of the period, thus providing a setting for understanding the progression of Mennonite thought.

Weaver's thesis, thoroughly documented in this book, is that a gradual acceptance of the penal substitutionary theory of atonement threatened to displace the earlier Anabaptist-Mennonite concept of salvation through identification with the nonresistant Christ on the cross. This is not to say that Mennonites at the end of the nineteenth century held the doctrine of nonresistance less firmly than before; but their theological rationale had changed. Compared to an earlier period, nonresistance was no longer as thoroughly rooted in their understanding of the atonement and salvation.

The consequences of this shift are even more evident in the twentieth century. So Weaver has included a brief essay especially on the work of Daniel Kauffman, who more than anyone else was indeed the bridge between the two centuries. Most interesting are the differences between Kauffman's *Manual of Bible Doctrines*, published in 1898, and his *Doctrines of the Bible*, 1928.

Even a cursory examination of those two books reveals the development. In the 1898 book Kauffman taught a generic doctrine of vicarious sacrifice by which Jesus "paid a ransom" and "bruised the head of the serpent, destroyed the works of the devil," "blotted out the handwriting," and "purchased redemption for the whole human race" (72). That book has chapters on regeneration as the outcome of the work of Christ, repentance, and conversion—all before a chapter on justification; and all those chapters precede one on "The Redemption of Man," which briefly discusses the atonement. A chapter on "Non-resistance" presents that doctrine as central to the gospel. Kauffman declared in 1898 that the "whole Gospel is a gospel of peace—peace with God, peace with the brotherhood, peace with all men" (206). Of course, following Mennonite tradition, "gospel" was essentially "teaching."

By contrast, Kauffman's 1928 book presents atonement as a penal sacrifice which God decreed as a "propitiation" to appease "the anger of a just God" (247). Following this discussion come the topics of redemption, faith, repentance, and justification, and then of conversion and regeneration—in that order. The shift in order marks the changing perception of the meaning and sequence of the salvation process. The 1928 book treats nonresistance under topics on the "Christian Life" and presents it as the *teaching* of Christ and the early church. With that development we are at least one half step away from a "gospel of peace."

The end of the process is clear already in the 1921 statement drawn up by the ("old") Mennonite Church's Virginia Conference and then adopted by its general conference. In that statement, which amounted to a confession of faith under the name "Christian Fundamentals," nonresistance is subsumed under Article xiii, "On Restrictions"—an article discussing the relation of church and state and other aspects of nonconformity to the world. Thus the statement treats nonresistance as but one aspect of nonconformity and reduces it to renunciation of "engagement in carnal warfare."

I have elaborated on these matters because, as Weaver himself recognizes, they highlight the significance of his study. The work of Leo Driedger and Donald B. Kraybill in *Mennonite Peacemaking* (1994) charts the developments further and from a sociological perspective. Weaver's study provides an excellent historical background for this continuing analysis.

—*C. Norman Kraus*
  July 1995

Series Editor's Preface

For the Studies in Anabaptist and Mennonite History series, this book by J. Denny Weaver serves two purposes. One is to help bring depth to the historical understanding of Mennonites in North America. As two book series—Mennonite Experience in America, and Mennonites in Canada—near their completions, the North American history of Mennonites is at something of a new stage. In the past there have been quite a few fine studies, but most have been straightforward stories of immigrations, of denominational and institutional development, of movement into missions and service, or of prominent leaders' lives. Among those studies the good ones have been quite valid and useful.

Now, however, we can expect more histories that deeply examine particular themes in life patterns and thought structures of North American Mennonites. Weaver's book is an excellent model. Not only does it examine how articulate Mennonites viewed atonement; as the title implies, it also demonstrates that on the whole they did not make the disjuncture between soteriology and ethics that has often appeared in Protestantism.

With that latter point, Weaver's book serves the second purpose: a deeper understanding of the theological perceptions that have made Anabaptism and Mennonitism a distinct tradition. How Protestant, really, have Mennonites been? In the case of the sixteenth-century Anabaptists, some scholars have of course seen them as the radical left wing of Protestantism; others have treated them as essentially so different that they were "neither Catholic nor Protestant." Meanwhile, there have been versions of Protestantism—the Puritan churches, the holiness movement, and others—which have strongly emphasized righteous behavior right along with salvation by grace. Scholars who classify some of these as "perfectionist" movements are likely to include Mennonites under that rubric.

Weaver has not cast his discussion of North American Mennonite thinkers into stereotyped formulas, but his treatment does throw light on the questions that gave such categories their rise. In the last half-century, Mennonites have been more and more ready to learn from other traditions. In the same period, Christians in those other traditions have increasingly recognized, from SAMH books and other sources, that the Anabaptist-Mennonite tradition has important understandings to offer all Christians. Mainly that recognition has emphasized Anabaptist-Mennonite teachings of peace, church, and practical discipleship. Weaver's book offers something more: an examination of how Mennonites have related such well-recognized emphases to a standard theological theme such as atonement.

A major strength of Weaver's work is that he develops his ideas in conversation with other scholars. He has attended many conferences where he has offered papers that in one way or another touched the central themes of this book. An article he published on this book's subject in *The Mennonite Quarterly Review* (1987) was a further case of such conversation. Not least, Weaver cooperated superbly with suggestions from readers and from C. Norman Kraus, the actual editor of this particular SAMH volume.

The SAMH editors deeply thank Kraus and Weaver for their hard work and fine cooperation. We believe readers will do the same.

— Theron F. Schlabach
  SAMH Editor-in-Chief
  The Young Center for the Study of
    Anabaptist and Pietist Groups
    Elizabethtown College

Author's Preface

This book is about theology, analyzing individuals not known for being theologians, who represent Amish and Mennonite traditions not known for having a history of systematic theology. The book is a product of my curiosity. When I first had to try teaching theology to college students, I began to wonder if Mennonites had anything unique to say about the classic theological questions. Although the route from the first inkling of that query to this book more than twenty years later is not a direct one, the book is in part an answer to that question. Yes, Mennonites do have something distinctive, if not really unique, to say to the classic theological questions.

In another sense, this book is a product of faith—perhaps even blind faith—that the Mennonite tradition would have something distinctive to say on the classic subject of atonement. Since the Anabaptist tradition was frequently praised for being more interested in practical living and discipleship than in "mere" thinking and theologizing, when I started reading I had no idea what, if anything, Mennonites might have said about atonement. More material emerged from my research than I had ever expected. In that sense, this book is the product of a surprise. As is obvious, it grew far beyond the article that I had hoped might be feasible.

This book is also a product of my hope for the Mennonite church. As a denomination, we live in exciting times. The church has more opportunities for witness and service than ever before in its history, and more resources for seizing those opportunities. The church has also undergone more cultural accommodation than ever before in North America. This accommodation means that the time of greatest opportunity for witness and service is happening at the time of greatest danger for the faithfulness—the identity—of the church. It is my hope that historical learnings from this collection of nineteenth-century Mennonite and Amish leaders can provide some guidance for our search for the nature of the faithful church as we prepare to enter the twenty-first century.

This book is also a product of love. I do identify with the wider Anabaptist Mennonite tradition that this essay analyzes. Beyond that, however, I grew to love and respect all the figures of this study. That was not always the case. Some of these figures, whom I chose for study because they represented a particular churchly or ethnic stance that I needed to fill out my grid, did not at first glance seem to be people for whom I would develop a great deal of sympathy. Immersion in their writings, however, gave me respect for the struggle of each one to understand what it means to be a faithful follower of Jesus and to work for a vision of the church founded on Jesus Christ. Thus while I, a modern person, could not survive in the church of a number of my subjects, I still grew to love and respect each one as a representative and a bearer of a part of the tradition to which I belong.

Because of that affection, in expressing my gratitude to the many persons who have made a contribution to the development of this manuscript, I want to start with the eight men whose materials I studied. Thank you David Beiler, John M. Brenneman, Heinrich Egly, John Holdeman, Johannes Moser, Jacob Stauffer, Cornelius H. Wedel, and Gerhard Wiebe for your contribution to this statement about Mennonite theology that attempts to speak to the believers church tradition in the late twentieth century. My contemporaries have also made many contributions to this work. I want to acknowledge and thank the following people, each of whom made a specific contribution to some facet of the development of the manuscript: Adolf Ens, John Friesen, Henry J. Gerbrandt, Gerald Gerbrandt, Ann Hilty, Harry Huebner, Gerhard Ens, Peter Fast, Erica Gellert, David Luthy, Richard MacMaster, Delbert Gratz, Burton Yost, James Satterwhite, Loren Johns, Perry Bush, Ezra Moser, John Moser, Naomi Claudon Vercler Luginbill, Rebecca Baumgartner, David C. Wedel, James C. Juhnke, Hilda Voth, Clarence Hiebert, John S. Oyer, Theron Schlabach, Paton Yoder, Amos Hoover, Paul Toews, Ray Gingerich, James O. Lehman, Rodney Sawatsky, Timothy Smith, Stanley Hauerwas, David Steinmetz, Donald Dayton, Evelyn Kirkley. I extend an apology to any others whose names I unwittingly managed to overlook.

In particular, I want to thank C. Norman Kraus, whose contribution to my work began when I first took an undergraduate course from him at Goshen College, and continues through the many helpful suggestions he made as the SAMH editor for this manuscript. In addition to this recognition of individuals, I am grateful for the Mennonite historical libraries at four institutions—Bethel College, Bluffton College, Canadian Mennonite Bible College, and Goshen College. In every instance, the personnel of these institutions went out of their way to accommodate even my smallest wishes as well as needs. I want to thank the American Academy of Religion, which awarded me a research grant to finance study in the C. H. Wedel materials in the Mennonite Library and Archives at Bethel College. And I want to thank the Bluffton College Study Center, which awarded me the two Summer Research Grants that funded research on David Beiler and John Holdeman, and in the materials of John M. Brenneman in the Mennonite Historical Library at Goshen College. Last but most important, I owe unending gratitude to my wife, Mary, whose faith, hope, and love endure in spite of and because of the creation of this manuscript.

—*J. Denny Weaver*
  Bluffton College
  Easter 1995

Keeping
Salvation
Ethical

1

Introduction

Only in the decade of the 1980s did Mennonites begin to feel comfortable discussing what they believed under the rubric of "systematic theology." The discussion—not infrequently a debate—has been both interesting and vigorous. By putting on public display its analysis of nineteenth-century Mennonite and Amish concepts of atonement within the wider context of Mennonite and Amish theology, this book joins that relatively new and still vibrant discussion about the nature of Mennonite systematic theology. The aim of this book is to develop a thesis about nineteenth-century Mennonite and Amish atonement theology that will have a clear imprint on the search for a modern Mennonite, peace-church theology.

The late nineteenth-century context is important. By focusing on this epoch, we gain a view of Mennonite and Amish theology before it passed over the brink into the maelstrom of changes provoked by modernity and the looming modernist-fundamentalist controversy. We observe their theology before its latent impulse toward the separation of ethics from salvation actualized itself as a result of modernizing changes. In two differing ways, therefore, this book concerns Mennonite and Amish theology on the brink.

Mennonites and Classic Theological Issues

At first glance, even studying nineteenth-century Mennonite and Amish views of atonement might appear misplaced or even unnecessary. For one thing, Mennonites have never been noted for having a theological tradition. In earlier epochs, Mennonite theology and Mennonite beliefs came in categories such as "Bible doctrines" or were defined historically by describing the beliefs of the Anabaptist founders.

Second, since Mennonites apparently lacked a tradition of theologizing and of systematic theology, it was assumed that what they did say on classic issues such as Christology or atonement would be in strict agreement with orthodox Protestantism, and that Mennonites would have nothing of their own to add. Note, for example, the words of Harold S. Bender, the dean of Mennonite historians in the 1940s and 1950s: "All the American Mennonite groups without exception stand upon a platform of conservative evangelicalism in theology, being thoroughly orthodox in the great fundamental doctrines of the Christian faith such as the unity of the Godhead, the true deity of Christ, the atonement by the shedding of blood, the plenary inspiration and divine authority of the Holy Scriptures as the Word of God."[1]

Bender's assumption about Mennonite espousal of orthodoxy's theology was foreshadowed and more recently echoed by a variety of Mennonite writers, including John Horsch, John C. Wenger, Cornelius Krahn, Robert Friedmann, Ronald Sider, Walter Klaassen, and Arnold Snyder.[2] If Bender and the others are correct, one would expect to find little that is either interesting or original on the classic issues in Anabaptist or Mennonite writings. Stated broadly, the argument of this book tests Bender's thesis that Mennonites only echo "conservative evangelicalism" on a doctrine such as atonement.

A significant dimension of both earlier and more recent discussions of Mennonite theology deals with the interaction of two sets of issues. One set concerns the classic questions of systematic theology, those which Bender called "the great fundamental doctrines of the Christian faith," including such doctrines as creation, sin, Christology, atonement and soteriology, and the Trinity. The second set of issues concerns the doctrines and practices which are specific, although certainly not unique, to the Anabaptist-Mennonite tradition. This latter list of issues includes such things as discipleship, nonresistance and pacifism, simple living, believers baptism, the church as a visible community, and separation of church and state or the rejection of an established church.

Questions for systematic theology concern the relationship of these two lists. Are the lists intrinsically related, or do they exist independently? With which set of issues do we begin in order to develop a comprehensive theology for the Mennonite tradition? For the Christian tradition? Is one of the lists a function of the other? Does one list limit the other? Do the items on the second list influence the conceptualization of the issues on the first list? Which set of issues receives priority in defining the essential nature of Mennonite theology in particular and of Christian theology in general?

As a corollary to defining Mennonites as orthodox on the classic questions, it was assumed that anything unique about Mennonite theology would appear only on the second list, the set of tenets dealing with ethics and practical Christian living. Harold Bender's list of these distinctive issues for Mennonites mentioned five: "the divine authority and adequacy of the Word of God; the necessity of a holy life in obedience to that word; the high calling and place of the church as distinct from the state; separation between church and the 'world'; and the abandonment of all carnal warfare and force and the actual practice of the gospel of love and peace."[3]

Some church leaders and historians even considered it a positive attribute to focus on these practical issues of obedience rather than on the theological questions.[4] Those espousing such views on (what is here called) the two lists assumed, therefore, that Mennonites would have nothing unique to say about the classic theological questions (the first list). It might appear, therefore, that a study of or search for distinct Mennonite and Amish perspectives on atonement is a quest for the nonexistent.

Recently a few scholars have begun to give greater attention to the theological beliefs of those Mennonites supposedly more interested in Christian experience and practical Christian living than in doctrinal formulations and systematic theology.[5] The present analysis of Mennonite and Amish theology in the latter half of the nineteenth century makes a major contribution to this modern discussion. The book dares to ask whether, in spite of the claimed agreement of Anabaptists and Mennonites with Protestantism on the classic theological issues, there still might be something unique about the way Mennonites dealt with their adopted or "borrowed" theology.

The study asks whether the things which have identified Mennonites—such as commitments to nonresistance, to believers baptism, and to a visible church—have any impact on the way they talked about things discussed by all Christians, specifically here Christology and atonement. By moving into such mostly uncharted areas, this study intends to open a new dimension for the study and understanding of Mennonite theology.

The question of what shapes a specifically peace-church theology for the Mennonite churches takes on another tone when one recognizes that there is a methodological presupposition behind the idea of the first list. Having a first list assumes that there exists a mainstream Christianity or a "Christianity-as-such." It follows that any additions to or departures from that mainstream Christianity become the distinct attribute of a particular tradition. Since Christianity-as-such supports doctrines on the first list, the burden of proof then falls predominantly on those who advocate items on the second list. These beliefs, after all, belong only to a few, while supposedly all Christians accept the first list. In the case of the peace churches, rejection of the sword then becomes such a "distinctive," something added to the "mainstream" Christian tradition that distinguishes the peace church from the mainstream—which does not, as a whole, avow pacifism.

This book rejects the idea of a "mainstream" which may assume priority and cast the burden of proof on the supposed "distinctives" of the Mennonite, peace-church tradition. Rather, I work with the assumption that there are only particular Christian traditions or particular Christian theologies. Each of these Christian theologies reflects or identifies with or builds upon some particular historical tradition, and reflects some particular context with roots at some particular point in time. Thus pacifism is specific to a particular kind of tradition, rather than being an addition to another, assumed mainstream theology. The following chapter will demonstrate that the classic satisfaction or Anselmian understanding of atonement is specific to the ecclesiology that emerged from what has been called the Constantinian synthesis; it did not arise out of the believers-church ecclesiology of the Mennonite and Amish peace-church tradition.[6] Recognizing that each tradition is a particular tradition means that each must then validate itself with reference to the narrative of Jesus. It is not right to assume the priority of a "mainstream" with only the "distinct" peace church needing to legitimate its theology.[7] The question for systematic theology then becomes, "Is Christian theology which is shaped by the assumption that Jesus' rejection of the sword is intrinsic to the gospel—is that theology different from theology which is not shaped by that assumption?"

This book delves into these historical and theological issues at two levels. First, the book is a history of doctrine. It intends to provide a description—with some analysis—of Mennonite and Amish thought from the previous century. At this level the purpose of the book is informative, and through its use of new primary source material, it considerably expands our knowledge of Mennonite and Amish theology in the latter half of the nineteenth century. As description, the book uses the doctrine of atonement to test Harold Bender's assertion that "all American groups without exception stand upon a platform of conservative evangelicalism in theology."

Second, since the conclusions drawn from that historical analysis speak directly to the modern discussions about the nature of Mennonite systematic theology, the book also has an apologetic agenda. It appeals to the historical description to argue a thesis relevant to the modern church. Stated generally, the thesis is that *nineteenth-century Mennonite atonement theology contained a latent threat to the peace theology and to the peace practice of succeeding Mennonite generations.* Their understanding of salvation stood, figuratively speaking, on the brink of losing its strong ethical component. While this danger remained implicit for the most part in the nineteenth century, the danger posed by the brink remains nonetheless real and still threatens the peace theology of modern Mennonites as well as their practice of peace in the modern world. The book also suggests a modern antidote to this threat: *the peace church should develop a systematic theology specific to peace-church assumptions rather than attempting to build on formulas that reflect one of the versions of "mainstream" theology.*

Since the book describes a perceived threat and poses an antidote, it does pursue an apologetic agenda. Others may attempt to draw different conclusions from the descriptive data. However, I proceed with due awareness that there is no wholly neutral description. Assumptions which shape the later argument do affect the material selected for analysis. Thus it is my hope that potentially differing conclusions about the meaning of the data will not lessen the informative value for all readers of the description of late nineteenth-century Mennonite and Amish theology. In any case, the book's twofold agenda addresses both historians and theologians.[8]

Methodology

Moving into the largely unmapped territory of nineteenth-century Mennonite and Amish theology poses some problems of methodology. The interpreter asks some modern questions of writers who, with one exception, did not usually lay out their abstract presuppositions, show awareness of a range of theological options, and then rationalize the one they chose. The book mostly deals with individuals who simply wrote what they believed. One may ask modern questions not addressed specifically by the earlier authors, and then discuss the results in terms of vocabulary and categories foreign to the original authors. Yet the interpreter must always keep in mind the possibility that the modern description may distort the meaning of the original. I hope that my awareness of the difficulty holds such distortions to a minimum. At the same time, one should remember that this hermeneutical difficulty is in no way unique to this study. The problem exists for any discussion of historical theology and for any historical discussion of theology.

I intend this book to work within the framework of the recent historiography of Mennonites in North America, and in particular of the four-volume work *The Mennonite Experience in America.*[9] Older Mennonite historiography primarily followed denominational history in linear and chronological fashion. The new research examines the experiences of Mennonites in terms of their responses to movements and events of the wider society in which they lived. While the present work follows denominational lines, it assumes and makes liberal use of the analysis of this new scholarship.

Selection of Subjects

The individuals analyzed in the following pages can be grouped in a number of ways. According to the denomination of origin, David Beiler (1786-1871) and Heinrich (Henry) Egly (1824-1890) were Amish, while John M. Brenneman (1816-1895), John Holdeman (1832-1900), Johannes Moser (1826-1908), Jacob W. Stauffer (1811-1855), Cornelius H. Wedel (1860-1910), and Gerhard Wiebe (1827-1900) were Mennonites of some kind.[10] Each man made his major impact or ended his career in a particular denomination.

David Beiler, who emerged as a leader of the Old Order Amish, was bishop in the Upper Pequea Amish congregation in Lancaster County, Pennsylvania. Heinrich Egly, bishop in Adams County, Indiana, led a group away from the Amish to found what was called for a time the Egly Amish, then the Defenseless Mennonite Church, and eventually the Evangelical Mennonite Church.

As a result of his constant traveling, John M. Brenneman, longtime bishop at Elida, Ohio, "in the third quarter of the century . . . was as close as anyone to being leader of North America's largest Mennonite branch, the 'old' Mennonite church,"[11] now known officially as the Mennonite Church. John Holdeman, baptized but never ordained in a Mennonite congregation in Wayne County, Ohio, separated from Brenneman's denomination in 1859 to found the Church of God in Christ, Mennonite, commonly referred to as the Holdeman Mennonite Church. Jacob Stauffer, minister at Groffdale, Pennsylvania, left the denomination of John M. Brenneman in 1845, to found the Stauffer Mennonite Church, the first of several Old Order Mennonite groups.

Johannes Moser, minister and bishop for nearly fifty years in the Swiss Mennonite congregation of Pandora and Bluffton, Ohio, and C. H. Wedel, the first president of Bethel College, each joined the

General Conference Mennonite Church. Gerhard Wiebe's following in southern Manitoba, Canada, took the name of the Chortitzer Mennonite Church, named after the Manitoba village in which Wiebe lived.

Ethnic origin and time of immigration produce another set of groupings. Stauffer, Beiler, Brenneman, and Holdeman represent the Swiss (and South German) Anabaptist tradition whose roots in North America reached back at least into the early eighteenth century. Heinrich Egly and Johannes Moser represent persons from the Swiss Anabaptist tradition, who immigrated to North America early in the nineteenth century and did not settle in the well-established Mennonite or Amish centers. Because of these two widely separated times of immigration of Swiss Anabaptist descendants, these groups referred to each other as the "American" Mennonites and the "Schweizer" or "Swiss" Mennonites. Egly arrived in Butler County, Ohio, in 1837, as a young immigrant from the territory of Baden in South Germany. In 1850 he moved to Adams County, Indiana, where he was ordained as deacon and then as minister. Johannes Moser was born in 1826 to parents who had immigrated from the Jura, Switzerland, in 1821. With his new wife, Moser moved to Putnam County, near Bluffton, Ohio, in 1852. He was ordained as minister in the fall of 1853, and as *Ältester* or bishop in 1864.

C. H. Wedel and Gerhard Wiebe are representatives of the Mennonite immigration from Russia to North America that began in 1874. Wedel, who immigrated with his parents at age fourteen, belonged to the more progressive, education-oriented people from the Molotschna colony, who settled primarily in central Kansas. Wiebe was the senior bishop or *Ältester* of the Bergthal colony, the more conservative group of Russian immigrants. Opposed to advanced education and uncomfortable with the Molotschna folk, Wiebe's Bergthal contingent settled in southern Manitoba.

A progressive-conservative scale cuts across these denominational and ethnic lines in yet another way. When conservative means a general effort to conserve Mennonite cultural traditions with as little change as possible, on the conservative end of the spectrum would be Jacob Stauffer, David Beiler, John Holdeman, and Gerhard Wiebe. Near the center of the spectrum stand Johannes Moser and John M. Brenneman. On the more progressive end of the spectrum is C. H. Wedel. Heinrich Egly retained a good deal of Amish culture while progressing in religious practice. Within the ethnic groupings, Beiler and Egly come from conservative and progressive ends of the Amish spectrum, while Stauffer, Holdeman, Brenneman, and Moser are ranged along a Swiss

Mennonite continuum. Wedel and Wiebe represent progressive and traditionalist ends of the immigrant Russian Mennonite spectrum.

The analysis uses revivalism and a particular, ritualistic form of conversion experience as a specific dimension of progressivism or willingness to adopt new practices. When revivalism is the indicator of willingness to change, the figures are ranged quite differently than they are on the usual progressive-conservative spectrum. With reference to the adoption of the new form of revivalism, the innovators are still Heinrich Egly but also include John Holdeman and John M. Brenneman. The conservatives who resist revivalism include not only Stauffer, Beiler, and Wiebe, but also Wedel and Moser.

The eight individuals on which this research focuses were selected in order to provide a variety of combinations of Mennonite ethnic identity and ecclesiastical stances. I examine one doctrine, atonement, for individuals across this spectrum of ethnic and denominational identities. By looking at the same doctrinal question in a variety of settings, I intend to learn to what extent there is—or is not—a common Anabaptist theological tradition underlying the varying church groupings.

All individuals selected for this study were active in the latter half of the nineteenth century. I have called that half century the eve of modernity. My goal is to survey representative Mennonite and Amish theological outlooks before they encountered the full brunt of the modernizing and Americanizing influences of the late nineteenth and early twentieth centuries. Such designations are never pure and clearcut, however. The development of the old order groups (Beiler and Stauffer) as well as Holdeman's conservative, pietist reform and Egly's revivalist, progressive reform—these are already early products of the confrontation with modernity.

For Wedel, the category stretches in other ways. While he was ordained in 1890, the earliest of his writings treated in this study appeared in 1899. In terms of methodology and education, his deep involvement in the beginnings of higher education—both as scholar and as teacher—within the Mennonite church distinguish him from the other seven subjects. Nonetheless, Wedel is included because his intent was still to describe and defend historic Mennonite faith rather than to reshape Mennonite faith on a modern or American framework.

Thus all eight subjects appear in the following extended analysis because they represent in some way Mennonite and Amish outlooks deeply shaped by their inherited, received traditions. To a lesser degree, they are touched by the looming modernist-fundamentalist controversy and the progressivist, technological and higher-education dominated society of twentieth-century North America. Thus the study concerns Mennonite and Amish theology perched, historically speaking, on the brink of modernity.

Testing the Thesis

Throughout the pages that follow, the argument of the thesis points to a real but mostly latent danger in the theology of the eight central figures—*a danger of separating ethics from atonement theology.* While this danger makes something of an appearance in the writings of Heinrich Egly, and in another way in C. H. Wedel's corpus, it became fully evident only in the theological formulations of later generations. To exhibit this culmination, chapter 6 introduces the outlook of John S. Coffman (1848-1899) and Daniel Kauffman (1865-1944) as an epilogue. More than any other single individual, Coffman made revivalism palatable to the Mennonite Church. Although he was a contemporary of several of the eight central figures of this study, Coffman's mature theological outlook was shaped much more by the modernizing impulses that confronted Mennonites at the turn of the century than by the inherited, received traditions that shaped the eight central characters of our study.

Daniel Kauffman became editor of the official paper of the Mennonite Church and served on all its important committees during the first four decades of the twentieth century. The three books of Bible doctrine, which constitute the heart of his theological corpus, display in graphic fashion the impact on traditional Mennonite theology produced by the forces of modernity. I use the writings of Coffman and Kauffman to display the actual theological consequences of the undertow toward separating ethics from atonement theology. This latent element is seen in the thought of the eight figures, comprising the majority of the book in hand.

All the central characters of this book were ordained men. Presumably they were more devout than the lay people to whom they ministered, though not necessarily more devout than other people who wrote for Mennonite church papers. Given the nature of the subjects and the sources, therefore, it is conceivable that study of other figures or of a different kind of sources might revise the picture drawn in this book of late nineteenth-century Mennonite and Amish theology.

Fresh Primary Sources

The analysis that follows breaks much new ground through its use of several sets of primary sources not treated in any other modern writing to date. These primary sources include two series of notebooks containing material from C. H. Wedel. His "Glaubenslehre," which most certainly would have been Wedel's systematic theology had he lived to publish it, exists in manuscript form in four notebooks. A similar series of three notebooks preserves Wedel's "Ethik."

David Beiler's 1861 treatise, *Eine Betrachtung über den Berg Predig Christi und über den Ebräer, das 11 Cap.*, became available in a 1994 Pathway reprint; this constitutes a second new primary source. A third set of heretofore unused primary sources in this study consists of the sixteen articles by Heinrich Egly in *Herold der Wahrheit* and *Christlicher Bundesbote* as well as the essays in his posthumously published *Friedensreich Christi.*

Finally, a fourth set of new primary materials is the sixty-four articles by Johannes Moser in *Herold der Wahrheit* and *Christlicher Bundesbote*, of which only two or three are noted in secondary literature dealing with Moser. Along with John M. Brenneman's more well-known writings, most of which appeared in both German and English, this study also makes use of several less-recognized ones in German that appeared only in *Herold der Wahrheit*. These new sources, when added to a new analysis of those previously known, enable the following essay to expand greatly our knowledge of Mennonite theology in the nineteenth-century.

Preview of Chapters

The doctrine of atonement serves as the indicator doctrine for this research. It is not feasible to compare every figure on every doctrine. Several reasons make atonement a particularly apt basis of comparison. For one, atonement is a classic doctrine that has belonged to all Christian traditions since the beginning of Christianity. On the other hand, in contrast to Christology, there are no early creedal statements that define acceptable and unacceptable positions on atonement. Throughout church history, Christian thinkers have suggested several images of atonement and posed a variety of positions with numerous nuances, as shown in chapter 2.

Only in the nineteenth century, with the early stages of what came to be called the modernist-fundamentalist controversy, have churchly traditions attempted to establish an official position. Thus atonement theology is an excellent indicator of theological orientation: it is a doctrine belonging to every Christian tradition, reflective of a variety of influences, and yet without official positions until the recent past. Assessment of Mennonite thinking on atonement provides a mark for comparison across Mennonite ethnic lines as well as a doctrine that situates Mennonites in relation to other strands of the Christian spectrum.

In what follows, the analysis of Mennonite and Amish atonement theology occurs in three stages, moving from broadest context to most narrow focus. In the first stage, in chapter 3, the essay sketches each nineteenth-century writer's worldview and attitudes on selected issues in North American society. These descriptions serve as the widest context in which to consider each character's understanding of atonement. Chapter 3 asks about the extent to which each Mennonite or Amish writer's understanding of theology interacted with and fits within the context of North American theology and the North American outlook.

Chapter 4 develops the theological context within which each writer understood the death of Christ. How does the death of Christ relate to soteriology, more broadly conceived, and to conversion and revivalism? How does the death of Christ relate to the nature of the church, to ethics, to resurrection and eschatology as understood by each of the Amish or Mennonite writers in question? This chapter asks whether things that distinguish Mennonites and Amish from the rest of Christendom—such as nonresistance and pacifism, visible church, and believers baptism—have an impact on the way Mennonites and Amish talked about the classic doctrines addressed by all Christians.

For several of the figures of this study, primarily those considered conservative, the worldview sketched in chapter 3 and the theological context described in chapter 4 are virtually synonymous, as I am using these categories. Except to provide a clear list of attitudes and practices to avoid, the North American society had not yet exerted any great influence on the way the conservative writers described their beliefs. For others, however, and there are some surprises, the impact had some significant and profound influences. Nevertheless, the line between chapters 3 and 4 is not always distinct. In some instances, the material in one chapter might fit just as appropriately in the other one. Thus, chapter 4 should be read with chapter 3 clearly in mind. The book develops the argument that the material of these two sections shows the uniqueness of Mennonite theology.

Finally, chapter 5 examines atonement in the narrowest sense, asking about the basic image which each individual used to explain what the death of Christ accomplished for sinful humanity. This chapter asks about the extent to which Mennonite images of atonement fit within the atonement categories as they have been commonly defined in the Western theological tradition. The material surveyed in this chapter is appealed to by those, such as Harold Bender, who would identify Mennonite theology with evangelical theology. I argue that while Bender may be correct in a narrow sense, marking that point of identity apart from the context of the material of chapters 3 and 4 greatly skews our understanding and interpretation of the uniqueness of Mennonite theology.

In the pattern of this book, I discuss each individual writer's theology in separate sections. One can obtain a systematic statement of a given subject's theological outlook by reading consecutively the section on him in chapters 3-5.

Recognizing the uniqueness—or lack of it—in Mennonite theology requires some awareness of the theological scene outside of the Mennonite world. Chapter 2 is a preliminary to developing a picture in some detail of the nineteenth-century Mennonite theological world. It sketches the history of the doctrine of atonement as well as some dimensions of the North American theological scene with which Mennonites were beginning to come in contact.

2

History of Atonement

History of Atonement: Traditional Version

Earlier this century, Swedish theologian Gustaf Aulén's *Christus Victor* (Christ the Conqueror),[1] began to lend currency to a threefold classification of atonement images. Identified as the classic theory or Christus Victor, the satisfaction theory, and the moral influence theory, each of the three is actually a family of views with several variants. With the exception of C. H. Wedel, the Mennonite and Amish writers of the nineteenth century did their theologizing within only one of the three families of images. Yet orientation in the history and development of the several atonement motifs will contribute to understanding the development of Mennonite and Amish discussions of atonement.

Christus Victor Motif

What Aulén called the classic view stressed the theme of *victory*. This atonement image used the image of cosmic battle between good and evil, between the forces of God and those of Satan. In that fray God's Son, Jesus Christ, was killed, an apparent defeat of God and victory by Satan. However, Jesus' resurrection turned the seeming defeat into a great victory, which forever established God's control of the universe and freed sinful humans from the power of sin and Satan. In their writings, many early theologians refer to this motif. Among them are some Eastern or Greek Fathers: Irenaeus, Origen, Athanasius, and the three Cappadocian fathers (Basil the Great, Gregory of Nyssa, and Gregory of Nazianzus), Cyril of Alexandria, Cyril of Jerusalem, and Chrysostom; and others from the Western or Latin Fathers: Ambrose, Augustine, Leo the Great, and Gregory the Great.

A variation of the victory motif depicted Christ's death as the *ransom* price paid to Satan in exchange for freeing the sinners Satan held captive. With his resurrection, Christ then escaped the clutches of Satan, and sinners were freed from Satan's power. However, paying a ransom assumes that even Satan has certain rights that must be respected. Another variation denies such rights and pictures the defeat of the devil by deception. Satan failed to perceive the presence of God or the Deity of Christ hidden under the flesh of Christ, analogous to the way a worm covers a fishhook or cheese baits a mousetrap. The devil assumed an easy prey, swallowed the bait of the humanity of Jesus, and was caught by the Deity hidden under the human nature. In these several images, the stress on victory through resurrection identifies this motif as Christus Victor. The designation of classic view acknowledges it as the dominant atonement motif in the early church.[2]

The Christus Victor motif faded away gradually after the sixth century. Reasons for the demise of Christus Victor usually suggested by writers on the history of doctrine include: (1) aversion to the idea that God would either acknowledge certain rights of the devil, or stoop to overcoming the devil through trickery; (2) discomfort with the motif's military and battle imagery; (3) incompatibility of either the image of a cosmic battle or a ransom payment to Satan within a modern cosmology; (4) lack of evidence of the victory of the reign of God in our world; (5) Christus Victor's dualistic outlook in light of a modern worldview composed mostly of "gray areas."[3]

The Satisfaction Theory

In his *Cur Deus homo* (Why did God become man? [1098]), Anselm of Canterbury (c. 1033-1109) explicitly rejected the idea that Jesus's death was a ransom paid to the devil. To replace Christus Victor, he developed the *satisfaction theory*. The collection of views related to satisfaction pictures Christ's death as an act performed on behalf of sinners to satisfy the honor of an offended God or as the payment of a penalty required of sinners by God's law. Since the penalty of death could not be paid by sinful humans, Jesus's death for sinners was vicarious. It was "propitiation" when the image is of the sacrifice offered to an offended Deity, and "expiation" when it concerns the sinners' guilt and penalty which are covered. Beyond atonement for individuals, Anselm understood the death of Jesus as the satisfaction of God's own justice in the universe.[4] This satisfaction atonement image likely originated as a reflection of the penitential system and the sacrament of private penance that was developing throughout the medieval era. On the surface, it also seems to reflect the image of the feudal lord who gave protection to his vassals but also exacted penalties for offenses against him.[5]

Anselm's image posed the death of Christ as the means to satisfy the honor of an offended God. In the following centuries, the divines of Protestant Orthodoxy developed the satisfaction theory within a strong legal and penal framework. They built on the stress Martin Luther and John Calvin placed on Christ's death as *penal suffering*, with Christ enduring divine judgment on behalf of sinners.[6] Christ's sufferings "were the penalty of the law executed on Christ as the sinner's substitute."[7] What Christ's death satisfied was the divine law. With satisfaction aimed at the law, the role of God was conceived in the mode of the trial judge who exacted the penalty demanded by the law, or as the prosecuting attorney who charged sinners with violating the law.

Opinions varied on how widely Christ's death brought benefit to humankind. Did the law require payment of an exact price equal to the accumulated sins of saved sinners, and thus the death of Christ could cover only the sins of the elect? Those who answer this question with yes argue that it is the only way to prevent Jesus' death from being an eternal suffering and death. Those who answer no argue that Jesus' death did not meet an exact requirement of law, but rather satisfied a general condition and established the possibility of forgiveness for those who would avail themselves of the provisions. In this case, the death did not actually cover all sins of all humankind but rather provided a way for God to forgive without setting aside the provision of the law.

This latter view is sometimes called a *general atonement*. A version of it was stated by Hugo Grotius (1583-1645), a Dutch legal theorist, in what he called the *governmental theory.* Picturing God not as judge but as Governor of the universe, Grotius argued that God need not exact every penalty stipulated by the law. Rather, by offering God's own Son as the example of penalty exacted by the law, God would be able to pardon sinners without a relaxation of the divine law.[8]

With an emphasis on satisfying either God as an offended party or legal obligations established by God's law, this family of views can go by the name of *satisfaction* theory of atonement. Focus on Jesus' death as an action in place of or as a substitute for sinful humankind makes it the *substitutionary* theory. Stress on Jesus' payment of the penalty that the law required of sinners or on Jesus' suffering the penalty which sinners deserved produces the *penal* theory of atonement. This family of atonement theories can also be designated as *Anselmian,* for Anselm, who made the first systematic articulation of it.

The Moral Influence Theory

Peter Abelard (1979-1142) developed the *moral influence theory,* also called the subjective view, as a specific alternative to Anselm's theory. Abelard disliked the stress on God's stern judgment required in the satisfaction theory, as well as the fact that it appeared to have a placated God, who had changed his attitude from judgment to love toward the sinner. For Abelard, the problem of atonement was not how to change God's mind toward the sinner, but how to bring sinful humankind to see that the God they perceived as harsh and judgmental was actually loving. Thus for Abelard, Jesus died as the demonstration of God's love. The change that results from that loving death is not in God but in the subjective consciousness of the sinners, who repent and cease their rebellion and running away from God. It is this psychological or subjective influence worked on the mind of the sinner by the death of Christ that gives this view its name of moral influence theory.[9]

Among these families of atonement theories, the death of Christ has four separate objects. For the classic view, in either the cosmic battle or the ransom versions, Satan is the object of Jesus' death. Among the versions of the satisfaction theory, Jesus' death is aimed either at an offended God or at the stipulation required by the divine law. For the moral influence theory, sinful humankind—and their distorted moral perception in particular—is the object of Jesus' death. This enumeration of the four objects of Jesus' death makes clear that there are truly different options for explaining atonement, or how the death of Christ affects those who claim the name of Christ.[10]

Atonement Debate

Since the medieval period, much of the atonement debate has been among those promoting some version of Anselm's theory or Abelard's. Some version of Anselm has been the majority view, for both Catholics and the communions of Protestant Orthodoxy. In the nineteenth and early twentieth century, it was given confessional status by Protestant fundamentalists and evangelicals. On much the same basis articulated by Abelard, nineteenth and early twentieth-century liberals advocated a version of moral influence theory over against the satisfaction theory of fundamentalism and evangelicalism. A primary example is Horace Bushnell's use of satisfaction terminology to argue for a moral influence theory of atonement.[11] In the twentieth century, Gustaf Aulén's *Christus Victor* initiated renewed visibility for the Christus Victor image. In recent years, several Mennonite writers have found it useful to some extent,[12] and my own theologizing builds on it extensively.

History of Atonement: Alternative Version

In a 1990 article for *Modern Theology*, I first proposed an alternative explanation to the traditional view on the demise of Christus Victor.[13]

This alternative explanation links the demise to the altered ecclesiology that emerged from a shift in the nature of the church. A series of changes began already in the second century and eventuated in the medieval church of Christendom. These changes are sometimes symbolized by the name of Constantine, whose Edict of Milan in A.D. 313 first designated Christianity a legal and tolerated religion of the Roman empire.[14]

Historicized Christus Victor

The early church, the product of an illegal religion based on claims about a criminal executed for sedition, clearly posed an alternative to the social structure of the Greco-Roman empire. The church's first confession stated that not Caesar but "Jesus is Lord." Such persons, who exhibited a higher loyalty to Christ than to Caesar, were excluded from Caesar's army, although as followers of Jesus, who had taught them to lay aside their swords, early Christians refused to bear the sword in any case. The church, an illegal social structure witnessing to the earthly dimension of the reign of God, comprises one element of the forces of God which confront evil and Satan in the image of Christus Victor.

Christus Victor and the Life of Jesus. Christus Victor used the otherworldly imagery of a cosmic battle. Yet interpretation of material at either end of the New Testament shows Christus Victor's clear correlation to the church and to the historical world. When the life of Jesus is understood as a making of the reign of God present in the historical realm, then the story of Jesus fits within a historicized version of Christus Victor. The motif appears clearly in the narrative of the temptation of Jesus in the wilderness. One may understand the account as an actual conversation of Jesus and Satan or as a metaphorical description of kinds of temptations that could divert Jesus' mission. In either case, the story concerns the reign of God present in Jesus. That reign contrasts with and confronts the structures of the world which oppose the reign of God.

In opening his public ministry at Nazareth (Luke 4:14-30), Jesus' use of Isaiah 61 poses the reign of God in social and historical terms—good news to the poor, release to captives, recovery of sight to the blind, freedom of the oppressed—as a contrast to the kingdoms of the world. That it is a clash of reigns is acted out in the expulsion of Jesus from Nazareth. In the course of Jesus' mission, healings, exorcisms, and nature wonders such as a miraculous catch of fish or stilling of a storm indicate the power of the rule of God over the physical and spiritual forces which enslave individuals, as well as over the created, natural order. The confrontation between reign of God and rule of Satan reached its culmination with the crucifixion. In apparent weakness, the reign of God as present in Jesus confronted strength. Brute force killed Jesus in what appeared, momentarily, to be a triumph for the powers of evil. Three days later God raised Jesus from the dead, displaying the power of God's reign over the ultimate enemy—death. The victory of resurrection inaugurated a new era for the reign of God in our history.

Christus Victor in Revelation. At the other end of the New Testament, analysis of symbols and their antecedents reveals the correlation between the historical church and Christus Victor in the book of Revelation. The element of cosmic confrontation and victory appear throughout, making the book virtually an extended, multifaceted statement of the Christus Victor image. Revelation 12 even uses the specific image of cosmic battle between the forces of God, led by Michael and his angels, and Satan and his angels. The triumph of Christ is proclaimed in 12:10-12. Another example of the victory motif appears in chapter 5, where the Lion and Lamb symbols both refer to Jesus—with Lion as the Conqueror and slaughtered Lamb as the means of conquering. The victory song of the heavenly creatures (5:9-10) celebrates the subsequent joining of people from all ethnic and culture groups into a "kingdom and priests serving our God," which "will reign on earth." In other words, celebrated here is the victory of the reign of God over the rule of evil, which slaughtered the Lamb, Christ.

The opening of the seven seals in chapters 6-7 culminates with celebration of the victory of God's reign over the forces which oppose it. Seals 1-4 depict various kinds of oppression and destruction, the highest level of evil appearing in the first scene of the sixth seal. Seal 5 shifts from an earthly scene to the viewpoint of the heavenly realm and the souls of the martyrs who bemoan the slowness of God in avenging their deaths. However, alongside the chaos and destruction pictured in the sixth seal also appears a much longer description of celebration which encompasses the entire seventh chapter. Scene one of chapter 7 depicts the gathering of the 144,000, with 12,000 from each of the tribes of Israel. The second scene portrays an innumerable multitude drawn from all the peoples of the earth.

These two multitudes represent the people of God, the first emphasizing its continuity with the Israelites, the second showing that the people of God assembled around Jesus embraces persons of all ethnic and cultural and language and national groups. The scene pictures these multitudes in celebration of the salvation by God and the Lamb. In seal 6, the juxtaposition of this celebration with the chaos and destruction of 7:12-17 strongly suggests a victory. The people of God celebrate the establishment of the reign of God over the accumulation of evil that mounted through seals 1-4 and 6. This celebration matches that of chapter 5, which acclaimed the victory of the slaughtered Lamb, the resurrected Christ.

Attention to the historical antecedents of the atonement makes it apparent that the confrontation and victory occurred in the historical world. The cosmic imagery thus depicts the universal and cosmic significance of events in our historical world. The sequence of seven seals corresponds to the Roman emperors from Tiberius (A.D. 14-37), during whose rule Jesus was crucified; through Caligula (37-41), Claudius (41-54), Nero (54-68), and Vespasian (69-79), to the short reign of Titus (79-81) or more likely Domitian (81-96).

When Revelation 6:2 says that the rider of seal 1 "came out conquering and to conquer," the reader eventually realizes that the rider did not conquer. The mere appearance of the word *conquering* constitutes an oblique reference to the death and resurrection of Jesus. His death was only a temporary or apparent victory for evil, occurring under the rule of Tiberius.

More directly with seal 2, the bloodred horse, the sword, and the act of taking peace from the earth refer to the threats posed by Caligula (Rev. 6:3-4). In addition to Caligula's provocations against Jews, the symbolism seems particularly to refer to events in A.D. 40. After decreeing that places of worship should be converted to shrines which acknowledged his deity, Caligula sent Petronius from Antioch with an army of more than two legions to march through Judea to install a large statue of Caligula in the temple in Jerusalem. The threat did not fully materialize. Petronius halted the march after lengthy appeals from the Jews, and Caligula died before his ordered removal of Petronius could be carried out.[15]

The symbols of famine in seal 3 certainly refer to widespread famines that occurred in several lands, including Palestine, during the reign of Claudius (Rev. 6:5-6). These famines are well documented in the literature of that time, including a reference in Acts 11:28.[16]

Nero followed Claudius as emperor. The double ugly riders named Death and Hades in seal 4, who kill with "sword, famine, and pestilence, and by the wild animals of the earth" (Rev. 6:8), most certainly depict Nero, who began the first imperial persecution of Christians. Nero made Christians the scapegoat for the great fire in Rome in A.D. 64, and his cruelty to Christians and others has become legendary. Among other things, he dressed Christians in the skins of wild animals to be torn to pieces by dogs, or used them as living torches to light the games and chariot races in his gardens or in the Vatican circus.[17] The bubonic plague claimed thirty thousand victims in one autumn during Nero's era.[18]

Following Nero, there was a break in the sequence of crowned emperors. The shift of viewpoint in seal 5 from earthly to heavenly realm recognizes that break, as it accommodates the civil war and efforts to gain the crown by Galba, Otho, and Vitellius (Rev. 6:9-11). None of the three managed to consolidate his hold on the imperial office in the period immediately following Nero. Vespasian finally attained the crown late in A.D. 69.

The next year, an imperial army under the command of Vespasian's son Titus sacked Jerusalem and destroyed the temple. From the perspective of Jews, the fall of David's city and destruction of the temple would produce virtually indescribable feelings of despair and tragedy, the end of life and civilization as they knew it—precisely the mood of the opening scene of the seal 6 (Rev. 6:12-17). Heavens and earth shake and shatter, while people of all levels—from the most powerful to the most lowly—flee in chaos and panic.

However, the sixth seal does not end with despair at the destruction of the city. A heavenly messenger stays damage to earth and sea until the servants of God have been identified, marked "with a seal on their foreheads" (Rev. 7:2). In other words, even in the midst of the worst imaginable tragedy from an earthly perspective, the people of God are known to God and ultimately will be vindicated.

Hence, the two multitudes celebrate. Celebration occurs in the midst of destruction. For the reader of Revelation, the message of the cheering throngs of chapter 7 is that for those who live within the resurrection of Jesus, the rule of God has already triumphed, and the people of God do not face ultimate despair. This is so even when they are confronted by the accumulation of evil experienced under the rule of Rome, even when that rule culminates with the destruction of Jerusalem and the temple. While earthly rule culminates in destruction, the rule of God has already begun on earth with a victory, the resurrection of Jesus. The heavenly voices announce: "Salvation belongs to our God who is seated on the throne, and to the Lamb!" (Rev. 7:10).

With the scenes of cheering throngs in seal 6, the writer of Revelation is making a statement about a historical event, the fall of Jerusalem. These celebratory scenes convey the message that in the grand scheme of things as defined by the reign of God, even the fall of Jerusalem pales in significance alongside the resurrection of Jesus.

This celebration leads to seal 7, which does not advance the chronology but begins a new cycle of seven. The epoch in which Revelation was written thus becomes clear, perhaps during the short reign of Titus, but more likely during the reign of Domitian. Meanwhile, Revelation delivers a cosmic and eschatological perspective on events in the historical world—the life, death, and resurrection of Jesus, and the confrontation between church and empire. The destruction and oppression which accompany the empire may continue, but so will the victory of the reign of God for those who see resurrection as a victory.

The symbols in Revelation 12 have similar antecedents in the historical arena. The twelve stars of the woman's crown recall the number of the tribes of Israel as well as the number of disciples. The number twelve designates the people of God: the Israelites, from whom Jesus is born; and then the church, which consists of those, both Israelites and Gentiles, who accept Jesus as Messiah. The dragon pursues the child. It is defeated by Michael and his angels and thrown down to earth, where it then pursues the woman. This dragon has seven heads, ten horns, and seven crowns. The description of the dragon fits well with Rome. The seven heads recall the seven hills on which tradition said the city was built. As listed above, seven crowned emperors plus three claimants (Galba, Otho, and Vitellius) make a total of ten rulers, corresponding to the seven crowns and ten horns on the seven-headed dragon.

Thus the imagery of chapter 12 again depicts the cosmic and eschatological dimension of the confrontation of Christian church and Roman empire. As the struggling and numerically insignificant church contemplates the might of Rome, the temptation is to despair. However, for those who perceive the resurrection of Jesus, the reign of God has already triumphed with the resurrection. While the earthly component of the confrontation continues, Christians need not fear death in an ultimate sense, the Revelator says, because in the resurrection the reign of God has already attained the ultimate victory.

Church Confronting Empire, Matrix for Christus Victor

The picture of the church as a social structure emerges from this survey of the narrative of Jesus' life in the Gospels and historical antecedents for the symbols of Revelation. This church posed an alternative to the social structure of the Greco-Roman empire.[19] Each of these entities solicited ultimate loyalty. The empire persecuted Christians because they professed a different loyalty. Christians presented a contrast to the empire precisely because they were shaped by the narrative of Jesus rather than by the demands of the emperor and the exigencies of the empire. My thesis is that *this confrontation between church and empire constitutes the historical matrix for the atonement image called Christus Victor.* This image portrays salvation as escape from the forces of evil, as being transformed by the reign of God and taking on a life shaped within the story of Jesus, who makes visible the reign of God in our history. This view of salvation understands becoming Christian (or identifying with Jesus Christ) and the discussion of ethics (or how Christians live) as two dimensions of the same question.

With the changes that began in the second century, Christianity evolved from the position of a suspect or despised minority to become the dominant religion of the empire. The status of the church shifted from object of suppression to sometime partner and quasi-supporter of the empire and the imperial office. Alongside the cessation of persecution as a mark of the shift, there was also the change in the attitude of the church toward the sword and warfare. While the early church rejected the sword, the church of the Constantinian synthesis rationalized use of the sword; the emperor fought in the name of Christ and, in part, for the defense of the interests of the church. Rather than posing a more-faithful-to-God alternative to the social order—the stance which underlies Christus Victor—the church had come to support the status quo with little critique.

Traditional historiography suggested that Christus Victor faded away because it was inappropriate to think of God either acknowledging certain rights of Satan or stooping to tricking the devil, or because the image of a cosmic battle was incompatible with a modern worldview. I find that explanation inadequate at best. The real reason for the demise of Christus Victor was the fact that the church no longer posed an alternative to the social order. Undergirding the Christus Victor motif as sketched here is the assumption that the church would exist as a counterproposal to the prevailing structures so compromised by evil. The cosmic imagery of Christus Victor is really a statement about the universal significance of the confrontation in history of Jesus and the early church over against the Greco-Roman empire. The so-called Constantinian shift is a label for the evolutionary changes that eroded the historical component of this confrontation. The historical confrontation was abandoned; the church no longer constituted a countersociety; the church now supported the imperial powers and worked through the prevailing social order. With all this, the cosmic imagery was left dangling and empty.[20] Emptied of its content, it would be abandoned as meaningless.[21]

Salvation Detached from Ethics in Anselm and Abelard

The axis of Anselm-Abelard has provided the parameters for much of the atonement discussion of the last millennium. At several junctures, the atonement motifs of Anselm and Abelard reflect their genesis in the post-Constantine church.[22] One such juncture concerns the location of Christian *ethics* in the atonement motif. For Anselm, the question that the death of Christ answered was how to satisfy the honor of an offended God. Anselm's solution required the death of a perfect human, while the divine nature of Jesus would give that perfect death complete efficacy for the sins of all humankind. For the penal version, the question for sinners was how to escape the penalty of death which their sin merited; and the answer was that Jesus bore the penalty as a substitute for sinners or in their place.

Those solutions to the atonement question require the essential categories of humanity and Deity, and situate them in the context of legal relationship between God and humankind. However, understanding atonement in terms of a legal construct removes it from our world or places it outside of the historical world in which we live. But it is precisely in that historical world that we discuss how to live in ways shaped by the reign of God. Stated another way, atonement defined in terms of a legal paradigm does not make use of what is learned about Jesus from the story-shaped and story-based Christology sketched above.[23]

Anselm's satisfaction theory does not make inherently necessary any specific or particular knowledge of the way Jesus was human or divine, nor does it require any particular knowledge of Jesus' teaching. Neither does the resurrection of Jesus figure as an integral dimension in Anselm's understanding of atonement. Certainly Anselmian atonement does not *deny* resurrection nor *reject* particular knowledge of Jesus' acts which portray *how* he is human and divine. But these particular dimensions are not inherently necessary to the discussion of atonement in the legal framework.

Abelard requires God to be present in Jesus so that the loving act of Jesus' death reveals the love of the Father. Yet his moral influence theory does not adequately explain why death is inherently necessary to convey the Father's love. Neither does it make use of the specific dimensions of the particular life and death of Jesus. Nor does resurrection constitute an intrinsic component of the moral influence theory of atonement. However, if we are to locate ethics with reference to the norm of Jesus, we need to know both the teaching and the particular acts of Jesus. The fact that those elements are lacking from the atonement motifs of Anselm and Abelard point to their separation of ethics from the story of Jesus and from salvation. In the post-Constantine church, *ethics became detached from Jesus;* precisely in that era, these atonement theories were developed.

Church Co-opted by Empire

The sword provides perhaps the most easily understood example of this separation of ethics from salvation. The *church accepted the sword* and acquiesced to the imperial army fighting in the name of Christ and under a banner bearing the cross. In so doing, the church had shifted the orientation of its ethics from Jesus to the exigencies of the social order. The functional question for ethics was no longer "How can we live within the story of Jesus?" but "What must we do to preserve the social order?" The normative reference for ethics had shifted from Jesus, who reflected *the reign of God;* to the emperor, whose policy was determined by the needs of *his empire.* Ethics had become separated from atonement and salvation, and the atonement motifs of Anselm and Abelard fit that context. This argument is not a claim that Anselm and Abelard were unconcerned about ethics. It is rather a recognition that their atonement motifs reflect a church which came to consider the content of ethics and the characteristics of the saved life *apart from* the teaching and the particular narrative of Jesus.

In contrast to satisfaction and moral influence theories, the historicized Christus Victor motif as sketched above anchors the discussion of atonement and salvation in the particular, historical life of Jesus. The story-based Christology that also constitutes a statement of Christus Victor uses the life of Jesus as its foundational categories. To be saved means to be located within the narrative of Jesus and to have a life shaped by that story. This approach pays particular attention to the way Jesus lived as a human. That life reveals the character of the reign of God, which Jesus embodies. In the historical realm, Jesus confronts evil, and the rule of God confronts the worldly realm. In contrast to both satisfaction and moral theories, Christus Victor needs the resurrection as an inherent part of the discussion; without resurrection, there is no salvation. In contrast to the satisfaction theory's focus on past sin and guilt, Christus Victor assumes that the saved person is both freed from past bondage to sin and freed for present and future life transformed by the reign of God.

Accommodation to Sin

Anselmian atonement fits the Constantinian ecclesiology in a second way. The post-Constantine church adopted a *minimal ethic* for Christians. Rather than envisioning a change in orientation, church leaders typically assumed that Christians would continue to sin in ways that reflect the fallen character of the social order. When theologians spoke of a debt payment or of satisfying the requirement of God's law, that accommodated itself well to the ongoing nature of sin. Debt payment cancels the residue of past sin (as well as original sin), but does not deal in a fundamental way with the future life of the Christian. According to such a construct, one can be saved and experience salvation at the moment, and yet at the same time not experience a fundamental transformation or reorientation of one's life.[24]

In contrast, a proper understanding of salvation begins within the context of social confrontation. It comes much closer to assuming a transformation or at least a reorientation of thought and action. To join the new society of the church is to adopt a new lifestyle, a way to think and act which contrasts with the fallen social order. The change may be only gradual, and it will always be in a process of becoming. The idea that the church poses a contrast is not a claim to perfection. However, it is (or should be) obvious whether one is intending to conform to the new social construct of the reign of God.

In part it is a matter of the view one has of failure or sin. If one assumes that the church should present a contrast, then failure or sin is recognized as an incomplete or imperfect witness to the reign of God. On the other hand, if the church's orientation is merely to support or work through the prevailing social order, then the church can excuse itself because of the world existing within the church. Hence, many say the church cannot really be different from the fallen social order, though sinners may nonetheless still claim to have their penalty paid or forgiven.

Individualistic Salvation

A third correlation of atonement motifs and ecclesiological images focuses on the extent to which salvation has an intrinsically social dimension. Salvation as understood by the Anselm-Abelard axis has a *primarily individual component,* whichever side of their argument one wants to pursue. The satisfaction or substitutionary theory of Anselm defines the problem of the sinner in inherently individual terms. The sinner owes a debt, and the debt is personal to that sinner. When paid, the sinner is saved. While for Anselm, Jesus's death does satisfy God's justice in the universe, that satisfaction does not change the individual nature of the debt-penalty arrangement with the individual sinner.

Abelard's moral influence theory is equally individualistic. Upon perceiving the loving death of Christ, the rebellious sinner perceives one's own alienation and rebellion and turns to God. In each case, the answer to sin envisions the status of the individual and God, and it is complete at that level. One can, of course, go on to discuss how that saved individual may or can or should engage in community and be socially responsible and establish relationships with other saved individuals. That social component, however, is logically an afterthought, something to consider *after* one has dealt with the prior, fundamental, and individualistic problem of personal guilt and penalty.

The absence of a social component to salvation fits with the Constantinian ecclesiology. Since the church had come to coincide with the dominant society, the church had lost the sense that salvation needed a social dimension over against or in witness to the Western social order. Stated another way, since the society was assumed to be Christian, the idea disappeared from view that the work of Christ envisions the transformation of institutions as well as individuals. Since society as a whole had been declared Christian, no perceived need existed to declare salvation as social. The focus on individuals and the individualization and personalization of sin and salvation followed as a natural consequence.

In contrast, Christus Victor, by assuming a church that posed an alternative to the social order, implies the creation of a *saved social structure* as an integral part of salvation. This structure is the church as the earthly manifestation of and testimony to the reign of God. It situates the discussion of sin and salvation within the clash of reigns, between the confrontation of the forces of good and the forces of evil. When we recall the specific context behind Revelation, it is the (social) institution of the church over against the (social) institution of the dominant society and the Greco-Roman empire. By understanding salvation within the framework of the victorious Christ, who makes present the reign of God, salvation is seen inherently to include saved relationships and structures as well as saved individuals.

Salvation in the church is personal and individual, of course, but it is the church which gives expression to and shapes that individual faith. To be Christian means to be a part of the church, a part of the movement whose existence is made visible because of its stance contrasting with the social order. The more clear we are about the specific historical reality of the confrontation between church and social order, the more clear it is that salvation has a social component or expression, belonging to the people of God. Hence, the work of Christ must be dealt with in such a way as to understand that social component as intrinsic to the work of Christ. It is that intrinsically social component of salvation which is lacking in the complex of the Anselm-Abelard approach to atonement.

The analysis in this section points to two sets of correlations. When it is a question of atonement motifs and ecclesiology, Christus Victor corresponds to alternative church ecclesiology while the motifs of satisfaction and moral influence are linked to Christendom ecclesiology. The second correlation is the location of ethics in the calculus of atonement motifs. Ethics is intrinsically a facet of atonement for Christus Victor, while ethics is unhooked from atonement in the satisfaction image and somewhat less so in the moral influence theory. The final section of the chapter applies this analysis to understanding the ethical and social concerns and the atonement theology of nineteenth-century American evangelicalism and revivalism.

Nineteenth-Century American Revivalism and Atonement

Revivalism shaped the religious ethos of nineteenth-century evangelicals, the majority Protestant tradition of the nineteenth century.[25] Evangelicalism in the nineteenth century had a strong moral and social concern. Revivalism provided the impulse for much of that social concern. Finney exemplifies these impulses.

Finney, Atonement, and Moral Concern

The foremost revival preacher of his era, Charles G. Finney (1792-1875) introduced into revivalism the so-called new measures, what Nathan Hatch called "techniques of hard-sell persuasion."[26] These new techniques included "protracted meetings" that continued for several days or weeks, the anxious bench at the front of the church where assistants could labor with those under conviction of sin, prayers and speeches by women in public and in meetings where men were present, and meetings conducted in an informal atmosphere with considerable religious frenzy.

While Finney made conversion central to revival, he believed that social reform was an appendage that would accompany revivalism. In particular, he preached against the social sin of slavery and became an ardent advocate of abolitionism from his location at Oberlin College, where he became professor of theology in 1835 and president in 1850.

Nineteenth-century evangelicals and revivalists had other social concerns as well. Finney also opposed smoking, drinking, and dancing. Other issues on the reform agenda of evangelicals were Sunday observance, opposition to Freemasonry, and the "purity campaign" against prostitution. Nineteenth-century evangelicalism had strong feminist impulses, and women were centrally involved in the various reform programs. There was also dissatisfaction with bourgeois church life. A concern for the poor is evidenced by opposition to pew rentals and the founding of the Free Methodist Church with free pews.

These impulses of social reform and concern for the poor drew inspiration from Jesus' words about preaching the gospel to the poor. The results were a strong critique of existing society and identification with class interests of the poor. Yet they were also deeply embedded in the social fabric of the time. For example, Paul Johnson's analysis of Finney's highly successful 1830-31 campaign in Rochester, New York, shows that the social reforms were part of the effort in the city to maintain a healthy social climate and stable working conditions in a time of economic growth and changing class structures.[27]

The decades after the Civil War saw the gradual disappearance of the reforming spirit of evangelicalism nourished by revivalism. Donald Dayton identified both general and particular factors that contributed to this demise and applied some general sociological analysis.[28] It is difficult to maintain intensity of effort for long periods of time, and to transfer first-generation zeal to later generations of reformers. No doubt the strictures Finney placed on "worldly amusements" caused some children to feel alienated from their society. This produced a greater desire to be at home in the dominant culture. Some converts from lower economic status used the discipline of an ordered life to rise in social and economic level; they may have chosen to insulate themselves against the impact of the lower class from which they had escaped and which now seemed to threaten their newfound status.[29]

However, beyond these general reasons, several unique factors contributed in significant ways to a declining impulse for social reform. For one, the Civil War provoked a reorientation toward issues of social reform. In part, revivalism and the revivalist impulse to reform in the pre-Civil War era reflected the general optimism of a young nation with seemingly endless frontiers to conquer. In the throes of that optimism, it did not occur to evangelicals that values from that society would conflict with each other. In Finney's early years at Oberlin, for example, evangelicals were committed both to the peace movement and to the antislavery crusade. However, the Civil War forced a choice between these two ideals, and the reformers opted for the antislavery campaign. In the process, they lost some of their optimism about the possibility of reform.

The antislavery impulse was also involved in a second way in the demise of the impulse for social reform among evangelicals and revivalists. Abolition of slavery was the most social of all the reformist issues supported by revivalism. The reformers saw slavery as the sin which most profoundly infected the social order as a whole. Reform issues that remained after the Civil War included temperance, anti-Freemasonry, the "purity campaign," and Sabbath observance. With the profoundly social sin of slavery eliminated, these remaining issues devolved into questions of individual and personal morality. Thus individual morality characterized later revivalist ethic in contrast to the social orientation of pre-Civil War revivalism.

Dayton's observations concerning post-Civil War changes in the reform impulse of evangelicals should be qualified by Herbert Gutman's analysis of Protestantism and the American labor movement. Gutman suggested that after the Civil War, the perfectionist evangelicalism of the Finney sort continued to drive the labor movement and gave it a sharp critique of changes happening in society. This evangelical impulse also distinguished labor's social protest from that of the social gospel promulgated by middle- and upper-class reformers.[30]

Accompanying this shift from a social to a primarily personal ethic, post-Civil War evangelicals experienced a profound disappointment. The optimistic revivalist and reformist movements had as a goal the development of a Christian society. After the American Revolution, the constitution officially barred the government from establishing any and all particular religions, including Christianity. Nonetheless, evangelicals expected that the revivalist movement, accompanied by a host of nondenominational and quasi-church structures sometimes called the "benevolent empire," would play the role in Christianizing American society on a voluntary basis. They envisioned a "Christian America," a kind of voluntary established Protestantism, with such principles as temperance, opposition to slavery, and Sabbath observance incorporated into the laws and cultural life of the nation.[31]

In the epoch following the Civil War, challenges began to emerge to this vision of a "Christian America."[32] Numerous European immigrants did not support the temperance movement, and both Roman Catholic and Jewish immigrants challenged the idea of a "Christian" America, actually a "Protestant" America. Dissident religious groups, such as the Latter Day Saints (Mormons), appeared on the scene. In addition, urbanization and industrialization created problems beyond the scope of the revivalist reform vision. The rise of biblical criticism and Charles Darwin's critique of the traditional views of human origins appeared to demonstrate for evangelicals the increasing secularization of American society. For the evangelicals, pre-Civil War optimism turned into post-Civil War pessimism.[33]

Some theological shifts both contributed to and reflected this growing pessimism. The most significant was the shift from postmillennialism to premillennialism. The reform activity of Finney and other revivalists was linked to postmillennialism. A good deal of the motivation for revivalist and reform activity came from the desire to prepare the way for the millennium and usher it in. That millennium itself reflected the vision of the perfect society which evangelicals expected to produce with their reform efforts. Finney, for example, proclaimed that if the church will "do her duty" in proclaiming the gospel and carrying out social reforms, "the millennium may come in this country in three years."[34] Integral to the early nineteenth-century evangelical vision was the idea of a Christian America whose complete manifestation would resemble the millennium.

This optimistic eschatology, which expected the revivalist-inspired reforms to prepare the world for Christ's return, collapsed after the Civil War. It was replaced by premillennialism, an eschatology that expected the near return of Christ to rescue believers out of this sinful world. Many evangelical leaders announced their conversion to the new eschatology of premillennialism. George Marsden illustrated this transition, for example, in terms of the successive presidents of Wheaton College. Jonathan Blanchard (1811-1892), who became president at Wheaton in 1860, was a postmillennialist and vigorous advocate of social reform. Late in his life, Jonathan softened his postmillennial stance and professed to believe "both theories and neither." Charles Blanchard (1848-1925) succeeded his father as Wheaton's president in 1882. The younger Blanchard opted fully for dispensational premillennialism, with attendant views on social reform.[35]

These two millennial positions have widely divergent views on the outworking of the divine will in the world. Postmillennialists emphasized God's grace and gradual transformation of society under the influence of grace. Premillennialists expected a radical and immediate transformation to the millennium, worked by Christ on the earth. Postmillennialists saw progress in such things as success in foreign missions and the spread of literacy. Premillennialists pointed to rising crime and social problems as evidence for an increase of evil in the world. Postmillennialists saw the world being transformed into the reign of God before their eyes. Premillennialists believed that no real transformation of the wicked world could happen until Jesus returned to inaugurate that change.

The shift between these two worldviews often had a profound impact on the social involvement of evangelicals. In the majority of cases, premillennialists tended to abandon programs of long-term social reform and focus on extensive efforts of preaching the gospel to as many people as possible before the expected soon return of Christ to begin the millennium. Evangelical energy had once gone into social reform and reform rallies; now that vigor was redirected into exegetical speculation about the timing of the return of Christ and into support of prophecy conferences.

Another theological shift that undercut social reform developed from the impact of so-called old school Presbyterianism, particularly the version known as the Princeton theology. This theology held sway at Princeton from its founding in 1812 until the split that produced Westminster Theological Seminary in 1929. Charles Hodge represented that theology in mid-nineteenth century. Finney's theology and reforms opposed Princeton theology, and Hodge pitted Princeton against Finney and the abolitionists and also against the women's movement that emerged from abolitionist efforts.[36]

Princeton theology was highly intellectual, understood faith largely in a doctrinal sense, and placed a high premium on orthodoxy and correct doctrine. While not anti-intellectual, Oberlin and Finney produced a different theology, more oriented toward questions of ethics, action, and doing right rather than thinking right. Hodge was deterministic, while Finney rejected the traditional Calvinist teaching and stressed free will.

Hodge and Finney differed in the relative emphasis they gave to sin and redemption. Finney placed greater weight on redemption and the power of God's grace to transform both sinful persons and sinful society. In contrast, the Princeton theologians were greatly impressed by sin in the world. They maintained that one implication of human depravity was that no person ever suffered as much as one's sins deserved. The Princeton theologians also resisted the idea that God's grace actually overcame sin in this life; they came close to making the sinful state normative.

This difference appeared in their attitudes toward women. Conscious of the impact of sin, the Princeton theologians tended to focus on the curse in the Fall narrative, arguing that the subordination of women in that text made subordination of women a universal principle normative for all of human life. In contrast, Finney and the Oberlinites saw the curse as descriptive of the sinful state from which people can be redeemed. Thus, women could and should be elevated to positions of equality, especially within the church. It was this emphasis on the possibility of redemption which supplied the theological support for Finney's efforts at social reform.

With its stress on the sin and the virtual impossibility of a trans-formed existence, Princeton theology reflected the tendency toward pessimism about social change that was also characteristic of premillennialism. Its ascendancy thus followed the growing pessimism after the Civil War.

Several of the Mennonite and Amish figures in the following chapters discussed some aspects of the revivalists' agenda of social reform. If not active participants, they at least supported to some extent such particular items of the revivalists' agenda as opposition to slavery, temperance, Sabbath observance, and opposition to Freemasonry. However, one dimension of the revivalists' social concern and efforts at social reform distinguished them markedly from the Mennonite and Amish characters who appear in the following chapters. For the revivalists, the primary focus of their social concern was American society. As noted above, their efforts to save sinners had the goal of building a Christian society, of creating a Christian nation. In contrast, Mennonites and Amish focused on building the church. This difference in social outlook appears, for example, with the issue of temperance. While more progressive Mennonites may have taken part to some extent in the temperance movement, more conservative ones refused to become involved because they opposed participation in worldly movements.[37]

The distinction between the expression of Christian social concern through church or structures of society appears most sharply for the question of war. As previously noted, the revivalist reformers were not pacifists. They supported the Civil War—on both sides, although the majority favored the Northern cause. Abolitionists opted, albeit reluctantly, to pursue that reform through war, as used by American and Western Christendom, rather than through means located within the narrative of Jesus. The revivalists conceived of their primary Christian social identity in terms of American society rather than in terms of the church. American revivalists thus had a modern "Constantinian" outlook.[38]

Underneath the competing views on social reform resides a theory of atonement, which comprises the central focus of this book. This is considered in the context of the evolution of the evangelical and revivalist attitude toward social reform, the shift from a postmillennial to a premillennial eschatology, and the growing influence of the more pessimistic Princeton theology. I want to sketch two versions of the satisfaction view of atonement from the North American theological scene. One version is that of Charles G. Finney, whose career covered the beginning of the Mennonite era of this study. An opponent of Princeton theology, Finney departed from Calvinism on the question of free will. His version of atonement was in line with the governmental theory. The career of Benjamin B. Warfield bridged the end of the Mennonite era of this study. Warfield's atonement theology continued A. A. (son of Charles) Hodge's opposition to the views earlier articulated by Finney. On the discussion of atonement, the disagreement between Finney and Warfield is an intramural argument within the satisfaction family of atonement views.

Charles G. Finney treats atonement in his lectures on systematic theology.[39] Both his specific statement of atonement and the larger context in which he situated the doctrine make quite clear that his approach is located within the cluster of views that stem from the satisfaction theory. More specifically, Finney advocated a governmental theory of atonement in line with the view of Hugo Grotius.

The lectures begin with Finney's description of moral law and moral government. That orientation constitutes the framework in which to understand his view of atonement. As Finney described it, laws provide rules of action. These rules he divided into "physical" and "moral." Physical laws deal with things which happen as a matter of course, without any decision or act of will, such as in the law of gravity. In other words, physical law applies to the material universe. In contrast, moral law rules actions which are voluntary and have moral implications. Sanctions secure conformity to moral law.[40]

Government is guidance or control in accordance with law. Moral government deals with administration of moral law. "It is the government of free will." The happiness of moral beings, and ultimately their holiness, depends on or is ruled by moral law and moral government. "Moral Government then, is indispensable to the highest well-being of the universe of moral agents, and therefore ought to, and must exist. The universe is dependent upon this as a means of securing the highest good." The one who may govern is the one whose attributes, "physical and moral," are best suited to government. Not surprisingly, Finney argues that God is the one who has the right and the duty to govern: "He is a Moral Governor,"[41] while human beings have the obligation to obey moral law.[42] After extended discussion of the various components of that obligation, Finney asserts that the essence of the moral law is expressed in love,[43] while the essence of disobedience is selfishness.[44] In his description of selfishness, he includes war and owning slaves.[45]

Finney presented atonement as "a very important feature of the moral government of God."[46] Under a system of law, the governor—in this case, God—provides for the protection of the law, and justice is the execution of penalties when the law is violated. Finney distinguished two kinds of justice—distributive and public. His rationale for a general atonement emerges from the distinction of these two kinds of justice. Distributive justice consists of applying, that is distributing, to each subject of government the full penalty required by the law. Public justice consists of protecting the public interest and the highest good by those acts which protect the integrity of the law. In other words, if some act or legislation is performed which upholds the integrity of the law, then that act or legislation can substitute for the full penalty which distributive justice would act. "Public justice thus makes exceptions as often as this is permitted or required by the public good."

Public justice, as understood by Finney, is not dispensing with justice nor with the concept of penalty. It is rather that because a substitute has been found or enacted, the distributive penalty can be forgiven because the integrity of the law is upheld by the substitute.

> Since the head of the government is pledged to protect and promote the public interests by a due administration of law, if in any instance he would dispense with the execution of penalties in case of a violation of the precept, public justice requires that he shall see that a substitute for the execution of law is provided, or that something is done that shall as effectually secure the influence of law as the execution of the penalty would do.[47]

As Finney understood the Governor's means of protecting the integrity of the law, the Governor's options are two: either exact all the penalties required of all subjects, or provide a substitute that will just as "effectively secure the influence of law as the execution of the penalty would do. . . . Either the soul that sinneth must die, according to the letter of the law, or a substitute must be provided in accordance with the spirit of the law."[48] When the substitute is found, and the sinner has returned to obedience, then public justice "demands that the penalty should be set aside by extending pardon to the offender."[49] While the offender still deserves punishment, public justice has spared the culprit the application of that penalty.

In Finney's understanding, atonement is that which satisfies the demand of public justice and thus provides the possibility of the pardon. To ensure that sinners cannot save themselves by their own human effort, a specific condition of this pardon is that it be "upon a condition not within the power of the offender" to effect. Public justice can consent to pardon only upon the provision of an atonement. "Atonement is the governmental substitution of the sufferings of Christ for the sufferings of sinners. It is a covering of their sins by his sufferings."[50]

Finney argued that natural law supports the idea of atonement. It is clear from natural law, for example, that God's own intelligence and character would be compromised if God made forgiveness possible to sinners on the basis of repentance only, without an atonement that satisfied the provisions of the law. Since the intent of the penalties of the law is to procure compliance, forgiveness without atonement would be tantamount to repeal of law.[51]

While Finney rejected the terminology of atonement as a "commercial transaction" or the "payment of a debt," he was not rejecting the idea of satisfaction. What he objected to was the idea from distributive justice, that Jesus suffered an exact amount demanded and determined by the full penalty of the law. Such suffering, Finney argued, would make Jesus' suffering eternal. "To suppose, therefore, that Christ suffered in amount all that was due to the elect, is to suppose that he suffered an eternal punishment multiplied by the whole number of the elect." Rather, he said, "the atonement of Christ was intended as a satisfaction of public justice."[52] Without paying the entire price, Jesus' death nonetheless constituted the substitute for that penalty which preserved the integrity of the law and allowed the Governor to proclaim a pardon.

These comments comprised Finney's answer to the view of Warfield, described below, who argued that Jesus' death did pay the exact, full price for sin. Warfield's view then means that Christ died only for the elect. In contrast, Finney's view described Christ's provision of a general atonement for all sinners, applicable to all who accepted it.

Finney's summary on the design of atonement is that "the atonement of Christ was intended as a satisfaction of public justice," so that the penalty required by the law could be set aside.[53] Once Finney established the atonement as the means for satisfying public justice, he developed further characteristics of atonement. These included its moral influence. "The atonement would present to creatures the highest possible motives to virtue. Example is the highest moral influence that can be exerted."[54]

Following his treatment of atonement, Finney passed to a discussion of human government. He explained how the institutions that organize human society reflect and are shaped by the moral law. The idea of human government, he said, is an intrinsic part of the natural order, a part of the providential and moral government of God. Intrinsic to human government is the use of force and violence to preserve order. And if it is necessary to preserve order, "it can never be wrong."[55]

Finney considered war a part of the necessary use of force to preserve order. He acknowledged that much war was unnecessary and therefore sinful. In particular, he characterized the recent war with Mexico as sinful. He also equated support for an unjust war with support for the intrinsically oppressive institution of slavery. To support either of these unjust institutions was to support sin. However, when war was commanded by God to preserve order, Finney said, then it was appropriate for Christians to participate in it as a part of the ordering function of government. Thus war might be necessary to preserve order; in addition, when government became oppressive, war was actually required to restore a just human government. He judged the war of the American Revolution to be one such justifiable revolution.[56] Given Finney's idea of a God-ordained war in the name of a good cause, one should not be surprised at the collapse of the peace movement at Oberlin in the face of the Civil War, as described above.

This description of Finney's atonement theology reveals that it fits within the observations made earlier about satisfaction theory.

1. The focus of atonement is an individual relationship between the individual and God, a relationship defined by legal parameters. That relationship defined in legal parameters is situated outside of the lives of Christians in history.

2. Finney's discussion of atonement does not involve ethics as an intrinsic dimension of atonement. War and slavery were examples of violation of the law. However, dealing with those violations was a matter of penalty, law, and satisfying public justice. In contrast to the Christus Victor model depicted earlier, Finney's atonement discussion preserved nothing of the particularity or narrative of Jesus.

3. On the other hand, Finney clearly believed that saved individuals, those whose penalty is forgiven on the basis of the satisfaction of public justice by the death of Christ, will experience a regeneration that results in moral impulses of social reform. However, in a way he did not realize, the shaping of social ethics and the reforming impulses came more from the American story than from the story of Jesus. That observation is particularly true for the question of war, and the choice

made by the abolitionists for the Civil War. The satisfaction theory of atonement, which relates the death of Christ to a relationship outside of the realm of human history and human life, allows this separation of salvation and ethics.

Warfield and Substitutionary Atonement for Individuals

Benjamin B. Warfield (1851-1921) wrote several articles on atonement and made clear his view that only the "substitutive" atonement first articulated by Anselm fully reflects the biblical data. Warfield considered all other views suspect. As a particular case, his substitutive atonement is posed as an alternative to the general atonement, which Finney represented.

One of Warfield's articles dealt with the terms *ransom* and the more popular terms *Redeemer* and *redeemed.* He argued that although the two terms derived from the same Latin root and are thus synonyms, *ransom* is the more precise term and best preserved the meaning of the original Greek term in the New Testament. In his view, ransom best preserved the idea that a soul is saved or redeemed "by the payment of a price," by the blood of Christ. Much of the article decried the diminution of the idea of "purchase for a price" in contemporary liberal theology, so that redemption or *Erlösung* was coming to mean only general deliverance, as it did in other religions. Emphasizing the purchase component, Warfield concluded the article by asking,

> Do you realize that Christ is your Ransomer and has actually shed His blood for you as your ransom? Do you realize that your salvation has been bought, bought at a tremendous price, at the price of nothing less precious than blood, and that the blood of Christ, the Holy One of God?[57]

In another article, Warfield dealt with atonement theories in terms of the history of doctrine.[58] Here he made it clear that Christ's "payment of a price" took place within the conceptual framework of Anselm's satisfaction theory of atonement. Both because the doctrine was so clear in the New Testament and because the early church was concerned with more pressing problems, it was not until Anselm in the eleventh century that atonement received a thorough explanation.

> Representing it, in terms derived from the Roman law, as in its essence a "satisfaction" to the divine justice, Anselm set it once for all in its true relations to the inherent necessities of the divine nature, and to the magnitude of human guilt; and thus determined the outlines of the doctrine for all subsequent thought.[59]

Summarizing developments with the doctrine, Warfield noted that its vital conceptions "were reduced to scientific statement by the Protestant scholastics, by whom it was that the complete doctrine of 'satisfaction' was formulated with a thoroughness and comprehensiveness of grasp which has made it the permanent possession of the Church."[60] In this "developed form," the doctrine thus

> represents our Lord as making satisfaction for us "by His blood and righteousness"; on the one hand, to the justice of God, outraged by human sin, in bearing the penalty due to our guilt in His own sacrificial death; and, on the other hand, to the demands of the law of God requiring perfect obedience, in fulfilling in His immaculate life on earth as the second Adam the probation which Adam failed to keep.[61]

The continuing description of this "double work" of Christ, aimed at both God and God's law, notes that it brings to bear on sinners "every conceivable influence adapted to deter them from sin and to win them back to good and to God." This includes proclamation of "full forgiveness of sin in the blood of Christ," by revelation of the spiritual world, by the example of his own perfect life, and "above all, by the purchase of the gift of the Holy Spirit for His people" as a power which will "supernaturally regenerate their hearts" and conform them "to His image."[62]

To place the satisfaction theory in relation to other, erroneous theories of atonement, Warfield categorized them according to the "person or persons" on whom the work of Christ terminates. This scheme produced five categories, ranged in "ascending order" of correctness.

The first has Christ's death "terminating upon Satan," the passé Christus Victor theory.

The second category understood Christ's death as "terminating physically on man." It assumed that Christ took on human nature, enabling sinners to be saved as "they become partakers (by faith) of this purified humanity."

In the third category, the work of Christ terminated "on man, in the way of bringing to bear on him inducements to action." This category included the moral influence theory.

The fourth category pictured the work of Christ as "terminating on both man and God, but on man primarily and on God only secondarily." This category included the governmental theories (such as Finney's), in which Jesus' death is understood to satisfy the conditions for salvation, but does not save sinners until they take the responsibility on themselves to make a response.

The final category contained the theories in which the work of Christ terminated "primarily on God and secondarily on man."[63] As far as Warfield was concerned, only theories which fit in this last category were valid, and even some of these had more validity than others:

> The Biblical doctrine of the sacrifice of Christ finds full recognition in no other construction than that of the established church-doctrine of satisfaction. According to it, our Lord's redeeming work is at its core a true and perfect sacrifice offered to God, of intrinsic value ample for the expiation of our guilt; and at the same time is a true and perfect righteousness offered to God in fulfillment of the demands of His law; both the one and the other being offered in behalf of His people, and, on being accepted by God, accruing to their benefit; so that by this satisfaction they are relieved at once from the curse of their guilt as breakers of the law, and from the burden of the law as a condition of life; and this by a work of such kind and performed in such a manner, as to carry home to the hearts of men a profound sense of the indefectible righteousness of God and to make them a perfect revelation of His love; so that, by this one and indivisible work, both God is reconciled to us, and we, under the quickening influence of the Spirit bought for us by it, are reconciled to God, so making peace— external peace between an angry God and sinful man, and internal peace in the response of the human conscience to the restored smile of God. This doctrine which has been incorporated in more or less fullness of statement in the creedal declarations of all the great branches of the church, Greek, Latin, Lutheran, and Reformed, and which has been expounded with more or less insight and power by the leading doctors of the churches for the last eight hundred years, was first given scientific statements by Anselm (*q.v.*) in his "Cur Deus homo" (1098); but reached its complete development only at the hands of the so-called Protestant Scholastics of the seventeenth century.[64]

Warfield's *Plan of Salvation*[65] added one additional element to his understanding of atonement. In this small book, he explained the divine decree for the salvation of the human race. The first chapter sorted out the several approaches to salvation. In ascending levels, Warfield defined a choice between two alternatives, each of which is the correction of an error at the preceding level. The first choice is between naturalistic and supernaturalistic approaches to the plan of salvation. Then for supernaturalistic approaches, one must choose between sacerdotalists (such as Roman Catholics) and evangelicals (most Protestants).

Among Protestants, one opts for either universalistic or particularistic approaches. At this juncture, the difference concerns whether God has planned actually to save particular sinners so that the grace of God always acts on particular individuals, or whether God has merely provided the general or universal possibility of salvation for those who avail themselves of it. As Warfield defined it, the issue dividing universalists and particularists was "whether the saving grace of God, in which alone is salvation, actually saves. Does its presence mean salvation, or may it be present, and yet salvation fail?"[66]

Finally, at the last level, Warfield divided the particularists between supralapsarians and infralapsarians. The point of difference concerned whether even at creation, God already considered human beings as sinful. The distinguishing point between supralapsarians and infralapsarians "is whether God, in his dealing with humans with reference to their destiny, divides them into two classes merely as human beings, or as sinners. The question is whether God's decree of election and preterition concerns men contemplated merely as men, or contemplated as already sinful men, a *massa corrupta.*"[67] After some discussion, Warfield restated the question as "whether God discriminates between men in order that he may save some [supralapsarians]; or whether he saves some in order that he may discriminate between men [infralapsarians]."[68]

At this juncture, Warfield opts for the infralapsarians. In his analysis, the supralapsarian version of particularism is inconsistent. If God created humankind with the intent of allowing some of them to fall and not be redeemed, and thus to end up outside the plan of salvation, that re-introduces into the supralapsarian version of particularism an element of the universalistic, that the atoning death of Jesus does not actually save but only establishes the possibility of salvation. Thus he concluded, "Infralapsarianism offers the only scheme which is either self-consistent or consistent with the facts."[69]

The following chapters of *Plan of Salvation* discussed the several options in more detail. In each case, a primary critique was that salvation whether by human effort or by a universalistic or general decree of salvation—one in which Christ's death provides the possibility of salvation to whomsoever will—is a denial of particular or substitutive atonement.[70] The concern for "substitutive atonement" is particularly evident in the final chapter that treats "Calvinism."

Particularism, which Warfield called a mark of Calvinism, means that the "saving operations of God are directed in every case immediately to the individuals who are saved. . . . God the Lord, in his saving operations, deals not generally with mankind at large, but particularly with the individuals who are actually saved."[71] On the other hand, denying particularism "is constructively the denial of the immediacy of saving grace, that is, of evangelicalism, and of the supernaturalism of salvation, that is, of Christianity itself. It is logically the total rejection of Christianity."[72]

Warfield's description of Calvinism recognized four versions of particularism—supralapsarian and infralapsarian, as well as two versions of particularism which are framed within a general or universalistic offer of salvation to all persons. Of course, he did not consider these four versions equally valid or innerly consistent. For present purposes, we can observe the role he articulated for substitutionary atonement without pursuing his analysis of the various particularisms. For Warfield, the problem with all but the infralapsarianism view was that they amounted to a denial of the efficacy of the "substitutive atonement."

He considered the governmental theory of atonement to be inconsistent because it featured a universal call and a particular atonement:

> All the substance of the atonement is evaporated, that it may be given a universal reference. And, indeed, we may at once recognize it as an unavoidable effect of universalizing the atonement that it is by that very act eviscerated. If it does nothing for any man that it does not do for all men, . . . then, it is obvious that it saves no man; for clearly not all men are saved. The things that we have to choose between, are an atonement of high value, or an atonement of wide extension. The two cannot go together. And this is the real objection of Calvinism to this compromise scheme which presents itself as an improvement on its system: it universalizes the atonement at the cost of its intrinsic value, and Calvinism demands a really substitutive atonement which actually saves. And as a really substitutive atonement which actually saves cannot be universal because obviously all men are not saved, in the interests of the integrity of the atonement it insists that particularism has entered into the saving process prior, in the order of thought, to the atonement.[73]

Warfield made similar comments about the postredemptionist view and other versions of particularism. He concluded that the important point for Calvinist particularism was

> that God's method of saving men is to set upon them in his almighty grace, to purchase them to himself by the precious blood of his Son, to visit them in the inmost core of their being by the creative operations of his Spirit, and himself, the Lord God Almighty, to save them.[74]

In other words, in Warfield's view, Jesus' death accomplished nothing if it is not immediately and directly applied to the ransom of particular sinners. In that redemption, Jesus accomplished something for them which they could not accomplish on their own initiative. And God, the architect of the plan, is the one who saves them. Warfield required a substitutionary atonement, by means of which God immediately and directly saved particular, sinful individuals.

While Warfield's theory of atonement focused on individuals, it was not limited to individuals. In the last pages of *Plan of Salvation*, he gave atonement a social or cosmic dimension. Individual persons "are not discrete particles standing off from one another as mutually isolated units." Instead, people "are members of an organism, the human race; and this race itself is an element in a greater organism which is significantly termed a universe."[75] Since God so loved the world, it is this universe which is the ultimate object of salvation. In God's plan the human race as a whole and the organism which is the universe will be saved. It is this understanding of salvation which is the "true universalism of the gospel."[76]

The salvation of a particular individual is a process, complete only at the sound of the last trumpet. Similarly, the salvation of the universe will be complete only at the last trumpet. Many souls will be lost in the course of that process. The goal, however, "to which the race is advancing is set by God: it is salvation." Warfield thus concluded by asserting that there is no contradiction between the claims that Christ died for his people and also for the world. The important point, however, is that salvation depends absolutely on Christ.

> But it must be punctually observed that unless it is Christ who, not opens the way of salvation to all, but actually saves his people, there is no ground to believe that there will ever be a saved world. The salvation of the world is absolutely dependent (as is the salvation of the individual soul) on its salvation being the sole work of the Lord Christ himself, in his irresistible might.[77]

Warfield clearly rejected the governmental theory of atonement held by Finney. On the other hand, it is nonetheless clear that their conflicting views of atonement reside within the broad family of satisfaction theories. Both conceived of the relationship of God to humans in terms of a legal construct. Each saw the death of Christ aimed both Godward and toward the divine law. Warfield would appear to have a much narrower view of correct atonement formulation.

Ethics Shaped by the Prevailing Social Order

Although we have only sampled two evangelical views, these observations appear to fit with Timothy Smith's hypothesis about the development of evangelical theology from nineteenth to twentieth century. Smith described atonement doctrine as evolving from a "broad synthesis of historic doctrines of the Atonement" shared by nineteenth-century evangelicals to an outlook that accepted "most emphatically, the doctrine of Christ's substitutionary sacrifice, in a form that implied that holiness was imputed but not imparted."[78]

I want to stress two elements of this combination of change and consistency. On one hand, in spite of earlier-noted changes in theology, social outlook, and attitudes toward reform, there was a certain consistency in the continuation of some version of satisfaction atonement. On the other hand, to emphasize the opposite side of the equation, in spite of the continuation of some form of satisfaction theory of atonement, there was significant change in social outlook and attitude away from ethics and reform.

This observation returns to the argument of the second section of this chapter, that satisfaction atonement is not a theological foundation which keeps salvation and ethics hooked together. Whereas Finney thought that the saved person would pursue moral reforms, such impulses are virtually nonexistent in Warfield's theology. The closest thing to any moral impulses in the context of Warfield's atonement articles are the brief mentions that for those who experience atonement, the Holy Spirit will "supernaturally regenerate their hearts" and conform them "to His image," and will make them into "a perfect reflection of his love."[79]

The comparison of Finney and Warfield illustrates once again how satisfaction atonement does not include particular ethics as an integral part of atonement and salvation. Nineteenth-century evangelicals assumed that being saved would eventuate in moral action. Yet there was no intrinsic link between the theology of Jesus' atonement and the particular ethics of Jesus. The formulation of satisfaction atonement theory allows persons to confess Christ for salvation, while unhooking ethics and ecclesiology from the particular ethic of Jesus. This observation does not mean that the nineteenth-century advocates of satisfaction atonement lacked a concern for ethics. On the contrary, as Smith and Dayton have shown, they pursued a vigorous program of social and ethical reform. It is rather an observation that the shaping influence of their ethics came *from the social order* rather than *from the narrative of Jesus* in a way that made Jesus' ethic intrinsic to atonement and salvation. For the nineteenth-century evangelicals, this particularly appears in their nonattention to pacifism.

Summary

The observations of this chapter provide a background against which to examine the outlook of the eight nineteenth-century Mennonites and Amish who comprise the heart of this study. The analysis will demonstrate that on one hand, they had an ecclesiology and an ethics that they understood to be intrinsically linked to the teaching and the narrative of Jesus. This ecclesiology and ethics correspond to the ecclesiology and ethics comprising facets of the Christus Victor atonement image that subsided after Constantine.

Yet on the other hand, even while maintaining this ecclesiology and ethics, all these Mennonites and Amish also used the language of satisfaction or substitutionary atonement, which originally developed within a quite different ecclesiology. The following will show the results of their efforts to hold together the ethics and ecclesiology from one theological tradition with the atonement theology of another theological tradition.

3

Worldviews Surrounding Atonement

Even the traditionalists among the eight Mennonite and Amish writers studied in this book engaged in conversation about issues in the North American environment. This chapter sketches those conversations on a variety of issues. Issues were selected for treatment either because they provide context for the discussion of atonement or because they provide relevant comparison among the eight subjects.

Jacob Stauffer

Jacob W. Stauffer (1811-55) abandoned the Mennonite Church in 1845 to found the group that carried his name, the Stauffer Mennonite Church.[1] It was the first of several Mennonite groups to identify themselves as Old Order Mennonites, following the *alte Ordnung,* the traditional church order and rules. Stauffer's church and his outlook appear clearly in the *Chronik* (Chronicle), which he wrote to explain and justify the origins of his church.

When Stauffer published his *Chronik,* Mennonites had not yet accepted revivalism as an instrument which could serve the church. That acceptance began to happen in the 1870s through the influence of John M. Brenneman and became widespread in the 1880s through the leadership of John S. Coffman. Stauffer did comment on camp meetings. He opposed any participation by Mennonites in such gatherings. With several preachers simultaneously in full voice, milling crowds of people, the cries and vigorous movements of those supposedly under the influence of the Holy Spirit, camp meetings in Stauffer's view were no better than "frivolous disorder (*eitel Unordnung*), with a dreadful

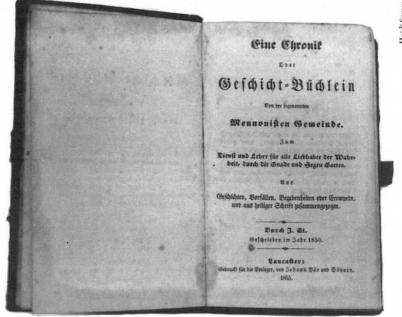

Heidi Sommer

Title page of Jacob Stauffer's Eine Chronik oder Geschicht-Büchlein.

crying and shouting and howling, just like the servants of Baal." Since God is a God of order, such noise and chaos could not be a worship service where one could obtain grace and blessing. One finds God not in the uproar of the storm nor in the disturbance of the earthquake nor in the raging fire, but in "a still and gentle blowing of the Spirit of God speaking to men, and giving them the commands they should follow."[2]

Beyond his distaste for the chaos of camp meetings, one can certainly surmise that Stauffer would support the theological opposition to revivalism that will be depicted in more detail for other figures in this study. His stress on a righteous life validating genuine repentance would clearly place him at odds with the idea that an experiential conversion indicated salvation, as developed by the later Heinrich Egly. Stauffer noted that many people have a "doesn't-matter spirit (*Machnichts-Geist*)," which claimed that external appearances do not affect one's inner relationship to God.[3] He would certainly agree with and underscore the idea expressed in some form by Johannes Moser and C. H. Wedel that a stylized, crisis conversion was really a form of pride and self-aggrandizement.

For Stauffer, the true indication of conversion was a changed life, rather than calling attention to oneself with a dramatic story of conversion or excessive movement and shouting. His stress on the necessity of discipline as the way to preserve the church meant that one could fall away from the faith. Thus Stauffer would certainly oppose the revivalist ideas of perfectionism and eternal security.

The Bible as history comprised a significant part of the perspective through which Stauffer viewed and interacted with the world. The line of transmission from the church of Jesus and the apostles to Stauffer's church was direct. He clearly considered himself a part of the biblical story so that both Old and New Testament stories applied directly to him and to his congregation. He admonished the "beloved reader to test in these confused and fallen times how truly necessary it is to pay attention to the teaching of Jesus and his apostles because so many such teachings, examples, and stories of Israel are in the Old Testament."[4]

Stauffer's outlook was shaped by the Bible in an immediate fashion, and his ecclesiological context was his worldview. An individual was either a follower of Jesus and shaped by the church, the Bible, and the example of Jesus and the apostles—or shaped by the world. Stauffer would not have understood nor known how to deal with discussions about the way in which philosophical assumptions about the nature of truth had shaped his scriptural exegesis or reflected his social context. In no way could he have considered C. H. Wedel's understanding of change and progress within the context of *Gemeindechristentum*, as explained in a following segment. The moderate voices of John M. Brenneman and Johannes Moser would already be too much. For the Old Order worldview of Stauffer, change meant diminution and dilution of the faith.[5]

Beyond these brief remarks on revivalism and the Bible, Stauffer's view of the disciplined church comprised the primary theological context in which to situate his understanding of atonement. As chapter 4 will make clear, his worldview was above all defined by the church—nonresistant, disciplined, separate from the world. This profound and exclusive orientation with the church distinguished Stauffer from the American evangelicals of chapter 2, for whom the social dimensions of Christian faith were expressed through institutions and structures of American society.

David Beiler

When the Old Order Amish separated themselves from the larger body of change-minded Amish in the 1860s, David Beiler (1786-1871) was a primary spokesman.[6] As was the case for Old Order Mennonite Jacob Stauffer, Old Order Amish David Beiler's worldview is also shaped in large part by his understanding of the Bible's story, which shows in both *Wahre Christenthum* (True Christianity) and *Betrachtung über den Berg Predig* (Reflection on the Sermon on the Mount). That biblical worldview was one oriented around salvation. It began with creation and was changed utterly by the Fall. Since then, the story of history has been God's efforts to overcome the effects of the Fall.

While the Old Testament contains some preliminary steps toward salvation—such as a law to obey—Jesus was God's real answer to the Fall. Beiler's world encompassed the Fall, and the life, death, resurrection, teaching, and example of Jesus. If one appropriated Jesus' sacrificial death and was reborn and obeyed his commands, then one overcame the Fall and would be saved. Stories from the Old Testament illustrated parts of the story of salvation, provided examples of human weakness and the need for rebirth, or showed persons who experienced true rebirth even before the coming of Jesus.

In his writing, Beiler is living in the world of the Bible. Thus he recounts Old (and New) Testament stories, not so much as past history, but as examples to show how God and God's world function. He did not spend a lot of space recounting the history of Israel. When he quoted the Old Testament, it was more likely to be a prophet's statement on the need to repent or change one's life, or a story in which an individual was punished as an example that God will punish modern people who do not obey God's commands.

There was something of a shift in emphasis and tone between *Wahre Christenthum*, written in 1857, and the *Betrachtung über den Berg Predig*, penned four years later. The first book contains meditations on such issues of concern to Amish as baptism and stream baptism, marriage within the church, vengeance and nonresistance, oaths, and church discipline, as well as frequent admonitions about the Fall, sin, and the need for rebirth. While disagreements about modernization were building which would eventually result in the Old Order Amish going their own way, in this work it seems that Beiler still has hope for the church, and that his words can preserve and safely guide the church.

Betrachtung über den Berg Predig has a somewhat more pessimistic tone. Throughout his comments on the Sermon on the Mount, Beiler frequently urges readers toward obedience and warns them that it is hard to obey God's commands; the natural man, without the grace of God, cannot obey. He emphasizes church discipline and the need to discipline erring members, and provides many biblical examples to show that the wicked are punished. Some begin in the true faith and then grow cold or become more interested in things of the world. Beiler cites warnings of Jesus and Paul about false prophets, divisions, and falling away in the last days, certain that he sees such prophecies fulfilled before his own eyes.

Such thoughts can reflect Beiler's attitude toward American society in general; most certainly they do reflect the elderly bishop's heightened discomfort with changes occurring in the Amish community, as the Amish brethren contemplated the first of the *Diener-Versammlungen*. This series of Amish ministers conferences met yearly from 1862 to 1876 and in 1878. They attempted to deal with differences arising within and among their congregations. However, the conferences were controlled mostly by the progressives, and the conservative-oriented grouping, for whom Beiler was a symbol, opted to go their own way and preserve the old order (*die alte ordnung*).

The New Testament, with the teaching, commands, and example of Jesus, is most particular about what the reborn must obey. Beiler's worldview was shaped by his understanding of the story of the Bible. That story centered on salvation from the effects of the Fall, and God's work to assemble the saved and obedient ones into his church. As was true for Old Order Mennonite Stauffer, in Beiler we once again observe an orientation in which Christian expressions occur through the church rather than through American social structures.

Gerhard Wiebe

In intent and format, Gerhard Wiebe's *Ursachen und Geschichte*[7] parallels Jacob Stauffer's *Chronik*, and David Beiler's "Memoirs," as well as John Holdeman's *History of the Church*, and Heinrich Egly's "Autobiography" in following sections. In each instance, the work offers the author's explanation and justification of his own church group, over against a larger body of the church which, he alleged, refused obedience to Christ and in some way abandoned the truth faith. In Russia, Gerhard Wiebe (1827-1900) became deacon (1854), minister (1861), and the second *Ältester* or bishop (1866) of the church in the Bergthal colony. He led the Bergthaler immigration to southern Manitoba, beginning in 1874, and retained churchly authority in Manitoba until his resignation from the office of bishop early in 1882.[8]

Ursachen und Geschichte offered the elderly ex-bishop's account of these events, along with his perceptions of the decaying state of Mennonites as they entered the twentieth century. His religious outlook was greatly shaped by his experiences as leader of the Bergthal colony, and by his perception of the relationship of Bergthal to the other Mennonite colonies in Russia. While his little book is not a comprehensive statement of theology, it does open a window into Wiebe's theological and religious outlook.

Bergthal had come into existence in 1836, as a daughter colony of Chortitza, the first Mennonite colony in Russia. West Prussian Mennonite immigrants from the area of Danzig had established Chortitza in 1789.[9] Molotschna, a second colony of West Prussian Mennonite immigrants, had been founded in 1804. For a variety of reasons, the Chortitza colony experienced a great deal of hardship in its early years, while Molotschna quickly prospered and outstripped the performance of Chortitza in a number of ways. Chortitza came to feel itself somewhat inferior to and even ridiculed by Molotschna.[10]

The problem of landownership affected both colonies. In order to

 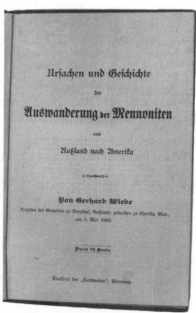

Cover and title page of Gerhard Wiebe's Ursachen und Geschichte.

ensure that farms would retain sufficient land to produce a livelihood, the original settlement provisions of 1789 prohibited the subdivison of farms. In effect, only one child could inherit the family homestead. There soon developed an unlucky and disgruntled majority of non-landowners, called *Anwohner*. To help redress the land problem, Bergthal was founded as a daughter colony of Chortitza. Stated in oversimplified fashion, the founders of Bergthal came primarily from the unlucky *Anwohner* of Chortitza.

Gerhard Wiebe was born in 1827 to *Anwohner* parents in Chortitza and moved with them to the Bergthal village of Heuboden in 1839. Wiebe reflected a group of people who had frequently thought of themselves as always second best, both as Chortitzans and *Anwohner*. We will presently observe the theological justification which Wiebe gave that supposed second-class status.

Wiebe began and ended the *Ursachen und Geschichte* with calls for obedience to the commandments of God. The protection promised by God to his people depended on obedience. References from the Old Testament illustrated both God's blessing and punishment of Israel, depending upon their obedience. And in Wiebe's own time, protection from God still depended upon obedience. The Bergthalers had survived the hardships of immigration, and he attributed that to the unity created by their obedience to the commands of God.[11] The scattering of the Mennonite churches to the four winds and the fragmentation of the two large congregations that remained in Russia resulted because they had ceased to listen to the Word of God.[12] He described the times of obedience and unity, and the current falling away from faith, which he perceived might even signal the end times. The consequences of obedience pervaded the entire account.[13]

The obedient life whose demise Wiebe lamented was characterized at least by nonresistance, humility and the absence of arrogance, and opposition to advanced education and worldly wisdom. All these characteristics were linked and intermingled by Wiebe in such a way that frequently to discuss one was to touch all of them. In his mind, humility provided the common denominator to which the other characteristics belonged.

Not surprisingly, Wiebe believed that Jesus exhibited a humble, unpretentious outlook. In fact, it was Jesus' humility that caused his rejection. "Had Jesus come in pride and magnificence (*Hoffart und Pracht*), then they would have accepted him."[14] Jesus also chose humble people as his disciples. They came from "the lowliest people, namely, fishermen and also a customs collector." None came from the "advanced school" of Gamaliel, which trained its students in "arrogance and self-righteousness." Because Paul had imbibed the teaching of Gamaliel's school, he had to be called "through thunder and lightning."[15]

Nonresistance belonged indelibly to the obedient, humble life. In the opening sentence of *Ursachen und Geschichte*, Wiebe gave the saving of "our children from military service and ruin" as the reason for emigration to North America.[16] In several different settings, however, he made nonresistance, humility, and opposition to advanced education one bundle of ideas. He characterized the change in the fourth-century church represented by Constantine as the beginning of a great battle in which "light and darkness exchanged places."[17] The struggle was between the false and true bishops, the former desiring guidance by the "state laws" while the latter held to "God's Word and command."[18]

However, the most serious offense of all in the fourth century, Wiebe wrote, concerned education. "The biggest error was committed by the church itself, . . . by its building of advanced schools; for here the Word of God and human wisdom were mixed together, and through this, simplicity and innocence decreased steadily. . . . So it was that after four hundred years the teaching of humility was transformed into an arrogant priesthood" preaching to please the emperor in exchange for an imperial supply of wealth.[19]

Some humble flames, such as Menno Simons, did flicker through the centuries, Wiebe maintained. Menno "held fast to the Lord's teaching" and was "meek and lowly."[20] Eventually Menno's legacy was carried to Poland and then to Russia. Wiebe quoted with approval a description of the demise of nonresistance among the Mennonites in Prussia that gave a scenario linking education and pride much like that he gave for the fourth-century church.

> The rich began to let their sons study in the advanced school of Danzig. From there they went to the Berlin university, and when they returned and were visited by their neighbors' sons, they would say to them, "Oh, you are only a boorish peasant." At the same time, they were so well dressed and bore themselves like military officers. The other youths did not need to be told twice, and so this worldly current swept into the congregation more and more, continually causing greater indifference. Finally our teachers were chosen from this educated group, and so we ourselves planted the germ of arrogance and pride into our schools, as well as into our congregations.[21]

In 1862, Wiebe said, the last nonresistant ones moved from Prussia to Russia.[22] In his accounts of both the fourth-century church and the Mennonite church in Prussia, the loss was nonresistance, but education was the culprit. Arrogance desired the prideful, higher education that undermined nonresistance, while humility and simplicity remained content to obey the Word of God and retain nonresistance.[23]

Signs of arrogance were not limited to support for education and the loss of nonresistance. Arrogant, educated ministers preached a repentance which touched the heart but accepted everything from the world.[24] Such preachers mentioned only a few words about the text, Wiebe said, and then to attract acclaim, they talked about the railroad, newspapers, and whatever is happening in the world.[25] Things which displayed arrogance or lack of humility included ostentatious display in clothing and fashions, buggies and coaches, marriage into other confessions, standing for and holding public office, and placing money at interest.[26] His critique of Mennonites for arrogance, education, and display applied both to the wealthy who remained behind in Russia and to the advocates of education in southern Manitoba.

In the case of Gerhard Wiebe, humility also apparently carried connotations of assumed personal inferiority. One senses that tone in his general descriptions of Bergthal interactions with representatives of the Molotschna colony.[27] That humility appeared when he agreed with the opinion of Molotschna representatives that he and other Bergthalers were an embarrassment when a delegation of Mennonites was called to meet with government officials.

> I was reluctant because I saw that they did not wish to have any of us go with them. Anyone can understand how a person feels when those whom he is supposed to accompany regard him as superfluous and not worthy of respect. Although I also felt unworthy, I was still a human being with feelings, but I, a miserable worm, would gladly have withdrawn from all this unrest. . . . I had firmly resolved to be humble and lowly, which I then was in all my imperfection, for I always stood behind the group and listened to their discussions. And should we actually be asked to have an audience with His Majesty, I would then again have liked to stand behind the others for protection, especially behind my dear *Ältester* Gerhard Dueck.[28]

His sense of personal inferiority also seems evident in his description of the great sin (not specifically identified but likely involving something of a sexual nature), which resulted in his resignation from the office of *Ältester*. He wrote that sin had led him to contemplate suicide, and that in his unworthiness, it was only the blood of Christ and the support of Jesus and his Holy Spirit that sustained him.[29]

Wiebe also put his opposition to education into apocalyptic language and imagery. Among the Bergthal Mennonites in southern Manitoba, there developed a movement in favor of founding a school. In 1891, H. H. Ewert,[30] progressive Mennonite educator from Kansas, accepted an offer to become principal of the new Mennonite Educational Institute at Gretna, Manitoba. This new school and its progressive leader represented for Wiebe the accumulated forces of the devil acting within the Mennonite world. He lamented the inroads among Mennonites made by the supporters of schools, noting that the

> schools and their founders do not stem from Bethlehem, where the three kings knelt at the manger to worship the child Jesus; rather, they stem from Babylon, that is, they produce confusion. Therefore, they can produce no other fruit than that which grows in Babylon's garden, the fruit of worldly knowledge and arrogance.[31]

Only three bishops remained true, Wiebe said, while the remainder sided with the worldly wise and their teaching.[32] When he noted again the three faithful bishops who had not abandoned Bethlehem, Babylon was revealed to be a specific Mennonite school: "The majority will have turned away from the simple Bethlehem and have gone over to Bethel College."[33]

In Wiebe's mind, opposing Babylon-Bethel meant to wage battle with the "prince of this world"[34] or the "prince of the air,"[35] who can be none other than H. H. Ewert.[36] According to the experience of many centuries, he opined, the church was now in the period of going "over into the kingdom of the beast (*zum Tierreich über*),"[37] which meant that "surely the appearance of the Lord is near."[38] For Gerhard Wiebe, opposition to education was serious business, with apocalyptic connotations, and he used imagery that linked his contemporaries to events he thought predicted in Revelation. Although he described the falling away differently, this sense of seeing end-time corruption in the church was like that of Jacob Stauffer.

In one particular area of his worldview, Wiebe was close to agreement with C. H. Wedel and John Holdeman. He may have paralleled these men in believing that a true, remnant church had existed throughout history.[39] At one point when Wiebe mentioned the changes in the church which began to occur in the fourth century, he seemed to say that the true church no longer existed. "In the tenth, eleventh, and twelfth centuries, sermons merely had the appearance of the gospel, and so the church had perished through human wisdom and philosophy."[40] The church was then restored, as God "kindled a light in southern France, through a man named Waldus [Peter Waldo]" and "God kindled a light in Bohemia, which was [Jan] Hus."[41]

Later, however, Wiebe used language that described the existence of a faithful remnant within the corrupt church through the centuries. As the church became corrupt in the fourth century due to the organization of advanced schools that mixed the gospel and worldly things, one door did remain open, in Philadelphia.[42] From that church the seeds were carried farther, "so that the Lord retained small congregations in hiding, here and there." The Lord Jesus kept the door open (Rev. 3:8) in countries such as France, Italy, Bohemia, Switzerland, Austria, Holland, Germany, Poland, Russia, and America. "The Lord has his own everywhere, though they are mostly hidden from the world." Wiebe then included himself and his readers in the "Philadelphia congregation."[43]

On the basis of these comments, it appears that Wiebe did entertain the idea that a true remnant had always existed. If so, at that point he agreed with Wedel and John Holdeman. Of course, his analysis and use of the idea was quite different from that of Wedel or even Holdeman.

Revivalism constitutes the final issue against which to consider Wiebe's understanding of atonement and as a point of comparison with the other figures of this study. Although his *Ursachen und Geschichte* made only a few, oblique comments in opposition to revivalism, they are sufficient to show his suspicion of it. He likely had revival preachers as well as educated preachers in mind when he commented,

> They preach repentance, but live in greatest arrogance, and try to cover up with the aura of Holy Scripture their belief that a person can go along with everything in the world, as long as his heart is not attached to it.[44]

Wiebe certainly had visiting revival preachers in mind when he wrote,

> A false preacher's fruit is always to bring something new. This is always done with an appearance of being a fine Christian, and so he prowls from flock to flock, in order to tear apart congregations.[45]

Mennonites in southern Manitoba faced three revivalist-oriented options, none of which had a significant, direct impact on Gerhard Wiebe's people in the East Reserve. During the winter of 1881-82, at the request of the *Kleine Gemeinde* bishop, Peter Toews, John Holdeman came to Manitoba and preached a revival. While Wiebe was concerned about the resulting fragmentation of the *Kleine Gemeinde*, that revival had little impact on his own people.[46] The second revival option came from the United States, in 1887, and frequently after 1890, in the form of the traveling preachers of the General Conference Mennonite Church. Mennonite Brethren ministers who began coming from the United States in 1883 constituted the third option.

Wiebe's churches in the East Reserve mostly escaped the effect of these revival movements. The revivalists had their greatest impact among the more progressive elements in the West Reserve. It is likely that the paucity of remarks concerning revivalism in *Ursachen und Geschichte* reflected the relatively small influence of revivalism on Wiebe's Chortitzer Mennonite churches.[47]

Putting all these observations together, one discovers in *Ursachen und Geschichte* an integrated worldview comprised of humility and simplicity, discipleship, nonresistance, and opposition to education. However, the integration was not so much that of a theological outlook as it was an understanding of the visible church. Wiebe did not defend nonresistance or humility or opposition to education by appeals to biblical authority. Much more, the church existed as the living extension of Christ and his disciples. It was a community defined and reinforced by lifestyle rather than by an explicitly biblical and theological rationale. Rather than appealing to biblical authority, Wiebe wanted to preserve a simple nonresistant people by opposing the outside influences which would enter via higher education.

In that context, his two references to atonement were an addendum to this package of the simple, obedient, nonresistant life. Arrogance belonged to the sins that were heaped on Jesus. For those sins Jesus had to undergo suffering and rejection from God. Jesus' death carried away the sin and punishment of those who violated the humble, obedient life. The atoning death of Jesus was more a means of dealing with the product of sin rather than an integral aspect of Wiebe's religious outlook. He did not link Jesus' manner of death to nonresistance, as did a number of the figures in this study. In comparison to American evangelicals, it is most obvious that Wiebe saw his conservative church rather than any North American public structures as the only avenue for the expression of Christian faith and social concern.

Cornelius H. Wedel

The synthesis of Mennonite history which C. H. Wedel[48] (1860-1910) prepared at the turn of the century presented his Mennonite worldview most clearly.[49] In its broadest dimensions, understanding of Wedel's soteriology requires setting it in the Mennonite context which he called *Gemeindechristentum* (congregation Christendom).

In his discussion of the catechetical questions on creation in *Meditationen*, his commentary on the Elbing Mennonite catechism,[50] Wedel noted the biblical texts which tie Jesus to creation so that "the mediator of salvation is also the mediator of creation."[51] The introduction to *Alten Testament* then situated the story of Jesus within human history. Wedel distinguished world history (the general working of God in history) from holy history (the realm of God's special activity and revelation). For Wedel, world history relates to holy history analogous to the relationship between the porch of the temple and the holy of holies.[52]

Christ is the middle point of history on which God's decree of salvation (*Erlösungsratschluss*) was focused.[53] Thus Wedel sought specifically to situate atonement within the realm of human history, and more specifically within Greek and Roman history. Within this history, *Gemeindechristentum* originated as the bearer of the legacy of the early church. He used *Gemeindechristentum* as the vehicle which gave the church its universal dimension.

Influenced by European scholars Ludwig Keller and Anna Brons, and by George C. Seibert, his professor at the Bloomfield seminary, Wedel called the apostolic Christianity to which Mennonites belonged *Gemeindechristentum*.[54] It is a form of Christianity which claims universality, he believed, and has existed in some form since the first century. In the third century majority Christianity became the church of the bishop, and in the fourth century it became a state church. But *Gemeindechristentum* continued to exist in the succession of groups which retained and maintained a New Testament understanding of the church. Mennonites emerged as the major sixteenth-century bearers of this believers-church Christendom, over against both Catholic and Protestant versions of state-church Christendom.

On the classic theological questions such as atonement, Wedel several times called Anabaptists and Mennonites orthodox. Yet he emphasized the relative unimportance of creedal or doctrinal formulations.[55] However, more important in describing *Gemeindechristentum* were such things as personal salvation, experiential faith, and practical Christian living. The religion of *Gemeindechristentum* had both internal and external components. The truly saved, who possessed heartfelt piety, were united by the Spirit into a community or congregation. Characteristics of this community included discipleship, apostolicity,

IN MEMORY OF
PROF. C. H. WEDEL,
PRESIDENT OF BETHEL COLLEGE.

BORN MAY 12, 1860.   DIED MARCH 28, 1910.

Memorial photograph distributed at C. H. Wedel's funeral.

voluntarism, progress, nonresistance, separation of church and state, freedom in religious doctrine, lay responsibility, and congregational authority.[56] In other words, *Gemeindechristentum* brought together heartfelt, individual piety with clear statements of traditional Mennonite emphases.

Wedel used *Gemeindechristentum* not to state orthodox theology but as a norm against which to interpret all of Christian history. It was a full-blown Christendom, which posed an alternative to state-church Christendom. Sixteenth-century Anabaptists were not, therefore, the originators of this orientation, but they were a movement which carried it forward. With roots in Judaism, Jesus established this church. Wedel linked the decline of *Gemeindechristentum* to the rise of the episcopal and papal and priestly church and then to the Constantinian shift.[57] Alongside that decline, the medieval sectarians preserved *Gemeindechristentum* in various forms and carried it through the centuries to the Waldensians, its purest medieval adherents. The Waldensians then spawned the various Anabaptist groups, Wedel believed, with the South German Anabaptists the ones most closely resembling the South German Waldensians.[58] Along the course of history, Wedel evaluated movements and developments on the basis of their reflection of *Gemeindechristentum*.

This larger entity of *Gemeindechristentum* constitutes the most comprehensive context in which to consider Wedel's atonement theology and his preservation of traditional Mennonite practices. *Gemeindechristentum* provided a social and structural entity which gave meaning and focus to individual salvation. It included not only a denominational identity but located that Mennonite denominational identity in a Christendom stretching throughout history from Jesus until Wedel's own time.

Wedel's soteriology featured an understanding of atonement very much in keeping with the discussion of evangelicals in chapter 2. It was the comprehensive outlook of *Gemeindechristentum* that kept that soteriology from absorption into individualist American, evangelical religious expression and instead plugged it into a free-church historical structure with a claim to universal reality. On the basis of material in chapters 4 and 5 (below), Wedel's theology could easily be identified with that of conservative Protestantism. He based salvation on the substitutionary atonement. His visible church, composed of individuals saved on the basis of the primarily individual-oriented substitutionary image of atonement, could easily end up with a focus on preaching and worship. That might nurture inner life and mediate salvation without

Heidi Sommer

Title page of vol. 1 (left) and cover of vol. 4 of C. H. Wedel's Abriss der Geschichte der Mennoniten.

Mennonite Library and Archives, Bethel College. North Newton, Kansas

Bethel College Bible class, ca. 1899-1900. C. H. Wedel's books served as texts in such classes. On the chalkboard is written, "Bibelkunde (Bible knowledge)."

saying much about specific external or behavioral manifestations of Christian faith in obedience to the teaching and example of Jesus.

In other words, Wedel's concepts of salvation and the church could drift into Pietism's church of saved individuals who stress individual piety and accommodate to the social ethics of the surrounding society. What saved Wedel's theology from that drift is the structure of *Gemeindechristentum*, which provided the locus of such Anabaptist-Mennonite themes as separation from the world, church discipline, nonswearing of oaths, love for enemies, and nonresistance. Wedel tended to locate these emphases in *Gemeindechristentum*, in contrast to our other subjects who locate these emphases more at the level of individual ethics and the nature of the church.

Gemeindechristentum preserved the Mennonite integrity of Wedel's theology in a second way. It provided a framework within which he could learn from the new, burgeoning turn-of-the-century scholarship without being reshaped by it. A number of articles that he published in the Bethel College periodicals displayed that capacity to retain his own identity while dealing with the new scholarship. In one, he reported his fascination with a visit to the University of Berlin to hear two lectures by the famous professor Adolf von Harnack. "It occurred to me immediately that one can learn a lot from him," Wedel wrote, even as he lamented the fact that the pastors of Germany were formed under such professors. Although highly learned, these professors showed little "solid grasp of the truth that God revealed in Christ."[59]

Wedel rejected the idea of scholars like Bruno Bauer, Ernst Renan, and David Friedrich Strauss, that the resurrection of Jesus occurred only in the minds of the apostles.[60] Wedel lamented that the new scholarship, building on an already-long history of interpretation, had "narrowed and shrunk our Lord's command to love enemies" to the point that it left room for "complete annihilation of enemies."[61]

Wedel was learning from the new scholarship while retaining his roots. As chapter 5 will demonstrate, he was fully aware of the various atonement theories but argued for substitutionary atonement, charging that "the new theology does not know how to deal with Jesus' suffering and death."[62] A series on Old Testament prophecy emphasized that the prophets spoke primarily to their own situation.[63] Two four-part series—one on New Testament criticism and another on the Gospel of John—display his familiarity with critical scholarship, the issues of historicity, the differences between John and the synoptic Gospels, as well as Wedel's willingness to learn cautiously from that scholarship.[64]

Parallel to his comment on Harnack, Wedel summarized his approach to new biblical scholarship after hearing a lecture which suggested that Jonah was an allegory and Ezekiel 40-48 was not a predictive prophecy. The lecture demonstrated, he said, how a serious Bible reader could get clues to a profound understanding of Scripture "from a healthy use of new discoveries and theories, while taking care not to follow the so-called 'modern' school blindly."[65]

The idea of learning without being captivated also applied to the natural sciences. Science need not hinder faith, Wedel said. Scientists can only "assert" that the world developed itself or that humankind developed from apes, but they cannot prove that. He cited scientists who profess faith in God and the wonders of nature created by God. "Such testimonies show," Wedel claimed, "that the natural sciences dare not be held up per se as hindrances to faith. It depends on the inner disposition of man, whether the wonders of nature lead him to God or away from God. For a Christian, nature is like the hem of God's garment."[66] It was *Gemeindechristentum* that provided Wedel with the orientation that enabled him to learn from the new while still preserving his Mennonite, free-church worldview.

Wedel's views on women do not figure directly in the discussion of his theology of atonement. Yet a sketch of his perspective on women is included here as a parallel to the following presentations of John M. Brenneman's and Johannes Moser's views on women, which do belong to the context of their atonement theology. Wedel held quite traditional attitudes toward women. He believed that their receptive temperament befitted them to stay at home, while the active temperament of men suited them for a profession and life in the world. Men deal with "matters pertaining to judgment," while women "are seldom strong in logic, but are superior in act and feeling."[67]

To "flee temptations," young people should "avoid a too-close relationship between the sexes."[68] In marriage, husband and wife each develop complementary dimensions of humanity. "With man it is the practical side of life; his head, his intellect, his will; he must go out into life to battle with life's adversaries." As a complement, women develop the "feeling, the heart." Women do not act logically "but through intuition, through tact." Together the husband and wife produce the "full idea of mankind."[69] The woman's place was clearly in the home. Before marriage "the woman should be trained to carry on household duties. It is dangerous for the young man not to learn to know his bride in a kitchen dress."[70]

While the spouses should have similar mental and spiritual interests, the wife should "accommodate herself to (*sich hineinleben*) the profession of her husband, although usually he will be better trained mentally and be above her in mental capacity."[71] The man is the "house priest," the head of the household and head of the woman, the first among equals in decision making. It is "unbiblical" to omit the woman's vow of obedience from the wedding ceremony. Within their dual roles, however, it is a partnership.

While the man goes out into the world, he is to protect his wife from the world's harshness. In her turn, the woman is the guardian of morals, the "conscience" of the man, the "priestess of all that is best in man." From her position as guardian of family morality, the woman "rules the world, for the greatest influence for the good as well as for the evil comes from the hands of women." Because of his superior strength, the man is to treasure and protect his wife. Nothing will ever remove these distinctions between the sexes, Wedel wrote. "The so-called emancipation of women is an error and ends in roughness and bestiality."[72]

In these views on the contrasting roles of men and women, Wedel was certainly in accord with the other subjects of this study. However, as following sections reveal, his description of women's roles seems less sharp-edged than the strident articles of Moser and Brenneman. And Wedel's caution against too-close association of young people with the opposite sex is a step removed from the stern warnings of Brenneman and Moser concerning the prideful conduct of woman and their capacity to mislead men. When Wedel suggested that a woman "with a tendency to finery" could burden a man, he balanced it by saying that a man who smoked, ran around a great deal, or was either miserly or wasteful with his money, burdened a woman who had "tender feelings and aesthetic tastes."[73]

One article suggests that Wedel could accept some change, within limits, of the traditional role of women. An article in *Monatsblätter* noted with approval the appearance of female poets in contemporary German literature. It was a characteristic of the times, he declared, that women who had previously prevailed in the quiet of the home should now properly have this opportunity in public life.

> And why shouldn't they here build hand in hand with men, with particular attention to the German song? If God has given them the gift of song, then we should listen to them as joyfully as to men.[74]

At the same time, Wedel did limit the sphere of women's poetry

and music. Women's efforts should not simply copy those of men, but
rather "poetically clarify their particular *feminine* sensitivity, their feminine sphere of life and worldview."[75] In the article, he also reproduced
two poems by women. The one he critiqued because it displayed a certain "bitterness" and failed to find that which makes one happy in affliction. He commended the second poem for having that capacity.[76] In
this article, though Wedel still thought primarily in terms of the traditional roles of women, his willingness to accept women in the new role
of poet suggests some openness to evolving roles for women.

Wedel often mentioned the values of the Americanizing concept
of progress, or expressed criticism of Mennonite groups who objected
to new ideas and institutions. He defended higher education as the way
to ensure the preservation of Mennonite values. Apparently the idea of
Gemeindechristentum enabled him to accept dimensions of American
progress, to underscore the necessity of education for the preservation
and continuation of a unique Mennonite identity, and to absorb some
of the new theological emphases while maintaining an essentially orthodox direction in classic terms. He did this in a way which preserved
Mennonite emphases when examined in the context of the whole.[77]

Modern interpreters, myself included, have made an effort to understand the concept of *Gemeindechristentum*, the six volumes of
Wedel's synthesis of Mennonite history, as well as his unpublished
"Glaubenslehre" (Dogma, a work of systematic theology), and "Ethik"[78]
(his systematic treatment of ethics), as parts of an integrated, whole
worldview. But "Glaubenslehre" is a work of theology. It provided the
history of interpretation for many doctrinal issues, and yet the manuscript did not mention *Gemeindechristentum*. Wedel apparently wrote
his theology without giving that concept explicit attention.

If *Gemeindechristentum* did provide a conceptual structure which
preserved a historic Mennonite dimension to his theology, the influence was implicit, and likely more evident to latter interpreters than to
Wedel himself. The same observations apply to the "Ethik." It considered Christianity's revealed ethic the culmination of the philosophical
ethics of the ancient philosophers. After its lengthy preliminary remarks, "Ethik" had long sections on both personal and familial ethics,
and shorter sections on the role of the Christian in the state and in relation to culture. Never, however, did the "Ethik" situate any of the discussion in terms of *Gemeindechristentum*.

Wedel died before American Protestantism had separated itself
into sharply defined fundamentalist and modernist or liberal camps.
The positions Wedel took, and the format of their presentation, made it

possible for later persons of several persuasions to claim Wedel as their own. For conservatives and fundamentalists, Wedel's quite orthodox theology in areas like atonement and Christology made him a symbol of a preliberal "golden age" in Mennonite education. On the other hand, his stress on culture, progress, education, and adaptation to changing circumstances enabled progressives to claim him as theirs.[79]

Then there is the C. H. Wedel that my analysis has revealed. While he used concepts and methodology borrowed from both conservative and progressive camps, this Wedel was defined by neither of those options. Instead, his writings show him as the purveyor of a unique synthesis of Mennonite identity, circumscribed by the label *Gemeinde-christentum*, which included both the basis for understanding separation from the world as well as a rational for a cultural presence within

Heidi Sommer

Monatsblätter aus Bethel College.

Fortsetzung des "School and College Journal," gegründet 1896.

| VIII. Jahrgang. | Newton, Kansas, Februar 1903. | No. 2. |

Ein geschichtlicher Ueberblick

Ueber die Auslegung der prophetischen Reden

C. H. Wedel article, "Ein geschichtlicher Überblick," in Monatsblätter aus Bethel College, *February 1903.* The "W" at end of article identifies Wedel as the author.

Page 1 of C. C. Wedel's first notebook containing C. H. Wedel's "Glaubenslehre." The title reads, "Kurze Einführung in das Studium der Hauptpunkte der christlichen Glaubenslehre."

that separation. This is an attractive position. Its idea of an ongoing, historical concept of the church, within which one can borrow and adapt from contemporary developments, has much to offer the contemporary church.[80] Since this interpretation of Wedel depends upon the entire corpus of his work (while the conservative and progressive readings rely on a selective reading), the Wedel of the Mennonite synthesis seems most true to the fixed legacy of his writings.

While the Wedel of the Mennonite synthesis best deals with his writings as a fixed entity, there is yet one more interpretation of C. H. Wedel to consider. One can argue that the "Glaubenslehre" and the "Ethik" were evolving in a different direction from the six-volume synthesis of *Gemeindechristentum*, and that at the time of his death, C. H. Wedel's theology was in flux. For example, over against Wedel's conservative theology of substitutionary atonement is a statement in the *Meditationen* which holds open the possibility of grace available to those in Hades.[81] My analysis shows that Wedel was open to such things as the partial truth of liberalism's preferred moral influence theory of atonement. He also welcomed the entry of women into at least one area previously dominated by men.

An even stronger indication of movement in a liberal direction might be Wedel's comments on the nature of religion. He called Friederich Schleiermacher one who stood on the borderline of error, but who nonetheless performed the positive service of opening new paths and new knowledge. Wedel adopted a view of religion reminiscent of Schleiermacher. True religion, Wedel believed, was revealed by God, and heathen religions (that is, non-Christian religions) came into existence when people followed their own human reasoning and fell away from the original consciousness of God.[82] Christian ethics does not contradict but completes the best of human understanding.[83] Such an understanding of religion opened to Wedel the possibility of seeing an underlying commonality among the world's religions. It gave him underlying assumptions more in line with liberalism than conservatism.

Finally, as evidence of a Wedel in movement, there is the direct testimony of an individual who knew him personally. A letter of January 7, 1917, by Bethel College professor David H. Richert to his brother Peter. H. Richert, a Bethel College board member, referred four times to C. H. Wedel and his theology that was evolving in a liberal direction.[84] David Richert wrote that he saw nothing wrong with a book to which Peter Richert had referred, and stated,

That even Prof. C. H. Wedel's views along these lines were undergoing a remarkable transformation during the last year, or two, of his life could clearly be seen by any one that came into as close contact with him as I had the opportunity to do. One day he remarked to me: "I do not preach everything I think about a certain thing, because people are not ready for it, and hence would only be alarmed." For example, he did not condemn those men that hold the view that the "immaculate conception idea" and the "Logos discourse" in the Gospel of St. John sound very much like Greek philosophy, because Wedel, as a thoroughgoing Greek scholar that he had become of late, knew very well what the Greek notions were."

A bit later David Richert noted that Wedel understood differing interpretations of Jesus' sonship. Wedel "granted that there might be another view concerning the sonship than he had been holding." And if Wedel granted that, David conjectured, then Wedel must also have granted that "the absolute Sonship of Jesus depended upon something more than the miraculous birth as recorded in Luke." Declaring himself indifferent to the "method" by which Jesus came into the world, David aligned himself with C. H. Wedel in accepting persons with conflicting views about Jesus' birth.

As long as he accepts Jesus as the messenger of God through whom we are saved from selfishness and sin, I shall call him my brother. I shall gladly tolerate, like C. H. Wedel did, his views in regard to whether Jesus was the absolute Son of God on account of this reason or that reason.

David closed the letter with one more appeal to the tolerant spirit of Wedel. "If it should come to such a thing, I hope the Board will be at least as tolerant as C. H. Wedel was in his day, as long as a man believes in Jesus as the UNIQUE revelation that was the most perfect revelation of God the world has ever seen." This letter from a personal acquaintance of Wedel lends strong plausibility to the idea that his theology was in flux at the time of his death in midcareer. While his written theology was far from a liberal theology, the apparent direction of his movement indicates that had he lived long enough, those who appealed to a progressive Wedel would eventually have been most correct.

Wedel's depiction of *Gemeindechristentum* and his conversation with developing historical scholarship gave him perspectives unique among the Mennonites and Amish characters of this book. Thus he was able to adapt or absorb a great deal from both European and North

American environments. Nonetheless, the intent of *Gemeindechristentum* to be a comprehensive believers-church Christendom over against state-church Christendom clearly distinguishes him from American evangelicals. The latter operated virtually from the perspective of a voluntarily established, state-church Christendom. On the basis of that distinction, Wedel is clearly more identified with his conservative Mennonite and Amish brethren than with American evangelicals.

The comprehensive character of *Gemeindechristentum* means that in his mind, expressions of the social dimensions of Christian faith and any use of the tools of historical scholarship occurred through a structure of the church rather than through institutions and structures of the world's social order. While that observation might not have remained true had Wedel lived long enough to give full expression to the elements hinted at in David Richert's letter, it is true for the C. H. Wedel reflected in his extant writings.

Johannes Moser

Johannes Moser[85] (1826-1908) was born to Swiss parents who had immigrated to Wayne County, Ohio, in 1821. For nearly half a century, he served as minister (ordained in 1853) and bishop (ordained in 1864) of the large Swiss Mennonite congregation located in Ohio between Bluffton and Pandora. The group had a meetinghouse at each end of the district, one in Putnam County and one in Allen County.

There have been few if any previous efforts to describe the theological outlook of the nineteenth-century Swiss Mennonite immigrants as a distinct group.[86] The numerous articles of Johannes Moser constitute an exception to the assumption that these Mennonite people wrote little. His writings provide a significant window into his theology before his Swiss congregation began to interact extensively with other Mennonites.[87] The articles reveal a clear doctrine of atonement as well as his views on a variety of other issues.

Johannes Moser did not write a comprehensive work that organized his theological outlook, as did David Beiler, John Holdeman, Jacob Stauffer, or C. H. Wedel. Yet Moser's numerous articles reveal a great deal about his responses to events and challenges from the wider society. On some issues, his views reflected traditionalist Mennonite positions. On others, he vigorously supported the progressives. The following discussion deals with traditionalist views and then progressive positions. By developing his progressive side, my argument revises the prevailing assumption that Moser was primarily a conservative force

Bishop Johannes Moser.

within the Swiss churches.[88]

Moser's opinion on revivalism came from the traditionalist side of the Mennonite spectrum. In his Swiss congregation between Bluffton and Pandora, Bishop Moser confronted revivalism directly. He opposed it. From his perspective, revivalism was a threat carried by representatives of other Mennonite traditions and aimed at his congregation. Heinrich Egly, founder of the Defenseless Mennonite Church, and the Reformed Mennonite followers of John Herr and Daniel Musser brought varying forms of revivalism or calls for a crisis conversion into Moser's community. They attracted a number of converts from his congregation. Many of the articles he published in *Herold der Wahrheit* and *Christlicher Bundesbote* portray elements of his opposition to the revivalists.[89]

Moser objected to revivalism for a number of reasons. He believed that the inner transformation of salvation was a lifelong process of nurture which took place within the loving embrace of the church. Several of his articles dealt with this process of nurture, with the patience and tolerance required by the nurturing leaders toward those growing in the faith, and with the disappointment of spiritual leaders when some fell away in spite of the best efforts of the shepherds.

The assumption that conversion consisted of a nurturing process constituted the foundation of Moser's objection to revivalism. A crisis conversion substituted a single event for a lifelong growth process that should continue "so long as we dwell in these earthly huts. The battle between flesh and spirit continues until the angel of death removes us from the battlefield."[90] The substitution of a single event for a lifelong process allowed one to claim salvation, he believed, without a significant alteration or reformation of one's previously sinful life.[91] Further, appeal to a crisis conversion substituted the notoriously unreliable criterion of feeling for the visible criteria of obedience to Christ as the means by which to validate conversion. Moser realized that feelings could vary greatly. "Even with all diligence, one does not always possess or experience joy in the Spirit to the same extent; for there are tests in which faith is tested without joyful feelings through seeming abandonment in struggle and suffering."[92]

Appeal to a crisis conversion also disturbed relationships both within a congregation and among neighboring congregations. Most of Moser's opposition to revivalism and a crisis conversion could apply generally. Yet his complaints and laments about disturbed interpersonal and intercongregational relationships appear to have been aimed specifically at the Reformed Mennonites and Defenseless Mennonites

Sam Amstutz collection, Swiss Community Historical Society, Bluffton, Ohio

Meetinghouse of the Defenseless Mennonite Church, in original location on Phillips Road between Bluffton and Pandora. Building was constructed in 1886 for congregation formed after Heinrich Egly and others had preached in the community and attracted some members from Johannes Moser's congregation. In 1939 this building was moved to Jackson Street in Bluffton, where it served as meetinghouse for the Defenseless Mennonites and then several other denominations. Later it was converted into a private dwelling.

whom he encountered.[93] Egly held revivalist preaching services in homes or school buildings and accused local ministers of being unsaved. Egly's meetings included more than one series in Moser's community of Bluffton, Ohio. In his last published article, looking back over several decades of pastoral experience, Moser called it a "loveless undertaking" for a visiting minister to come to a church and convince someone who had already had an experience of being a child of God that the experience was invalid merely because the individual had grown into the faith and could not name a time and place of conversion.[94]

Moser likely had in mind the practice of Heinrich Egly when he argued that baptism should not be repeated if one fell away and then returned to the faith, or if one had been baptized without having experienced a crisis conversion. Egly did rebaptize people who joined his congregation if their previous baptism had occurred without a conversion experience as Egly defined it.[95] Likely Moser was protesting the Reformed Mennonites when he reported that they visited individual members of his congregation, raising doubts where none previously existed about the member's current pastor and present experience of salvation. For those visits, Moser wrote, the visiting missioners often sought "to take weak women[96] prisoner, observing in particular the time when the men would not be at home."[97]

While Moser made these sharp critiques, he also expressed openness to mutual acceptance of diverse religious expressions—both individual and congregational. This could happen if preachers and congregations could bring themselves to accept each other in love in spite of differing approaches to conversion.[98]

Alongside the revivalist contribution to congregational conflict, Moser's additional comments about divisions and disturbed relationships within a congregation likely reflected two other congregational conflicts. One was the conflict in the Swiss congregation of Sonnenberg in southeastern Wayne County, Ohio. Moser had moved from there to Putnam County in 1852, while his mother and a number of siblings remained at Sonnenberg. By the late 1860s or early 1870s, it was becoming clear that a majority of Sonnenberg stood by the traditional ways, while a minority of the congregation advocated a more broadminded and "liberal" outlook. Support of the liberal-leaning Wadsworth Institute was a key issue.

Other specific issues included Sunday schools and support of home and foreign missions. Finally on May 19, 1886, S. F. Sprunger, progressive minister from Berne, Indiana, assisted the progressive minority to organize themselves into a separate congregation, called Salem. It had eighteen charter members, and grew to fifty within the first year. Each of the two congregations had one of Johannes Moser's brothers as a deacon. Salem soon joined the progressive General Conference Mennonite Church. Harsh words and feelings reverberated between the Salem and Sonnenberg congregations for years.[99]

The second congregational conflict involved Moser's own congregation in Bluffton and Pandora, which experienced some difficulty over the same kind of issues. Potentially controversial issues included support for higher education, biblical interpretation, use of English, and congregational organization and governance. Prior to 1893, the congregation had had a rather informal organization. On January 2, 1893, they adopted a constitution written by Moser[100] and began to hold annual business meetings. Beginning with the second congregational meeting of 1893, the minutes contain repeated admonitions from Moser about the need for love and harmony in the congregation. While the minutes do not record the specific cause, it is evident that tensions must have existed for some time.

Starting with the 1897 minutes, there is discussion of the desire of members in Pandora to build a new meetinghouse. In June 1903, Moser resigned from his ministry after nearly fifty years in office (but did express "willingness to continue preaching as far as his strength permitted"). At that time, the large congregation with a single organization was alternating worship services among three different locations—in Bluffton; at Ebenezer, two miles west of Bluffton; and at St. John, two miles east of Pandora. For several years already, petitions to hold simultaneous preaching services on Sundays or to build another meetinghouse in Pandora had been voted down at the congregation's annual meetings. Finally in April 1904, the year after Moser's resignation as elder, 141 members in Pandora signed a resolution of independence from the congregation and invited S. F. Sprunger from Berne, Indiana, to help organize them into a new and separate congregation, Grace Mennonite Church.

A dispute exacerbated the tensions in the Swiss congregation and precipitated the withdrawal of those who formed the new Grace Mennonite congregation. It resulted from the formation of Bluffton College and likely reflected disagreements within the congregation about higher education. In 1898 a committee had been appointed by Middle District Conference to procure land and funds for a college at Bluffton. The dispute began at the conclusion of the committee's work, when a committee member submitted a bill for two year's work at two-thirds time. He claimed that he had worked as an employee of the committee, but the committee had considered his work a donation. The committee member filed a lawsuit, which was eventually settled out of court.

However, members of the congregation then filed a complaint with the church council against four members who had supported the lawsuit. The four were excommunicated, but they filed a lawsuit for reinstatement. In a decision accepted by all parties, the four were reinstated, but then they became leaders of the new Grace congregation.[101] The conflicts in the Swiss congregations in Wayne County and in Bluffton-Pandora, with Moser barely able to stave off the division of his congregation until he retired from office, certainly provided the backdrop to several of his articles that dealt with issues of love and conflict.

Moser's seven-part series in mid-1884, "Gedanken über Spaltungen"[102] (Thoughts on schisms) seems clearly written with the Sonnenberg conflict in mind. The length of the series testified to the depth of his concern. The series abounds with pastoral concern and brotherly and fatherly admonitions to accept one another in love. In part 1, for example, he noted how all hear the same preacher and have their souls saved by the same Redeemer. All agree to counsel each other in weakness and in love—elements which comprise the relationships that make the household of God one body and one spirit. These people engage in friendly relationships, worship, pray, and sing together, serve each other in need, bury their dead together, and so on.

But sometimes, in the midst of this brotherly service, as hair begins to gray, the enemy tries to produce enmity. In that case, Moser suggested, they may need to tolerate a difficulty, so as to avoid offending a brother. Perhaps, he hoped, one might be willing to confess himself the more wrong rather than demand change. Then reconciliation and fellowship could be restored, and the covenant of love and peace could become closer than before. Four years latter Moser expressed similar sentiments in describing the attraction of love and good works. He also noted that posing ultimatums, "to here and no farther," violated the Spirit of God.[103]

Moser's remarks about the advisability of a confession of faith for a congregation seem directed, at least in part, toward congregational conflicts. A stimulus for the article no doubt came from developing a constitution and confession for his Bluffton-Pandora congregation.[104] A major point in favor of a congregational confession of faith, Moser maintained, was that it provided a foundation which would hold the congregation together while the members differed on individual items. With the central affirmations intact—and he assumed that all agreed on such central issues as the nature of salvation and nonresistance—it was clear that God would not abandon them because of disagreements in their individual works. Meanwhile, from the human side, the order of the day was to strive for unity. The real error, he admonished, "is in not *desiring* unity" (Moser's emphasis).[105]

Moser's "Festigkeit in Prüfungen (Steadfastness during trials)" focused on disputes in the congregation. One senses the tension he felt in his own congregation when he questioned why some members seemed so closed to each other, with people standing side by side without wanting to interact. Since they have a common confession, such coldness should not be present. Love is lacking, he suggested, and it undercuts the congregation's belief in nonresistance. In resolving disputes, he said, it was actively working for unity which gave meaning to one's words about unity. One showed love for the congregation not by criticizing but by working for unity.[106] One of Moser's last articles, written only a few months before he resigned his ministerial office, returned to the idea that actions rather than words about love were the basis of conflict resolution.[107]

Moser's opposition to the inroads of revivalism identified him with the traditionalists on that issue. Yet his words on love and striving for unity displayed an understanding of the church in line with that of the emerging, progressive General Conference Mennonite Church. On one hand, he was clear about the central core of beliefs, and he was willing to use admonishment and discipline as the means of protecting the core. On the other hand, Moser also clearly sensed the inadvisability of rules sternly enforced. He counseled patience and tolerance with those who tried but fell short of the expectations of the church. Apparently he was willing to tolerate significant amounts of diversity and individual differences for the sake of preserving the larger unity of the congregation. It is a testament to his personal patience, presence, and leadership that the long-brewing schism in the Bluffton-Pandora congregation was postponed until after the elderly bishop had retired from his office.

A further dimension of Moser's traditionalist outlook was his strident opposition to stylish dress and jewelry, particularly for women. He equated stylish dress with pride, often with considerable sarcasm. Pride and finery were hindrances to missions. "If Christians give no image of lowliness (*Niedrigkeit*), who will do it then?" Moser asked.[108] Pride goes before a fall, he said, and worldly fashion constituted one of the primary enticements to sin. What caricatures one sees, he wrote, "particularly of the female sex," depictions that "would be considered a horrible birth defect if they were born that way."

An artist would have a hard time making a painting even of the hat of a stylish woman. Its size already betrays it, looking like

a hen's nest on a haystack, so very puny and small that it can give shade from neither cold nor warmth, just sitting on top like a tree frog to show people that the wearer knows how to be stylish. If something symbolic is there, then the bird feathers must indicate that they want to fly. However, I believe that they would have done better if they had allowed the poor birds to live and left the flying to them.[109]

In his hostility to stylish dress, and in making women the primary targets of this opposition,[110] Moser was clearly aligned with the traditionalist elements in the Mennonite churches.

Church discipline constituted another element of Moser's traditionalist view of the world. His particular points on which to exercise church discipline would not have satisfied the Old Order men David Beiler and Jacob Stauffer or conservatives such as Gerhard Wiebe and John Holdeman. Yet it was a church discipline which maintained traditional positions and took the visible church seriously. Moser wanted to handle as much of the confrontation and correction of erring persons as possible in private. Public accounting was necessary only when private admonishment failed. He believed, in any case, that one should move slowly to a public accounting.

On one hand, while the external conduct depended on the inner condition, one could also conform externally without a changed heart. But on the other hand, since one cannot see into the heart and know fully the inner condition which produced external behavior, one should exercise great patience in nurturing weak faith.[111] This stance was clearly not the *alte Ordnung* outlook of the Old Orders, but Moser did believe in church discipline.

Moser's conviction that nonresistance belonged to the essence of the Christian life is another element of his traditionalist Mennonite worldview. His articles reveal that he never wavered in that conviction. Chapter 4 will describe in some detail Moser's position on nonresistance in the context of his theology of atonement.

In at least two instances, his commitment to nonresistance comprised the foundation for other positions that also located Moser in a traditionalist Mennonite camp. For one, in materials written together with Peter Schumacher and published in *Herold der Wahrheit* and *Herald of Truth*, Moser opposed jury duty for Christians. The letters were provoked by an item in the March 1, 1891, issue of the two periodicals stating that the Mennonite church prohibited jury duty only in cases involving the death penalty. Joseph Steiner, a member of Moser's Swiss congregation in Bluffton, had paid a fine of $10.00 and submitted to ten days in prison rather than perform jury duty.

The materials subsequently printed from Steiner, Schumacher, and Moser explained why the position of the Swiss church in Bluffton was more stringent than that stated in *Herold der Wahrheit* and *Herald of Truth*. The first point of the argument was that the kingdom of Christ is a kingdom of mercy and peace. Christ has given an example of lowliness, meekness, and patience that they are to follow. Second, in that kingdom of peace, Christians "live by the mercy of God alone." If they truly live on mercy, Moser wrote, they cannot then judge others. Only God may judge.[112]

Moser's assumptions about the inseparable linking of atonement and nonresistance also provided him with a critique of some facets of the dispensationalism and premillennialism becoming visible among Mennonites at the end of the nineteenth century. While Moser did not use those specific terms, he referred to the belief of some persons in a future thousand-year reign of Christ. Moser specifically rejected the idea that nonresistance belonged only to that future kingdom of Christ, or that Christians were currently bound by Satan in such a way that they could not now practice nonresistance.[113] Though he confessed to not understand the meaning of the numbers and prophetic texts of the book of Revelation, he believed that the peaceful nature of Christ's kingdom and Christ's followers was clear:

> If his followers [do not forgive their enemies], who will do it. . . . Shall Christ's followers remain bound by the power of Satan and then be freed from him only for a thousand years and only then be ruled by Christ?[114]

In Moser's view of eschatology and the work of Christ, it was clear that the kingdom with all its implications had already begun, and that those who claimed Jesus as Savior had to follow his nonresistant example beginning in the present, not waiting until a future millennium. Either Christ's lordship had already begun, or it does not begin at all. On this issue, Moser was in agreement with his revivalist nemesis Heinrich Egly, as well as with the conservative John Holdeman.

Moser also expressed opinions on some of the emerging issues in the theological discussions in the latter half of the nineteenth century. For one, he opposed evolution, and defended material in the Bible against the claims of science. He argued for the existence of hell and the devil. In Moser's mind, these positions were all linked as facets of the same argument. For example, he claimed,

> The Word of God teaches us who the author of evil is, whose enticement and working we see and experience in a painful manner. Those people who recognize no hostile power and simply want to deny the existence of the devil, and teach that everything is the way God wanted it, etc. (so that God would also be the author of evil—a horrible thought!), and is gradually evolving to a higher stage and form: these also deny the Fall and thus also the Mediator and Redeemer![115]

After rejecting the idea of evolution, Moser discussed the Bible:

> If one could believe such a theory of evolution, then one would also have to accept that such men, who want to assault the Bible in this way, have become apes. They also want to place their science over the Bible through ancient artifacts, layers of earth, and a few excavated skulls, etc. However, they say nothing of excavations which support the Bible. Natural scientists who are believers have already thought much about nature and science, and what kind of objections these might have against the Bible. Rom. 1:20. And when seen with spiritual eyes, the entire universe testifies to the truth of the Bible. The Bible is also shown to be God's revelation through its own history. The fulfillment of prophecy and thousands of facts show that the Bible is God's revelation and truth.[116]

Ten years later, Moser wrote that while much in Scripture is incomprehensible, it has remained steadfast through a variety of circumstances. All contradictions have been compared and explained, and "what remains beyond our understanding, we accept in childlike faith." Those who support evolution, he said, merely want to be lord of the Scripture.[117]

At the same time, Moser was not unalterably opposed to science. He noted a national exhibition which would bring together all the creations of humanity,[118] and he allowed that some human discoveries were for the good, for which God should be thanked. At the same time, however, he declared that even something so small as a grain of wheat made a mockery of a man's discoveries and art. Anything that people accomplish was really the result of the wisdom of God, and human wisdom would never fully plumb the wisdom of God.[119]

These views on sin, evil, the devil, evolution, and the Bible clearly locate Moser within the conservative theological tradition, a position he shared with the large majority of Mennonites in the nineteenth century.[120] At the same time, it is also clear that he was aware of devel-

Article "Mission," by Johannes Moser, identified as "Joh. Moser," in
Christlicher Bundesbote, *May 5, 1892.*

oping theological arguments outside the Mennonite society. He adopted the language and the views of the nascent fundamentalist movement on these issues. Moser seems to have been less open to the findings of the rising historical scholarship than was C. H. Wedel. But as the following discussion will show, he was less rigid in holding to an unchanging, static worldview than was John Holdeman.

Material discussed thus far under the heading of Moser's worldview puts him in the traditionalist Mennonite camp and in agreement with the conservative side of the American evangelical theological spectrum. Another set of issues gave him a good deal of affinity with parts of the Mennonite progressive agenda.

Bishop Johannes Moser vigorously supported missions, one of the principal goals of the progressive General Conference Mennonite Church. His first article for the new General Conference Mennonite periodical *Christlicher Bundesbote*, which began publication in 1882, dealt with the subject under the title "Ideas on missions and congregational relationships."[121] His strongest defense of the idea of missions appeared in the first section of a three-part series of articles that appeared in *Christlicher Bundesbote* in 1892.[122] He anchored missions in biblical authority, Christology, and atonement, making missions an intrinsic part of what it meant to be Christian.

The 1892 article used Acts 16:9 as text. Missions occurred

throughout the Bible, Moser wrote, from the divine plan for mission given in the promise after the Fall to the eventual defeat of the old serpent, in Revelation 20:10. The command to practice missions occurred throughout prophecy, as in Isaiah 62:6-7; 61:11; 54:[13]. The prayers and promises for mission were fulfilled to the utmost in the coming of Christ, "the greatest of all sent ones." Jesus Christ came and fulfilled his mission to redeem humankind. When he left, he commanded his disciples to take the message of salvation to the entire world. That mission was carried out with great zeal in the apostolic period, and the command applies just as much in the present. The call which Paul answered, to "come to Macedonia and help us" (Acts 16:9), should appeal just as much to modern hearts, Moser said.

At the most profound level, missions depended on atonement. Since we participate in the divine nature through Christ, Moser said, we should carry the message of mercy to the unsaved, just as Christ was merciful to us. Motivation to missions also came from reflection on the suffering and persecution experienced by the forefathers. Living now in a time of freedom, Moser asked, how can one now avoid carrying out the command of Christ? Heathen practices—such as burying a wife with her dead husband—make missions an urgent matter.[123] He returned to such themes again in an article of 1899.[124] Moser was always clear that nonresistance belonged integrally to the gospel and must not be compromised for the sake of numbers in missions.[125]

While Moser clearly supported missions as an inherent part of Christian practice, his support of missions had another dimension as well. It was integral to his attack on the Reformed Mennonite Church. In a word, Moser accused the Reformed Mennonites of hindering missions. The multiple ways in which the Reformed Mennonites stood in the way of missions comprised nearly all of his first article on missions in *Christlicher Bundesbote*. John Holdeman was also a target in the same article. The Reformed Mennonites or Herrites, whose spokesman was Daniel Musser, did not do mission work, claiming that the command of Christ applied only to the apostles.

Further, Moser objected to both Reformed Mennonites and Holdeman Mennonites because each claimed to be the only true church. When each beats down the other as well as all other churches, he claimed, that hinders the cause of the gospel. Judging others severely was no guarantee that the accusing party remained free of error. Further, to insist that churches be painted in dark colors did not advance the cause of the kingdom of Christ. Moser's tolerant attitude shows in this instance. Even when Mennonites disagreed at some points with other denominations, one could still accept that which was good in the other tradition. Examples of such disagreements noted by Moser included the number of sacraments, or whether the sacrament was a visible sign of invisible grace. One need not reject the good with the bad, as was done when a church claimed to be the only true church.[126]

These accusations against the position of the Reformed Mennonites recurred in the series of three articles of 1892. Moser could use harsh words. The opponents of missions were actually yoked with unbelievers in that opposition, he wrote. Further,

> it is remarkable in this time that an entire congregation or fellowship sets itself as a whole against missions, particularly when it occurs among those who claim to be possessor and owner of the holy vessel (*heiligen gefässe*) and to be the only bearers of saving truth; who look with suspicion on all spiritual contacts with others and represent them as the whore of Babylon, beasts from the underworld, and antichrist. . . . Such people are judged by their own words: (1) since the accusations are not true, they themselves stand where they would place the others; (2) and in the case that the accusation is true, why do they not then fulfill Christ's last commandment (Matt. 28:19-20), if they are the ones who possess and are responsible for the glorious vessel (*herrlichen gefässe*) and want to be the bearers of saving truth? If they have received so much, why do they take the five pounds and hide it in a handkerchief in the earth?[127]

Moser's defense of missions was undoubtedly sincere, and he forthrightly supported the several Mennonite mission efforts. It appears, however, that the theme of missions also provided him a specific issue with which he could vigorously attack the church that caused significant difficulties for his ministry in the Bluffton-Pandora community. Moser had presented missions as a command of Christ and anchored missions in atonement theology, as chapter 4 will show. In response, the Reformed Mennonites registered a basic disagreement—beyond peripheral matters, where they could agree to disagree. The failure of the Reformed Mennonites to support missions handed Moser an issue by which he could return the kind of charges the Reformed Mennonites leveled against him: disregard for the Bible and the teachings of Christ, toleration of unbelief, and links with unbelievers. However, whatever personal impulses may have reinforced Moser's conviction, support of missions was a position on which he agreed with the Mennonite progressives.

In addition to missions, Moser supported other parts of the progressive, activist agenda at the turn of the century.[128] He actively supported the Sunday school. The Bluffton congregation held Sunday school in both north and south meetinghouses.[129] Reports in *Christlicher Bundesbote* of Sunday school conventions held in Bluffton mentioned his addresses. The power of the Sunday school teacher, Moser said, came from the zeal to lead souls to the Lord. A Sunday school teacher should empower students through a good example.[130] Late in his ministerial life, he included Sunday schools as one of the good undertakings in a congregation which reflected God's blessing.[131] Along with his support of Sunday schools, he also warned about the importance of doing such things with proper decorum, though he admitted that more noise and enthusiasm could be expected from children than from adults.[132]

Moser gave explicit support to the development of higher education within the Mennonite churches. His name appeared among a Putnam County list of early supporters of Bethel College.[133] When the Middle District Conference of the General Conference Mennonite Church began discussing the formation of its own college, he wrote for *Christlicher Bundesbote* to give strong support to the idea. His advocacy dealt with religious and church issues: the importance of including religious training in the curriculum, the amount of time teachers spend with students, the importance of having Christian teachers, and the idea of preparing young people for service in the church. Moser gave

From *Bluffton College: An Adventure in Faith, 1900-1950,* edited by faculty members.

Laying the cornerstone of College Hall at Bluffton College, June 19, 1900. Johannes Moser gave the dedicatory prayer.

practical advice on the necessity of making good plans, and he commented that since young people are going to get education some place to function in the modern world, it is better to provide a Christian school for that education.[134]

Finally, Moser appealed for wide support. Since he and others had contributed to the faraway school in Kansas because it was good for young people, he invited those far away now to contribute to the school in the Middle District.[135] Moser's support for the school reached a fitting culmination on June 19, 1900, when he uttered the dedicatory words at the cornerstone laying of Central Mennonite College,[136] renamed Bluffton College several years later.

Moser also supported the use of English language in church, another part of the agenda of Mennonite progressives. He believed that since the language of the wider society was English, part of the curriculum of the new school should be conducted in English in order to enable young people to function in the wider society in such roles as teachers. At the same time, Moser still cherished the German language and argued that the new school's curriculum should also teach German.

> I have heard no one complain that he could speak German, but I have heard several lament that they could not. . . . One who speaks both German and English is ahead of those who know only one language. A sober, upright young German-English youth has an advantage in a store and in almost any business, both in the German settlement and also as teacher and preacher.[137]

Moser's practical approach to the use of English gave him affinity with the camp of the Mennonite progressives.

Moser vigorously supported the idea of Mennonite periodicals. His own activities provide ample testimony. From his first article in *Herold der Wahrheit* in 1867 until his final article in *Christlicher Bundesbote* in 1905, his writing appeared in sixty-four separate issues of those periodicals. Eleven titles, some with multiple parts, appeared in 21 issues of *Herold der Wahrheit*, with 38 titles in 43 issues of *Christlicher Bundesbote*. He also encouraged others to write for the *Christlicher Bundesbote* and saw the periodical as a tool for advancing the cause of Christ. Moser concluded an article on hell with words in support of having a church periodical. It nourished congregations, the correspondence section helped people to know each other almost personally, and the subscription price was worth it since the *Christlicher Bundesbote* encouraged readers in the work of the Lord. One need not

Central District Archives, Bluffton College, Bluffton, Ohio

Early postcard photo of Ebenezer Mennonite Church (completed 1883) near Bluffton, Ohio, as it appeared in Johannes Moser's time. The sign on the building reads, "Mennonite Church 1883."

Herman Kindle collection, Swiss Community Historical Society, Bluffton, Ohio

Postcard photo from 1906 or 1907 of First Mennonite Church (completed 1906) in Bluffton, Ohio. Johannes Moser worshiped and perhaps preached here before his death in 1908.

Photo of St. John Mennonite Church (completed 1889) near Pandora, Ohio, as it appeared in Johannes Moser's time. The General Conference met here in Johannes Moser's time. The General Conference met here in 1893 when Johannes Moser's Swiss congregation of Bluffton-Pandora joined the General Conference Mennonite Church.

Ebenezer, St. John, and First were the three meetinghouses of the Swiss congregation of Bluffton-Pandora at the time of Johannes Moser's death in 1908. A congregational directory of 1903 listed the names of 840 baptized members of the congregation, which worshiped in the three meetinghouses. A 1913 directory listed 880 members. In later years, members who worshiped at these three meetinghouses organized themselves into independent congregations, and 141 members withdrew in 1904 to found Grace Mennonite Church, Pandora, Ohio.

be an expert in spelling to write for the *Christlicher Bundesbote*, Moser added. "The editor can correct it, and he can, if we are not too self-satisfied, improve the meaning and make it more understandable."[138]

As noted earlier, Moser drafted a constitution and confession of faith for the Swiss congregation in Allen and Putnam counties. Developing a written constitution aligned him with the new kind of authority prescribed by the Mennonite progressives.[139] He anticipated that the congregation would join the progressive General Conference Mennonite Church. Moser took a pastoral approach to a constitution and confession of faith. It was not written in order to exclude, nor did writing such a statement mean that the author or congregation claimed perfection or absolute certainty of truth. Instead, the statement was a goal and a direction toward which the congregation should strive. In that way, a confession could serve as a means for church unity.

At the same time, Moser said, a confession had to be clear where clear truth existed. Thus a proper confession should reject infant baptism and a Lord's Supper like the Catholic's, which withheld the cup from the laity. It should also prohibit swearing of oaths, divorce, military service, membership in secret societies, business practices such as selling liquor, and allowing women to preach.[140] A church without a constitution and rules implied that all positions were equal. Such a church would have no real relationships either within itself or with others.[141] The congregation adopted the constitution during a meeting in the St. John meetinghouse on January 2, 1893.

In all of these items related to the agenda of the progressive Mennonites, Moser took positions in line with the relatively new General Conference Mennonite Church. That affinity came to fruition on October 2, 1893. Having adopted a constitution in anticipation of the event, the congregation now voted 195-32 to join the General Conference. The vote was timed to coincide with the hosting of General Conference by the Bluffton congregation soon afterward.[142]

These items in which Moser identified with the progressive agenda all concern things that he supported. In two other instances, his oppositions also identified him generally with the progressives. He joined the growing, turn-of-the-century Mennonite opposition to the use of tobacco. In rather vivid language, he described enslavement to the lifelong tobacco habit, the unsightliness of meetinghouse floors spotted with tobacco juice, stale smoke in rooms and on clothing, the emptiness of drawing in smoke merely to blow it out and of paying money to suck powder up the nose and then blow it out again, and the preference for offering oneself to God rather than to the desire for tobacco.[143] Moser also opposed use of alcoholic beverages.[144]

Moser's involvements with other congregations also seem to reflect both his traditionalist and progressive dimensions. For one, as has already been noted, he was a major factor in the conferences of the Swiss congregations. He was a cosigner of a conservative-oriented conference statement of 1879 which questioned S. F. Sprunger's progressive direction and support of Wadsworth Institute.[145] That action reflected Moser's traditionalist dimension.

An involvement that implied a more progressive orientation occurred in 1871. In that year, Moser visited the young Bethel congregation in Morgan and Moniteau counties in Missouri. Bethel had been founded four years earlier by progressive elements of the Sonnenberg

Swiss congregation from Wayne County, Ohio, along with persons from more longstanding American Mennonite congregations in Virginia, Pennsylvania, Indiana, Illinois, and Ontario.[146] In the spring of 1871, the young congregation experienced a series of disagreements. One concerned foot washing, not practiced by the Swiss, but considered important by those the Swiss called the "American" Mennonites. While the Bethel congregation had earlier agreed to grant "each one liberty of serving God according to his custom and conscience," in 1871 a peaceful separation into two congregations was agreed upon.

Moser was invited to help organize the Swiss congregation, which retained the name and full title to the church property.[147] During the August visit, he served communion, helped to write a congregational constitution, and assisted in the election and commissioning of a young minister, P. P. Lehman Jr. To better prepare for his calling, Lehman spent a year at the Wadsworth Institute before taking up work as minister at the Bethel church in 1873.[148] Bethel joined the General Conference in 1881. While this separation into two congregations was primarily a matter of sorting out along ethnic lines, it is clear in this instance that Moser was assisting a rather progressive-oriented Swiss congregation.

This survey of Moser's outlook in relation to the Mennonite traditionalists and conservatives reveals a combination of views. Although he agreed with some aspects of each agenda, it would be incorrect merely to see Moser as a moderate. On some issues he supported the traditional positions, on others he clearly advocated the progressive agenda. His overall impulse moved the church in a progressive direction. His attitude of patience and tolerance toward lapses, while continuing to uphold clear positions as a goal, allowed the movement in a progressive direction to proceed. It is not at all surprising that his congregation eventually joined the progressive General Conference Mennonite Church.

Long before Moser's Bluffton-Pandora congregation joined the General Conference, his contributions to the two Mennonite periodicals appeared to reveal that preference. Between 1867 and 1885, he contributed to 21 issues of *Herold der Wahrheit*, the periodical published from Elkhart by John F. Funk which functioned as the voice of the majority, modern Mennonites and Amish. However, already in 1882, the first year of its publication, Moser wrote an article for *Christlicher Bundesbote*, the new periodical of the General Conference Mennonite Church. Although he did not write for the *Christlicher Bundesbote* again until 1887, after 1885 he produced only one other item for

Herold der Wahrheit, the 1891 article concerning Joseph Steiner's sentence for refusing to do jury duty.[149] Meanwhile, material from Moser appeared in another 43 issues of *Christlicher Bundesbote*.

Some have suggested that Moser acted as a conservative force within the Pandora-Bluffton Swiss congregation, guiding but perhaps delaying their movement toward the General Conference.[150] This assessment was offered, however, without awareness of the full publication record of Johannes Moser. A perusal of the content and pattern of Moser's writings indicates that he was far from retarding his congregation's evolution toward the General Conference. On the contrary, it seems arguable that Moser was actually prodding toward the General Conference a congregation with factions of both progressives and traditionalists.

A noteworthy incident in Wayne County provides a symbolic conclusion to this analysis of Johannes Moser. In late November 1889, three years after the bitter schism that produced Salem alongside Sonnenberg, Moser was in Wayne County to attend the funeral of his aged mother. Johannes's brother David was deacon of the progressive Salem congregation, while their brother Jacob J. served the more conservative group at Sonnenberg as deacon. Johannes was persuaded to stay and minister in the community, dividing his time between the two congregations. At Salem, he spoke at the midweek meeting on 20 November, on Sunday evening 24 November, and on Tuesday of the following week. He spoke at Sonnenberg on Sunday morning, as well as at the Sonnenberg Sunday school that day, and again at Sonnenberg on Thanksgiving day.

The dramatic moment occurred on Sunday morning, 24 November, when the Salem congregation canceled its own service and crowded into the old Sonnenberg meetinghouse to hear the revered bishop Johannes Moser preach, while sitting alongside their erstwhile co-religionists and protagonists whom they had abandoned to form Salem. His sermon undoubtedly addressed both factions. As it was later reported, he spoke on the text, "Ask, and ye shall receive," with the main theme described as "every person seeks something, but unfortunately, too often it is not the one thing that is most necessary."[151] It was quite obvious that Moser had retained the reverence and respect of both the progressive Salem and the traditionalist Sonnenberg. This analysis, depicting both his traditionalist and progressive sides, indicates how he could retain the respect of both sides in the Sonnenberg-Salem schism, although it would be only four years until his Bluffton-Pandora congregation would cast its lot with the progressive General Conference.

This survey also reveals clearly that Moser's worldview is a Mennonite one. Traditional Mennonite positions characterize his understanding of the church. He believed in the authority of the Bible, discipleship, nonresistance, a simple and humble lifestyle, and church discipline. The church might reflect something of the progressive Mennonite agenda—support for higher education, missions, Sunday schools, English language. However, it was still the church and not American society through which Moser understood that a Christian expressed the social dimensions of what it means to be Christian. At that point, Moser was clearly with the Mennonites rather than with the American evangelicals described in chapter 2.

John M. Brenneman

In the last half of the nineteenth century, the largest group of Mennonites were the descendants of Swiss immigrants who had arrived in Pennsylvania in large numbers early in the previous century. These people comprised the majority of the Mennonites who began moving south into Virginia later in the eighteenth century, and west with the moving frontier into Ohio, Indiana, and Illinois beginning early in the nineteenth century. John M. Brenneman (1816-95), longtime bishop of the Salem Mennonite church in Elida, Ohio, represents this largest group of American, Swiss-derived Mennonites. His numerous articles, many reprinted in booklets or books, provide a good look into his theology.[152]

For the most part, Brenneman's many articles dealt primarily with the nature of the Christian life and the shape of the church, the believing family of God. He also recognized and handled, sometimes indirectly, some challenges from the wider American society and from other religious traditions. A review of what Brenneman said about the Christian life and the nature of the church will show how he faced issues posed by the world.

Brenneman looked at the church as the family of God, converted persons, brothers and sisters united together in Christ. His first article in the initial issue of *Herald of Truth* and *Herold der Wahrheit* likened the church to the family of God. He touted the papers as a way for the scattered family to maintain acquaintance with each other.[153] The theme of the church was one of his primary concerns. The church is built of professing Christians. Confessing one Christ as the foundation and one Spirit of Christ should produce one, unified church, Brenneman said. However, for a variety of reasons, divisions exist in the

The meetinghouse of John M. Brenneman's Salem Mennonite Church, near Elida, Ohio, built in 1883. Although in its original location, this building was turned 90 degrees on its base. More recently, members added several sections and covered it with brick.

body of Christ. Some members are not truly converted, and others have remained only babes in Christ. Members receive the gifts of the Spirit in different measure, and some members have lost their first love for God and the church.[154] All members should work to overcome these divisions and produce a united body.

All members have a role as laborers or builders of this church, but the ordained ministers have the primary role. "Preachers are especially called laborers in the Scriptures."[155] Brenneman's many preaching trips to scattered congregations reflected that priority, as well as his accompanying exhortations for more ministers to visit these scattered brothers and sisters.[156] His understanding of unity and fellowship bridged the prevailing organizational boundaries; he included the Amish and the Swiss in his travels and in his promotions of church unity.[157] Brenneman's cautious support for the idea of a general conference of Mennonites also reflected the goal of a unified church, one that would include Mennonites, Amish, and Swiss.[158]

When people moved, Brenneman believed that they should give the church first priority. When a contingent of three families with twenty-four persons moved from Elida to Iowa, he ordained one of the men as minister so that the new little flock would not lack spiritual nurture.[159] He counseled emigrants to avoid the mistake of Lot, who moved where the good land was and neglected the worship of God. Rather than merely seeking out the best land, "it is much better to remain united and connected with the church, with food and raiment barely sufficient, than to venture among the ungodly and worldly minded, where we might perhaps accumulate great wealth, but in the end 'lose our own souls.' "[160]

Finally, understanding the church to be composed of brothers and sisters in Christ should make it impossible for Christians even to contemplate killing each other. "Alas, how questionable is it then that Christian believers, who stand under a common order or confession of faith or fellowship, can directly in war so deplorably shoot deadly weapons at each other in order to kill and do all manner of harm to each other, as frequently happened in the last American war. Are these the gentle followers, disciples and lambs of Christ?"[161] This nonresistant church, composed of repentant, converted sinners and united across many miles into Christ's body by God's Spirit, constituted Brenneman's tangible identity and his spiritual home. It was this body that he was building and this body in which he lived and this body which shaped the way he looked at the world.

While Brenneman did not mention nonresistance in every statement about conversion or the nature of the church, nonresistance clearly belonged in an ineradicable way to his understanding of the gospel and of the church. The most visible instance of his complete commitment to nonresistance was the long sermon, *Christianity and War = Das Christentum und der Krieg*, which he published in the midst of the Civil War.[162] The booklet began with Peter's call to follow the example of Christ (1 Pet. 2:21). It left no doubt at all that following the example of Christ—being Christian—meant that Christians could have nothing to do with war. Using a wide variety of Scripture texts, Brenneman argued that the penitent and regenerated individual, who partakes with Christ of the Holy Spirit, and who imitates the practices, walk, and conversation of Christ, cannot participate in war.

This regenerate individual follows the positive command of Christ to love one's enemies.

> To "love our enemies," is a positive command, wherein Christ has also "left us an example that we should follow his steps." The ungodly cannot love their enemies, neither can they follow Christ's steps; but to love their enemies is the characteristic of all true Christians.[163]

Love of enemies gives evidence of conversion and possession of the Spirit of God.[164] Brenneman wrote that nonresistance belonged to the gospel which missionaries should proclaim, and that Mennonites should not support missionaries who considered warfare a Christian duty.[165] Jesus' words on nonresistance from the Sermon on the Mount sat high in Brenneman's list of one hundred commands given by Christ and the apostles,[166] and they appeared in the "counsels of God," which defined the Christian life.[167]

Beyond rejecting participation in war, Brenneman also called for Christians to remain uninvolved in the political processes. They ought to avoid the party spirit created by elections, not to mention the discord that results from the war. Christians should not identify themselves with political names like Democrat or Republican nor allow themselves to be divided by political matters. It is also inconsistent, he continued, for nonresistant Christians to help choose men for office who would use deadly weapons. Thus Brenneman counseled,

> Therefore be separate, and touch not the unclean thing. . . . Let us, by our walk and conversation, declare plainly, that we seek a heavenly country; and let us not be entangled with the trifles and follies of this present evil world, so as to neglect the "one thing needful."[168]

At the same time, Brenneman expressed both national loyalty and a certain amount of social concern. Christians should be loyal and faithful citizens, obeying the worldly government in all things that did not contradict the laws of Christ, as well as paying all lawfully enacted taxes. Further, they should provide reassurance to the government that it need never fear rebellion from the "Defenseless Christians."[169] Writing in the midst of the Civil War, the point about rejecting the idea of rebellion put Brenneman and his fellow Mennonites on the side of President Lincoln and the duly constituted, legal government.[170] Further, Brenneman even confessed that nonresistant Mennonites might have a modicum of responsibility for the unrest of the Civil War.

His discussion used the story of Jonah, with the ark of safety—the church—analogous to the boat on which Jonah slept. As Jonah's disobedience caused the turbulence which threatened the boat, sin caused the turbulence of the war that currently threatened the church. Since the Lord has permitted the sea of the American people to become tempestuous as punishment for sin, we Mennonites need to "humble ourselves," Brenneman wrote, and ask whether Mennonite idolatry—putting more trust in the power of man than in the living God—has not contributed to the national sin. Perhaps "if we confess our sins before

God, with sorrowful hearts, and like the Ninevites cry mightily unto Him," God might spare the nation as he would have spared Sodom and Gomorrah for the sake of ten righteous persons.[171]

Brenneman considered suffering and tribulation a mark of God's people, "from righteous Abel down to the present time."[172] Tribulation served a purpose for the church. Not all members of the church are genuinely Christian. The fire of tribulation will destroy "the wood, hay, and stubble [that] denote those professors of Christianity that are not truly converted," while it refined "the precious stones in the house of God [who are] the true children of God."[173] At times, punishment, such as war and famine which God lays upon the godless, also strikes believers. In the case of the righteous, however, it works to their good, out of love, in contrast to the destructive effect that it has upon the wicked.[174] In the nature of the narrow path Christians walk, they experience persecution and opposition, as well as temptations from Satan.[175] Finally, Brenneman explained, tribulation belongs to the counsel of God that describes the Christian life. It serves the purpose of making believers humble and teaches them dependence on God. "The counsel of God demands that his children should in this life pass through great tribulation, trials and afflictions, to keep them humble, that they might feel the great need of his help."[176]

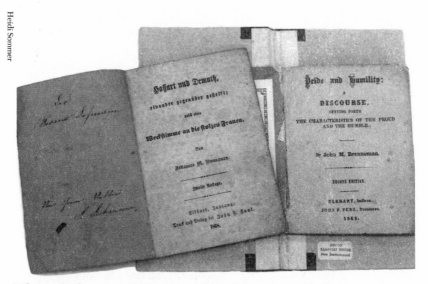

Photo of title pages of German and English versions of John M. Brenneman's Pride and Humility.

Humility as a characteristic of the regenerated Christian comprised a well-known dimension of Brenneman's worldview.[177] He gave his best known articulation of the humility vision in a three-part article, *Pride and Humility = Hoffart und Demut*, that appeared in both language versions of *Herald of Truth* and was subsequently reprinted several times as booklets in each language. Funk promoted these booklets in the pages of his periodicals.

In *Pride and Humility*, Brenneman articulated his understanding of salvation. Taking 1 Peter 5:5 as his text, he divided humanity into two classes, the proud and the humble, which are as opposed to each other as "day to night."[178] Since pride caused the Fall of Adam and Eve, pride constituted the first or original sin, while humility described the state of the restored, regenerated believer. "Thus by pride man fell, and it is only through humbleness of heart that he can be restored."[179]

Throughout history, God has always resisted the proud. As examples of the proud so resisted, Brenneman included "our first parents," Cain, the wicked before the great flood, the people of Sodom and Gomorrah, King Pharaoh, Miriam when she spoke against Moses, the "mutinous faction of Korah, Dathan, and Abiram," Haman, Nebuchadnezzar, Belshazzar, Herod, the Jews of Capernaum, and the "many thousands" of contemporary people who refuse to yield to the gospel of God. God resists such pride "with various plagues; as war, famine, pestilence, earthquakes, sickness, and punishments in various ways too numerous to be recounted here." Ultimately, Brenneman wrote, God will resist them at the final judgment.[180]

After Brenneman identified pride as the problem, he turned to what he called "the more agreeable part" of 1 Peter 5:5: God gives grace to the humble. The description followed the process of salvation that will be described in more detail in chapter 4. As a result of the calling and chastening of God, the sinner became aware of one's own wretched and lost condition, with a burden of sin "too heavy to be borne." In that state of helplessness, the now "truly penitent and humble heart" could turn to God and make a commitment to serve God to the end. To that humble supplicant, God then gave the grace which resulted in regeneration of the sinner.

> Through grace we are regenerated, and born anew, and made heirs of his eternal and heavenly kingdom. . . . He gives grace to them in this life, inasmuch as he pardons their sins and blesses them in body and soul with all manner of good gifts; and in the life to come he bestows on them eternal and heavenly gifts and possessions, and eternal joy, rest, and happiness.

Only the humble received this grace, and it was grace, according to Brenneman, precisely because the humble sinner was sinful and had done nothing to merit God's acceptance and regeneration.[181] He then listed five reasons why his readers should become humble: their sins, Christ's commands, God's promises, God's threats, and the example of Christ. Christ's example included washing the disciples' feet, and ultimately, humbling himself on the cross.[182] This description of the proud and the humble confronted the readers with a choice: "God's grace, or to be resisted by him." Brenneman concluded, "I hope we will choose his grace."[183]

The virtue of humility appeared in several ways throughout Brenneman's activities and his articles. It gave him a personal diffidence which could produce a somewhat distorted version of events. For example, when he reported on the several addresses given and subjects discussed at the annual conference held at the Yellow Creek Mennonite church in Elkhart County, he described his own activities as, "I also attended three evening meetings."[184] More accurately, he had delivered the main conference sermon and spoken several other times to overflow crowds.[185]

In 1868, he had helped the Virginia conference to adopt a resolution that allowed remarriage for a person divorced for reasons of adultery. Two weeks later, the Indiana conference reached a contrary conclusion, and Brenneman received a good deal of criticism for his stance. He was quick to ask forgiveness. While his apology did not retract his position, it affirmed his submission to the will of the church. He declared that he had never acted on his view, "nor did I ever have any intention of doing so without the counsel and consent of the brethren."[186] The last item Brenneman ever published in the Mennonite periodicals was a warning that to praise ministers for a good sermon could lead to pride.[187]

By far the most visible example of pride mentioned by Brenneman was "external adornment," which covered a multitude of sins. Pride manifested itself by "a man's actions, deeds, and manner of deportment." It was

> clearly visible in the needless splendor, costliness, and magnitude of house, barns, &., which are sometimes highly ornamented, and painted in a variety of colors, merely to make a magnificent show. It is frequently also to be seen in the manner in which houses are adorned and furnished . . . with all kinds of new-fashioned, ornamental, and costly furniture, floors overspread with brilliant and showy carpeting, windows decorated with fine drapery, and walls adorned with pictures.

Such unacceptable adornments also included any pictures or like-nesses of people,[188] which stirred up lust of the eye, ostentatious display when serving guests at table, and ornamental coaches and carriages.[189]

Beyond these signs of pride, stylish clothing and adornment of the body drew Brenneman's particular ire as signs of pride. "Especially does pride, when it exists in the heart, manifest itself very plainly in the manner of dress and in the costly array with which poor dying mortals strive, frequently beyond their means, to decorate themselves, in order to gain the respect and esteem of a proud and wicked world."[190]

He rejected the idea that such stress on external appearance gave Mennonites a religion that consisted "entirely in their manner of dress." Were that actually true, he said, they would be in a sad state indeed, for if dress carried their Christianity, "they would not have any at all." Instead, a true Mennonite believed that "true Christianity is to be found only in the humble and regenerate heart." External appearances, therefore, do not and cannot save. They are, however, evidence that the heart within is genuinely humble and regenerate, since such a heart will "feel an aversion to, and abhor, all needless ornament and extravagance in dress."[191]

The theme of dress and bodily adornment appeared throughout Brenneman's writings, with frequent admonitions to avoid such prideful display. His concern to maintain a standard of plain dress helped fashion his respect for the Amish.[192] For Brenneman, pride manifested in external adornment constituted the great evil that presaged the end of the world.[193] In addition to brief comments in a number of articles, he devoted several full tracts to the subject. He singled out women for particular admonition on this sin in "Eine Weckstimme an die stoltzen Frauen."[194] Disaster awaited complacent women in Isaiah 32:11. That disaster Brenneman applied in near apoplectic fashion to the

> great majority of women of the present day. For who can show us a time since the creation of the world, in which there was more pride, pomp and extravagance to be seen among the female sex than now? And all the preaching, admonishing, reproving, warning and writing against the abominable vice seems to be well-nigh in vain; indeed in many it seems only to excite to laughter.[195]

This is not a laughing matter, he warned. If their daughters were in physical danger from fire or water, warnings would go out. Even more so should the daughters be warned about "their terrible pride and vanity" with which they are walking on the broad road that leads "to the abyss of eternal fire, into hell and eternal damnation."[196] Johannes Moser would no doubt have approved. The article "Der äusserliche Schmuck verboten," issued a similar warning, declaring that nothing was more clearly forbidden in the Scriptures than external adornment of the body.[197]

The intensity of Brenneman's feeling on the issue appeared in a short statement on "Pride and Fashion." He began by quoting a paragraph from another source which decried dressing up children in silks, laces, and other fashionable items. He used that comment as the basis for his own warning that children frequently suffer from insufficient dress, when "head, arms, neck and breast" are uncovered for reasons of style. But he was not finished there. Mothers who dressed in such fashion, he opined, would likely complain of the cold. Brenneman's exceedingly dire conclusion:

> There is no doubt at all, but that the lives of thousands of innocent children have been shortened by this very sinful and shameful fashion. O! when will such mothers become sensible and merciful? The sixth commandment says, "Thou shalt not kill." Sisters take the hint.[198]

Alongside pride, idle talk and frivolous activity constituted another dimension of worldly life that Brenneman believed regenerate Christians should avoid. A short chapter in *Plain Teachings* argued that Christians ought not to laugh aloud. We do not read that Jesus laughed, he said, but it does say that he wept, whereas wicked men laughed Jesus to scorn. Christians should follow the example of Jesus. Further, our laughter should turn to mourning when we think of the many unconverted souls which daily pass into eternity. "It is unbecoming and unsuitable for Christian professors to laugh aloud, or to say or tell any thing to cause others to laugh." Both such activities left a dim light before the world.

Brenneman did not go so far as to condemn to hell those who laughed (as he did the proud who adorned themselves). Yet "unnecessary laughing" was something for which one could "pray to God for forgiveness" and for "grace and power to abandon it."[199] It was reported that in one instance, Bishop Brenneman withheld a name from the lot for bishop because the potential candidate "was fond of joking and laughing" as well as using tobacco.[200]

One wonders about Brenneman's ability to maintain such a laughless posture. Many years later, his nephews said that he "was seldom if ever heard to laugh aloud."[201] His family was not without enjoyment, however. Sophia, Brenneman's daughter, described an evening of family fun, which included a spelling bee in which Brenneman pronounced the words. "I just wish you could have all bin her," she wrote to relatives, "We had such a good time of spelling and singing duch [German]."[202] Sophia's words imply that her father shared in the enjoyment. His words do allow for such enjoyment, provided the socializing is understood in the proper manner.

On one hand, it was preferable, Brenneman counseled, to enter the house of mourning, where one may help someone, or see things which move one to think about one's life and relationship to God, rather than to enter the house of feasting. On the other hand, Christian friends may come together in a Christlike manner at a common feast, provided that it honor God and avoid excess, and that they be "quite [quiet], peaceable, and sociable together, and not turn the feast into a frolic."[203]

No comprehensive study exists comparing the humility outlook across the several Mennonite traditions, from Bergthaler Gerhard Wiebe to the outlook described in the Swiss Mennonite tradition of Stauffer, Holdeman, and Brenneman. They have a great deal in common in defining this attitude as integral to the meaning of Christian discipleship. At the same time, however, further research would no doubt reveal some differences. I perceive that Wiebe tied humility more to specific deeds and symbols than did the Swiss. Particularly for Brenneman, humility was more an outlook that colored every dimension of life. Perhaps with Holdeman and Stauffer, the more tradi-

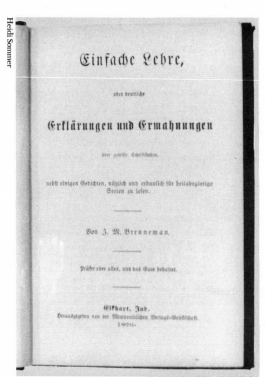

Heidi Sommer

Photo of title page of John M. Brenneman's Einfache Lehre.

tionalist of the Swiss figures in this study, Wiebe saw humility as a barrier against the outside, non-Mennonite world. In contrast, John M. Brenneman saw humility more as a means of dealing with the world, a way to provide a witness of Christian obedience when one contacted the world.

In reading Gerhard Wiebe's *Ursachen und Geschichte*, one develops a rather strong impression that for him humility implied a lack of individual self-worth, that it required Wiebe to believe he was truly inferior to other people. In contrast, humility meant not inferiority to Brenneman but rather constituted a recognition that all that one does is subject to error. Thus belonging to the church should mean a willingness to submit to the correction of the church. For Brenneman, humility did not prevent one from acting or speaking but rather defined how one acted and spoke.

Brenneman took specific positions on at least four theological controversies. He asserted a symbolic view of the Lord's Supper and rejected the Catholic doctrine of transubstantiation.[204] He asserted baptism by pouring and rejected the requirement of immersion.[205]

Positions on two remaining issues have implications for Brenneman's understanding of salvation. Two of his last significant articles opposed the Calvinistic doctrine of eternal security, and the revivalist, holiness doctrine of perfectionism or entire sanctification. He published "Sanctification" in 1880 to describe a middle ground between those who claimed such a high degree of sanctification as to be without sin, and those who made light of sanctification.

To sanctify meant, Brenneman explained, to be made clean and set apart for holy use. As such, it applied to every Christian. Sanctification, which Brenneman called another way to describe conversion or regeneration, depended upon the linking of atonement, repentance, and conversion. Since this was the case, sanctification, a visible external change in one's life, could not be avoided. On the other hand, sanctification was "progressive" and described a process which continued throughout the Christian's life on earth. Thus, to claim perfect holiness would in fact contradict all the biblical texts which speak of growth in grace.[206]

"Hope," first published in 1885, presented Brenneman's arguments against the doctrine of eternal security. The Christian's hope of heaven, he wrote, depended upon the experience of rebirth. When an individual has experienced genuine rebirth, that same person can and will know that the Christian hope of heaven is founded on experience of rebirth. What one could not know, however, was whether one will continue to hope until the end. Brenneman rejected the idea of "some professors of Christianity [who] claim to have attained to a much greater privilege than hope, namely to a positive certainty that future glory will be their portion." He asked, "But who would venture to say that he is positively sure that he will remain faithful unto death?" The implied answer was "no one." For that reason, the Christian must always be on guard to nourish his or her spiritual condition.[207]

While Heinrich Egly did not teach eternal security as such, he did maintain that the believer should have certainty of salvation. It appears that Egly would find Brenneman's understanding of the Christian hope just as unacceptable as he found the hope of Johannes Moser.[208]

Brenneman was an advocate of the Sunday school, and he invited John F. Funk to Allen County to help organize the first Sunday school in the Ohio Mennonite Conference, in 1868.[209] Brenneman also supported evangelistic or revival work in Mennonite congregations. In a number of instances, the series of meetings he preached were all but "protracted meetings" or revival meetings. John S. Coffman, the foremost Mennonite revival preacher in the last quarter of the century, regarded Brenneman as "the pioneer, the forerunner in evangelistic work."[210] One reason for establishing the Sunday school was to teach German. However, Brenneman advocated use of English when needed to retain young people or build the church.[211] He was also an advocate for a general conference to unite the majority stream of Mennonites and Amish. Brenneman strongly supported the publication of a Mennonite denominational periodical.

These positions all identified Brenneman with the developing Mennonite progressive agenda of the third quarter of the nineteenth century. On the other hand, the Brenneman described by this survey of his entire literary corpus is not at all defined by the single adjective "progressive." In many instances, he had a decidedly conservative or traditionalist outlook. It can be argued that he filled the progressive forms of Sunday schools, revival meetings, denominational periodicals, and English sermons with quite traditional content. His theology clearly reflected the received Mennonite tradition. Theron Schlabach was certainly correct when he called Brenneman "very much a link between an older Mennonitism and a newer."[212] The foregoing analysis suggests that the link was welded most firmly to the traditionalist side.

This survey reveals that Brenneman had a great deal in common with Johannes Moser, who also had both traditionalist and progressive dimensions. The sense of a long tradition prevented Brenneman from any serious idea of following his progressive side into the fledgling

General Conference Mennonite Church. Working out of a religious worldview similar to Brenneman's, Johannes Moser did follow the progressive dimension of his outlook into the General Conference. As the son of Swiss immigrants, Moser did not have Brenneman's sense of belonging to a long American tradition, and it was thus easier for Moser to join the General Conference.

Perhaps it was the generational difference within the Mennonite church in America as much as anything which accounted for the fact that these two men of similar outlook, who knew and respected each other, opted for different conference affiliations. In each case, however, a similar understanding of the visible church obedient to Christ certainly defined the theology of them both. As was true for Moser and others, Brenneman's view of the church distinguished him from American evangelicals of chapter 2. Not only did Brenneman maintain an absolutist view of nonresistance, but he clearly perceived that Christian social expression was exercised in terms of the church rather than through the structures and institutions of American society.

John Holdeman

John Holdeman (1832-1900) withdrew from the Mennonite Church of John M. Brenneman in 1859 and founded his own church, the Church of God in Christ, Mennonite.[213] It is often referred to as the Holdeman Mennonite Church. To a large extent, Holdeman's theological perspective, displayed in the view of the church detailed in chapter 4, constituted his worldview. As he defined the true church, it is the agent of salvation which is God's answer to the problem of the Fall. Christ's example, teaching, and commands describe the life and practices of that church, which must be followed and obeyed if one would be saved. Although Holdeman's church practices differed in their details from the other conservative manifestations, his outlook shared a great deal in common with the worldviews of Jacob Stauffer and David Beiler.

At one point, Holdeman shared a view of church history with C. H. Wedel and probably Gerhard Wiebe. Like them, Holdeman believed that the true church had "always existed"[214] in an unbroken line of succession from Jesus until the present. The line passed through the medieval sectarians to the Waldensians. Menno joined the Waldensians, so that "the Waldenses and the Mennonites . . . were the only true, visible Church of God in the sixteenth century." This church was carried for a long while by the Mennonite church until decay set in. This decay,

Pencil sketch of John Holdeman made between 1978 and 1981 by Linda Jackson, art instructor at Tabor College. Jackson first made pencil sketches of facial structures based on ideas gleaned from photos of Holdeman's two sons and daughter. She then made revisions until the image matched the appearance of Holdeman remembered by his granddaugher Florence Lawson, Hutchinson, Kansas. In her late 80s when the sketches were drawn, Lawson was 12 when John Holdeman died. She had lived with her grandparents for many of those 12 years. The original sketch is in the possession of Clarence Hiebert, who graciously made a copy available for this book.

Holdeman claimed, necessitated his separation from them and the formation of his Church of God in Christ as the contemporary manifestation of the true church.[215]

Holdeman provided more discussion about the true church than Wiebe's few remarks. In contrast to Wedel, who depicted *Gemeindechristentum* as a comprehensive Mennonite outlook which enabled Mennonites to incorporate culture and new learnings, Holdeman used the idea of a continually existing true church primarily as the basis for rejecting other Mennonite denominations.[216]

Holdeman had a strong concept of separation from the world. He had no interest in adjusting to the world nor even in looking for some aspects of the world that could be brought into the church in a transformed fashion to further the agenda of the church. In spite of his sense of having built a wall against the world, however, Holdeman's worldview shows traces of a philosophical system that was much more modern and American than he would have admitted. In several instances, Holdeman used language reminiscent of Commonsense philosophy and seemed to anchor his doctrine in presuppositions that echo that philosophical system.

George Marsden identified two presuppositions of Commonsense philosophy that undergirded the social order of mid-nineteenth-century America: there is one unified system of God's truth, and all persons who exercise common sense can know that truth. For evangelicals, of course, the Bible constituted the primary source of God's truth.[217] Although John Holdeman did not appeal specifically to Commonsense philosophy, several of his comments seem to echo its presuppositions.

Holdeman's preface to *A Mirror of Truth*, his last comprehensive book, opened with the lament that truth has been dimmed and distorted in these last days by false teachings which opposed truth. That truth was, he continued, "an intrinsic reality, which is vested in God and which has been revealed to us by the prophets, by Christ, and by the apostles."[218] Such truths included the universality of death produced by Adam's Fall, and the remedy of the Fall provided through Christ. Those truths Holdeman considered incontrovertible.

> To teach differently is to invent falsehood, because there is no reality in such teachings. Also in all other matters which we have been taught—if we teach different from that which we have been taught of God, we teach falsehoods and become false teachers, opposing His revealed truth.[219]

Because he intended his book to reflect this revealed truth, Holdeman called it *A Mirror of Truth*.[220] Such comments seem to ring with a different tone than that of other traditionalist Amish and Mennonites, even when Holdeman attempted to harmonize them with nineteenth-century Mennonite humility through references to his own "infirmity," the "fear and trembling" with which he undertook the book, and the mistakes revealed in his previous writings.[221]

Similar and perhaps more distinct echoes of the presuppositions of Commonsense philosophy appeared in the chapter entitled "Concerning Truth."[222] There Holdeman defined truth as "genuine fact" and falsehood as "something which is not reality and consequently nothing at all." Truth comes from God "who cannot lie," and thus "all that He has said, taught, and done from the beginning is truth." Proverbs 30:5-6 indicated clearly, Holdeman wrote, "that everything that is added to the pure Word of God is a fabricated falsehood."[223]

In following paragraphs he explained that true doctrine will be preserved in the church by true teachers. Holdeman gave the sources for divine truth: the voice of God's Spirit, angels, prophets, God's Son, apostles, and ministers of the Word of God.[224] Finally this short chapter closed with a list of doctrines which Holdeman considered to be true. The content of the list was about what one would expect for conservative Mennonites of the era. What is remarkable is that Holdeman called these doctrines incontrovertible statements of absolute "truth," or of "real fact."[225]

Such echoes of Commonsense philosophy are not prominent throughout *A Mirror of Truth*, and there can be no claim that Holdeman appealed directly to Commonsense philosophy.[226] However, he was a step beyond other Mennonite and Amish writers studied here in his use of terminology which reflected an American idiom. His personal library contained between fifty and one hundred volumes, which may well have given him access to contemporary American thought.[227] Along with his adoption of the modern practice of revivalism, Holdeman likely borrowed some assumptions of writers shaped by presuppositions of Commonsense philosophy. In any case, his defense of truth in *Mirror* was different from David Beiler's and Jacob Stauffer's appeal to tradition. Holdeman's defense of truth also had a different orientation than the foundation in experiential faith and the Bible; this was apparent in his first major book of doctrines, the *Old Ground and Foundation*. Holdeman's way of defining only one truth, with all things definitely either right or wrong, had a new tone not present in other Mennonite writers of his era.

In spite of Holdeman's incipient use of a Commonsense assumption borrowed from other Americans, he employed it to underscore his ideas about the church. He clearly held that all dimensions of Christian faith are expressed through the church and not through the institutions and structures of North American society. This will become even more clear in the analysis in chapter 4 of the theological context in which Holdeman put atonement.

Heinrich Egly

Primary sources for the theology of Heinrich Egly (1824-90),[228] founder of the Defenseless Mennonites, include a series of articles or essays, an undated tract, and an unpublished "Autobiography" written in April 1887.[229] Analysis of these materials reveals a tension between the principles of his progressive Amish tradition and the revivalist orientation which he adopted. That tension appears only when one compares the viewpoint of his published articles with that of the "Autobiography," which reflects the outlook most removed from the Amish tradition of his roots.

Egly penned the "Autobiography" as an elderly churchman reminiscing about his life and the church he founded. He claimed to write "in the name of Jesus, . . . to His honor alone," and presumably at the urging of his children.[230] Much of the manuscript consists of descriptions of his many preaching trips, and reports of conversations and events related to the trips and the meetings he led and preached. In these reports, Egly's revivalist emphasis on conversion is obvious and frequent. The sequence of acknowledging the atoning death of Christ, confession of sin and repentance, conversion, and reception of the Holy Spirit is clear throughout.

Rather surprisingly, however, nonresistance and love of enemies as evidence of conversion does not appear in the "Autobiography." That absence is particularly striking in light of the strong emphasis on love of enemies and rejection of vengeance that occurred frequently in the articles he wrote for *Herold der Wahrheit.* As treatment of his theol-

Artist's conception of Heinrich Egly by Clarence D. Diller. Working from a group photo of the children of Heinrich Egly, Diller sketched the son who most resembled the father. The photo is in Albert and Anna Egly, compilers, Egly Family Record, *between pages iv and v.*

ogy in chapter 4 will show, these articles reveal a tight linking—a virtual fusion—of conversion grounded in the atoning death of Christ with traditional Mennonite and Amish understandings as represented by the stance on humility, nonresistance, and pacifism. It appears that the Heinrich Egly reflected in his "Autobiography" had already evolved quite far in the direction his church would go toward validation of rebirth by the felt experience of conversion. This was replacing validation through nonresistance and a humble daily life, as variously described by Stauffer, Beiler, Moser, and Brenneman.

The difference between the majority of Egly's articles and the outlook of his "Autobiography" points strongly to the conclusion that a shift occurred in his theology under the influence of revivalism. Earlier in his career, he validated conversion with reference to the traditional Mennonite and Amish teachings about obedience to Christ. But the later leader of a conversion-oriented denomination tended to focus on a heartfelt conversion itself as the mark of genuine rebirth for a child of God. The Heinrich Egly of the "Autobiography" was significantly more revivalist than Amish and Mennonite in his theology.

Theron Schlabach claims that during Egly's lifetime, except for a new emphases on conversion and inner experience, "his people appear to have learned from revivalism without departing radically from Amish faith and practice."[231] Schlabach's assessment is generally correct, and Egly certainly did not abandon or reject nonresistance. Yet the analysis here shows clearly that his espousal of revivalism and revivalist doctrines opened the doors wide to the major changes which occurred in the era immediately following his death. This espousal of revivalism was one of the first stages in what George Marsden called "a classic case of a transformation from an Anabaptist to a fundamentalist Protestantism."[232]

Among the figures of this study, John M. Brenneman belonged to the camp of those who accepted revivalism in some form. On the necessity of conversion and on the fact that a genuine conversion would have tangible manifestations, Brenneman was as insistent as Heinrich Egly. What separated them was the way in which the conversion manifested itself. Egly came more and more to stress the sensory, heartfelt nature of conversion as the indication of its reality. In contrast, as evidence of genuine conversion, Brenneman continued to retain his emphasis on the righteous life of the converted person, testified to by such evidence as plain dress and love of enemies. That focus gave Brenneman an affinity for someone like Johannes Moser, even though Moser expressed significant reservations about revivalism. Brenneman supported revivals within a congregation, in contrast to Moser. Moser's pastoral tolerance coupled with Moser's and Brenneman's shared belief that lifestyle demonstrated genuine conversion, would give them a common concern about Heinrich Egly.

Egly's "Autobiography" reveals that he had evolved quite far in a revivalist direction. At the time of his death, he still perceived the social dimensions of Christian faith in terms of church rather than being expressed through North American institutions. However, by removing a social form such as nonresistance from salvation and focusing on a crisis conversion, he opened the door wide to a different assumption about the church. If salvation is focused on personal experiential faith, it can be expressed in a church that poses an alternative to the social order but also in one which supports the social order. Thus Egly was evolving toward a stance like that of the American evangelicals of chapter 2, for whom Christian faith is personal. However, the social expression of Christian faith is expressed in terms of the North American social order.

Summary

In this chapter we have observed eight examples of Mennonites or Amish who in some fashion depicted the church or the Christian life in ways which specifically distinguished it from the social order of North America. As will be articulated more fully for them in chapter 4, the two Old Order men, Jacob Stauffer and David Beiler, envisioned a church shaped by quite traditional Mennonite and Amish principles, a church disciplined and separated from United States society. The same is true for Gerhard Wiebe, who was distinguished by his strong opposition to formal education. John Holdeman worked for a similar church, but with a slightly more American idiom as well as a more experiential conversion to underscore the traditional Mennonite beliefs and practices.

While Johannes Moser and John M. Brenneman accepted more kinds of learning and experience from North American society, they too envisioned a disciplined church that was clearly distinguishable from North American society. Although using historical and theological categories gained through his considerable education, C. H. Wedel also developed the idea of a church clearly distinguishable from the social order. In every instance, these seven men made pacifism, nonresistance, or opposition to war a mark of the faithful church.

Heinrich Egly presented a somewhat different image. Although still formally committed to the practice of nonresistance, that commitment was not articulated in Egly's latest writing. For him, the experience of a crisis conversion had replaced the more practical emphasis on love of enemies as evidence of genuine rebirth to a child of God. He was evolving toward an ecclesiology in which the church could support the institutions of the social order.

As chapters 4 and 5 will demonstrate, all eight subjects discussed salvation and ethics on the basis of some version of satisfaction atonement. Note the contrast between seven subjects including nonresistance and pacifism with the saved life, and Egly omitting it from the definition of the saved life. At some remove, this contrast runs parallel to the erstwhile pacifist abolitionists who came to support the Civil War, or to the comparison between Charles Finney's moral concern and B. B. Warfield's individualistic emphasis. The contrasts are relevant for the discussion of atonement. In all these instances—whether Mennonite or Amish or American revivalist or American evangelical— a common foundation in satisfaction atonement and the attendant understanding of salvation did not produce a common understanding of ethics and the role of ethics in the saved life.

4

Context for Atonement

Chapter 3 sketched some attitudes and perspectives of the eight principal figures of this study for selected issues related to the way they faced the North American environment. That material comprises the broadest context in which to consider their understanding of atonement theology. The present chapter now brings a narrower focus as it explores the particular theological context in which each of these eight situated his understanding of atonement.

Jacob Stauffer

Stauffer in Old Order Mennonite style viewed the disciplined, nonresistant church as composed of humble and repentant sinners, separated from the world, and following the commands of Jesus. That constitutes the theological context in which to consider his understanding of atonement. The purpose of the *Chronik*, as given by Stauffer, was to produce salvation, "to seek the salvation of the undying souls of all humankind."[1] The chapters in Stauffer's part 1 outlined his understanding of church and salvation. In his mind, as demonstrated by the theme of the book's first chapter, the salvation of souls begins with separation from the world and church discipline to protect and preserve that separated church.

Stauffer's view of church discipline mirrors his understanding of God as a God concerned with both mercy and judgment. He expressed dismay at those who will not humbly submit themselves to the Word in obedience to Jesus Christ. They claimed, according to Stauffer, that "this and that don't matter (*Dieses und Jenes macht nichts*)," and they refuse to obey the Word in all its parts.[2] However, in his mind, such an attitude was merely a defense of known sin, as one chose consciously to

Jan Gleysteen and Amos Hoover

View of Pike or Stauffer Mennonite Meetinghouse, showing the original stone center portion of the building, in which Jacob Stauffer preached.

do things prohibited in the Scriptures. Stauffer considered such practice a clear misuse of God's grace and mercy, which the gracious and loving God must punish. Such willing sinners need to remember that the God of grace has also said, "Vengeance is mine, I will repay."[3]

Stauffer believed that discipline served the good of the church. The primary focus of the second chapter of *Chronik* is his belief that without discipline, the church cannot stand.[4] He used the images of a wall and of a fence to depict the way discipline and separation protect the church. Describing the majority Mennonite church of his day, he wrote, "The walls of this city, vineyard, or congregation have become full of holes, and the fence (namely the *Ordnung*,[5] which is the Word of God) has been broken and torn down, so that all can wander in and over them."[6] In other words, without the discipline of separation and shunning, all manner of worldly elements enter the church, and the church ceases to be distinct from the world.

Separation and discipline were really two facets of the same process: separation from the evil world and purification of the church when an element of the world is discovered within the church. Stauffer called separation and discipline "a firm foundation and command from Jesus and his apostles in the treasured Word of God (Matt. 18; 1 Cor.

View of Pike or Stauffer Mennonite Meetinghouse from the cemetery, with Jacob Stauffer's gravestone in foreground.

Gravestones of Jacob Stauffer and his wife, Lydia, (Martin) Stauffer, in cemetery of Pike or Stauffer Mennonite Meetinghouse near Hinkletown, Pennsylvania. After Jacob died, Lydia took the name Brubaker.

Jan Gleysteen and Amos Hoover

5)."[7] Cutting away the unfaithful branch or offending member, he added, prevents damage to the remainder of the congregation. Stories from the Old Testament illustrate the necessity of purging and separation of the sinner.[8]

According to Stauffer, the basic motivation behind discipline was love. Discipline is practiced for the good of the offending sinner. Its intent is to bring the sinner to repentance, so that the offending person can be restored to the fellowship of the church. As long as restoration fails, then discipline fulfills its other function, preserving the purity of the church. It is still motivated by love for the offender, however, since the excommunicated or separated person is subject to God's punishment, and punishment serves the purpose of bringing the sinner to recognize one's own sinful condition. The hope is always the restoration of the sinner to fellowship, so that the offender may again experience the grace and mercy of God.[9] Such elements of discipline appear repeatedly throughout the *Chronik*.

Once he established discipline, namely, excommunication and shunning, as the foundation of the church, Stauffer began in chapter 3 to describe the process whereby the soul is saved within the separated and disciplined church. Salvation depends on genuine repentance. Stauffer rejected the sham of repentance that consists of words alone, the opposite of genuine repentance. According to Stauffer, in the Mennonite churches whose walls have broken down, even mortal sins (*Laster- oder Todsünde*) are dealt with by merely expressing repentance orally before the congregation.[10]

In Stauffer's mind, true repentance goes beyond mere words to express itself in fruit and signs. The first such sign consists of humbling oneself before God, with much self-accusation and great anguish of heart for sins committed. As a second sign, the sinner laments and confesses his or her sinful condition before God and then begs for forgiveness. The final sign is the most telling: the penitent sinner begins a new life. "Thirdly, it is a true sign of repentance (*Busse*), if one seeks to take up a new life and behavior in Christ Jesus, and becomes truly small, lowly and humble (*recht klein, niedrig und demüthig*); if one abandons sin and lives righteously."[11]

The heavy stress on discipline and the expectation that repentance will manifest itself in a holy and righteous life did not make Stauffer's religion merely an external one. He stated clearly that salvation depended on faith, not on works.[12] The new life does not result from human effort; it is impossible without the inner working of God's Spirit. The one who takes up the new life

> will be renewed daily both within and without; he receives new eyes, to make a living confession of God's majesty, power, and holiness, goodness and love in Christ, and to perceive more clearly his own nothingness and imperfection, and the vanity of the world. He receives a new heart, to love and obey God as his highest good and Jesus as the most worthy treasure and Redeemer, through which he also has received new power, joy, and peace in his mind.[13]

Stauffer obviously considered salvation an internal matter brought about by the Spirit of God and founded upon the death of Christ. However, for Stauffer, most important was to stress the external manifestation of that salvation, which provided a specific clue to the inner condition. The condition of the heart, whether pure or wicked, cannot fail to manifest itself.[14]

As noted, the external characteristics of the saved life include willingness to submit to the church and its discipline, and separation from the world.[15] A comprehensive but idealized description of that saved life appeared in Stauffer's depiction of the church of the persecuted Swiss Mennonite immigrants who began coming to North America in 1709. Although mostly poor, they survived the hardships of life in remote areas. Since their eyes and hearts were full of the love of God, God's love strengthened their courage and blessed their work so that soon they had cleared a great deal of land and prospered. They thanked God for having led them to a land where they found complete freedom of conscience.

These people "led a life pure, upright, and separated from the world, in the fear of God." They treated one another with love and took in and supported the needy. Since they wanted their children to remember and follow the wisdom of their ancestors, the martyrs, they tried diligently to provide their children "patterns and images of humility, meekness, and lowliness, so that the church of God would continue to grow, and through repentance to God and faith in Jesus, their children would be prepared for eternal life."[16] Although the Revolutionary War threatened their military exemption, they did not lose it. For that they were grateful, and their way of life continued to be separated from the world.

Their separation included discipline and punishing the works of darkness. It also included refusal to participate in worldly government, coupled with a willing payment of all fees and taxes. They believed that God had ordained the civil authorities (*Obrigkeit*) to use the sword to punish evildoers and to protect the good. Hence, they should submit to these worldly authorities in all things which were not contrary to the word and will of God. On the other hand, they did not seek honor, friendship, love, or fellowship with the world, but instead followed the example of the Lord and Master Jesus Christ in "meekness, humility, and lowliness." For them, worldly pride was an "abomination" entirely contrary to God's "holy Word, counsel, will, and command."

As Christ's sheep, they loved their enemies and blessed them, did good to those who hated them, and prayed for those who persecuted them. They refused to curse those who cursed them. They endured suffering as a mark of God's approval. They trusted God and laid their cares on the Lord. As much as possible, they remained blameless before the world. They took seriously Paul's words about not being yoked with unbelievers, and they avoided all appearances of evil. As a result of this kind of life, the Lord was with them and blessed them richly.[17]

This description by Stauffer is obviously a highly idealized version of the immigrant church, based upon scriptural texts, and depicted as the pristine church from which the majority Mennonites of his own day had degenerated. Nonetheless, it displays the external dimensions of the church and salvation that he wanted to preserve with discipline.

Stauffer also provided ample descriptions of the antithesis of the saved life and pure church. Things punishable included lust of flesh and eye, prideful lifestyles, and pride, pomp, and display of all kinds. More specifically, it included costly jewels and display items for children and houses; fancy, immodest, and fashionable dress; jewelry; lying and cheating to take money from companions; cursing and swearing; frivolous and foolish and nonsensical talk; playing musical instruments for fleshly enjoyment;[18] buying insurance for their buildings from worldly insurance companies; holding worldly offices; sitting on juries, and ruling in worldly courts and disputes; lawsuits about material goods; participation in elections and campaigning for candidates who will bear responsibility for the sword; use of the newspapers to publish warnings that land is off limits to hunting and fishing, and then backing up the prohibition with the force of civil authorities; and lightning rods on buildings.[19]

Such prohibitions are more than individual interdictions. All reflect the outlook and attitude of humility, a strong sense that the humble Mennonite did not assert political or economic power over others in ways that did not fit with nonresistance and the rejection of lawsuits. Most Mennonites in the nineteenth century adhered to the principle of humility. However, Stauffer's views put him at the conservative edge of the Mennonite spectrum on these issues.[20]

This is the context in which to consider Jacob Stauffer's understanding of atonement: the disciplined, nonresistant church, composed of humble and repentant sinners, separated from the world, and following the commands of Jesus. At the most general level, the death of Christ made possible salvation within this disciplined church. While Stauffer did not articulate that idea in these words, it is clear that if he assumed the satisfaction theory of atonement (which seems to fit; see below), he would understand that the forgiveness made available by the atoning death of Christ constituted the foundation of salvation within the disciplined church.

Further, Stauffer tied the atoning death of Jesus directly to the discipline which preserves the church. Not only is separation and discipline a command of Christ and a betrayal of Christ when not practiced,[21] but the gospel which saves immortal souls is "overthrown and lost" when discipline is not practiced as Stauffer envisioned it.[22] Stauffer explained why Romans 13 does not allow holding of public office by nonresistant Christians: "If you want to find the basis for disciplining the brothers who hold worldly office, then seek it in the gracious gospel and apostolic teaching, which Jesus sealed on the cross with his blood, and his holy apostles after him, and also many others; there you will find the basis to punish such a brother."[23]

The link Stauffer made between discipline and atonement is further clarified by examining the direct contribution which the disciplined church makes to salvation. Numerous times he described discipline—specifically, excommunication and shunning—as something practiced for the salvation of immortal souls. Social ostracism, when done out of a spirit of love and concern, will shame the sinful one and bring about repentance and a bettering of life, that is, salvation. Discipline thus works to save immortal souls. Stauffer called the discipline of excommunication and shunning "the best medicine for the poor wounded soul, through which the fallen sinner comes to repentance, remorse, and suffering for sin, and to confession of truth."[24] Thus, consideration of Stauffer's view of atonement must fit within the ecclesiology of a church that is protected by church discipline, namely, excommunication and shunning.

Eschatology contributed an additional facet of Stauffer's clear belief that the church must be disciplined. He did not engage in eschatological speculation about the time of the end or about the identity of antichrist. Like Gerhard Wiebe, however, Stauffer supposed that the corruption he found in the "nonresistant churches (*wehrlosen christlichen Gemeinde*)," that is, in the Mennonite fellowship he had abandoned, constituted the falling away which Jesus and the apostles had prophesied for the end times. Separation and shunning, Stauffer said, would protect the church against that falling away.[25] Those who did not keep the commandments of the Bible, he continued, "are betrayers of the teaching of the apostles and of Jesus," and one who is outside of the teaching of Jesus in this way "has no God."[26] Since the leaders of the church have not "kept house (*haushalten*)" by punishing evildoers through the practice of shunning, the church has fallen and become corrupt.[27]

Stauffer further underscored the point that the church should punish evil and practice discipline by providing a number of Old Testament stories in which God either desired the punishment of evil or also enacted the punishment. These narratives include the accounts of the plague following the sin of David, the defeat of Israel after the deceit of Achan, the death of Eli and his two sons, and Samuel's failure to exterminate the Amalekites. For Stauffer, these examples showed clearly that the contemporary church must punish erring members.[28] Such actions of discipline and punishment are part of the direct contribution which the church makes to the salvation of immortal souls.

As depicted by Stauffer, God is a God of judgment and punishment. Stauffer described God, for example, as the God who "became angry at the violation of his words, orders, and commands."[29] It can be observed without great elaboration that such a view of God corresponds to the image of God in the satisfaction atonement motif, in which God's act through Christ looks out for the punishment of sin and the preservation of the integrity of the law.

While Stauffer advocated nonresistance as a command of Christ, it also belonged to the theological context of Stauffer's understanding of atonement. Nonresistance was one of the beliefs most strongly emphasized by Stauffer throughout the *Chronik*. Frequently he referred to Mennonites as the "nonresistant church (*wehrlosen Gemeinden*)." For Stauffer, nonresistance clearly meant much more than the refusal of military service. It was an attitude which the humble believer brought to a wide variety of situations and problems. Beyond obedience to a Bible text or a command of Jesus, Stauffer considered nonresistance an intrinsic dimension of Jesus' redeeming work, thus giving the gospel a "nonresistant foundation (*wehrlosen Grund*)." Stauffer called the reader to notice

> how patiently the innocent Lamb of God, Jesus Christ, suffered for us, all the while having access to all of the power of the authorities and all the force of heaven and earth; he could have chastised all his enemies with a word and punished them with death. However, to show us a defenseless pattern and example, he suffered ridicule, shame, and beating, not seeking to avenge himself but praying for his enemies and loving them until death.[30]

Thus Stauffer located the foundation of nonresistance in the atoning act of Jesus Christ and thus made nonresistance inherently central to following Jesus.

While Stauffer undoubtedly assumed the satisfaction atonement motif, his theology was driven by his understanding of the nonresistant, separated, disciplined church. The church shaped the theology in which atonement appeared in a consistent way. As Theron Schlabach has said, "For persons not too locked into progressivist assumptions to appreciate it, Jacob Stauffer constructed an intelligent and coherent system of Old Order ideas."[31] Stauffer's Old Order outlook, his actual Mennonite theological identity, is not accounted for if one only notes his assumption of satisfaction atonement. Superficially observed, that would seem to align him with the evangelicals. However, recognizing humility and nonresistance as intrinsic dimensions of Jesus' atoning death distinguishes Stauffer's version of satisfaction atonement from most of his North American contemporaries.

David Beiler

The sermons in Beiler's first book, *Wahre Christenthum*, contain more traditional theology than the four sermonic reflections in *Betrachtung über den Berg Predig*. Most of what one can learn about his understanding of atonement comes from the first source.

Letter dated July 3, 1861, from David Beiler to Jacob "Schwartzentruber" (Schwarzendruber). After the greeting, the first sentence of the letter begins, "Ich David Beiler bin heute 75 Jahr alt, und kann ich erinnern mehr als 60 Jahr zurück (I, David Beiler, am 75 years old today, and I can remember more than 60 years ago)."

According to Beiler, the covering of sin and punishment accomplished by Jesus' sacrificial death established the condition which makes the new birth possible. When Beiler discussed the salvation which results from sacrificial death and new birth, he had a clear, twofold concern and emphasis: the necessity of rebirth or conversion, and the nature of the saved life which resulted from the saving work of Christ. For Beiler, the righteous life is the primary evidence that a person has indeed been saved. In his writing, every mention of atonement in the narrow sense—Jesus' substitutionary bearing of sinful humanity's deserved penalty or punishment—was a prelude to emphasis on rebirth or conversion and the saved life.

Two things occupy Beiler's remarks on the saved life. First, it happens only as a result of rebirth or conversion—an inner, subjective component. Second, it is a life of external submission and obedience to the word and teaching and example of Jesus.[32] Beiler's long meditation on the third chapter of John[33] perhaps best illustrates this relationship of the internal and the external. Yet in all of his discussions of the topic, the various dimensions of the saved life appear in interwoven and interrelated fashion.

By rebirth or new birth, Beiler understood a work of God in the heart of the individual sinner. It happens by the grace of God and through the Spirit of God. It has an experiential component which the reborn person senses while becoming oriented to Christ and living in Christ. The sinner's heart and mind are transformed with the result that the sinful inclinations of the flesh are overcome. The individual becomes a new creature in Christ and thus will follow obediently the commands of Christ. Beiler quoted abundantly from Scripture to describe the reborn person and the changes that occur as one's mind becomes conformed to the word and will of God.[34]

For Beiler, following Jesus—living a righteous life—is not possible without rebirth. He wrote concerning Nicodemus's question about the means of rebirth:

> We cannot speak with spiritual power about the new birth and its working and its fruits and teach it to others without first having experienced it, and thereby come to a true conversion and change of heart; that is, that we have buried the old man of sin and death, and are resurrected with Christ to new life; that we can truly say with Paul, "I no longer live, but Christ lives in me." We must participate in Christ through faith, and allow him to work in us.[35]

The covering of sin and punishment accomplished by Jesus' sacrificial death established the condition which makes the new birth possible. Beiler's comments on atonement occurred in that context, as here:

> Thus the new birth and rebirth is a work of God in man, through illumination from above. . . . It is good also to observe that as man is not born naturally into the world without anguish and suffering. Thus in the same way, the spiritual rebirth cannot happen without anguish of soul; . . . when we observe the difference between righteousness and godlessness. And how much God hates all sins, whether secret or open, and will punish them with eternal pain and torment. And also how he made his innocent Son suffer so much in order to redeem the sins of Adam and Eve and the whole world. . . . And when one reaches such a state of repentance, . . . then he will be reborn of water and Spirit.[36]

Beginning with the opening sermon of *Wahre Christenthum*, a recurring theme throughout the book is the sinful state of humankind and the legacy of the Fall. Throughout his chapters are frequent sorrowful references to the sinful nature of the natural person, not reborn. This sense of sin gives great urgency to Beiler's words about the necessity of rebirth. Sinful people cannot save themselves. Only an act of God through God's Spirit can transform the sinner into an obedient child of God.

Awareness of sin makes rebirth possible. At the point when one confronts the hopeless state of sinful humanity and realizes that human effort can do nothing, then one can turn to God for help. In his meditation on Matthew 18, Beiler stated,

> The first teaching is: repentance and betterment of life, abandonment of sins, and believing on the Word of God, confessing Christ as the Son of God, that he is the one through whom man was created in the beginning, and through whom he is redeemed (*erlöset*). . . . And that no other means of eternal salvation is given by which we can be saved, except for the perfect sacrifice (*vollkommenen Opfer*).[37]

New birth can occur "when one is illuminated from above . . . so that he confesses his spiritual poverty and his sinful manner and nature; and confesses that nothing good dwells in his flesh. . . . Then without doubt an earnest and righteous repentance will follow." When that state of mind is reached, then "God for Christ's sake will send all and forgive us and loose us (we would like to say) from the bands with which Satan has long bound us."[38]

For Beiler, after the necessity of new birth, the other significant aspect of salvation was the obedient life which demonstrated that new birth has occurred. Frequently he rolled new birth and the obedient life together into one package. It is the obedient one whom God can save, and it is the saved, reborn ones who are obedient. "Thus all reborn Christians must be so minded that they follow the command of Jesus Christ in all obedience."[39]

Surprisingly, the language of new birth is little present in *Betrachtung über den Berg Predig*,[40] and atonement terminology appears relatively infrequently, such as *offered, Mediator, reconciled (versöhnet), redeemed (erlösen),* and *Redeemer (Erlöser)*.[41] The Fall, or the effects of the Fall on all humankind, is clearly present, both in specific references[42] and in the heavy consciousness of human sin that permeates the book. The answer to sin focuses on the need of the sinner to recognize spiritual unworthiness or spiritual poverty (*geistlich Armuth*) and that such a natural, unredeemed, spiritually impoverished individual can accomplish nothing.[43] Such a condition can be countered only by the grace of God.

One of the major salvific themes running through these sermons is the stress on obedience to Christ's word, commands, and order (*Ordnung Christi*)[44]—an obedience made possible by grace. Accompanying that emphasis are such themes as repeated reminders that external things and external forms are meaningless without an obedient heart,[45] the need to persevere in the faith, the dangerous temptation posed by the allure of Mammon and worldly pleasures,[46] the great tribulation and corruption which abound in these last days,[47] the fact that true Christians are strangers and pilgrims in the world,[48] and the necessity of proper discipline in order to protect God's people.

Such sentiments clearly reflect Beiler's malaise about the direction in which the Amish communities as a whole were going. Such concerns for obedience also add to the context in which to situate his understanding of atonement. Whether he spoke of rebirth or of the grace of God that overcame sin, the result of Christ's atoning death for the true Christian was a life of obedience to the teaching, commands, and order of Christ.

Along with emphasizing obedience, Beiler's concept of new birth in *Wahre Christenthum* also had a cognitive content. When he said that reborn Christians obey the command of Jesus Christ, that included not only an oral confession but believing with the heart. However, that believing was not confined to actions. The reborn one must believe that "Jesus Christ is the eternal wisdom of God, in whom the fullness of deity dwells bodily, and which is the image of the invisible God."[49]

The first sermon in *Wahre Christenthum* filled out the content of that christological statement at some length.[50] Beiler followed a trinitarian outline. He noted the infallible being (*unfehlbares Wesen*) of God, and God's eternal power and deity which are visible in the creation of the world. Beiler's christological statements followed a traditional pattern of confessing the eternal deity (*ewigen Gottheit*) and the true humanity (*wahrhaftigen Menschheit*) of Jesus. About the deity of Jesus, he wrote that in some inexpressible way, Jesus was born of the Father before the foundation of the world and is one with the Father, with "the same power and lordship, one will and being from eternity."[51] The eternal Jesus worked with the Father in the creation of all things visible and invisible.

Beiler linked the humanity of Jesus to God's work of salvation (*Erlösungswerk*). When the time was right for that work, the message came to Mary about her coming pregnancy by the Holy Spirit. Beiler's Scripture texts on the humanity of Jesus included John 1, and the apostles' references to Jesus as a *Mensch* and a *Mann*.[52] He became a suffering person, who got hungry, thirsty, and tired on trips, and was like us in everything except sin. He became lower than the angels, a humiliating condition.

Beyond the traditional christological categories of humanity and deity, Beiler used language reminiscent of the celestial flesh Christology of Menno Simons. Beiler declared that while he confessed the humanity of Jesus in the flesh, his confession differed from that of the scholars (*Gelehrten*), who believe that he received his flesh and blood from Mary. In contrast, Beiler said, Jesus "was not from Adam's sinful flesh, even if the Scripture calls him the seed of the woman."[53] He called such scriptural language figurative, similar to calling Jesus a vine or a rock. Beiler then added that Jesus "came from heaven,"[54] as was written in John 1.

One other time in *Wahre Christenthum*, Beiler used similar phrases to describe Jesus, as in the sermon on John 3:

> I believe that if we are to understand the sense and basis of his [Jesus'] words [in John 3:13], we must accept that Christ Jesus is come from heaven, and his body or flesh was not from the earth as ours is. He was not of Adam's sinful nature, who was submitted to death and decay. He was, as John said, the Word become flesh.[55]

Such comments correspond to what has been called the celestial flesh of Christ. Since Beiler had quoted Menno as an opponent of pride,[56] it is a reasonable conclusion that he had read and adopted Menno's Christology.[57]

Beiler concluded the discussion of Christology with a trinitarian statement. No one can call Jesus Lord unless he has Christ's Spirit. Three from heaven give that witness: "The Father, the Word, and the Holy Spirit. And the three are one." On the basis of these witnesses and much Scripture, Beiler believed that "the Father, Son, and the Holy Spirit is one true God from eternity, even if the Scripture identifies different works for them,"[58] the Father as Creator, Son as Savior and Healer, while the Holy Spirit works in believers as happened at Pentecost.

Even though Beiler's understanding of belief had a cognitive dimension, he emphasized obedience.[59] References to the omnipotence of God, the heavenly origin of Jesus' humanity, or the deity of Jesus were primarily for the purpose of underlining the authority of the Scripture-based word or command or example which the believing individual must obey. Thus believing that Jesus was the eternal Son of God was not a dogmatic requirement as an end in itself. It was rather the reason why one must obey what Jesus taught if one would achieve salvation.

Beiler's view of obedience came to be recognized as the Old Order Amish outlook. Obviously it included nonresistance to evil. He devoted the entire fourth chapter of *Wahre Christenthum* to nonresistance, and to the necessity for the Christian to obey that command of the Redeemer. In *Betrachtung über den Berg Predig*, the teachings of nonresistance and love of enemies are counted as contrary to the inclination of natural or unsaved persons. Obeying this command is only possible through God's grace.[60]

Further, occupying a central place in the saved life was the virtue of humility, which Jesus exhibited in his incarnation, and which every believing individual should reflect. Those two mean that obedient disciples of Jesus do not use the worldly law courts to settle disputes. They do not swear oaths, and they do practice church discipline. Believing individuals will not marry outside the church. If one member of a marriage becomes converted, it is expected that the believer will leave the unbelieving spouse with the hope that the spouse might some day also repent and be saved.[61] This humility theme appears in *Betrachtung über den Berg Predig* in several ways—in the repeated reminder that we bring nothing into the world and can take nothing out of it;[62] the admonition to be satisfied with food and clothing and to avoid the jealousy and envy that come from the desire for material things;[63] and the frequent calls to acknowledge spiritual poverty.

In his "Memoirs," written in 1862, not long after he completed the *Betrachtung über den Berg Predig*, Beiler provided a rather nostalgic description of his vision of the saved life.[64] At age 75, he reminisced about the way things had been in the church 60 years earlier. The old church stressed simplicity in many areas of life. People walked to church barefooted, rather than riding in light pleasure vehicles and wearing fine shoes and boots. Clothes were made at home, with homespun cloth. They used simple implements on the farms. Basic knowledge of reading and writing satisfied educational requirements, and they did not spend months at a time in school. Houses lacked decorations; they ate from plain dishes. He added more on a simple lifestyle. Beiler's intent was not simply to list individual prohibitions. He wrote as a representative of the Old Order, for whom the many changes of modern times indicated pride and self-aggrandizement. In contrast, humility marks the life of the truly reborn person. Like Jacob Stauffer, David Beiler posed the *Ordnung* as the answer to change.[65]

Beiler's description of the inner subjective component of conversion[66] made clear how his Amish people might be vulnerable to a revivalistic conversion. However, focus on such a crisis conversion itself would change the pattern of entry into the church, and stress on the experiential component of conversion would change the means of identifying who was a Christian. Beiler held that Christians were those who obeyed Jesus nonresistantly and submitted to the teaching and discipline of the church, not those who merely described a specific kind of religious experience. Thus while Beiler's writing revealed a somewhat larger role for experiential religion than did Stauffer's, Beiler nonetheless retained a focus on the disciplined church and the saved life, parallel to the outlook of Old Order Mennonite Jacob Stauffer.

Concluding comments about David Beiler are parallel to those about Jacob Stauffer. While Beiler assumed the satisfaction theory of atonement, other impulses oriented his theological outlook. In his theological scheme, atonement as a doctrine was the necessary prerequisite to conversion and obedience. However, atonement received minimal attention in his writing. He stressed the necessity of conversion and the life of obedience to the will of God which followed conversion. At that point, his outlook resembled Old Order Mennonite Jacob Stauffer. If one makes allowances for different detail in characterizing the saved life and the saved church, the outlook of Stauffer and Beiler is compatible with that of Gerhard Wiebe, described below.[67] Beiler's theological outlook was shaped by the church of the converted, humble, nonresistant, disciplined believers, obedient to the teaching and example of Jesus. This outlook is not accounted for if one only considers Beiler's assumption of satisfaction atonement, which would seem to align him with the evangelicals. Atonement is a precondition to the saved life, but does not contribute to understanding the nature of that life.

On the other hand, Beiler's outlook displayed a noteworthy contrast to his Amish brother Heinrich Egly. While the two Amish both believed in conversion, they eventually came to different means of authenticating it. For Beiler that authentication came in the form of the humble, obedient, nonresistant life lived by the converted one and preserved by the *Ordnung.*[68] Early in his career, Egly fused the experience of conversion and the obedient life. Over the course of his ministry, Egly came to focus on the experience of conversion itself.

Gerhard Wiebe

Gerhard Wiebe was not a trained theologian. As the description of his worldview in chapter 3 showed, he considered higher education a primary threat to the church. Not surprisingly, while Wiebe's *Ursachen und Geschichte* was clearly a religious document that conveyed his great concern for the church, it does not contain a great deal of specifically theological material.

The material developed in chapter 3 described several aspects of Wiebe's worldview, and the few observations to follow in chapter 5 reveal his basic assumption of a satisfaction atonement motif. Beyond that, *Ursachen und Geschichte* says little about the theological context in which he put atonement.

Cornelius H. Wedel

Situating C. H. Wedel's understanding of atonement in the wider context of his theology displays his considerable theological acumen and knowledge of church history. He attempted both to situate atonement in relation to a number of other doctrines and also to integrate some Anabaptist-Mennonite ideas into this outlook.

Wedel followed the conventional Protestant interpretation by calling the law a schoolmaster for Christ. By showing the depth of sin and the enslavement of humankind to it, the law prepared the way for Christ by causing a yearning for "a Rescuer, a Redeemer, a Savior," a desire for the goodness which could first come only through Christ.[69]

Wedel sought to deal with atonement as a part of Jesus' life and also in the context of Christology. In the *Meditationen*, Wedel called atonement the heart of the catechism.[70] However, he followed the catechism in providing commentary on the teaching of Jesus and events in his life. Wedel intended to integrate the atoning work of Jesus into his life as a whole; hence, he called Jesus' death the last and most important of all the good things he had done.[71] Further, following the specific discussion of atonement, Wedel recognized the importance of holding atonement and resurrection together. He wrote that resurrection assured forgiveness of sins and sealed Jesus' mediatorial role, as well as defeating death and verifying his messianic mission.[72]

The ascension then allowed Jesus as high priest to enter heaven as "the substitute for humanity (*in Seiner stellvertretenden Beziehung zur Menschheit*)" and to offer his own blood for their sin, thus making their freedom from sin eternally valid.[73] Wedel certainly considered atonement integrated into the whole life of Christ. He said that it is of greatest importance that the Christian religion has its foundation in the historical appearance of Jesus on earth. Thus young Christians often begin their knowledge of salvation with the Gospels, in which are found the roots of the Christian's strength.[74]

These themes receive expanded treatment in the "Glaubenslehre." Wedel declared that preparation for salvation began in Judaism, with the call of Abraham. The history of Israel revealed the divine ways of God while God's covenant with Israel and the attendant worship ceremonies foreshadowed the coming perfect salvation.[75] As a part of this discussion, Wedel described how human thinking leads away from religious thinking and toward heathenism, which encompasses all efforts at human salvation outside of God's way. The reality of human sin and inability of people to save themselves necessitate divine assistance. For that reason, God sent his Son as a sacrifice for humankind.[76]

At this juncture, Wedel dealt with Christology. He described Jesus as the Son of God who became man, was like us in all things except sin, and died to make the sacrifice necessary to atone for sin.[77] True to the logical requirement of the sacrificial theory of atonement, Christ was both divine and human.

Alongside Christ's deity, Wedel made an effort to locate Christ in the historical realm. His discussion displayed a certain tension between a historical description of Jesus and the ahistorical satisfaction atonement motif, which is built on a legal construct. He demonstrated that Christ was a historical personage[78] and included a long section on "The Main Aspects of His Life."[79] However, when we assess his work from the recent perspective of narrative theology, it is evident that this section did not really deal with the particulars of Jesus' life. After noting the event of the virgin birth, Wedel's description of Jesus' life followed an outline that included his sinlessness, omniscience, physical weaknesses, his spiritual and mental life, and his friendships. Rather than focusing on the particularities of the life of Jesus, that is, the particular way in which Jesus was human, Wedel simply expanded the traditional description of Jesus as human and divine.

After sections on the creedal categories of suffering under Pilate,[80] the descent into hell, and resurrection,[81] he included a section on Christ as a sinless human.[82] Again, rather than appealing to the particulars of Jesus' life, Wedel opined what Jesus must have been like since he was sinless. At this point his theology displayed a certain tension as he attempted to take an ahistorical atonement which uses a legal structure and its attendant ontological Christology, and fuse that with a more historical description of Jesus' life and work.

Wedel's treatment of Jesus as Son of God included a description of christological developments through the first six centuries of Christian history.[83] In these discussions, Wedel was at home in the language of the traditional categories of the humanity and the deity of Jesus. At the same time, he freely acknowledged both the historical intrigues and the philosophical speculations which occurred in the centuries after the New Testament. He said, for example, that the teaching concerning the two natures was lodged within a philosophical frame of reference "whose biblical correctness can hardly be substantiated by Scripture." While the church put the divine-human personality of Jesus into philosophical categories which would address the heathen, "the personality of the Lord was missing (*Persönlichkeit der Herre fehlt*)" and consequently "that did not constitute a scriptural solution."[84]

Wedel listed a number of erroneous attempts to resolve the divine and human problem, including Menno Simons' belief in the celestial flesh of Christ.[85] Further sections dealt with Christ in terms of the categories of prophet, priest, and king.[86] Out of the discussion of Christ's priestly office, Wedel developed his doctrine of atonement.

The effort to hold atonement and the historical life of Jesus together is obvious in Wedel's *Neuen Testaments*. There, as would be expected, he covered the life of Jesus in much detail and identified the historical cause of Jesus' death as the unified act of all the guiding political parties. Wedel intended to conflate historical and theological causes (or world and holy history) when he wrote that "God used this triumph of human evil to work out the salvation of humanity."[87]

Wedel had a frequent and strong emphasis on the inner nature and experiential quality of true faith.[88] Experiential faith and the regenerate life of the believer constitute another component of the wider context in which one should examine Wedel's statements on atonement. This faith is developed through a confrontation with the whole Christ and personal appropriation of his death and resurrection, a confrontation which changes humankind. The encounter begins with the historical appearance of Jesus on earth, but ultimately is not based on ideas, teachings, and opinions. In the life and work of Jesus is the self-revelation of God to humanity, and the believer meets the God-man who redeemed humanity and is now raised to the right hand of God.[89]

As chapter 2 showed (above), in the governmental or general version of the satisfaction atonement theory, the atoning death does not actually change the relationship between God and sinful humankind. Instead, it creates the *potential* for a changed relationship which is not actualized until the sinful individual chooses to appropriate the effect of Jesus' atoning death. Wedel devoted considerable effort to explaining how an individual comes to actualize or possess the salvation made potentially available by the death of Christ.

In the *Meditationen*, he claimed that the salvific power released by Christ's death becomes real for an individual "only when the individual person enters into a personal relationship to Christ (*nur dadurch werden, dass der einzelne Mensch in persönliche Beziehung zu Christo trat*)," so that the person surrenders his enmity toward God and has his will changed into that of a servant of God.[90] Although the saving work of Christ must become the possession of the individual, a person cannot obtain it of one's own volition. The impulse is a divine one. "According to the clear testimony of Christ and his apostles, the personal appropriation of salvation is the work of the Holy Spirit."[91]

As Wedel discussed Jesus' kingly office in *Meditationen*, he described the kingdom of God as "a spiritual appearance (*geistige Erscheinung*)." It began with "an inner change and a renewal of the heart (*inneren Umänderung und Erneuerung des Herzens*)" of those who believed on Jesus.[92] A primary characteristic of the kingdom of God was the experiential quality of the faith which it worked on individuals. However, Wedel did not leave the kingdom of God and the religious experience associated with it to be only inner and experiential. He clearly expected the inner experience to result in a changed external behavior. True inner faith will manifest itself in the way the regenerate person lives.

In the section of the catechism which deals with the life and conduct of the believer, Wedel noted that "it is quite natural that the inner disposition will express itself externally in things both done and left undone."[93] As part of that expression, he underscored such traditional Mennonite emphases as love of enemies and nonresistance to evil, avoidance of government service, avoidance of the oath, and willingness to suffer.[94] The description of the relationship of inner faith and its outward expression from the *Meditationen* has a good deal in common with the other subjects of this study.

Analysis of "Glaubenslehre" adds a great deal to our understanding of how Wedel thought the atoning death of Christ was appropriated, and to the relationship which he saw between inner and outer faith. While his remarks leave him in the same atonement tradition as the other subjects of this study, Wedel developed a more nuanced view.

In "Glaubenslehre," Wedel described a two-part process through which the repentant sinner appropriates the death and resurrection of Christ. On one hand, appropriation of the salvation made possible by the death of Christ cannot happen through human effort. It is a divine effort, worked by the Holy Spirit. "The Spirit of God must appropriate this possession for man." On the other hand, "man has the primary responsibility." Scripture provides evidence for each side of this apparent contradiction.[95]

In some way, the two impulses must work together. The individual possesses the grace of salvation as a gift, without earning it, while it is equally true that "without the individual's own act, one cannot come to Christ. . . . If one remains far from grace, it is his own fault and his own deed for which he is made responsible by God because he has not desired to come."[96] Wedel recognized that his emphasis on divine initiative implied predestination. "Yes indeed," Scripture teaches predestination, he wrote, but not in a way that removes human responsibility.[97]

Wedel moved from his description of the two-part process by which atonement is appropriated to his description of the "plan of salvation (*Heilsordnung*)."[98] Much of the discussion dealt with issues related to personal appropriation of salvation, including conversion.

Wedel's first point concerning the specific personal appropriation of salvation was that there can be no prescribed pattern of conversion.

> Notice that in Scripture, we do not find a mechanical conversion path (*einen mechanischen Bekehrungsweg*), on the basis of which each Christian must run through a prescribed order of sharply distinguished conditions, so that later he can give the time and hour at which he mounted each step.[99]

While Christ is clearly the only way to God, at the same time "many paths lead to Christ." Frequently, Wedel claimed, one does not notice the initial inner working of the Spirit of God, and "the beginning of the kingdom of God is like a seed grain that takes root in the heart overnight and develops in all stillness, like a sweet secret." The analogy of a plant that grows in a variety of directions clearly indicates that there can be no thought of a "patterned (*schablonenhaftes*) conversion." The differing relationships in which people stand to the gospel make a stereotyped conversion impossible: the hostile Paul in comparison to the seeking John, or a heathen in contrast to someone raised in a Christian family.[100]

Although Wedel rejected the idea of a prescribed model of conversion, he did identify three stages of the process: a preparatory stage, a renewal stage, and a growth stage.[101] The preparatory or "calling (*Berufung*)" stage encompassed the general invitation to all sinners offered through the gospel; this included all the ways, often imperceptible, that the Spirit of God works in the heart.[102] Earlier, he had emphasized that while God sometimes draws near to people in special ways, as God did with Paul, God's Spirit works with people primarily through things already present in the world. These means include our natural organs of communication through which our understandings, feelings, and imagination are stimulated, through hearing the gospel at school or when one reads about it.[103]

Wedel's second stage, awakening, corresponded to conversion, as that was understood by John M. Brenneman or Heinrich Egly. For Wedel, awakening occurred when the individual "comes to oneself and becomes repentant." Wedel used the term "awaken" specifically, making the prior state analogous to sleep, when one was unaware of the surroundings. When the "sleeping" sinners "awaken," they come to a realization of their sin and estrangement from God. For those deep in sin, this awakening is usually quite spirited, but it "also can be done in an artificial or even feigned way, as has been observed in the so-called revival meetings of the Methodists."[104] The idea of an awakening does have a biblical basis. It is by definition "transitory (*vorübergehend*)," and although not the fullness of conversion, it does mark the turning point, when a person has chosen to follow the path of grace rather than to sink again into spiritual sleep and ultimately spiritual death.[105]

In the third stage, growth, one goes on to true knowledge of one's sinful self and the saving God. These three stages contribute to each other, as feelings of sorrow contribute to repentance, while faith contributes to strengthening the will.[106]

Parallel to his critique of an excessive emotionalism at awakening or conversion, Wedel also placed limits on the emotional or sensory component of repentance. True repentance (*Busse*) belongs to the process of inner change, as the Holy Spirit leads the sinner from the old life to a new life in God. Included in repentance are feelings of the burden of sin, sorrow for sins, and a profound sense that the sins are indeed one's own. Under the impetus of these feelings, the sinner asks forgiveness on the basis of the merit of Christ, and resolves to begin a new life.[107]

However, Wedel pointed out that the New Testament term translated *Busse* actually means "to change one's mind." Thus *Busse* has taken on distorted meanings as a result of Catholic use of the term. And pietist circles, for example, speak of "soul struggle (*Busskampf*)," which has come to mean "a very profound doubt bordering on anguish," which culminates in a sudden breakthrough. Wedel warned against such applications. While there may be some truth to such a struggle of the soul, he wrote, most of it is a struggle to repent for those who do not want to leave their sins and humble themselves before others. Meanwhile, many converted people do not experience such profound feelings of struggle.

"Soul struggle" is not a biblical word, Wedel pointed out, and one should guard against "a mechanical dwelling on this practice." Many Christians worry that their anguish is not deep enough. In response, Wedel said,

> One must rely on grace, and not attempt to build certainty of salvation on an inner feeling of sorrowful repentance (*Bussangst*). Our certainty of salvation does not rest on our feelings of repentance, . . . but on simple, childlike faith in the merit of Christ.[108]

In the following section, Wedel stressed that faith was worked in people by the Holy Spirit, and that the basis of salvation was what Christ did "for us," and "not on our works, nor our feeling of repentance, nor our churchliness."[109]

In a section on "conversion and rebirth (*Bekehrung und Wiedergeburt*)," Wedel returned in another way to the relationship between human and divine effort in the plan of salvation. According to Wedel, when the Bible speaks of "conversion," it deals with "man's will," and envisions an individual's own decision to turn to God. In contrast, "rebirth" is a work of God and refers to the action of the Holy Spirit, through which an individual's "inner being is changed to its very roots."

Conversion and rebirth reach their culmination in justification. Once again, he reminded readers that for most people, this process of rebirth comes to fruition "in a subdued and quiet way."[110]

Wedel also stated positions on two other issues raised by the revival movement. He rejected the idea of an instantaneous conversion. While conversion can be a specific, life-changing event, it is clearly only the beginning of a lifelong process. He stressed the fact that life in a state of grace was a life of progress and growth. "The Christian can never ever rest on his conversion, thinking that with it his life's struggle has reached its end."[111]

In a parallel way, Wedel emphasized that holiness was a double-sided activity, of turning from sin to God, and of dying to self in rebirth and resurrection as a new person.[112] He made this process analogous to learning to play a musical instrument,[113] or to the way an initial foothold in an alien land is gradually expanded by an invader until the whole country is conquered.[114] "The formation of a perfect, holy character is a lifelong task, on which the Christian must work with great earnestness."[115] More important than an oral confession is a lived faith, a faith active in love.[116] Thus he rejected explicitly the idea of a uniform kind

Alexanderwohl, the meetinghouse of C. H. Wedel's home congregation north of Newton, Kansas, as it appeared ca. 1895.

of conversion. This process of growth in grace leads toward perfection, a state which is never attained, but toward which the Christian grows throughout life.[117] In these views, Wedel is in line generally with the critique of revivalism offered by an Old Order Mennonite like Jacob Stauffer as well as the more moderate critique from John M. Brenneman or Johannes Moser.

The limits which Wedel put on revivalistic and experiential forms did not develop in a vacuum. They had both family and ecclesiological dimensions. About 1880, a schism developed in Wedel's congregation of Alexanderwohl, founded in 1874 just north of Newton, Kansas, by the immigrant community from Alexanderwohl in the Ukraine, South Russia. Wedel's father, Cornelius P. Wedel, led the breakaway group to found a Mennonite Brethren congregation nearby. Most of the Wedel family joined the father in the breakaway, while C. H. stayed with the original congregation.

The Mennonite Brethren, whose roots reached back to 1860 in the Russian empire, emphasized "spiritual renewal through heartfelt conversion"[118] as well as baptism by immersion (another item which Wedel rejected as a required form).[119] Hence, one dimension of C. H. Wedel's limitation on conversion was without doubt to counter the Mennonite Brethren impact on his own family and congregation as well as on the larger Russian Mennonite tradition with which he identified.

Analysis of Wedel's concept of the church will complete the wider theological context within which to consider his understanding of atonement. As primary point, he called the church the "locus of salvation (*Heilsanstalt*)." Since the ascension of Jesus, Wedel explained, "the Christian church is the means through which the Holy Spirit mediates the blessings of the kingdom of God to humankind."[120] The church is a fellowship of those who believe in Christ, whose faith is nourished by preaching and sacraments. While it has its foundation in the Old Testament, it is also a new manifestation of the kingdom of God, which is broader than the church. God's kingdom began before time and includes the realm of angels.

However, from Pentecost throughout history until the return of Christ, it is in the church that the kingdom of God is present on earth and among humanity. Since it is normal that people of like interests congregate, faith in Christ should obviously compel Christians to unite on the basis of their common faith in Christ. Thus the confession of Christ as the Son of God is the cornerstone of the church, and Christ is its head. The "Holy Spirit cares for those who exercise his office of teaching and discipline."

The foundation of the church on faith in Christ, and the care of it by the Holy Spirit demonstrate clearly that the church is more than an accidental assembly. "The church is thus not merely an association of friends (*nicht ein beliebiger Verein*)," but a divine creation, an institution which joins together those who believe in the power of the divine Christ, which has its particular marks of recognition in calling on Christ and in baptism and the Lord's Supper."[121] In Wedel's thought, the church is both the conveyor of and the culmination of salvation. It mediates the salvation of Christ to humankind, and it unites within itself those who experience that salvation. Wedel's atonement theology thus finds its most complete expression in the doctrine of the church.[122]

While Wedel presented essentially a theology of atonement in line with conservative orthodoxy, he was not polemical about it. Further, as the discussion in chapter 3 demonstrated, he was also open to integrate elements of other theological perspectives into his essentially conservative framework. James Juhnke was certainly correct when he wrote that "it was not [Wedel's] style, either in his personality or his theology, to be rigid and polemical. He was secure in his own beliefs and open to new learnings."[123]

With allowance for the much more educated form of Wedel's theology, his understanding of atonement and conversion had a number of similarities to other individuals of this study. All of these subjects shared a foundation on the satisfaction or substitutionary atonement. They all assumed that focus on atonement alone was an incomplete understanding of salvation, and that individuals who properly seized upon the atoning work of Christ went on to manifest it in the way they lived. His integration of satisfaction atonement and personal salvation into a communal understanding of the church has much in common with other figures of this study. His specific objections to revivalist forms certainly found a clear echo in the analysis of Johannes Moser and even Jacob Stauffer in the previous chapter. The other subjects would differ somewhat with Wedel on the particular external forms and practices of the church. Nevertheless, Wedel's stress on the church as a divine creation within which saved individuals find their home would certainly meet approval of the other subjects.

At the same time, Wedel did not integrate ethical concerns, and nonresistance in particular, into the doctrine of atonement as much as did any of the other subjects. At that point, he is closer to Protestant theology than the other subjects. Wedel's theology opens the door to treating ethics and theology as separate categories. In the beginning of the "Ethik," he said that while ethics and dogma are "closely related," they have distinct functions.

In dogma (*Glaubenslehre*) we deal primarily with what God has done for man, in ethics with that which we become or should become. In the former it is God's personal revelation, in ethics it is what we through grace can and should become for him. . . . If dogma deals with the great love that God has for us, "This have I done for you," ethics turns to the question, "What are you doing for me?"[124]

Wedel emphasized that Christians must go beyond the beginning event of conversion to engage in a lifelong process of growth. Yet he did not appeal in "Glaubenslehre," for example, to the nonresistance of God or of Jesus in the act of atonement as foundation for that growth process. He did not use pacifism, nonresistance, and love of enemies as evidence of genuine conversion and the true church to the extent of the other individuals of this study.[125] The "Ethik" clearly identified the teaching and example of Jesus as the culmination of ethical teaching. Nevertheless, when Wedel discussed peace-related issues such as self-defense, pacifism, capital punishment, and government service, he based his views more on biblical authority and assumptions about the natural order than on theology which grew out of atonement.[126] This distinction ought not be pushed too far, however. In *Meditationen* he did note ethical components of the saved life,[127] and he stated clearly the principle that genuine conversion will manifest itself in a saved life.

The fact that Wedel did not spell out ethics in this discussion of conversion and the Christian life demonstrates perhaps as much about the satisfaction theory of atonement as it does about Wedel's ethics. As was argued in chapter 2, this theory of atonement clearly opens the door to the possibility of separating ethics from salvation. While Wedel's theology of atonement was vulnerable to that problem, he certainly had no intention of developing a theology which weakened the traditional Mennonite ethical stance. The larger framework in which Wedel situated his thinking succeeds in holding the two together when his theology is viewed as a whole.

In "Glaubenslehre," it is the concept of the church, a divine creation encompassing individuals saved by grace, that keeps Wedel's atonement from devolving into individual salvation, completely apart from visible manifestations and outside of the visible church. However, as shown earlier, the concept of *Gemeindechristentum* was the most distinct and also the most significant aspect of Wedel's outlook, and the element which gave his outlook its most distinct Mennonite orientation. The most distinctive component of Wedel's thought was not his use of traditional theological categories of Christology and atonement but his situation of the Mennonite ecclesiological tradition in the world via *Gemeindechristentum*.

Johannes Moser

Moser did not discuss atonement merely to lay out a doctrine of the work of Christ. Instead, his effort reflected his larger intent for the article "Über die Wehrlosigkeit,"[128] and the more general orientation of his theology. The discussion of atonement occurred primarily within Moser's understanding of nonresistance, and to a lesser extent, as a function of his ecclesiology. For Moser, the substitutionary death of Jesus exemplified the nonresistance which stands at the heart of what it means to be a disciple of Jesus. He intended his remarks on atonement as a statement of the foundation on which nonresistance stands.

Moser anchored nonresistance in the affirmation that "Christ is the head of his church (*Christus is das Haupt seiner Gemeinde*)." The head taught nonresistance to his disciples and exemplified it in his person. Thus Moser believed that one who read the Scripture carefully would certainly see that "the entire context (in promise and fulfillment) teaches nonresistance."[129]

The retributive aspect of Old Testament law constituted one means God used to show sinful people their need for a Redeemer. Thus the law required retribution for sin, and the wars and tribulations which God sent against wicked people constituted his legally required response to sin. When the Israelites who attempted faithfulness experienced that punishment, Moser believed, their desire must have been acute for a Redeemer who would stop the cycle of retribution by suffering in their place and fulfilling the law. The stern law thus created a strong desire for a Redeemer (*Erlöser*) who would bring complete forgiveness and a peaceful kingdom.[130] In other words, for Moser, violence and retribution belonged intrinsically to the law and to the Old Testament.

In contrast, by submitting to the law and fulfilling its requirement for retribution, Jesus halted the cycle of violence and retribution. He inaugurated a new covenant with a different orientation. Grace replaced law, peace could reign in the hearts of people, and they would be free from the wrath of God and the curse of the law.[131] The atoning work of Jesus established a new way to live. That way originates in the Spirit of Christ and is modeled on Christ's atoning work. Moser's gospel, as defined within a sacrificial view of atonement, was thus inherently nonresistant, inherently a gospel of peace.

Heidi Sommer

Monument on site of first meeting-house (constructed in 1840) of the Swiss Mennonite congregation between Bluffton and Pandora, Ohio.

Heidi Sommer

Close-up photo of plaque which commemorates the first Mennonite meetinghouse of the Swiss congregation between Pandora and Bluffton, Ohio. Bronze plaque made in 1959 by Bluffton artist John P. Klassen.

Moser's major point—his primary reason for discussing atonement —was that the atoning act of Jesus happened *nonresistantly*. The one proclaimed by the prophets, who would bear our sins in our place, performed that act "without murmuring and without retaliation (*ohne Murren und ohne Wiedervergeltung*)." Atonement was inherently nonresistant. Further, any persons who would be followers of Jesus must be motivated and regenerated by his Spirit, the same spirit of nonresistance. Thus Moser concluded, "In this sense the entire context of Scripture teaches nonresistance."[132]

The foundation of nonresistance in atonement theology is less evident in Moser's other major statement on nonresistance, a series of three letters written to his brother Abraham[133] about twelve years prior to "Über die Wehrlosigkeit." Abraham had posed to Johannes a version of the oft-cited dilemma about use of violence in defense of a helpless loved one, in this case their aged parents. The question was stated so as to assume the rectitude of resorting to violence.[134] Johannes's answer in the three letters stated a variety of arguments. He argued that precipitous use of violence precluded God's providential intervention. He challenged the assumption of the question, namely, that violence would succeed quickly. In actuality, Johannes said, one cannot foresee the chain of events unleashed by the resort to violence.

Beyond this sort of logical and rational argumentation, Johannes used a great deal of biblical material, with frequent appeals to the example, teaching, and authority of Christ. While he based nonresistance firmly in the revelation of Jesus, in these letters Moser made appeals directly to Christ's authority, but without spelling out the foundation in atonement theology as he did later in the essay "Über die Wehrlosigkeit." Without the explicit foundation of atonement, however, he still referred to Jesus in these three letters as *Erlöser* (Redeemer) and *Mittler* (Mediator) and used other language reminiscent of the satisfaction theory of atonement.

Moser's two major statements on nonresistance were separated by about twelve years. One can conjecture that some development of his thought occurred during that time. The more explicit spelling out of atonement in the later piece may constitute an effort to give additional depth and conviction to the doctrine of nonresistance which Moser considered absolutely essential. In any case, nonresistance as intrinsic to the gospel and the saved life is evident in Moser's articles to the end of his writing life.[135]

One could perhaps point out some inconsistency in God's activity as Moser understood it. In the Old Testament, Moser accepted the law

The opening lines of Johannes Moser's third letter on nonresistance,
"Vertheidigung der Wehrlosigkeit," written for his brother Abraham,
and published in Herold der Wahrheit, *August 1867. Photo shows title,*
Moser's name written as "Joh. Moser," and the address to Abraham as
"Lieber Bruder (dear brother) Abraham J. Moser!"

as the unquestioned beginning point. He saw God's activity change in relation to it, with God sometimes calling, sometimes punishing, acting in both loving and retributive ways. Moser's view certainly warrants the traditional charges leveled against the penal theory by advocates of the moral influence theory of atonement: that it envisions God as harsh judge rather than as loving father, and that it pictures a change in God's attitude toward sinful human beings.

When Moser interpreted Christ's death as meeting the requirements for halting the cycle of retribution, it was the legal construct of atonement rather than a continuous work of God that remained intact. From this side of the Christ event, however, Moser made Christ's non-resistance the unquestioned norm, to which everything else must conform. Moser put the law in the position of preparing the way for nonresistance, and he interpreted the traditional sacrificial view of atonement so that it taught nonresistance as an inherent dimension of the gospel of the forgiveness of sins. He discussed atonement not only as a doctrine but as the foundation of the nonresistant life that he considered a sine qua non for all who claimed to be disciples of Christ. The

John Moser

House on family farm of Johannes Moser north of Bluffton, Ohio. In his retirement years, he occupied the small room on the right. The house has been remodeled and relocated on the farm since this photo was made. Moser's great-great-grandson David Moser and his wife, Jenny, now live in the house and work the farm. David and Jenny's daughters, Bess and Sara, are the sixth generation of Mosers to live in the house.

Barn built on the family farm of Johannes Moser.

Heidi Sommer

(*Above*) *One of several hewn 60-foot supporting girder beams that still hold up the floor of the barn built by Johannes Moser. This beam may symbolize Johannes Moser—although virtually unknown in modern times, he remains an important, foundational contributor to the ongoing Mennonite tradition.*

(*Right*) *View of hewn timbers inside Johannes Moser's barn, showing post and portion of 60-foot, supporting girder beam. Note axe marks.*

Heidi Sommer

final sections of "Über die Wehrlosigkeit" as well as the second part of the three letters emphasized repeatedly that nonresistance was central for the saved life.

Moser emphasized both internal and external components of atonement and salvation. On one hand, inner transformation is essential, and without it no salvation exists. The sacrificial death of Christ is the foundation for this inner transformation. The heart, the primary source of human evil, must change if evil is to be overcome. On the other hand, the inner life will necessarily manifest itself in external behavior. However, the externals do not guarantee salvation, since one can conform outwardly without a corresponding inner change. Those who make a great deal of their conversion experience can still dress in a glitzy, modish manner that hardly reveals a genuine inner change. However, genuine change within cannot fail to produce an external manifestation, while evil works clearly show that no inward transformation has occurred.[136]

The link between atonement and inner cleansing that manifested itself in external action tied directly into Moser's ecclesiology. Stated quite succinctly, in his understanding the most complete experience of salvation occurred within the church. In an article on the church, Moser linked atonement to the formation of the church. The spiritual house is built of living stones; individuals become living stones before God can form them into the church. "That house is costly: the founder purchased the right for us with his blood."[137] Preparation for the spiritual house happens in the heart, worked by the Word of God. While that inner process is invisible, and not understood completely even by those who experience it, they know they are reborn for the spiritual house.

However, that experience of salvation, rebirth, is incomplete outside the church. "These [reborn] people have a desire to be taken into the spiritual house because they know that the inner must also have an external expression, and that one house guest serves to admonish and strengthen another."[138] This communal expression and experience of salvation is one of the motivations for missions. "Since it is God's will that all people should experience spiritual blessing, all members of the household [church] should work diligently to bring those coming after us and all those outside into the house (for God's promises are given to the church and not outside of it)."[139] Similar comments opened another article on the "Haus Gottes":

God is the founder of his community (church), and his promises are given to it. Of course, under certain circumstances separate, isolated individuals, who have entered God's fellowship through genuine repentance and faith in Jesus Christ, can stand in the promise (Luke 23:42). However, if the opportunity presents itself, Christ's teaching and example obligates them to join a visible, external Christian community.[140]

Clearly for Moser, the inner experience of salvation, which begins with substitutionary atonement, receives its most complete fulfillment within the visible church. While a free-standing Christian is possible, that person's situation is an exceptional state that should be improved at the earliest possible moment. At the same time, atonement itself does not build the church. Instead, the church is formed of saved individuals, whose reborn state depends on the substitutionary death of Jesus. Such indirect linking of atonement to the building of the church was stated another way by Moser: after completing "all that was necessary for the salvation of poor, fallen men," Jesus returned to the Father from whom he had come. His followers who remain on earth then work for the kingdom of God.[141]

The analysis in this section demonstrates that while Moser assumed a satisfaction and penal substitutionary motif, it was located within and shaped by two central, inherited Mennonite principles, nonresistance and a community-based concept of the church. These latter two themes much more than the satisfaction atonement motif indicate the real orientation of his thought.

John M. Brenneman

When John M. Brenneman's satisfaction atonement motif is examined in the context of his wider theology, it becomes apparent that atonement is one of three intrinsically related elements in his soteriology. First, atonement itself, the satisfying, propitiatory death of Christ, established the condition which makes forgiveness available to the sinner. Second comes repentance. Repentance, sorrow and remorse for one's sin and for having offended God, is the condition of mind that enables the sinner to take advantage of the forgiveness made possible by atonement. Finally, there comes conversion, which Brenneman described in several different ways.

In conversion, God acts to change an individual who has repented and taken advantage of forgiveness. This conversion or new, changed life will manifest itself in the outward and external dimensions of the way the Christian lives. Together these three elements, atonement, repentance, and conversion, describe the how and why of salvation. They constitute an inseparable triad in Brenneman's theology. To isolate any of the three from the others distorts his view. In his mind, to isolate any of the three would distort the way of salvation and threaten a soul with eternal damnation. The following considers several dimensions of the two elements of repentance and conversion, and their relationship to atonement.

One of Brenneman's earliest articles for *Herald of Truth* and *Herold der Wahrheit* carried the title "Repentance." Brenneman took his text from the conclusion of Paul's sermon to the Athenians, in which Paul said that while God had previously winked at ignorance, God "now commandeth all men everywhere to repent" (Acts 17:30). Brenneman stressed repentance as a command from God binding on all people of all times and places, "which none may neglect with impunity."[142] Repentance was the necessary attitude which preceded forgiveness of sins. He described repentance as "a true and heartfelt sorrow for past sins, as committed against God; and at the same time, in deep humility, confessing the same before him, and earnestly praying to him for forgiveness."[143]

Further, repentance "is not a mere outward confession of our sins, but a deep, heartfelt, and painful sorrow and mourning on account of them. A truly penitent sinner abhors and loathes himself."[144] Repentance was the first doctrine taught by Jesus.[145] Peter taught repentance at Pentecost; Paul considered repentance and faith the two fundamental articles that he stressed.[146] God gives the command to repent in at least five different ways: by God's Spirit, which operates upon the minds of all people; by God's word, sent from heaven; by ministers, who are called to be messengers of peace to sinners; by the "chastening rod of affliction;" and finally, by the "awful judgments" God has sent over the earth, such as "sword, famine, pestilence, earthquakes," when the milder callings and chastisements failed to produce results.[147]

Only when sinners repent does the atoning death of Christ become efficacious for them and their sins can be forgiven.

> Repentance . . . seems to be the first command to man after his fall; because by sin he separated himself from God. Therefore it is necessary that men repent in order that they may have their sins blotted out, and be again restored and united to God through Jesus the great Mediator and Savior of sinners. If they will repent, then he will be their Redeemer and Savior. But if they will refuse to repent and be saved by him, he will finally be their awful judge.[148]

Brenneman's articles contain numerous similar comments which link repentance and access to the atoning blood of Christ.

Brenneman understood repentance as the basic, correct response to sin, he understood the call to repentance as a command issued by God. Hence, it hardly comes as a surprise that Brenneman tied repentance to a great many issues. For example, a task like writing for *Herald of Truth* provided an opportunity to fulfill one's duty to call sinners to repentance.[149] Repentance was the basis of learning to control one's tongue.[150] Brenneman provided a list of Jesus' miracles, organized under twenty headings, in order to certify Jesus as the Son of God in whose name repentance and forgiveness of sins was preached; the article then concluded with a call for the impenitent to repent.[151] In another article, the command to "repent and believe the gospel" headed a list of some hundred commands from Jesus and the apostles.[152] One of his last major articles, "A Noble Determination After a Conflict," carried a list of commands and requirements which sinners must follow to escape everlasting destruction. The command to "repent and turn to God" leads the list.[153]

For Brenneman, repentance belonged integrally to conversion and the new life following repentance. Experiencing conversion and a changed life constituted one of the primary proofs that the sinner has truly repented and is not making a merely formal confession of sin. In numerous articles, he made explicit the connection between repentance and conversion.

Repentance was the focus of the article "An Encouragement to Penitent Sinners and Joy over Their Conversion." In the preface to its reprinted edition, he stated that the purpose of the booklet was to show sinners how to be converted, the process on which their eternal destiny depended, and to show that the conversion process began with repentance. "As we are so plainly taught in the Holy Bible, that the sinner must repent and be truly converted to God, in order to become happy in eternity, the Author earnestly begs the reader that he would attentively and seriously examine the following discourse."[154] The tract provided abundant citations of biblical materials—on the need for repentance and the remorse which leads to it; on God's love in sending his Son to die for sinners; on the many things Jesus did among the people, for sinners; and on the repentance and turning which constitute the proper response to Jesus.

While repentance and conversion are distinct dimensions of the process of salvation, Brenneman's theology linked them inseparably:

Photo of license issued by the state of Ohio, authorizing John M. Brenneman as a "regularly ordained MINISTER OF THE GOSPEL of the Denomination commonly called Mennonite" to perform marriages in the state of Ohio.

The word *repentance* in our text [Luke 15:7], signifies more than merely acknowledging our sins with our mouths before men; it means a deep, heartfelt sorrow for sin, which will cause the sinner to "go mourning all the day long," for where true repentance exists, the sinner will most painfully feel the burden of his sins, will feel deeply stricken and bowed down because of them, and is brought into such a penitent and mourning condition, as will cause him now to forsake and sincerely hate sin, and earnestly to pray for forgiveness of the same; and by the influence and power of God's Spirit and true faith in Jesus, he now turns, or becomes converted, from darkness to light, and from the power of Satan unto God, and through his Holy Spirit becomes changed and renewed; yea, is born again, and thus is translated into a spiritual, godly and heavenly state and life, that he from henceforth will walk in newness of life.

For a true, evangelical, heartfelt repentance, which alone is pleasing to God, and a true conversion, belong together, and are so closely connected, that it is impossible to separate them, because where true repentance exists, or has taken place, there is also a true conversion to God.[155]

The tract continued with biblical examples and citations on the important and inseparable link between repentance and conversion. "Thus turning and repenting were connected. And although, we do not always find these sentences together, the one is nevertheless generally included in the other."[156]

The two entities of repentance and conversion form an inseparable triad with atonement. Repentance is the act whereby the sinner comes to acknowledge one's total helplessness and comes to express complete dependence on God for salvation. Atonement has already established the basis for forgiveness of sin. With that condition met and the sinner now confessing helplessness and remorse, God then has the freedom to convert and change and regenerate the sinner, who is reborn as a child of God. In faith the sinner believes God and trusts God for salvation, and believes that God's pronouncement of forgiveness and conversion is true. Various versions of that process appear throughout Brenneman's articles.

Brenneman applied this process of salvation to the Old Testament as well as the New. Prior to the coming of Christ, people were justified in anticipation of Jesus' coming redemption. Brenneman posed and answered for himself the question of how justification happened before the atoning death of Christ: "I would answer that it was through faith in the promised Redeemer who was to make the atonement; like Abraham, who 'believed God, and it was counted unto him for righteous.' "[157]

In Brenneman's theology, conversion was clearly a sensory experi-. ence. The sensory dimension, however, is not the primary validation of a genuine conversion. While conversion is clearly heartfelt, it is the visible life of the believer that provides the primary testimony to its authenticity. He noted several kinds of testimony to the presence of heartfelt repentance and conversion by the Holy Spirit. The presence of spiritual love indicates genuine conversion: love toward God, toward Jesus Christ, toward all children of God, and even for one's worst enemies.[158] A change in outlook from pride to humility is an important indication of conversion.[159] Modest dress testifies to conversion and rebirth.[160] Conversion and new life are manifested by obedience to the entire edifice of external behaviors which Brenneman believed the Scripture requires of believers.[161]

Brenneman's great stress on obedience to God's or Christ's commands would seem to open him to the charge of legalism. That charge appears appropriate when he notes that the commands call for acts that sinners must do *if* they would be saved or if they are to demonstrate true repentance. Yet Brenneman himself insisted that human beings cannot save themselves, and he explicitly rejected a salvation based on works.[162] One's emphasis must be on required obedience to commands from Christ or Scripture in the context of the triad of atonement, repentance, and conversion. Only thus can Brenneman perhaps begin to dodge the problem of legalism and salvation by works.

When one recalls how Brenneman put together atonement and conversion, the strong command to obey as the basis of salvation is not contradicted. He understood atonement—Jesus dying in order to satisfy the law and pay the penalty—as something that happened while all people were sinners. It happened entirely apart from anyone's acceptance of it. Thus this substitutionary, atoning death was an act of grace, wholly unmerited by sinners. However, to take advantage of this offer to escape punishment, one must repent (the first command) and be born again. That rebirth subsequently demonstrates itself through willing obedience to Jesus' commands.

Clearly, for Brenneman, atonement and conversion or rebirth must belong together theologically. Atonement without rebirth is a salvation apart from and separated from a holy life. A claim to conversion or rebirth without atonement would clearly be salvation that disregarded God's justice and the requirement of the law. In Brenneman's theology, as long as atonement and conversion remain linked, he could maintain that salvation is by grace and apart from merit.

The components and process of salvation—atonement, repentance, conversion—are a constant and continual theme throughout the articles Brenneman wrote for *Herald of Truth* and *Herold der Wahrheit*. He related virtually every other idea or interest to that triad, as themes which either helped or hindered the proclamation of the salvation that God offered to lost sinners. In his articles, a frequent admonition or question concerned the state of the reader's soul and one's preparation for death and meeting God. Several times he used instances of sudden, unexpected death as the basis for a plea to be ready to die.[163]

For practical purposes, concern with salvation in its broadest theological context constituted Brenneman's worldview. It was the stance from which he looked at the world and divided it into two parts, the righteous and the wicked.

John Holdeman

John Holdeman was much more explicit about his understanding of atonement than were the other figures of this study, except for C. H. Wedel. Yet Holdeman shared with the others the general pattern of making atonement a facet of the broader concerns about repentance, conversion, and a lived faith. But even with his much more explicit attention to atonement, Holdeman's principal concern was still the obedient life following conversion rather than the articulation of a doctrine of atonement for doctrine's sake. At the same time, there was some evolution of thought from the early *Old Ground* to his later *A Mirror of Truth*, a change which tended to distinguish Holdeman from his Mennonite and Amish counterparts. This section will explore both these points.

Holdeman began *Old Ground* with a discussion of the complex of ideas related to repentance, regeneration, and the Christian life. The outline starts off with "Of True Repentance."[164] Similar to the thought of the other individuals we have observed, Holdeman maintained that conversion began with repentance, a heartfelt sorrow that one has offended God and transgressed God's commandments. The proper response to sin is repentance, and Holdeman quoted a number of biblical references about the need for sinners to repent. In response, God gives "a new heart and a new spirit" and the sinner is converted.

While Holdeman described a highly experiential conversion, his experiential version was not externally exuberant. He believed, as did the other individuals of this study, that genuineness of conversion was validated not by the experience itself but by the way one lived following conversion. Thus he explained in *Old Ground* that conversion is not a shouting of joy, or a great pretension, but a change of heart. To abstain from evil and to do good, to take the commandments of God upon oneself and walk therein: this is the conversion that is based on Scriptures. The right sign of true repentance is to experience and feel one's sins, being troubled therewith day and night, praying to God for forgiveness and leaving off sinning and commencing to do good. . . . If we have no such fruits of repentance, we are yet in the old way. . . . Repentance and conversion is not the moving of the outward body in jumping and shouting, but a moving of the power of the soul, which moves to the laying off of the sins in the flesh, and to the putting on of Christ.[165]

In his discussion about repentance, conversion, and the subsequent saved life, Holdeman assumed atonement. For example, he noted that "Christ, the Messiah has come, to redeem us from our sins, through his blood, and open to us the way to heaven. Therefore approach him with a full assurance of faith."[166] However, he did not here or elsewhere in this book lay out a full statement of atonement. The first full treatment of atonement came later, in *History of the Church*. Following these first sections in *Old Ground* on repentance, conversion, and faith, Holdeman dealt with a range of issues describing the saved life.

Sections on the saved life treated baptism as a command of Christ, which testifies to faith and makes one a member of the church of God; and the Lord's Supper and foot washing, which testify to the unity of the church and are practiced in response to a command of Christ. The rest of the book picked up issues such as the calling and sending of ministers, regeneration, refusal of oaths, plain dress, rejection of insurance and lightning rods, strict separation of church and state, marriage within the church, refusal of interest, church discipline, and so on.

With allowance for Holdeman's particular slant on the issues, the outline of concerns in *Old Ground* resembles that of the other traditionalist nineteenth-century Amish and Mennonites who began with repentance and conversion as the basis of a changed, reborn life.[167] The absence of a fully articulated doctrine of atonement is noteworthy. While he obviously assumed atonement,[168] its articulation is nowhere nearly as complete as in the sections of the later *History* and *Mirror*. In his first long work, it is significant to observe, Holdeman stressed the character of the life of the saved person.

In the *History*, where he did provide an extended discussion of atonement, Holdeman treated the penal and substitutionary atonement as God's answer to the Fall, and atonement was therefore a part of salvation history. Like John M. Brenneman, Holdeman believed that in

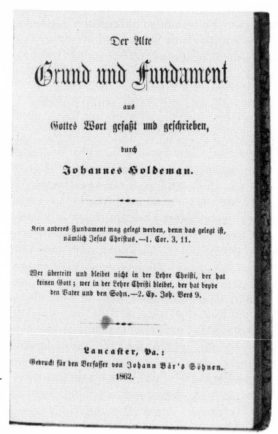

Heidi Sommer

Title page of John Holdeman's Der Alte Grund und Fundament.

the Old Testament, sinners were saved on the basis of belief in God's promise of atonement in Christ. History then became, for Holdeman, the preparation for Christ's sacrificial death. After sufficient time under the law to demonstrate his unrelenting opposition to sin, God sent Jesus to die as a sacrifice. Thus even though Holdeman went beyond his Mennonite brothers in being quite explicit about penal atonement, his outline in the *History* still reflected the received Mennonite and Amish focus on salvation history. He in no way hesitated to describe God as a God of punishment who demands blood as the price of reconciliation.

However, in *Mirror*, Holdeman's third major work of doctrine, the outline itself underwent something of a change. Rather than beginning with salvation history, the book started out on a note much more in harmony with historic Protestantism.[169] His long opening chapter carried a much more Protestant-sounding title: "On Belief in the Triune God—of Father, Son and Holy Spirit—and what they teach us."[170] It began with a discussion of attributes of God: unchangeableness and omnipotence,[171] goodness and wisdom.

Holdeman used some christological language reminiscent of the Nicene formula, writing that before Jesus was born in the flesh, he was "a light of the real light, God of the true God."[172] Further, Holdeman's discussion of Christology reflected other dimensions of the classical debates not always found in historic Anabaptist and Mennonite writings, concerns such as preexistence.[173] He established that the attributes of God also apply to the Son and the Holy Spirit.[174]

Holdeman's trinitarian discussion also has a soteriological dimension. When he showed that the divine attributes of God also applied to Jesus—preexistence, compassion, righteousness, omnipotence, goodness, wisdom, and so on—in every instance Holdeman argued that the sacrificial death of Jesus was the foundation on which the divine attribute was based.[175]

In sum, by the time Holdeman wrote the initial chapter of *Mirror of Truth*, he had adopted a bit of the vocabulary and outlook of traditional Protestantism.[176] The concerns in this chapter also have parallels with Menno Simons' tract, "Confession of the Triune God."[177] Holdeman admired Menno greatly, and the issues Holdeman chose to mention may also reflect Menno's discussion of the triune God. Nonetheless, opening *Mirror of Truth* with this chapter constitutes a change in the traditional Mennonite outline.

Following this opening chapter in *Mirror of Truth*, on the triune God and issues in Christology, Holdeman turned to the traditional concerns of nineteenth-century conservative Mennonites: repentance, conversion, true faith lived out, baptism, Lord's Supper, foot washing as a requirement, nonresistance, avoidance oaths, discipline and shunning, and so on. While the perspective on these issues was clearly Holdeman's, the issues remained those of the traditionalist Mennonite agenda of the nineteenth century.

The discussion of each particular theme is more succinct in *On Redemption* than in *A Mirror of Truth*. Yet *On Redemption* follows the traditionalist outline, beginning with atonement, the plan of salvation, and developing the other issues out of it. With his death and resurrection, Christ effected sanctification and redemption, which Holdeman interpreted as essentially the same process.

He used present and future dimensions to distinguish his under-

Clarence Hiebert

Two views of John Holdeman's church in Wayne County, Ohio, as it appeared in 1968, while in use for storing farm equipment.

standing of redemption from that of the holiness tradition. Holdeman called "present redemption" the forgiveness of sins, while "future redemption is being delivered from our vile body containing the seeds of sin, namely, inherited sin, or the inclination in the flesh to sin."[178] Future redemption will happen only with the resurrection.[179] His main point with the present-future distinction was to show that even redeemed Christians cannot escape sin. This provides the basis for rejecting the idea from the holiness tradition that "by a second work through sanctification," a sinner can be "made as pure as Adam was before he fell."[180]

Holdeman tied the redemption worked by the sacrificial death of Christ to lived faith and to the church. Each redeemed person is a "member of Christ, and a member of his church, and is to be joined into one organization with all saints."[181] The church thus belongs intrinsically to the work of Christ. "Christ died, not only to save sinners, but also to gather together the children of God into this one body."[182] This linking of church to the work of Christ provided the bridge that Holdeman made between redemption and the ordinances, practices, and doctrines of the church. While no one is saved by the performance of any external ordinance or command or outward work, a redeemed person nevertheless "must fulfill all the commands of God through the saving truth."[183]

The various ordinances and practices of the church become what Holdeman called a "consequential truth."[184] The performance of them does not save, but since their performance is a part of God's saving truth, failing to perform them demonstrates that one has not been redeemed. Thus they "follow as a consequence on the faith in the saving truth of Christ."[185] The consequential truths included baptism, Lord's Supper, foot washing, nonresistance, amillennialism, nonswearing of oaths, marriage, excommunication, and shunning.[186] Among these, he singled out nonresistance as the particular mark of redemption. "The doctrine of nonresistance is the mark or standard whereby we are to know whether we are indeed the disciples of Christ."[187] While the particular manner of making this point was Holdeman's, the basic point was one he shared with the other individuals of this study.

As previously noted, the process of conversion as understood by Holdeman was highly experiential although not externally exuberant. The experiential dimension defined one problem he had with the Amish. As he saw it, many of their members and ministers were "baptized unconverted."[188] He applied the same critique to the old church he had abandoned.[189] Holdeman described his own conversion in some detail, actually a series of conversions, visions, and intense struggle, which had occurred over an extended period of time.[190] What distinguished him was not the stress on conversion itself, but the quite experiential, emotional intensity of it, combined with his experience of and faith in dreams and visions as means of direct revelation.[191]

This emphasis on conversion gave Holdeman some initial similarity to Heinrich Egly. Both shared the requirement of an experiential conversion, and Holdeman noted that since Egly's group had separated, it had come closer to Holdeman's. They apparently had more than one conversation about merging their two groups. Egly wrote that they had hoped to unite but "could not agree again about water baptism." He held to 1 Corinthians 12:13 for his own position. Egly also charged Holdeman with claiming to have the only true church, and with leaving the church in which he was baptized in order to start "a church of his own without any calling of the church."[192]

Holdeman's comment on Egly brings a bit of clarity to their disagreement. It appears that Holdeman made rebaptism of Egly a requirement of merger, and Egly refused. Holdeman stated,

> We cannot acknowledge Egly's baptism received of the church that had but few living members,[193] and of which I already wrote that we could not accept it as the Church of God since its separation from the true Church. . . . The future will decide, as I hope, how wrong they did [*sic*] in laboring separately from us. God desired them to unite and labor with us, no doubt, but they were not willing because of some of our infirmities. . . . In doctrine, they have come nearer to what we hold from time to time, but we cannot yet agree. May God help that we may become united.[194]

Analysis of Egly in chapter 3 showed that Holdeman and Egly came to differ significantly at another point. While probably neither recognized it, Egly's stress on experiential conversion evolved to focus much more on the conversion experience itself, with less stress on the traditional Amish and Mennonite issues related to a visible and lived-out faith so important to Holdeman. Holdeman maintained the idea that conversion was to a new, reborn life described by the list of Christ's commands.

Christology is another crucial point in Holdeman's theology. Holdeman belonged to the small number of Mennonites and Amish after the sixteenth century who accepted and defended Menno's celestial flesh Christology.[195] His acceptance of Menno's Christology is much clearer in the original *Spiegel* than in the English translation.

One of Holdeman's principle christological concerns was to demonstrate the deity of Jesus,[196] that "he is God."[197] Holdeman's argument consisted to a large extent in claiming that the Jesus who appeared on earth had a prior existence in heaven, to which he then returned after his resurrection. He cited the three births of Jesus—in eternity, of Mary, and his resurrection[198]—and the fact that his deity was preserved throughout the three, so that the term "birth" dare not allow one to conclude that Jesus had a birth like a natural child.[199]

Note his attention to the prepositions, reminiscent of Menno's "born out of but not from" Mary,[200] when Holdeman wrote about Jesus:

> His manifestation in the flesh is called a birth because He was conceived by the Holy Ghost in the pure virgin Mary and out of her was born as a man, although not as a created being like us but rather as God-man. The Word, or God, became flesh, and in this flesh He suffered, died, was buried and resurrected from the dead.[201]

Holdeman assured readers that Jesus even described himself as "being the same before, and during His manifestation in the flesh, and after His ascension to heaven."[202] For Holdeman, Jesus' flesh clearly descended from heaven. "Because the Son of God did not take his flesh from the earth and was not earthly, but he was rather the Lord himself from heaven, thus he did not face corruption and when he was killed he was raised again from among the dead."[203]

The celestial flesh and the deity of Christ do not stand as doctrines for their own sake in Holdeman's theology. The atoning death of Christ was the reason for asserting his origin and character.[204] Christ had to become flesh in order to make the payment necessary for the salvation of sinful humankind.

In another context, the divine origin of Jesus served to confirm the authority of his teaching. Much of Holdeman's attention to questions of conduct for Christians and his defense of the practices of the church depended on finding an authoritative word or a command of Christ. That is, something is true and must be obeyed or practiced because it was given by Christ. While Holdeman defended these commands and practices in other ways as well, his most weighty argument was to imbue them with the authority of Christ.

Nonresistance to evil and a total rejection of any hint of involvement with government and secular authorities was one doctrine grounded in the authority of Christ.[205] However, Holdeman also integrated an assumption of nonresistance into his understanding of atonement. This theological argument included his understanding of the relationship between old and new covenants, and between law and the gospel. Under the law and the old covenant, Israel was required to use capital punishment against serious offenses or "presumptuous sinners."[206]

However, Israel was overcome by the Romans and therefore no longer had kingly power,[207] and Jesus fulfilled the law in a once-for-all fashion. Hence, there was no longer any need for the exercise of capital punishment nor the exercise of secular authority by Israelites or Christians since the time of Jesus. This logical and theological assertion of nonresistance dovetails with Holdeman's defense of the same points on the basis of the authority of Christ.[208] Under the old covenant, love meant to fight with the sword; now love has a new meaning. "Christ died as a defenseless lamb on the cross out of pure love toward us, and did not allow Peter to defend Him by the sword."[209]

Holdeman's commitment to nonresistance also supplied the basis for his rejection of premillennialism. He considered it a gross contradiction for Christians to accept war in the present while arguing that Jesus' teaching about nonresistance belonged to a future kingdom. Any future kingdom of peace, he declared, must be "the manifestation of the saving truth contained in the gospel." Since that is the gospel which the present church proclaims, it is impossible to contend "for war now and universal peace in the millennium."[210] His additional discussion included scriptural arguments against varying dimensions of the premillennial program.[211] Thus for Holdeman, nonresistance was both a doctrine to be believed and an integrative principle which exerted influence on other aspects of his theology.

In this section we have observed that, with the exception of C. H. Wedel, John Holdeman had a more complex context for atonement than did the other figures of this study. In addition, he went a great deal further than his coreligionists in articulating doctrine as truths to be believed. These aspects of his thought distinguish him from them. Yet one needs to recognize Holdeman's understanding of atonement and his conviction that it is the external life of the believer which provides the most sure evidence of conversion. Such views clearly place him in the same theological tradition as his fellow Mennonites and Amish, with similar understandings of the church and the lived faith.

Heinrich Egly

Similar to John M. Brenneman, Heinrich Egly understood atonement as part of a multistaged process of salvation. First, Jesus' atoning death made possible the forgiveness of sins, something no works or hu-

Einladung.

Hiemit bestellen wir, so Gott will, eine Versammlung am 14. Oktober 1883 und am 15. und 16. halten wir Conferenz, um miteinander den wahren seligmachenden Glauben aus Grund Gottes Wort miteinander zu betrachten und besprechen. Und in dieser Conferenz soll Jedermann das Vorrecht haben, Fragen zu stellen oder zu beantworten, doch in der Ordnung und nach Gottes Wort. Folgende sind Gegenstände unserer Berathung: Buße und Bekehrung; das neue Leben; Ausgießung des heiligen Geistes; und wie weit, nach der Lehre Pauli (Röm. 6, 7. 8, 22), wir erkennen und glauben mögen u. s. w. Auch was noch in den Wiedergebornen bleibt zu tödten und abzulegen nach der Rechtfertigung, um Christi Nachfolger zu sein.

Wir wünschen mit dem Grund den wir bekennen als wehrlose Christen oder Mennoniten mehr bekannt zu werden, und laden daher freundlich ein, uns an jener Zeit zu besuchen und der Versammlung beizuwohnen.

Gäste, die auf der Fort Wayne u. Richmond, oder auch auf der Grand Rapids Eisenbahn kommen, belieben an Berne Station auszusteigen.

Heinrich Egly,
Geneva, Adams Co., Ind.

Heinrich Egly's open invitation to the October 14, 1883, conference of the Defenseless Mennonite Church, as it appeared in Herold der Wahrheit 10.17 (Sept. 1, 1883): 265.

man effort of any kind could accomplish. At this point, Egly assumed the satisfaction image of atonement and saw it as a component of two additional emphases. Second, sinners have access to that forgiveness when they recognize their hopeless and sinful condition and repent. In response to this repentance, God pours out the Holy Spirit on the penitent sinner, and the sinner undergoes the experience of conversion, of being remade as a child of God. The atoning blood of Christ has made new birth and Spirit possession possible. Third, the converted sinner experiences the joy of the Lord, and is enabled to lead a life of obedience to the commands of Christ. While this process of conversion is visible in some way in a majority of Egly's articles, he described it with various images and types, and with some shifting of emphases.

Most Mennonites and Amish of Egly's era, and certainly all the individuals treated in this study, stressed the necessity of conversion.

What distinguished Heinrich Egly from most others, except for John Holdeman, was the focus on a crisis, experiential, or felt conversion.[212] A visitor to Egly's home congregation in Geneva, Indiana, noted that an experienced conversion was a requirement for baptism and membership.[213]

Egly believed that a newly converted believer would experience the new birth vividly, with immediate assurance of salvation and visible fruits of the Spirit.[214] His first article placed a great deal of stress on the need to experience certainty in the heart as the assurance of forgiveness of sins. The visible evidence provided by abandoning a sinful practice, even years before, is not enough. Perhaps it is merely advancing age, he wrote, that deprives one of the vigor to sin! For repentance and conversion to be genuine, the sinner must undergo a deeply felt experience in the heart. That experience is the prerequisite for teachers and parents who would punish sin in their hearers and children.[215]

Thus Egly admitted both the necessity of conversion and the possibility that merely advancing age might account for the absence of some sins. These remarks may reflect the controversy which compelled Egly to organize a separate Amish group. As he became increasingly convinced about the necessity of a heartfelt conversion, Egly expressed willingness to rebaptize persons who had earlier received baptism without such a conversion. In his mind, the first baptism, without benefit of such a conversion, had occurred "without repentance," and a person baptized in that way had no more assurance of forgiveness of sins "than the one that was baptized in infancy."

His willingness to rebaptize challenged the validity of other ministers and their congregational practices. It provoked opposition and intervention by the annual Amish *Dienerversammlungen* (ministers' meetings, which began in 1862). Eventually, in the fall of 1865, Egly withdrew from his congregation at Berne, Indiana, along with about half of the members, and organized them into a new group.[216]

In his biblical exegesis, Egly was fond of discovering types or images in the Old Testament. He had several Old Testament images for conversion. For one, he used the Flood story: Noah building the ark, the preservation of Noah in the ark, the outpouring of water from above, the destruction of sinful flesh through this water, the culmination with Noah's thank offering for his salvation. This account constituted "a clear type (*Vorbild*) of rebirth and entry into the church (*Gemeinde*) of God."[217]

In another instance, Egly used three Israelite festivals as images of the conversion process. The Israelites commemorated the Passover, in which God saved them; the reception of the law at Sinai, fifty days after Passover; and the Feast of Booths at the conclusion of the grape harvest. According to Egly, these three festivals foreshadowed three components of the Christian life: Easter, in which God through Christ redeemed sinners, while awareness of the law brought sinners to repentance and faith in Christ; Pentecost, at which time the Holy Ghost was poured out, purifying hearts and sealing them as believers and true heirs of God; and last, a continuing enjoyment of the Lord and the fruits of the Spirit.[218]

Egly's view of conversion shaped his opinion of other church leaders. He considered ministers such as C. H. Wedel or Johannes Moser to be unsaved since they believed that conversion could happen gradually as a result of nurture or that feeling provided an untrustworthy validation of one's salvation. In the "Autobiography," Egly characterized Moser, whose congregation had been the target of Egly revivals, as a preacher who "had no assurance of his salvation in his heart" and called him an "instrument through which [Satan] worked against us."[219]

His favorable comments about John H. Oberholtzer's movement appear to be based not on Oberholtzer's espousal of modern culture but on what Egly considered revival-like preaching. "Oberholzer and his fellow preachers preached mightily. . . . They preached about repentance and change of mind and life." Egly also praised William Gehman, early supporter of John Oberholtzer and, after splitting from Oberholtzer, a founder of a group that later became the Mennonite Brethren in Christ Church. Egly noted Gehman's "great zeal" in preaching and also Gehman's support of prayer meetings. In dealing with Gehman's separation from Oberholtzer due to the latter's opposition to prayer meetings, Egly quoted, apparently with approval, a letter he had received from a J. G. Stauffer, which expressed mild chastisement upon Oberholtzer's position.[220]

One of Egly's problems with the so-called sleeping preachers, whose nickname came from their practice of preaching while in a trance, was that they preached obedience without stress on conversion.[221] A revivalist-style experience of conversion clearly shaped Egly's theological outlook and shaped the matrix he used in evaluating people and movements. At this point, his evaluation resembled John Holdeman's critique of Amish ministers who lacked conversion. Other Mennonite and Amish ministers did indeed consider conversion important and necessary. Yet Egly and Holdeman differed from them, not in emphasizing conversion, but in requiring a specifically revivalist-style, crisis conversion.[222]

The first meetinghouse of Heinrich Egly's newly established Defenseless Mennonite Church, erected near Berne, Indiana, in 1871. The congregation used this building for ten years.

Egly did not believe that feelings saved. In fact, he stressed repeatedly that redemption was a matter of grace, a gift of God. On the other hand, he was also aware that he was subject to the charge of making feelings the basis of salvation. While his first published article stressed conversion, he said that a person found certainty of forgiveness of sins "in his heart and in the Word of God."[223] The main point of his one independently published tract was that salvation depended on faith in the blood of Christ, not on feelings. "The ancients were convinced by faith and not feelings."

After noting a number of things which are acquired through faith, Egly wrote,

> Now after a saved soul is convinced of salvation in Christ's blood and death, of redemption and forgiveness of sins, of judgment and punishment, and has put on Christ through baptism with all its costly promises of the Holy Ghost, then it receives certainty. As soon as a soul loses sight of Jesus, the only goal and power, and focuses on itself and listens to poisonous influences, so soon does it lose the witness (or the feeling as some call it). Now the joy is lost, courage falls, . . . in that love and trust in Jesus fail.[224]

It is quite clear that while inner feelings were an inherently necessary dimension of conversion in his understanding, feeling was the product rather than the producer of conversion.

Feeling was not the only sign of conversion. Early in his ministry, Egly stressed that conversion would manifest itself through obedience to all the commands of Christ. Thus, while he differed from most other Mennonites and Amish of his era by insisting upon a particular style of conversion, the results of that conversion resembled closely what others, including his nemesis Johannes Moser, also expected of conversion.

Almost all of Egly's articles in *Herold der Wahrheit* reflected the fusion of heartfelt conversion and Mennonite-Amish issues. In his first article, he identified participation in frivolity as a major indication of lack of genuine conversion. A man, young or old, had clearly not yet crucified the flesh if he gave himself to foolishness, emptiness, impurity, pride, and intemperance, or laughed at those who did. Therefore, "one sees thoughtlessness in speaking and laughing after the worship hour, in stores, and things are said and done that will produce damnation if they are not abandoned."[225] John M. Brenneman would certainly have agreed that laughing and frivolous activity could not come from a truly converted heart.[226]

While Egly's articles barely mention the necessity of plain dress and other instances of traditional plain living, he retained these emphases early in his ministerial career.[227] In 1887, members of his congregation in Berne, Indiana, voted not to allow organs in their homes.[228]

In his second article for *Herold der Wahrheit*, Egly listed the entire range of distinctive Mennonite and Amish practices as evidence of a truly converted heart. As a text, he used Jesus' words, "If you love me, keep my commandments" (John 14:15), spoken to the disciples at the Last Supper. At that point, Egly said, the disciples did not yet have the power to understand and obey. That power came at Pentecost, when they received the Holy Ghost. He used Peter as one example. In Gethsemane, Peter wanted to fight the soldiers; after Pentecost, Peter was among those who held themselves back and prayed for enemies (Acts 5:40; cf. 4:24-30). Only the love and Spirit of Christ enables one to keep such commands of Jesus, Egly declared.

Further commands of Jesus which the converted one will obey included baptism, keeping the Lord's Supper, and the practice of foot washing. Love of enemies, however, was singled out as the key indicator of conversion. "Can you love your enemy, and pray for him from the heart, . . .? If you can do that, then Christ's Spirit is within you and gives birth to it through his power." If not, "it is as clear as sunshine that your heart has not been recreated and renewed by God."[229]

In Egly's next article, he used an Old Testament type as the basis for listing the commands which regenerated Christians would obey. As the Israelites were commanded to eat all of the Passover lamb, so Christians, who are the spiritual Israelites, are commanded spiritually to eat all of Christ. That spiritual eating, empowered by the Holy Spirit poured out at Pentecost, consists of obeying all the commands of Christ. Repentance heads the list, followed by believing that the blood of Christ has made possible forgiveness of sins. The converted one then proceeds to Christ's commands regarding baptism, the Lord's Supper, washing the saints' feet, nonresistance to evil, and love for enemies. Of these commands, Egly singled out loving one's enemies as the supreme test of whether one was willing "to eat the entire lamb."[230] In his early articles, he consistently made nonresistance and love of enemies the ultimate test of genuine conversion.[231]

Egly also developed an eschatological dimension of the fusion of conversion and Mennonite-Amish emphases. As the complete title of the sermon "Vom Friedensreich Jesu Christi" indicated, its main point was to emphasize that the peaceable kingdom of Christ had *already* begun, "as soon as Christ had made his offering on the cross."[232] He quoted a number of Scripture texts to demonstrate that Jesus was the Prince of Peace and that the kingdom prophesied in the Old Testament had already begun and would have no end.

In particular, he identified the atoning death of Christ on the cross as "the great chain (*die grosse Kette*)" that bound Satan, as given in Revelation 20:14.[233] Egly's intent was to refute the premillennial argument which would postpone obedience to Jesus' commands to a future thousand-year rule of Christ. He wanted to emphasize the present and immediate manifestation of the new birth. Since the kingdom of God has already begun, a newly converted believer would experience that new birth vividly, with immediate assurance of salvation and visible fruits of the Spirit. Obedience to the commands of Christ belonged not to the future but to the already-present kingdom of God.

More attention to the death of Christ would produce more Christlike living. "Oh, that the death of Christ could be more evident in us, then Jesus' life might also be more visible; as death was powerful for the forerunners, but life is now evident in the church."[234] Evidence that one truly has a converted and purified heart and new life included "humility" and patience towards one's bitterest enemies. None who truly repent can "still avenge themselves with the sword, or with government, or scolding and threats, or beating."[235] Thus Egly's stress on conversion fused with peace theology led him to oppose premillennialism.[236] Both Johannes Moser and John Holdeman made similar arguments.

Thus the fusion of conversion and peace theology is evident in many of Egly's published articles. In contrast, the section on Egly in chapter 3 described the virtual absence from his "Autobiography" of nonresistance and other distinctive Amish-Mennonite practices as he listed evidences of genuine conversion. In the light of the altered perspective reflected in the "Autobiography," some dimensions of the articles also appear to take on a different hue.

Egly wrote a sharp critique of the so-called sleeping preachers[237] which appeared in the General Conference Mennonite paper, *Christlicher Bundesbote*. Among his points of critique, he accused Noah Troyer and John D. Kauffman of preaching works of the law, failing to preach about redemption (*Versöhnung*) through Christ, denying that Christ paid (*bezahlt*) for sins, and lacking personal assurance of salvation.[238] Such critique can reflect Egly's movement away from a fusion of atonement, conversion, and Mennonite-Amish practices and toward a validation of salvation by heartfelt conversion. Other factors no doubt also played a role in Egly's critique.

This article was the first that he sent to the new *Christlicher Bundesbote*, still in its first year of publication. Its appearance there was certainly in response to the support John F. Funk's two papers, *Herald of Truth* and *Herold der Wahrheit*, gave to Troyer and Kauffman.[239] In a following article for *Christlicher Bundesbote*, which dealt with a question raised by his sleeping-preacher article, he referred to the shift of the early church away from the teaching and ordinances of Christ. However, his description of the fallen, papal church reflected revivalism more than Mennonite and Amish emphases on nonresistance. He asserted that when the church had lost true life, "form and appearance (*Form und Wesen*) took its place, and opinion and reason ruled, so that the victory of Christ was weakened."[240]

More clearly indicative of Egly's movement away from the fusion of conversion and nonresistance are the introductory comments in the last of the three items he published in *Christlicher Bundesbote*. The title of the article asks why so few Christians are happy and blessed (*glücklich und selig*). The primary thrust of the article was that confessing Christians, who acknowledged forgiveness to be a free gift from God as a result of Jesus' redeeming death, should be happy and blessed in their surrender to Jesus. Knowing that they need no longer pursue works of the law, they can be happy and blessed in their hearts. As the Holy Spirit works through them, they will be light and salt for the earth, and the Father in heaven will see their good works and praise them.

Absent is any specific indication that conversion as a work of the

Spirit will be revealed through obedience to the commands of Christ, including the loving of one's enemies.[241] Without the "Autobiography," this article would likely appear as an additional facet of the view displayed in the majority of Egly's published articles. However, when read in light of the "Autobiography," the article seems to reflect the later Egly, who had replaced nonresistance with a crisis conversion experience as evidence of rebirth.

The shift indicated by the "Autobiography" is also instructive when analyzing the articles reprinted in *Das Friedensreich Christi*. Five were reprints from *Herold der Wahrheit*, and three were new, presumably unpublished sermons in the possession of son-in-law and editor Jacob Schenbeck. Commitment to the tradition of nonresistance is visible as an integral part of the reborn life in the initial piece, "Vom Friedensreich Jesu Christi," as well as in "Ein neu Gebot," and in "Only One Gospel," the final selection. This latter essay was previously unpublished and is the only extant Egly item in English. Nonresistance, loving enemies, and forsaking vengeance do not appear explicitly in the other five items of the little book.

Though one may assume that nonresistance is present in the several references to obeying "all the commands of Christ," one would not know that without having read the entire Egly corpus. In this little book, *Das Friedensreich Christi*, items selected for publication carry relatively few explicit references to nonresistance. This is noteworthy in light of the fusion of conversion with nonresistance and love of enemies that is quite evident in Egly's written corpus as a whole. One can speculate that son-in-law and editor Schenbeck selected items for reprinting that reflected, no doubt unwittingly, the new orientation which the church was assuming at the time the book was edited.

In that light, Egly's introductory comments in "Etwas vom lebendigen Glaube," another previously unpublished item, are telling:

> In speaking and writing, the fruits of rebirth should be emphasized more. We have enough emphasis on the confession that Jesus is God's Son and also that Jesus came to save sinners. But there is not enough emphasis that I myself am a sinner but am now a child of God, and that I now have his Spirit as a seal of faith.[242]

Noticeable by its absence is any indication that possessing the Spirit as a seal of faith will result in baptism, Lord's Supper, foot washing, and loving enemies. Instead the article focuses on such things as the fact that sins are no longer held against the penitent sinner, and that the reborn one experiences peace and joy in the Holy Spirit. Once again, read only in the context of Egly's published writings, this article might be seen as filling in an additional component of the whole. Read in light of the "Autobiography," it looks much more like another indication that revivalism had reshaped Egly's thought.

The analysis of this section demonstrates quite clearly that Heinrich Egly did not intend to neglect or abandon the inherited Mennonite and Amish understanding of nonresistance, pacifism, and rejection of war for Christians. Those items are quite evident in his articles, and he linked his inherited Amish-Mennonite understandings to his new, adopted emphasis on a crisis, heartfelt conversion. Even Johannes Moser, whom Egly considered unconverted, and conservative Amish David Beiler, who had previously abandoned his progressive Amish brethren, would have supported Egly's linking of conversion and nonresistance, even as they rejected his requirement of a revivalist-style, crisis conversion.

However, chapter 3 (above) showed that his "Autobiography" lacked certain Mennonite-Amish distinctives. Comparing that late work with his earlier articles clearly demonstrates that Egly's outlook underwent significant development. In assessment, using language that Egly would not recognize, one dimension of that development was that ethics was becoming detached from the understanding of salvation. Evidence of conversion shifted from a saved life of following Jesus to the experience of a crisis conversion. As noted in chapter 2, such a shift could occur without challenge from the satisfaction atonement theory which Egly espoused.

Summary

In this chapter we have observed the theological context in which each of the eight subjects situated his doctrine of atonement. For the most part, that context reflected the writer's inherited Mennonite or Amish understandings related to the church and its characteristics such as humility or discipline or simplicity or nonresistance.

More than the other seven, Wedel's theological context concerned itself primarily with classic questions about atonement. However, when Wedel's theological context is related to his larger concept of *Gemeindechristentum*, all eight of these subjects are seen to deal with atonement in a context which reflects their inherited traditions of a visible peace church with a clear emphasis on pacifism and nonresistance.

The following chapter deals with the theology of these eight men on the narrow question of how their various atonement images compare with the images of the three classic families of atonement identified in chapter 2. The analysis will show that little of what characterized these men as Mennonite or Amish theologians is reflected when one considers only the classic atonement images.

5

The Theory of Atonement

Chapter 2 described three families of atonement theories: the classic or Christus Victor image, the moral influence theory, and the several versions of the satisfaction theory. Among these families of atonement theories, the death of Christ has four separate objects. The classic view envisioned Satan as the object of Jesus' death. Among the versions of the satisfaction theory, either an offended God or the stipulations of the law are the objects of Jesus' death. For the moral influence theory, sinful humankind—and their distorted moral perception in particular—is the object of Jesus' death. That matrix of views and objects of death informs the description of atonement images for the eight primary characters of this study whose views fall almost exclusively within the satisfaction theory, and more specifically, with the version of satisfaction known as general or governmental atonement.

Jacob Stauffer

Nowhere does Jacob Stauffer articulate a theory of atonement, nor does he even provide a complete statement of what the death of Christ accomplished. He even seems oblivious to the historic discussions about the nature of the work of Christ and virtually unaware of the nature of a systematic discussion of such theological issues. Nonetheless, several bits of evidence in the *Chronik* indicate Stauffer's affinity for the satisfaction theory of atonement.

In at least two separate passages, Stauffer employed language usually associated with an Anselmian viewpoint. As the foundation for the love which the first disciples of Jesus had for him, Stauffer noted, "How very important the salvation purchased in such a costly way (*das theuer erkaufte Heil*) was to their immortal souls."[1] In the page-long greeting

Jan Gleysteen and Amos Hoover

View from the east, showing Pike or Stauffer Mennonite Meetinghouse and the fully enclosed horse barn of Jacob Stauffer's time. It is believed that this is the only such Mennonite barn to have survived.

which introduced part 3 of the *Chronik*, he extended many divine blessings and encouragements in name of Father and Holy Spirit, through Jesus Christ. He then called Christ "our Lord, Redeemer (*Erlöser*) and Savior, who gave himself for our sins, in order to redeem (*erlösete*) us from this present evil world."[2]

The use of *Erlöser* and *erlösete* to identify Jesus and his saving act may be the only appearance of these terms in the *Chronik*. To these examples of satisfaction terminology, one might also add Stauffer's quotation of Hebrews 12:24, which called Jesus "the mediator (*Mittler*) of the new covenant, whose sprinkled blood speaks better than the blood of Abel."[3]

Other remarks reflect in a more general way a satisfaction orientation toward atonement. For example, Stauffer mentioned the certain punishment due those who knowingly disobey Jesus' commandments and thus "crucify the Son of God and thus esteem as impure the blood of Christ through which they are sanctified."[4] In denying that he preached a salvation by works, Stauffer stated that "we are saved through the grace and merit (*verdienste*) of Jesus, and only by his blood are our sins washed away (*durch sein Blut allein die Abwaschung der Sünden haben*).["5]

These brief indicators and several quoted examples do not constitute an effort by Jacob Stauffer to articulate a theory of atonement. They do indicate, however, that his theology appears to rest on assumptions of the satisfaction atonement motif. If questioned about atonement theology, he would no doubt have expressed agreement with or a preference for the satisfaction theory. At the same time, it is accurate to point out that little that really characterizes Stauffer's thought is given when one indicates his agreement with satisfaction atonement. While atonement doctrine would link him to evangelicalism, it misses the specific understanding of the Christian faith that results from Stauffer's belief in the disciplined, humble, nonresistant church.

David Beiler

David Beiler's *Wahre Christenthum*, a series of meditations and sermons, has much more explicit theological content than Jacob Stauffer's *Chronik*. Although Beiler's *Betrachtung über den Berg Predig* contains less such theology, it nonetheless reflects *Wahre Christenthum's* perspective on atonement. While Beiler did not discuss atonement as a distinct category, parallel to Stauffer, it is quite clear that Beiler assumed the satisfaction theory of atonement.

Terminology and phrases that reflect the satisfaction theory appear in most of the ten chapters of *Wahre Christenthum*. The family of terms related to *erlösen* occurs rather frequently. We note here a few of the more explicit examples. The announcement to Mary of her coming pregnancy was made when the time was ready for the beginning of the "great work of redemption (*das grosse Erlösungswerk*).["6] Through the Son who is "Savior and Healer (*Heiland und Seligmacher*)," "all has been atoned for (*versöhnt*) whether in heaven or on earth." Beiler then quoted a Scripture text which calls Jesus "our Shepherd and High Priest, our Mediator and Redeemer and Intercessor (*Mittler und Versöhner und Fürsprecher*).["7]

Several pages later, Beiler noted that Jesus "paid (*bezahlt*) what he was not guilty of, . . . [and thus] redeemed (*versöhnt*) all believing, obedient people with God."[8] When explaining why the baptism of John the Baptist differed from that of Jesus, Beiler wrote that during John's era, the "perfect sacrifice (*vollkommene Opfer*)" had not yet been completed. "Through his own blood [Jesus] found eternal redemption (*Erlösung*).["9] "I believe that the sins of Adam and Eve were atoned for (*versöhnt*) by God; the record (*die Handschrift*) which stood between man and God was taken away, and the two were made one—thus was the great work of salvation (*Erlösungswerk*) completed."[10]

A rather explicit use of penal substitutionary imagery occurs in a paragraph in which Beiler denied vigorously the possibility of salvation by any human efforts.

> For the only means to reach or to obtain salvation is Jesus Christ; for he is the Lamb of God who bears the sins of the world (*das der Welt Sünde trägt*). He was wounded for our misdeeds and beaten for our sins, and the punishment lays on him (*und die Strafe liegt auf ihm*) so that we might have peace, and through his wounds we are healed. We have all gone astray like sheep, each in his own way; but the Lord threw all our guilt on him (*aber der Herr warf unser aller Schuld auf ihn*).[11]

Although Beiler used biblical language, he seemed to assume here the Anselmian idea of Jesus being punished in place of sinful humanity.

In remarks about what constitutes worthy participation in the Lord's Supper in *Betrachtung über den Berg Predig*, Beiler also used something approaching penal substitutionary language. In the Supper, one participates spiritually in the suffering and death of Christ, which he endured like a patient lamb:

> The righteous for the unrighteous, the pure for the impure, the innocent for the guilty, the Son of God for men. And the reason that Christ had to suffer such an offense, and not just a mildly painful death, was the sins of Adam and Eve and of the whole world.[12]

Beiler's most extensive discussion of atonement appears in his meditation on the story of Jesus' conversation with Nicodemus in John 3.[13] While it is clearly not an articulated statement of Anselmian atonement, the motif of a substitute punishment or substitute payment of a deserved penalty does seem to underlie such statements as this:

> [One should observe] how much God hates all sin, whether secret or open, and will punish them with eternal pain and torment. And also how he made his innocent Son suffer so much in order to redeem the sins of Adam and Eve and the whole world.[14]

> As Paul showed, the sin of Adam is carried through to all men because all have sinned. And thus it was established in the counsel of God that through Jesus Christ all should be redeemed (*erlöst*) from the sin of Adam and Eve.[15]

What was said about Jacob Stauffer applies to David Beiler as well. These brief quoted examples do not constitute an effort to articulate a complete theory of atonement. Yet the remarks do indicate that if questioned about atonement theology, Beiler would certainly have expressed agreement with some form of the satisfaction theory. But true for Beiler as it was for Stauffer, emphasis on satisfaction atonement, so as to define Beiler as evangelical in theology, would fail to account for the core of his concern: the disciplined, humble nonresistant church and the Christian's life of discipleship. That core much more fully characterized Beiler's faith and theological orientation.

Gerhard Wiebe

At two separate locations in *Ursachen und Geschichte*, Wiebe used atonement language. Both occasions indicate that his atonement assumptions fall within the category of penal, substitutionary atonement. The first instance comes in the course of Wiebe's description of the events leading up to the Bergthal immigration from Russia. At one point, the czar convoked Wiebe. As he waited with much fear, trembling, and trepidation in an outer room for the meeting with the czar, an aide came with a brush and proceeded to clean Wiebe's clothing from head to toe, including his boots. Of the thoughts racing through his mind, Wiebe could describe only one: "That's how you will some day be inwardly cleansed when you will appear before the King of Kings. Only there no servant will clean you; you must be washed by the blood of Christ alone."[16] The image of a substitutionary atonement, with Jesus' blood cleansing the individual of sins, seems clearly to stand behind Wiebe's choice of words in this instance.

Wiebe's second explicit use of atonement imagery comes close to making the penal dimension explicit. In the immediate context of explaining why he opposed the use of Christmas trees, he used as an example the gifts of the three wise men who sought out the baby Jesus in Bethlehem. According to Wiebe, the first gift, gold, which must be purified by fire, represents the cleansing and purification sinners must undergo in order to enter the kingdom of heaven. That cleansing takes place through the Holy Spirit "and the blood of Christ." The gift of incense symbolizes the gospel, which is to pervade and affect the entire world.

Finally, in mentioning the gift of bitter myrrh, Wiebe made explicit the motif of punishing sin. Myrrh signified Christ's

Chortitzer Menno-nite Church, built in 1896 at Randolph, Manitoba. Although Gerhard Wiebe had resigned as bishop, he worshiped in this building. His gravestone is in the left foreground.

Orlando Hiebert

Gravestone of Gerhard Wiebe, in cemetery of Chortitzer Mennonite Church, Randolph, Manitoba.

Orlando Hiebert

terrible death on the cross; yes, those were our sins which made his end so bitter, because when He stood before Annas and Caiaphas, they spat in His face and slapped it, and our sins were there too; and when they brought Him before Pilate, where they tortured Him some more, then my sins and your sins, dear reader, were also there. And when He was being whipped, our sins were also present. And when He carried the heavy cross to the place of execution, then this Lamb of God carried my sins and yours; and when He broke down under the weight of the cross, he sank under the weight of our sins also. And when he was being nailed to the cross, our sins were also there. And when His last hour came, the Lord cast all of our sins on Him in that terrible condition, so that He cried out: My God, My God, why hast Thou forsaken me?[17]

In this vivid image, Wiebe did not lay out the legal framework explicitly; yet it seems clear that he saw Jesus bearing the sins of humanity and experiencing the punishment required by God's law as retribution for those sins. "The sacrifice had to take place," he wrote, "for the sins of the whole world, also for me and you, dear reader."[18]

At the same time, Wiebe's description of the death of Jesus might be said to echo the element of victory from the Christus Victor atonement motif. Perhaps better stated, he included a bit of a victory motif alongside the language of sacrifice and satisfaction. When Jesus expressed the anguish of being forsaken,

> Satan took advantage of the opportunity. He thought: Now God has cast Him out, and so he wanted to crush Him with all our sins and to kill Him.[19] That was an agony which no man can describe, much less bear. But the sacrifice (*Opfer*) had to take place for the sins of the whole world, also for me and you, dear reader; and as He said: It is finished, He bowed His head and gave up His spirit. Through bitter suffering and dying He overcame death, devil, all our sins; because through His blood He reconciled (*versöhnte*) us with His and our Father, and so we can be saved from our sins only through Christ and His shed blood.[20]

While Wiebe here attached the victory motif to Christ's death without mention of resurrection, this is a statement of victory over the devil. As chapter 3 described, that victory over the devil is important since it means that the Christian need battle only the devil's agents as princes of this world, princes whom Wiebe saw within his own Mennonites in southern Manitoba. But however one understands the element of victory in this atonement passage, Wiebe concluded it with language which assumed substitutionary atonement.

In the two instances where Wiebe used explicit atonement language, his imagery reflects the motif of penal, substitutionary atonement. While he mentioned the sins heaped on Jesus, who must of necessity be crushed by them, Wiebe did not actually state that Jesus' blood or his death was the required payment demanded by God or by God's law. Along with the substitutionary motif was also the element of victory, but attached to the death rather than resurrection. However, it is also quite evident that Wiebe used atonement language without awareness of alternative images and motifs. He stated what he believed without reflecting on the wider theological implications or consistency of his beliefs.

In the school constitution which Gerhard Wiebe helped to draw up around 1878, the Elbing Catechism[21] was one of the required textbooks.[22] The catechism states that Jesus "died for our sins." It calls his death a "sacrifice (*Opfer*) for the sins of the entire world which he has completed in eternity for those who will be saved." The catechism says that the suffering of Jesus began "in the night when he was betrayed by Judas in the Garden of Gethsemane." His anguish was a result of the fact that "the Lord threw all our sins upon him," and that the Savior had to die on the cross "in order to save us from the curse."[23] The description of Wiebe's view of atonement based on the two passages from his *Ursachen und Geschichte* indicates that his theology of atonement stood in harmony with the parallel questions in the Elbing Catechism.

Wiebe likely would not have understood the questions of the classic debates on atonement. In any case he would have considered those debates an example of the "worldly" or "secular" wisdom taught in advanced schools.[24] Yet he would have wanted his thoughts to align themselves with the catechism required as a text in the elementary schools he supported. Once again, it is true that while Wiebe's atonement theology fits evangelicalism, his focus on a humble, nonresistant church, without formal education, as described in earlier chapters, places him in a different theological camp, with the other subjects in this study.

Cornelius H. Wedel

Among C. H. Wedel's published writings, the most explicit references to atonement occur in *Meditationen*, his commentary on the Elbing Mennonite catechism. Since Wedel's comments follow the questions of the catechism, the *Meditationen* does not itself reveal his own outline. However, his unpublished "Glaubenslehre" reveals clearly that his conceptualization of atonement corresponded to the catechism's structuring of salvation on a classic outline of creation, Fall, and redemption. He had accepted that outline as his own.

Wedel's doctrine of atonement clearly falls within the category of the satisfaction theory, and his discussion covered the central points of the Anselmian doctrine. At the same time, Wedel posed one corrective to his understanding of Anselm's view. He also affirmed both truth and error in Abelard's moral influence theory of atonement.

Wedel began the discussion of atonement in "Glaubenslehre" with a statement of the universality of human sin.[25] In the *Meditationen*, he noted that the unity of the human race explains why redemption (*Erlösung*) is possible.[26] Although created in the image of God, Adam and Eve sinned, thereby corrupting the entire human race. Subsequently, each individual recreates that Fall in one's own life, and all individuals are unavoidably corrupted by sin. As a result, the entire human race lacks the power to do anything about its sinful and lost condition.[27]

While grounding atonement in the universality of sin reflects the traditional approach to the satisfaction theory, Wedel's formulation of it also shows that he offered a specific critique of Anselm. He acknowledged that much in Anselm's theory is "correct." However, for Wedel, Anselm began at the wrong place. Anselm began with the honor of God and said that "sin was an offense against the divine majesty."[28] The correct, biblical foundation, Wedel declared, was actually that the "righteousness (*Gerechtigkeit*)" of God reveals human sinfulness. For Wedel, the point is to shift the responsibility for the necessity of the sacrifice of Christ, from God to humankind. It is not God's offended honor but rather "the sin of humanity" which necessitates Christ's sacrifice.[29] Quite deliberately, therefore, he began his discussion of atonement with a lengthy analysis of human sin.

Gravestone of C. H. Wedel, in cemetery of Alexanderwohl Church.

In the *Meditationen,* Wedel summarized atonement as a guilt offering which paid the debt owed for human sin. Only God possessed the capacity to save sinful humanity, and he did not leave them in their lost condition. As an act of grace, and because of his love, he sent his Son to redeem (*erlösen*) them. It was a plan of salvation (*Erlösungsplan*) which no human mind could have conceived or carried out. This plan required a sinless and guilt-free man who would experience the wrath of God and die in the place of humankind and "with this infinitely great sacrifice pay and atone for (*bezahlen und sühnen*) their otherwise deadly burden."[30] Wedel said that Jesus gave his life as a great "guilt offering (*Schuldopfer*)"[31] and that he has "paid our debt (*bezahlte unsere Schuld*)."[32]

In the "Glaubenslehre," Wedel expanded on these themes considerably.[33] Jesus is the Mediator in heaven, whose work encompasses the offices of prophet, priest, and king. As prophet, he witnesses to himself and the kingdom of God through teaching and miraculous deeds. The apostolic witness to Christ concerning his life and work continues this prophetic office.[34] The heart of Christ's atoning work he performed as priest, which included both his atoning death and his continuing work as heavenly Mediator.

> As the high priest the Lord himself sanctified his own through his holy life, [and] through his suffering and death accomplished the work of reconciling mankind with God and the redemption of his own from the power of sin. Since then he represents his own before [the throne of] God and blesses them.[35]

In "Glaubenslehre," Wedel devoted considerable discussion to atonement in terms of satisfying the demand for punishment of sin.[36] Sin is punished so that sinful humanity may be freed from the deserved punishment which separates people from God. Punishment is not removed but rather borne by Jesus. Only then is the power of sin removed. To atone for sin means, he wrote, "to take the power of death away which resides in it and separates us from God." Since God's anger resides in the power of death, "atonement must be a bearing of the collective sins of humankind so that sin receives its deserved punishment, and God's anger can work itself out—and in this way sin becomes powerless."[37]

The sacrifices in the Old Testament provide a foreshadowing of the final sacrifice performed by Jesus. As the blood of the animal covered the sins of the individual and was accepted by God in the place of the deserved death of the sinner, so Jesus' whole life constituted a bearing of sin, and in his death he bore God's anger against sin.[38] This death of Christ was clearly substitutionary, one done in the place of sinful humanity which cannot satisfy its own deserved punishment. Seven times Wedel described Jesus' death as substitutionary (*Stellvertretung, stellvertretend*).[39] While Jesus died as a man who represented humankind, in Wedel's theology his was also a substitutionary death; Jesus submitted to the punishment which sinful humanity deserved.

His summary in the *Meditationen*, given as the correct response to erroneous theories of atonement, brought these motifs together:

> As a pious Israelite observed the innocent sacrificial animal which suffered death in his stead, and in his mercy God accepted such a substitute (*Stellvertretung*) and counted it as acceptable—thus shall humankind confess Christ's suffering and death as the greatest, most complete expiation (*Sühnung*) of their sin.[40]

A few questions later in the catechism, Wedel again used the language of guilt removal. There he claimed that Jesus' death was not merely a witness and sign of God's love but an all-encompassing act of atonement or expiation (*Sühnetat*) for the infinite guilt of humanity, an atoning act which required suffering at the hands of God. "On Golgatha, Christ became the object of divine wrath; divine righteousness worked itself out fully and completely on him, which brought about the redemption of humankind (*Erlösung der Menscheit*) from the curse of sin." The one who could bear such a load of sin, Wedel continued, must be both sinless and also human (*ein Genosse des menschlichen Geschlechts*), "in order to represent humankind (*um für dieses Stellvertretend einstehen zu können*)."

He called the expiatory death of Christ "an eternally remarkable wonder of divine wisdom and love."[41] Such comments show that from the narrow perspective of explaining the meaning of the death of Christ, Wedel clearly adhered to the sacrificial theory of atonement with his one correction of Anselm. While he shared that orientation with the other figures of this study, his statement of atonement shows much more the nuances of a learned theologian.

Once he had anchored atonement firmly in the concept of a substitutionary sacrifice, Wedel also accommodated several motifs from Abelard's moral influence theory to explain how Jesus' work may become the possession of sinful humanity. Somewhat parallel to his evaluation of Anselm, he also called Abelard's theory one with "which much is true" but nonetheless "onesided (*einseitig*)." The problem was that Abelard placed "all the emphasis on the Love of God" and had a "lax" concept of sin.[42] At the same time, Wedel preserved Abelard's emphasis on love, calling it the "framework (*Rahmen*) which surrounds the sacrificial suffering of Christ."[43] The death of Christ is a revelation of the love of God. Jesus' atoning death enables God to be gracious "because Christ's unfathomable sacrifice of love bore the sins of humankind and has paid for our sins."[44]

In a further assimilation of an Abelardian motif, Wedel acknowledged the necessity of a change in humankind's perception of God alongside the Anselmian focus on God's changing attitude toward sinful humanity. "It is not only a matter that God's relationship to man should change (that is, instead of being angry he now is merciful to man), but it is also a matter of a new relationship of man to God."[45] To pay the penalty of sin, Jesus had to enter the earthly realm and be subject to it. His power was somewhat freed of those limitations, however, in miracles, but primarily in his death and resurrection. Individuals then come to possess that power when Christ transfers to them the powers of his personal life which he exercised while on earth, and they receive the power of the Holy Spirit.[46]

However, Wedel's summary used more of Anselm than Abelard:

> Christ atoned for our sins and thus made our atonement, so that it may be properly said that God is reconciled; through the sacrifice he redeems us from the power and rule of sin. As sinners we see in God a God of wrath, but as soon as we accept the sacrificial death of Christ, we see in him a God of love. Through the acceptance of salvation, our atonement is completed.[47]

In addition to his analysis of Anselm and Abelard, Wedel took pains to reject what he considered salvation by human effort, primarily the effort of intellectual knowledge. Among such futile attempts to articulate salvation through human wisdom, he included the philosophical studies of Plato, Buddha's self-renunciation, the Stoic's excellence and virtue, and the more recent efforts to find truth in art and nature. However, no amount of knowledge can remove the guilt of humankind,[48] he said; salvation must come from God.

Wedel also noted and rejected other specific approaches to atonement. He acknowledged that the early church believed that Jesus' death had purchased humankind from the devil. He rejected this version of the classic view, saying that Christ's word cannot be understood as "ransom (*Lösegeld*)."[49] Wedel also rejected what he called a rationalistic approach. This theory would claim that Jesus' death was simply the final seal on a life dedicated to the good of humanity, and that he thus died as a martyr simply because of his calling, because he was a friend of his people. In that case, he wrote, Jesus' death would have meaning only for himself and would produce no new relationship between humankind and God.[50] In addition, Wedel critiqued the Socinians, who attacked Christ's high priestly office and shared the Pelagian error that sin is only a mistake in training. He noted and rejected more recent philosophical efforts by Schleiermacher, Kant, Hegel, and Ritschl which variously emphasize love, deny the wrath of God, and empty the cross of its meaning.[51]

In contrast to all other subjects of this study, Wedel presented a nuanced espousal of the satisfaction theory of atonement. He discussed a variety of approaches to atonement by name, and responded with systematic questions in mind. None of that theological processing, however, seems particularly impacted by his assumptions about *Gemeindechristentum* or the rejection of violence. On the surface, his comments about atonement seem to be much in line with the classic evangelical discussion of atonement. Yet this description of Wedel's views on atonement theory does not reflect the real orientation of his thought: *Gemeindechristentum* and the church.

Johannes Moser

While Johannes Moser never mentioned Anselm or referred to any theory of atonement by name, he clearly had a sacrificial, penal substitutionary view. On the narrow question of the object of Jesus' death, he clearly understood it within framework of required punishment for having broken prescribed law. In the first half of the two-part article "Über die Wehrlosigkeit,"[52] he discussed atonement explicitly. It supplied the foundation for a rather literalistic reading of other aspects of Old Testament history and prophecy.

Moser said that the Mosaic Law was a harsh taskmaster, demonstrating to the Israelites their sinfulness and causing them to desire a Redeemer (*Erlöser*). The law still exercises that function, he wrote, while the resultant consciousness of sin makes it impossible to face God freely and unafraid. That sense of sin caused Paul to rue his miserable condition and to value the Redeemer highly. Moser then called the redemption of fallen humanity from this unhappy and sinful state the "central characteristic of the entire Scripture."[53]

Front page of July 16, 1908, issue of The Pandora Times, with two-column story and picture on the death of Johannes Moser. Headline, top left, reads, "Rev. John Moser Called Home." The article stated that Moser's funeral at the St. John Mennonite Church "was no doubt the largest ever held there, as 500 persons, by actual count, could not gain admittance" while "by actual count" there were 385 rigs conveying persons who attended the service.

Heidi Sommer; *The Pandora Times*, from Don Schneck

The various trials and tribulations which sinners encounter constitute one of the ways by which God shows sinners their sinful state and need for redemption. According to Moser's demonstration of this function of tribulation within the Old Testament, it made a substitutionary suffering by Jesus inherently necessary. Adam and Eve no doubt regretted greatly their fallen circumstances and fate. In the midst of that regret, then, God promised a future Redeemer. That promise carried God's children throughout Old Testament history, while the Mosaic Law served as the ongoing reminder of their need for the future Redeemer. The heavy-burdened hearts (*bedrängte Menschenherz*) waited

Heidi Sommer

Gravestone of Johannes Moser and his wife, Anna Lehman, in the cemetery of St. John Mennonite Church, one mile east of Pandora, Ohio.

in hope for the one whom all the prophets proclaimed, "the one who would bear our sins in our place."[54] The Redeemer described by Moser was clearly a substitutionary one, and Jesus' death was submission to the penalty required by the law.

A bit later, Moser returned to the theme of Christ's substitutionary suffering. He noted the difficult path which the Redeemer had to take to lead sinners back to the throne of grace. Jesus as the high priest, who was like humanity in all things except sin, "had to take up in our place the battle against all the power of death and hell; in our place he had to carry the guilt and feel the pain of sin."[55]

For Moser, the reconciliation and forgiveness (*Vergebung und Versöhnung*) made possible by the death of Jesus provide the basis for the calming of a sin-troubled heart. A sinful person truly finds rest only in the justification (*Rechtfertigung*) which Christ accomplished. For this reason, Paul valued grace so highly.[56]

Moser's most complete explanation for the death of Christ appeared in the essay "Über die Wehrlosigkeit." Describing atonement in the retributory, penal framework was not limited to that article, however. It was a position which Moser retained and referred to a number of times, virtually to the end of his years of writing. In articles confirming the reality of human sin and of the devil, Moser stated again the idea that under the Old Testament and old covenant, God punished evil. That led some in Israel to hope for the coming Redeemer, who would make mercy possible.[57]

A significant characteristic of unbelief, he thought, was the opinion that the penal suffering of Jesus was unfair or made God out to be a harsh judge.[58] While unbelievers may declare it unjust and foolish "that one must do penance for the sins of others," it is not nonsense when it is done out of mercy and love.[59] Elsewhere, the language of the satisfaction theory occurred without reference to the framework of law and retaliation in comments Moser made on the Lord's Supper. Each taste of bread and wine is a recollection of "justification, purification, salvation, redemption, etc. . . . . A remembrance that with his body and blood he purchased us in a costly way."[60]

Moser's comments on atonement contained hints of other motifs. In "Über die Wehrlosigkeit," his reference to the high priest noted the battle against death and hell, with an implicit assumption that the battle was won. There is, however, no reference to the resurrection as the source or emblem of victory. The following sentence added the motif of love. He declared that Jesus' entire being taught and demonstrated love for sinners. The words of forgiveness he spoke on the cross testified to his divine origin and mission.[61] Thus Moser's orientation within a sacrificial view of atonement was not merely a narrow focus on the element of substitution. It is clearly an Anselmian view, however, without explicit reference to other theories of atonement. At that point he was quite like his contemporaries.

In terms of the satisfaction motif, Moser's position on atonement was perhaps remarkable only for his desire to see the biblical material as a whole. That emphasis appears in his belief that because of the repeated punishment they experienced, the Israelites would be waiting anxiously for the one who would suffer and die for them. As was true for figures already discussed, Moser's use of penal substitutionary atonement imagery clearly aligns him with evangelicals on that issue. At the same time, this observation does not account for that which truly characterizes his thought. As chapters 3 and 4 demonstrated, Moser's regulating principles came from the nonresistant church, which posed a visible contrast to the social order. The heart of his doctrine of atonement was the nonresistance of Jesus.

John M. Brenneman

Brenneman clearly assumed the satisfaction theory of atonement, and made it an integral part of his theology. He believed that Jesus' death paid the penalty for sin and thus enables the sinner to escape from deserved punishment. Yet in spite of the vivid language of satisfaction, Brenneman did not refute any other theories of atonement, or even appear aware that there were other ways to approach atonement doctrine.

Brenneman's first article in the first issue of John F. Funk's new periodicals[62] dealt with atonement. Following an assertion that "sin and iniquity made a separation between God and man," he wrote, "Christ is the mediator between God and man (1 Tim. 2:5); and by offering up himself, and shedding his precious blood upon the cross, he has made such a full and complete atonement (*vollkommene Versöhnung*) for sinful man, that the apostle Peter was perfectly safe . . . to pronounce peace upon 'all that are in Christ Jesus.' "[63]

Brenneman's essay "The Unanswerable Question of the Great Salvation"[64] made his satisfaction atonement motif quite explicit. He took the title from Hebrews 2:3, which asks, "How shall we escape if we neglect so great salvation?"[65] What one cannot escape if one neglected salvation, he said, is the deserved punishment of death. Adam's fall placed all people under the power of Satan, sin, death, and condemnation. God's law established the provisions violated by these sinners, as well as the proscribed penalty. "The law imposed a penalty upon the transgressor; for if any one transgressed the law of Moses, he must die, without mercy, under two or three witnesses." Later in the essay, Brenneman added, "I think the passages quoted should be sufficient to convince us that there is, surely, great danger of punishment, from which the disobedient cannot escape. . . . It is terrible for all impenitent sinners to fall into the hands of the living God."[66] Salvation then means to be rescued from the danger of punishment, and to be in a "condition of safety, security, happiness, and blessedness."[67]

The obvious way to escape the punishment decreed by God's law, according to Brenneman, was to accept Christ's satisfaction of the demand of the law as one's own deliverance. He said that after Jesus had proclaimed salvation and finished his life on earth, Jesus "permitted himself to be nailed to the cross by the hands of sinful men, where he sacrificed his holy innocent life and precious blood, for our ransom, and propitiation for our sins and for the sins of the world (*zur Bezahlung und Versöhnung für unsere und der ganzen Welt Sünde*)."[68] "He will forgive us our sins, if in faith and a penitent mind, we turn to him, and he

will make us pure and holy through his Spirit and the blood of propitia
tion (Versöhnungsblut). He also makes us free from the condemnation
of sin, and no longer holds us accountable for them."[69] How can we neglect such great salvation? Brenneman asked. "If we are not eternally
saved, it is our fault, for God hath done his part."[70]

One other text demonstrates clearly Brenneman's explicit acceptance of the satisfaction atonement motif. In "An Encouragement to
Penitent Sinners and Joy over Their Conversion," an essay that appeared in both English and German versions, he posed and answered
the question of how sinners are justified. Following a citation of Romans 3:24, 28 on being justified by faith apart from the law, he added
an explanation: "To be justified then means to receive the full pardon
and forgiveness of our sins, and by faith in Christ, and through, or on account of his atoning blood to be received into the favor of God as just or
righteous."[71]

Such a comment demonstrates Brenneman's clear acceptance of
the satisfaction motif of atonement. That conclusion becomes even
more certain when one notes that the quoted statement appeared only
in the English text, as an addition to the earlier German version.[72]
When he thought of adding glosses to biblical texts, those explanations
moved in the direction of making the satisfaction motif more explicit.[73]

Brenneman did not at all flinch from the fact that the satisfaction
theory of atonement clearly casts God in the role of judge and inflicter
of punishment. In a statement of "Good Advice to the Young," he admonished youth to remember especially that the God who loves them
is also "a sin-punishing God, where sin is not forsaken and heartily repented of." While God is a "sin-pardoning Creator" for the penitent
and for those who truly believe, such a God dare not show mercy to the
unrepentant:

> You must remember him to be just what and as he is, namely, a holy and
> just Creator, who will in no wise clear the guilty, or save sinners in any oth-
> er way than upon the conditions laid down in his holy and infallible
> word. . . . Learn to know his true character, namely, that he is a sin-
> punishing God, and that he "resisteth the proud," and will punish all those
> who forget him.[74]

His article, "The Unanswerable Question," emphasized the possibility of punishment.

> Our text clearly implies that there is great danger before us, from which
> the careless and unconcerned who disregard this proffered salvation can-

not possibly escape. . . . There is really before us a great danger, a terrible punishment, from which all impenitent, unbelieving, and those who only make a show of religion . . . cannot escape.[75]

Following a chronicle of biblical examples of divine punishment, Brenneman wrote, "I think the passages quoted should be sufficient to convince us that there is, surely, great danger of punishment, from which the disobedient cannot escape."[76]

In addition to these explicit references to the satisfaction motif in Brenneman's writings, scattered throughout his corpus are comments too numerous to mention where the satisfaction motif is apparent as an underlying assumption. The way he referred to the Lord's Supper also reflected the satisfaction motif. In most of his numerous trip reports, he described participation in the Supper as "a commemoration of our crucified Redeemer and Savior (*Gedächtmahl unseres gekreuzigten Erlösers und Seligmachers*)," or in memory of the "sufferings and death of our blessed Redeemer."[77]

Heidi Sommer

Consideration of one other text completes the description of Brenneman's atonement theology in its narrow focus. In "Das Osterlamm,"[78] he discussed the Israelite Passover Lamb as a type of Christ. Along with the fact that the lamb and Christ were both without blemish, innocent and blameless, the blood of each also saves and protects from punishment. His description of that saving blood identified the punishing God of the satisfaction motif.

Gravestone of John M. Brenneman in cemetery of Salem Mennonite Church, near Elida, Ohio.

Thus he [the Lord] will pass over and spare all those who are marked and sprinkled with the blood of the lamb on the doorposts of their hearts, should He one day come with a great plague in order to punish all those who are still in their original, sinful condition, and have not yet been purified of their sins through the sprinkled blood.[79]

The material of this section demonstrates conclusively that when analyzed in terms of the traditional atonement categories, John M. Brenneman assumed and used only the satisfaction theory of atonement in a penal substitutionary form. At the same time, that description does not relate what truly characterized Brenneman's thought: the humble, nonresistant church, which focused on the saved and obedient life of the believers.

John Holdeman

Quite like the other individuals of this study, John Holdeman assumed and accepted the satisfaction theory of atonement. However, his rather mechanical and stilted description of it went beyond any of them in expounding on the details of the legal satisfaction of God's broken law. He had a much greater stress than the other men on the penal dimensions of Jesus' atoning death. Holdeman's earliest major statement of the transaction occurs in the first chapter of his *History of the Church of God*, where it is an integral part of the story of creation and Fall.

Creation began in heaven with the angels, some of whom fell and are irrevocably lost.[80] A fallen angel then tempted Adam and Eve, causing them to fall. Since God did not want them to remain in that lost state, he promised them a Messiah, who would redeem them from their sins. Those who believed the promise were restored to the status of sons of God. Eventually there was more falling away, until only eight righteous persons remained, the family of Noah. While the flood eliminated all the wicked for a time, Satan again caused the fall of some of the sons of God and propagated his evil kingdom with them. Nonetheless, God always retained his seed and his children, and the special covenant with Abraham gave them adoption, law, glory, and the service of God.

Prior to Christ, the children of God knew that God's justice demanded death as the penalty for sins. Presumptuous sinners paid for their sins with their own deaths. Animal deaths covered inadvertent sins, while they waited for the time when Christ's death would pay for

Clarence Hiebert

Two views of writing desk owned by John Holdeman.

210 / Keeping Salvation Ethical

the sins of the whole world. The animal deaths thus served as a type of the future offering of Christ. The children of God were saved on the basis of their faith that the Messiah would indeed pay their penalty for them at some future time.[81] No sin, guilt, or penalty was actually covered, however, until Christ's death. Before the giving of the law to Israel, each person could function as his own priest in offering animal sacrifices. After God elected Israel as his priestly nation, he chose priests from the tribe of Levi to offer sacrifices for all. These animal sacrifices continued in accordance with the law, until Christ's once-for-all sacrifice eliminated the need for them. Thus Christ's death fulfilled all the offerings required by the law.

In Holdeman's theology, the death of Christ was clearly both substitutionary and penal. He referred repeatedly to the fact that "Jesus took our guilt on himself," or that "the punishment of our sin was laid on Him," or that "Jesus Christ must take the guilt upon Himself . . . to free us from our guilt." That results in "acquittal from our punishment of sins."[82]

The ideas of a penalty owed to God, and of God as the judge who metes out punishment, were central to Holdeman's outlook. His view of atonement reflected his view of God as judge. God's law established death as the penalty for sin. While an animal's death paid for sin committed in ignorance, "presumptuous sinners" paid for their sins with their own deaths. This punishment by death and the carrying out of "severe judgments" by God against wicked sinners "both among the Jews and Gentiles" represented the eternal punishment which God will dispense in the last day.[83]

Holdeman even implied that the time of the incarnation was determined on the basis of the time necessary for God to make that demonstration of justice and judgment. After that, the death of Christ could then make redemption available in its fullness.

> When God had sufficiently manifested His righteous judgments to introduce His gospel, then He sent His Son in the likeness of sinful flesh to condemn sin in our flesh through sin (that is, through His sin-offering, wherein He was made sin for us) and made Him to be sin for us.[84]

Even when Christ appeared to pay the penalty once for all, Holdeman's view of God remained essentially intact. Jesus had paid the Great Penalty. While God's provision for paying the penalty of sinners revealed that God has a merciful dimension, God remains a God of justice and judgment who demands death as the penalty for breaking divine law. What has changed is that through Christ, God's children can now escape the penalty. Since Jesus has paid the penalty once for all, the need for animal sacrifice was removed. God's children need no longer exercise capital punishment to show that God does not take sin lightly.

John Holdeman's view of atonement remained unchanged in *A Mirror of Truth*. He still understood atonement as substitutionary and penal.[85] He still appeared unaware of other theories of atonement. He contended vigorously for some positions which had sparked a great deal of controversy—for example, against baptism by immersion, and for a Christology resembling that of Menno Simons. However, he did not argue against another theory of atonement or in other

Clarence Hiebert

Gravestone of John Holdeman and his wife, Elizabeth, in cemetery of the Lone Tree Church of God in Christ, Mennonite congregation, McPherson County, Kansas.

ways indicate that he had knowingly chosen one among several options. Describing the penal substitutionary atonement was not a matter of rationalizing the choice of a doctrine but rather a discussion about the foundation and nature of salvation itself.

In similar fashion, *A Treatise on Redemption* also sketched a penal, substitutionary approach to atonement. This plan of salvation, "predicted by the prophets," sets out the idea that "sin must be paid with the price of death." "God, the Father of Christ, required Christ to die and taste death for every man, as a price for souls."[86] Quite clearly for Holdeman, to discuss salvation was still to discuss the penal substitutionary atonement.

However, at one juncture in *On Redemption*, he took one small step beyond his earlier atonement statements. He acknowledged, obliquely, that there were other theories of atonement. Without listing those theories and without responding to their points, he acknowledged their existence when he asserted,

> Though some professors of Christ deny that Christ died in our stead, and made an offering to satisfy God and His Father, to redeem and release us from sin, it is nevertheless so plainly taught in the Holy Scriptures, that I cannot see how any person who denies this can be a true christian [*sic*].[87]

It is obvious that Holdeman assumed a version of the satisfaction theory of atonement. But as has been said repeatedly, that observation does not adequately characterize his thought as depicted in chapter 4. Holdeman is basically oriented by the humble, converted, disciplined, nonresistant church.

Heinrich Egly

Like the previous figures, Heinrich Egly accepted and used the satisfaction atonement motif. Furthermore, like all but C. H. Wedel, and John Holdeman's indirect reference to other motifs, Egly did so without mention of Anselm, other atonement theories, or apparent awareness of atonement as a subject for theological rationalization. References to the atoning death of Christ are sprinkled throughout a majority of Egly's articles in *Herold der Wahrheit* and *Christlicher Bundesbote* as well as in his "Autobiography." These comments clearly reveal his orientation within a satisfaction motif, with variations of imagery but without a sharply articulated atonement theology.

Egly reported that Jesus' disciples had peace and comfort in him, since their sins were forgiven "through Jesus' blood."[88] As the Passover Lamb, Jesus was slaughtered on the cross and his blood shed "for forgiveness of sins."[89] In "Vom Friedensreich Jesu Christi,"[90] Egly referred several times to Christ's "offering" or "sacrifice"—in such expressions as "when Jesus made his offering on the cross (*die Zeit dass Jesus sein Opfer gethan hat am Kreuze*)" or "the sacrifice of Jesus (*das Opfer Jesu*)." Rather than finding salvation in works, self-will, or doing as one pleases, salvation is found only in the "sacrifice and merit of Christ (*das Opfer und Verdienst Christi*)" and his grace.[91]

The natural or still sinful self needs to be redeemed (*erlöset*) from sin.[92] Egly wrote that it was only after Pentecost that the disciples had true understanding of Christ's "work of salvation (*Werk der Erlösung*)," and that apart from the Spirit of Christ, no one understands "the merit of Christ and his sacrifice (*dem Verdienst Christi und seinem Opfer*)."[93] Egly called the Paschal Lamb whose blood protected the Israelites in the night before the exodus a type (*Vorbild*) which Christ fulfilled. When discussing Jesus as the true Passover Lamb, he used the terminology of the satisfaction motif. One who is not "reconciled (*versöhnt*) to God through the blood of the Lamb" is unworthy to partake of the Lord's Supper, the parallel to the Passover supper.[94]

In another article, Egly referred to the faith which carries to the soul the word about "reconciliation, Christ's sacrifice, and merit in his blood (*Versöhnung, Christi Opfer und Verdienst in Seinem Blute*)."[95] Egly criticized the so-called sleeping preachers[96] for lying because they supposedly claimed that "Christ had not paid for all our sins but only prepared the way to heaven." It is not true, he said against the sleeping preachers, that a soul can come "truly to redemption (*Erlösung*) and adoption as a child of God and Christ" through speaking.[97] In a quite clear reference to satisfaction, he shared his testimony: "Little by little God worked [in me] the faith to grasp Jesus Christ and his merit, sacrifice, and blood."[98]

Such language certainly puts Egly's assumed view of atonement within the orientation of the satisfaction theory. But it is not clear how much he thought in terms of an offering to an offended God, or payment of a substitutionary penalty which met a legal requirement. He also connected satisfaction language to the Passover and Israel's exodus from Egypt.

Material throughout Egly's "Autobiography" augments these observations.[99] One instance comes from his description of a conference session which met in Livingston County, Illinois, on 26 September 1882. He described the deliberations as though they constituted a consensus of the gathering. Two questions dealt directly with soteriology. The first question in the open discussion concerned the reason that all people are sinners. The second question dealt with the way to be made right before God. That process included acknowledgment of sin, belief in the gospel, asking God for grace and mercy and forgiveness of sins. Such things require divine initiative, not human initiative. Then he used language reflecting the satisfaction theory of atonement:

> But man cannot do it himself, it must be given to him by God. . . . Through faith we accept what Jesus Christ did for us, in whom we have redemption through His blood, the forgiveness of sins, according to the riches of His Grace, by believing and accepting this will take away the curse and the

Herold der Wahrheit.

Eine religiöse Monatsschrift.

„Wie lieblich sind die Füße derer, die den Frieden verkündigen.“

Jahrgang 14.—No. 12. Elkhart, Indiana, December 1877. Ganze Nummer 168.

First page and signature at end of
Heinrich Egly's "Vom Friedensreich
Christi" in Herold der Wahrheit *14.12*
(Dec. 1877): 1-3.

burden of sins. . . . Now the cloud is taken away and we are redeemed through the blood of our Great Shepherd, Jesus Christ, . . . for which we thank and praise Him for saving us from punishment and from serving sin.[100]

Another time, Egly referred to messages he had preached in the area of Allen-Putnam County, Ohio, where under his inducement a number of persons felt compelled to leave the old church—the congregation of Johannes Moser—because it did not teach the new birth.[101] After noting the baptism of eighteen persons, and then communion with them, Egly praised the Lord as the source of the results. "He is the Shepherd and Bishop of our souls, through His blood is our redemption and the forgiveness of sins."[102] That language again situates Egly's view of atonement within the satisfaction theory.[103]

One paragraph in the "Autobiography" summarized a traditional outline of salvation within the satisfaction theory. Egly noted the universality of sin and of human depravity, God's patient work to draw sinners back to himself, God's leading them to repentance, and making known through God's love what Jesus Christ had done for them. God then forgives sin "through the shed blood of Jesus Christ," and the sinner is now one of God's children and possesses the nature of Christ.[104]

While these brief comments by Heinrich Egly do not lay out in detail a doctrine of atonement, they indicate rather clearly that he assumed atonement within the framework of the satisfaction theory. But once again, it is necessary to observe that characterizing Egly only on the basis of an image of atonement does not accurately assess his thought. More telling is the material from chapter 4 in which his real emphasis on atonement was the fusion of atonement with a saved life marked supremely by love of enemies and nonresistance. Chapter 3 showed how later in life his focus on nonresistance abated.

Summary

Chapter 5 has examined the atonement motif for eight selected Mennonite and Amish writers of the last half of the nineteenth century. In every case, these writers assumed some version of the satisfaction atonement motif. Although it was not their language nor their agenda, they could all be classified as holding a general theory of satisfaction atonement, and as working with what Charles Finney called public justice rather than distributive justice. Those observations, if they were all that we knew, would locate Mennonite and Amish theology squarely within the theological camp of Protestant orthodoxy and conservative or evangelical Protestantism.

At this level, the assertions of Harold S. Bender and others are correct that "all the American Mennonite groups without exception stand upon a platform of conservative evangelicalism in theology, being thoroughly orthodox in the great fundamental doctrines of the Christian faith such as . . . the atonement by the shedding of blood."[105] However, chapters 3 and 4 show the inadequacy of such a characterization. While their atonement doctrine, when measured against the classic images, does align these eight men with evangelicalism, the observation in no way identifies what is distinct or unique in the outlook of these Mennonite and Amish writers.

My discussion has arrived at this one conclusion on the relationship of Mennonite and Amish theology to the theology of the evangelical wing of Protestantism. Questions in other areas are still open. Chapter 6 develops briefly a historical culmination that was reached only in the epoch following the nineteenth-century focus of this study.

6

The Separation
of Atonement and Ethics

Throughout this book we have observed the link which Mennonites and Amish attempted to maintain between atonement and ethics.
For the most part, the individuals surveyed did maintain that bond. At
the same time, the analysis pointed toward two different ways in which
ethics had the potential to become separated from theology: via doctrine, and via crisis conversion. While the beginning stages of that separation appeared in different ways in Wedel and Egly, the situation actualized itself to a much greater extent among those individuals who
were more impacted by the confrontation with modernity at the turn of
the century. Two cases illustrate that development.

John S. Coffman

The writings of John S. Coffman (1848-99) provide one clear example. More than any other individual, Coffman made revivalism acceptable to the Mennonite Church. While he was active during the last
two decades of the century, so that his career overlapped with several
of the eight individuals of this study, three points highlight the difference between the more modern outlook of Coffman and that of the
eight subjects on which this study focuses.

First, Coffman was aware of competing theories of atonement, and
he rejected all of them except for the satisfaction theory, which he accepted with emphasis on the vicarious and substitutionary nature of
Christ's death.

Second, and more significant, while he clearly believed that nonresistance belonged ineradicably to the Christian life, he defined salvation primarily in terms of the escape from deserved punishment which is made possible by Jesus' vicarious death. "Through the atonement the soul is made to live in purity before God and is saved from banishment forever from God, which it has merited through sin."[1] When he did explain an ethical dimension to the substitutionary atonement, it was not, as the majority of writers did in this study, via a stress on the saved life as validating salvation, or through an affirmation that without a righteous life one has not appropriated the death of Christ and is not saved. Instead, Coffman stressed that the righteous living of obedience to the commands of Christ was what one owed to Christ as the result of having *already been saved* by Christ from the deserved penalty of sin.

Third, Coffman introduced the term "restriction" as a separate category in which to put the commands of Christ such as nonresistance, not seeking vengeance, nonswearing of oaths, and not being conformed to the world.[2] This development allowed salvation, having one's penalty paid by Christ's death, to go in one category; then how one acted, ethics, went into another category (the restrictions), what one offered to Christ as an obedient response to salvation.

In effect, the restrictions *moved ethical issues from the heart of the gospel to its periphery,* making them questions one discussed after one was saved. When one compares these three aspects of Coffman's thought with the writers in this study, it is clear that the potential separation of ethics from the theology of atonement and salvation displayed by our eight writers had actualized itself in the thought of John S. Coffman.[3]

Daniel Kauffman

A complete separation of atonement and nonresistance appeared quite graphically over the course of the three volumes of Bible doctrine written or edited by Daniel Kauffman (1865-1944).[4] The evolution of thought through these three volumes reflects the increasing influence of the modernist-fundamentalist controversy on Mennonite theology of that epoch.

His 1898 *Manual of Bible Doctrines* still has a good deal in common with the subjects of this current study. With allowance for Kauffman's greater awareness of theological discussions and a more comprehensive outline, Kauffman still stressed such things as the necessity of conversion and a changed and righteous life, and of repentance as the beginning of that life.

Kauffman's minimal treatment of atonement subordinated it to repentance and conversion. He used John S. Coffman's category of "restriction" for nonresistance and did not discuss nonresistance as a part of atonement. Yet he did consider peace and nonresistance to be inseparable dimensions of the religion of Jesus. "It is difficult to conceive how any professing Christian can get the idea that it is right for any one under any circumstances to harm his fellowman."[5]

In the 1914 text on *Bible Doctrine*, Kauffman's outline had shifted to reflect much more the beginning point of orthodox Protestantism. Atonement became an independent doctrine discussed in its own right, with the sacrificial view the only one judged to accord with Scripture and reason. "Restrictions" gained in status to become part of a section title. While the restriction of nonresistance was a "fundamental principle of the Gospel as taught by our Savior,"[6] Kauffman made no real effort to spell out how nonresistance belonged to the gospel. It had become a principle to accept on the authority of Jesus, after one had accepted Jesus' penalty-paying death.

In 1928 the third volume, *Doctrines of the Bible*, atonement as a doctrine was still prominent, with separately titled paragraphs on Jesus' death as ransom payment, propitiation, substitute, and advocate. Erroneous views of atonement were rejected in favor of a correct view, which had to make adequate provision for cleansing by blood through Christ's "vicarious suffering" and "substitutionary sacrifice." While the term "restriction" barely appeared,[7] nonresistance was discussed only in a chapter listed under the category of "Christian life." There was no mention at all of nonresistance in the earlier sections that dealt with issues related to atonement and salvation.

In other words, over the three decades represented by his three volumes, Kauffman's theology devolved from one which still had significant aspects in common with the nineteenth-century writers to a theology which appears to have fallen sway to the very error that the nineteenth-century writers feared. Kauffman came to see atonement as an independent doctrine. Thus one could discuss the essence of salvation based on atonement without dealing with the nature of the saved life. A potential danger that the nineteenth-century writers sought to avoid had come to fruition in the theology of Daniel Kauffman.

Summary

Along with this description, it needs to be pointed out clearly that in none of these instances of potential or actual theological separation of ethics and nonresistance from the heart of the gospel did any of the individuals explicitly reject or even question nonresistance. All, including Heinrich Egly and Daniel Kauffman, whose writings reflect the separation most clearly, maintained a commitment to nonresistance, love of enemies, and forsaking of vengeance, as part of the normal expectations for Christians. What changed, eventually, was the way in which they supported nonresistance, and the way they described its relationship to atonement, the work of Christ. Chapter 7, below, will underscore the problematic dimension of that change.

7
Conclusion

Thus far, this extended essay has analyzed past experience. In focusing on the theology of nineteenth-century Mennonite and Amish leaders, it fits into the category of study sometimes called the history of doctrine. It has asked questions of doctrine and analyzed the theology of individuals who, with the exception of C. H. Wedel, did not pose the issues in this form. The answers to those questions have enabled the description of a number of heretofore uncharted vistas of Mennonite and Amish theology.

Asking such theological questions of nineteenth-century people is also a new experience for people today. It has been assumed that leaders from the epoch covered by this study had little to contribute to the modern theological agenda, at least little that was interesting or significant. This final segment presents a variety of observations and conclusions for the contemporary believers church. I have drawn them from my analysis of atonement theology and salvation in the works of these particular eight nineteenth-century Mennonite and Amish writers and preachers. These judgments are offered with due awareness that extending the research to additional subjects might well bring different nuances to the discussion.

A Significant Theological Legacy
With the exception of C. H. Wedel, the subjects of this study did not have a systematic theology as scholars have come to understand it. These nineteenth-century writers did not attempt to develop an all-encompassing, comprehensive outline of systematic theology, and they did not deal with theology as an abstract entity possessing a validity in and of itself. While Holdeman came closer than the others, except for

Wedel, Holdeman was still listing and describing his traditional beliefs more than developing an integrated systematic theology.

Nonetheless, this essay has demonstrated that these self-taught writer-preachers attempted to think systematically and logically about their beliefs and the Christian life. Their writings and reflections contained a great deal of theology. All of them had presuppositions, a received Mennonite faith, which they sought to apply systematically to faith and life. They have left a significant theological legacy upon which late twentieth-century people so inclined can draw.

Wedel for Gemeindechristentum, Not State-Church Christendom

In contrast to the other seven figures of this study, the writings of C. H. Wedel displayed a good deal of what we now think of as the methodology and content of systematic theology. He discussed presuppositions, examined alternative views, and made a reasoned explanation and defense of his position. Hence, Wedel belongs more to the beginning stages of the modern project of developing a systematic theology for Mennonites than to the end of premodern Mennonite theology.

On the other hand, as indicated, Wedel shared with the other subjects of this study the presupposition that learnings from the Anabaptist-Mennonite tradition should shape the contemporary face of the church. His integral assumption was that one builds on the Anabaptist-Mennonite tradition precisely because Mennonite theology and practice was based on the New Testament and therefore displayed significant differences from state-church or Christendom theology. This impulse received the most complete expression in Wedel's depiction of *Gemeindechristentum*, an approach that allows one to learn from all of church history while remodeling those learnings within a historical construct shaped by free-church Anabaptism.

Satisfaction Theory, General Atonement

As chapter 5 demonstrated, when the question of atonement was posed in terms of the classic theories of atonement, it is obvious that all these nineteenth-century Mennonite and Amish subjects espoused some form of the satisfaction or substitutionary theory of atonement, associated traditionally with the name of Anselm. To explain atonement, they used different sets of terminology and a variety of images. They envisioned Jesus' substitutionary death sometimes as satisfying an offended God and sometimes as paying the penalty required by God's law. Yet in every instance, these men espoused an understanding of atonement fitting within the cluster of views grouped as satisfaction or substitutionary theories.

To a man, their particular positions were located in the camp of those who envisioned Christ's death as a *general atonement* which all sinners might claim. They did not espouse a particular atonement in which Christ died for the sins of the elect only. In large part, their statements about atonement were unpolemical, given with no explicit reference to Anselm and with little or no awareness of the history of atonement doctrines. Wedel is the only one who analyzed competing theories of atonement. Holdeman acknowledged their existence but did not discuss them. For the most part, one has much the sense that when the nineteenth-century Mennonite and Amish writers assumed and used the language of satisfaction or substitution, they believed themselves to be explaining the basis of salvation itself.

They may have assumed the satisfaction atonement theory rather than explicitly justifying it. Yet one could argue on the basis of the findings of chapter 5 that Mennonites should be grouped theologically with evangelicalism. If the content of chapter 5 were all that we knew about the outlook of these eight Mennonite and Amish leaders, it would make sense to define them primarily as evangelicals and to emphasize that Mennonite theology is evangelical theology. But we know more.

Atonement, Nonresistance, and the Lived Faith

The nineteenth-century Mennonite and Amish subjects of this study held to nonresistance and the lived faith as the historic center and foundation of the Christian faith. This characterized the Anabaptist movement of that century. It affects how these writers linked atonement and obedience.

Obedience More Distinctly Mennonite Than Satisfaction Theory

The use of the language of satisfaction or substitution was non-polemical and unselfconscious. This fact opens the door to a different conclusion. The satisfaction or substitution theory of atonement should not be considered a distinctly Mennonite position. It is not the one inherently necessary view on this theme for Mennonites to espouse. These subjects all assumed the satisfaction atonement motif. Yet if one paints them chiefly as Anselmian or as holding the satisfaction theory of atonement, that does not adequately characterize their theology.

As the analysis of chapter 4 demonstrated, atonement filled a specific theological niche for these writers. It was not a doctrine that could be isolated and made to stand alone. When these eight figures talked about atonement, it constituted the initial step of a process that reached culmination only with a life of *obedience* to the commands of Jesus. To define their theology of atonement as Anselmian or satisfaction or substitutionary, as though their atonement motif alone defined their emphases, would be to skew their theology in precisely the manner they wished to avoid. Stating the problem in a modern way, to lift out atonement alone would be to detach that part of theology from ethics, which is also supposed to be theological. However, separating ethics from theology was precisely one of the things these eight men most wanted to avoid.

Nonresistance a Touchstone of the Saved Life

What provided the specific orientation for the theology of these eight writers was the material identified in chapters 3 and 4 (above), which described the context in which they put atonement. One overarching presupposition shared by all was the belief that commitment to Christ—being Christian—would inevitably and of necessity manifest itself in the way an individual lives. That lived expression of Christian faith was modeled on the life and teaching of Jesus.

Further, as a specific application of the model and teaching of Jesus, all eight subjects agreed that nonresistance, love of enemies, and refusal of military service constituted an intrinsic and clear dimension of that saved life. They did differ on certain other dimensions or details of the saved life, such as appropriate dress, the exercise of discipline in the congregation, holding Sunday schools, or the extent to which the church should use the form of revivalism. Nevertheless, all were committed to a visible Christian life.

This study frequently used *nonresistance* to show how inherited doctrine impacted other dimensions of their theology. For example, commitment to nonresistance constituted one of the reasons which led Moser, Egly, and Holdeman to reject premillennialism, even when they did not fully fathom or know how to deal with the specific arguments about millennialism and predictive prophecy.[1] Commitment to nonresistance was one of the impulses which led Wedel to look for an alternative to state-church Christendom. Seven of the individuals in this study explicitly integrated nonresistance to some extent into their atonement theologies, though in differing ways. Wedel, the most progressive, located it in his widest perspective but did not make it a specific dimension of his atonement theology.

Theology Expressed in the Lived Faith

To state the last point in another way, the analysis of chapter 4 clearly revealed that Mennonites and Amish were not creedal churches. They did not define the true church in terms of abstract beliefs, and measure faithfulness on the basis of wholehearted assent to particular doctrinal formulations. It is this noncreedal and nondogmatic orientation and the stress on a *lived faith* which has sometimes been interpreted as the absence of a recognizable Mennonite theology. While they had a theology, it was the obedient life which comprised and expressed the distinct dimensions of their theology.

How Mennonites Differ from So-called Evangelicals

In contrast to the eight subjects of this study, many Christian traditions do not make a lived faith the integrative principle of theology and the context within which to consider atonement. Most do not hold to nonresistance as a specific application of the lived faith. However, it was that linking of salvation theology (soteriology) with ethics which was a distinctive characteristic of the theology of these nineteenth-century Mennonite and Amish writers.

It is appropriate to identify historic Mennonite theology as a particular manifestation of the believers-church or free-church or alternative-church tradition. This is better than identifying historic Mennonite theology in terms of the evangelical wing of majority Protestantism (the possibility posed above). Suppose one stresses the commonality of Mennonite and Amish theology with a so-called evangelical theology that rejects nonresistance as lived faith. Then one has already moved to the periphery the central assumptions of all eight subjects of this study. Such "evangelical" doctrine is not the good news, the gospel of the Gospels and the rest of the New Testament, the evangel proclaimed by the Mennonite and Amish subjects in this study.

Instead, it is crucial that we depict Mennonite and Amish theology in terms of the believers-church or alternative-church tradition. Such a classification enables one to preserve the specificity of the theological tradition, and to *retain nonresistance and the lived faith as the intrinsic center and foundation of Christian faith.* Precisely this is the position of the eight subjects of this study. My analysis has demonstrated that the Anabaptist-Mennonite tradition does indeed have an identifiable way to do theology, distinct from Protestant orthodoxy and evangelical theology.

Anabaptism Impacted by Pietism and Revivalism

The foregoing analysis of nineteenth-century theology of atonement has identified two different ways potentially to separate ethics from salvation theology: via doctrine, and via crisis conversion. These observations concerning the potential separation of soteriology and ethics, whether arising from doctrine or from a stereotyped conversion experience, have implications for the historical question about the impact of Pietism and revivalism on Mennonite and Amish churches. Seventeenth-century Pietism, which assumed orthodox theology and emphasized an experiential faith compatible with a revivalist conversion experience, has received both negative and positive reviews from Anabaptist-related historians and theologians.

Robert Friedmann argued that the influence of the experiential faith of Pietism helped Mennonites to abandon evangelization and to emphasize inner joy and outer peace with the world. He claimed that this became a substitute for the radical way of the cross in original Anabaptism. For Friedmann, the pietist influence meant "apparently, the gradual disappearance of that concrete Christianity which had been the goal of the original Anabaptists, and the substitution for it of an emotional Christianity which no longer caused the authorities of state or church any trouble." It paved the way for them to become "*die Stillen im Lande*."[2]

Ernst Crous seconded Friedmann's assessment of the differences between Pietism and Anabaptism.[3] Although Friedmann and Crous were not speaking about Heinrich Egly, their observations appear to fit the shift depicted in later Egly's focus on conversion apart from nonresistance.

Not surprisingly, writers who speak for Anabaptist groups with a root in Pietism have seen fewer problems with it than did Friedmann or Crous. Church of the Brethren theologian *Dale Brown* investigated such charges as subjectivism, individualism, withdrawal, and other worldliness in the founders of Pietism, primarily Philipp Jakob Spener (1635-1705) and August Hermann Francke (1663-1727). Brown concluded that while the seeds of the problem are found in Spener and Francke, the founders themselves avoided the pitfalls. Thus modern Anabaptist groups can, with appropriate awareness of the negative potential, properly own the inherited, positive dimensions of Pietism.[4]

Martin Schrag developed a similar rehabilitation of Pietism, using Brethren in Christ origins in colonial North America as the basis for his conclusions. Schrag's intent, like Brown's, was to show that outright acceptance or rejection of Pietism by Anabaptists was not the only option, and that Pietism ought not to be considered inherently dangerous to Anabaptism.[5] The rehabilitation efforts by both Brown and Schrag assumed what *Carl Bowman* called a "balanced" view, that it is possible to find a "creative tension between Anabaptism and Radical Pietism with neither side getting the upper hand."[6]

Recent Mennonite writers have also rehabilitated Pietism vis-à-vis Mennonitism. *Richard MacMaster* described a German pietist subculture of colonial Pennsylvania in which the Mennonite churches "swam as fish in water." The Mennonites and Brethren maintained nonresistance and accepted social ostracism during the Revolutionary War. Hence, it is quite clear, MacMaster showed, that participation in the pietistic subculture of Pennsylvania did not undercut their willingness to suffer nor their commitment to historic Anabaptist principles.[7]

Similarly, *Theron Schlabach* showed that Pietism and pietist forms were thoroughly intermixed with Anabaptist emphases among nineteenth-century Mennonites, and thus "helped to lay a groundwork for commitment to Mennonite tradition."[8] When Carl Bowman surveyed the efforts by Brethren scholars to rehabilitate Pietism, he included the analyses by Mennonite scholars (as identified above). He assessed the outcome as attempting to show that the best alternative was a balanced blend of Pietism and Anabaptism.[9]

Carl Bowman, however, posed an alternative to these efforts either to identify Anabaptism or Pietism as the essential one, or to discover the proper balance or blend of the two. Previous scholarship has assumed, Bowman argued, that the two movements were "religious crosscurrents," one of which usually prospered at the expense of the other, with a few commendable instances of balance between the two. In contrast to the crosscurrents assumption, Bowman suggested that Pietism and Anabaptism are "mutually reinforcing currents." This approach would explain how "heightened (or lessened) spirituality may produce heightened (or lessened) obedience and church commitment; radical spirituality may yield radical or dissenting religious practices; and that such practices may reciprocally nurture such spirituality."[10]

By showing how Holdeman or early Egly used a pietist-like, experiential impulse to reinforce commitment to nonresistance, my observations in chapters 3-4 support Bowman's thesis that Pietism and Anabaptism can reinforce each other. At the same time, by showing how an emphasis on conversion gave the later Egly a way to focus on salvation apart from nonresistance, my analysis also demonstrates how pietist or revivalist experiential emphases can undercut historic Anabaptist Mennonite emphases. I suggest that the historical argument about the impact of Pietism is not, in the first order, a function of Pietism itself. It depends, rather, upon the prior understanding of the gospel and the church in which the pietist modes and methods are adopted.

Suppose the pietist idiom is introduced into an ecclesiology and an understanding of the gospel which considers the social dimensions of salvation as intrinsic, with nonresistance and pacifism as the obvious test case. Then pietist forms can strengthen the commitment of individuals to that church. Figures of this study such as John Holdeman and John Brenneman illustrate this category, as does the early Heinrich Egly.

Suppose the understanding of the church and the gospel allows for the development of an inner and individual spirituality essentially complete within the individual and separated from ethical expression. Then in such cases, Pietism clearly has the potential to undercut the social components of the gospel and of lived Christian faith. The direction taken by the later Heinrich Egly illustrates this result. In previous chapters, I have shown how satisfaction and substitutionary atonement allow for salvation to become unhooked from ethics. This then constitutes part of the theological foundation for a church whose social ethics is separated from the understanding of salvation. In this situation, there is a definite change in ecclesiology.

The way in which a focus on some component of experiential faith can undercut a theology of peace and nonviolence has clear implications for the continuation of the contemporary peace church as a peace church. To maintain a tradition of pacifism and nonviolence, *the church needs to be explicit about its peace theology* rather than assuming that it will be included or subsumed under some other emphasis such as evangelism or spirituality. There is not a more important conclusion to draw from these pages.

Discipleship Without Loopholes

In none of the noted instances of potential or actual theological separation of ethics and nonresistance from the heart of the gospel did any of these eight subjects explicitly reject or even question nonresistance. This needs to be underscored. All, including Heinrich Egly, maintained a commitment to nonresistance, love of enemies, and forsaking of vengeance. They counted this as part of the normal expectations for all Christians. What changed, eventually, was the way in which they supported nonresistance, and the way they described its relationship to atonement in the work of Christ.

An Anabaptist Corrective to Western Atonement Theory
For the eight writers studied here, the real orienting principle of their theology was that a commitment to Jesus Christ must be lived out. A Christian expressed allegiance to Christ by *living like Christ and following his teaching*. All of these men shared this principle, which acted as a glue to hold together the two ideas of satisfaction atonement and nonresistance, even though in other theological traditions these two doctrines are not linked.

In most theological traditions, it is actually stressed that sinful humanity cannot follow the impossible ideal of Jesus' teaching and example. In that case, Jesus' propitiatory, substitutionary death as a penalty or payment covers the guilt of inadvertent failure to fulfill the impossible ideal. His death is also supposed to cover the guilt of a presumed necessary evil such as killing in war.

It made a difference when these Mennonite and Amish writers insisted that atonement and salvation must be expressed in a life that includes nonresistance. Their inherited Anabaptist emphasis on discipleship and a visible church provided a corrective to the satisfaction theory of atonement inherited from Western Christendom. In my view, this is the ecclesiology of Christus Victor (see chapter 2), correcting or modifying atonement images inherited from Christendom's ecclesiology and soteriology. It is this clear modification of the satisfaction, substitutionary view of atonement which makes most obvious why the distinct character of the theology of these individuals is not adequately identified by labeling them simply as "evangelicals." Doing the latter unjustifiably fuses them together with the conservative part of the spectrum of North American Protestantism.

Pacifism Marginalized If Mennonites Labeled Evangelical
To use a doctrine such as atonement to claim that Mennonites are actually part of evangelicalism has the potential to weaken the commitment to peace, nonresistance, and nonviolence as inherent dimensions of the gospel. A significant part of the Christian spectrum espouses the satisfaction theory of atonement while explicitly rejecting the Mennonite and Amish commitment to nonresistance and/or nonviolence. In a parallel way, a major part of the Christian spectrum espouses and requires a crisis conversion, in company with the older Heinrich Egly, but goes on to reject the belief that conversion to Christ must include nonresistance, love of enemies, and forsaking vengeance.

Suppose one appeals to a doctrine such as atonement or to a patterned conversion experience and takes that as the basis for claiming commonality with traditions which reject nonresistance and nonviolence. In so doing, one has already relegated the commitment to nonresistance and nonviolence to the periphery of the gospel and what it means to be Christian. To assert that one has full Christian identity with those who do not espouse pacifism is in effect to place the questions about the rejection of violence, nonresistance, and nonviolence outside of the central core of Christian beliefs.

Ethics Prior to the Rest of Theology

Thus nineteenth-century Mennonite presuppositions about the lived faith modified the classic atonement theology. The way this happened illustrates the truth of several recent statements about the relationship of ethics and the other theological disciplines. For one, it fits within *George Lindbeck's* description of a "cultural-linguistic" approach to doctrine. In Lindbeck's model, the "regulative principles" of a religion exist as a "grammar" that shapes the entirety of life and thought. It is not one's inner experience which produces doctrines. Instead, the inherited, communal realities shape one's inner experience and commitments. While inner and outer experiences exist within a dialectic relationship, it is the external which is prior to the inner. Lindbeck's model stresses the degree to which human experience is shaped by cultural and linguistic forms.[11]

In the case of these nineteenth-century Mennonites and Amish, their given was the nonresistant story of Jesus. They placed themselves into that story, which shaped their behavior and moved them to modify the received doctrine of atonement. They understood Jesus in terms of his story in the Gospels, rather than in terms of abstract doctrine or the legal transaction of satisfaction atonement. Precisely because of this, they assumed that claiming the name of Jesus meant to live like Jesus, to put themselves into his story. When they included themselves in the narrative of Jesus in this way, it was inconceivable that they could claim to accept Jesus and not live according to the teaching and example of Jesus. It would be akin to an athlete claiming to be fully committed to basketball while spending one's time playing on the school volleyball team.

A second major statement on the relationship of theology and ethics comes from *Stanley Hauerwas*. Influenced by Lindbeck, Hauerwas argued that it is not the case that we develop a theology, and then move on to develop the ethical implications of that theology. On the contrary, ethics, or the way one lives, gives expression to the ultimate values, that is, the theology to which one is really committed. Hauerwas related the oft-repeated legendary story of a resident of Shipshewana, Indiana, who was confronted by an evangelist and asked if he was saved. After some thought, the [Amish] Mennonite farmer wrote out a list of ten people who knew him. The Mennonite suggested that the evangelist ask these people whether he was saved, since he would not presume to answer for himself.[12]

The point is that Christian faith is lived, and that theology emerges as the Christian community's reflections on what it means to live under the reign of God. In contrast to the various ways of finishing a systematic theology and then proceeding to ethics, Hauerwas wrote,

> I wish to show that Christian ethics is not what one does after one gets clear on everything else, or after one has established a starting point or basis of theology; rather, it is at the heart of the theological task. For theology is a practical activity concerned to display how Christian convictions construe the self and the world.[13]

Using the framework depicted by Hauerwas, the nineteenth-century Mennonite and Amish writers were committed to the narrative of Jesus and assumed it as their normative tradition. They placed themselves within that story. When they talked about salvation, they did so by using the traditional, inherited language about satisfaction of penalty, and so on. However, their assumption about living within the story of Jesus required them to *modify the received atonement doctrine* so that it contained or reflected an ethical dimension, not really intrinsic to the satisfaction language. Their sense that a commitment to Christ was lived meant that the abstract theology of atonement should be restated in such a way as to give it a lived dimension.

James Wm. McClendon Jr. has written a third major statement which makes ethics intrinsic to theology. He uses a "baptist" perspective, preserving the historic term *Täufer* for what others have called "radical Reformation," "Anabaptist," "believers church," or "free church." McClendon has argued that the baptist perspective will produce a theology distinct from the theology developed by the churches of Christendom. McClendon's initial point is that the

> theology of the church is not the standpoint, basic point of view, theology of the world. The church's story will not interpret the world to the world's satisfaction. Hence there is a *temptation* . . . for the church to deny her "counter, original, spare, strange" starting point in Abraham and Jesus and to give instead a self-account or theology that will seem true to the world on the world's own present terms.[14]

McClendon summarized the relationship of the three traditional branches of theology. A primary characteristic of baptist theology is that ethics should come chronologically first, stating the common life of the community. Second, doctrine then describes and expounds the foundation of that common life. Third is apologetics.

> On this view, we begin by finding the shape of the common life in the body of Christ, which is for Christians partly a matter of self-discovery. . . . That is ethics. We continue with the investigation of the common and public teaching that sanctions and supports that common life by displaying its doctrinal height and breadth and depth. That is doctrine. And we end by discovering those apologetic and speculative positions that such life and such teaching call forth. That is philosophical theology or apologetics. Yet like the rest, the last-named of these . . . is without value except as it leads back to the new that comes in Christ.[15]

The Eight Subjects Did Have a Theology

These nineteenth-century writer-preachers *did* have a theology. This is shown in the way the eight individuals shaped atonement on the basis of their assumptions about the narrative of Jesus. From yet another perspective, the descriptive terminology of Lindbeck, Hauerwas, and McClendon makes this clear. With the exception of C. H. Wedel, it was not a systematic theology as that genre is used today. Nonetheless, they clearly had a theology, and they thought systematically about their beliefs and the Christian life, applying logically and devoutly their inherited assumptions about lived faith. Since not all Christian traditions make nonresistance an explicit and integral dimension of atonement theology, that specific combination is a distinctive characteristic of the theology of these nineteenth-century Mennonite and Amish writers.

So What Now?

With the nineteenth-century Mennonite and Amish writers, we still want to affirm a commitment to live within the story of Jesus. We affirm that the church founded on Jesus will pose a witness to the world, an embodied contrast to the world, a critique of the social order. We affirm that inherently part of the gospel of Christ is the good news about peace and reconciliation within the reign of God.

Developing a Theology for Mennonites

These observations all point to a very important implication for the contemporary task of cultivating an integrated theology for Mennonites. There are a number of calls for modern Mennonites to develop a systematic theology on the basis of the supposedly more "universal" or "catholic" creeds or formulas of Nicaea, Chalcedon, or the Cappadocian Fathers, which are shared with all of Christendom.[16]

However, we are not looking for the mere presence of a common item of Christology or atonement, or mere agreement with a formula held longer and by more people. That does not guarantee either completeness or truth or faithfulness. If such were the case, the present survey of nineteenth-century Mennonite leaders' use of the satisfaction theory of atonement would demonstrate that Mennonites belong in the camp of Protestant orthodoxy. In fact, this essay has demonstrated that historically, Mennonites represent another kind of theological tradition, one not properly accounted for by merely including them in one camp or another on the conservative side of the theological spectrum.

Mennonites and Amish have taken it seriously that in Jesus one sees the essence of the reign of God and the nature of God's work in the world. They made nonresistance or nonviolence an integral part of their discussion of the work of Christ. In that linking of atonement and nonviolence, they distinguished themselves from the orthodox tradition. They could not be part of an orthodoxy that used satisfaction atonement to save individual souls but removed ethics to an entirely different level of understanding, based on the prevailing social order rather than on Jesus and his gospel.

I maintain that the current development of a systematic theology for Mennonites should begin with the specific aspects of the Mennonite tradition, rather than with a more "universal" creed from another tradition. The foregoing analysis of eight nineteenth-century views of atonement shows that way of doing theology. Following the received pattern, this developing theology for Mennonites will not simply identify with some version of Christendom's theology. Instead, it will stress the way in which imitating Christ, rejecting violence, and loving enemies reshapes the doctrines held by the heirs of established-church Christendom.

When one defines contemporary theology for Mennonites in terms of some supposedly more universal catholic orthodoxy, this poses the same inherent danger as did (the later) Heinrich Egly's or Daniel Kauffman's separation of salvation and ethics. This is true even if it happens in another form. One may seek identity in terms of doctrine which does not make explicit the central emphases on the lived faith and nonviolence. But then these emphases are by definition relegated to the margin of the Christian life.

Further, the modern situation poses an additional challenge. Mennonites are becoming culturally assimilated and are much less of a Dutch-German-Swiss ethnic tradition. Hence, there are fewer visible reminders of the inherited idea that salvation and nonviolence are intrinsically connected. Without obvious reminders such as German language or plain clothing as boundary markers, it becomes much easier to focus on what is held in common with other confessions—an early creed, for example. That may allow the commitment to peace and nonviolence to slide to the periphery. It may give members permission to abandon that commitment altogether. Thus, in line with the pluralism and relativity of North American society, the historic commitment to nonviolence simply becomes an "option" for the few so inclined.

Theology from Within the Hermeneutical Community

It is both appropriate and necessary for the Mennonite churches to develop an identity that is no longer limited to a Dutch-German-Swiss ethnic identity. However, without the visible marks of ethnic distinction, it will be more necessary than ever to make explicit the inseparable nature of peace, nonviolence, and the gospel. As beginning principles, a systematic theology for the contemporary believers church will need clearly to articulate its commitment to live within the narrative of Jesus.

Stated another way, a modern theology for Mennonites needs decisively to acknowledge the hermeneutical community within which and from which theology is developed. With that commitment clearly in mind, we then move to express the theology and to examine the world from the perspective of that commitment to live within the story of Jesus. That is not a task restricted to ethnic Mennonites with Swiss, Dutch, or German surnames. It is an ecumenical task that engages all persons who claim the name of Jesus Christ.

Starting from Anabaptist-Mennonite Presuppositions

These eight individuals, as well as Coffman and Kauffman, did succeed in maintaining a commitment to nonresistance alongside satisfaction atonement. Since they did, some may argue that it is thus proved that satisfaction atonement does work for Mennonites, and that it ought to be retained and affirmed. My reply is to point out the assumption behind that argument. As indicated in chapter 2 with reference to American evangelicals, one can stand on satisfaction atonement and support war. Just as assuredly, Johannes Moser could argue that satisfaction atonement eventuated in absolute pacifism. One does not get to nonresistance and pacifism and rejection of the sword unless one makes it an assumption based on the narrative of Jesus prior to the discussion of atonement.

Thus, to argue that satisfaction atonement should be seen as compatible with pacifism and nonviolence is already to be developing theology on the basis suggested (two pages above, "Developing a Theology for Mennonites"). I called for us to begin with presuppositions from the Anabaptist-Mennonite tradition rather than from a creed or motif from a supposedly more universal tradition. When beginning from those presuppositions, we ought to be free to develop alternatives to the satisfaction theory which are true to the biblical story in general and to the narrative of Jesus in particular. Stated another way, if Mennonites do not share the ecclesiology of Christendom, they ought not to be obligated to accept the particular atonement motif that developed from Christendom's ecclesiology.

Developing Alternatives to the Satisfaction Theory

The satisfaction theory of atonement contains inherently the possibility that salvation become separated from ethics. The nineteenth-century Mennonite and Amish writers demonstrated that it is possible to keep the two patched together. However, if we truly believe that salvation in Jesus Christ does not depend on a specific theory of atonement, then we are free to explore other ways of expressing atonement issues and themes (see chap. 2, note 10). Theologians of the church should be free to look for better ways to express the theology of atonement, Christology, ethics, and the nature of the church. According to Hauerwas, this is "a practical activity concerned to display how Christian convictions construe the self and the world."

The task of a modern theology for Mennonites is precisely that of developing an understanding of atonement and Christology which reflects a commitment to live within the story of Jesus. Our nineteenth-century ancestors began that task, and this study has examined their efforts. We do not dishonor their efforts if instead of copying their product precisely, we search for a new formulation of atonement. Chapter 2, in the section "History of Atonement: Alternative Version," provides the foundation for a more biblical theology of atonement. That version assumes nonviolence, the church as a visible witness to the reign of God, the church as an alternative society to the church of Christendom that simply confirms the prevailing social order, and the understanding that salvation and ethics compromise two dimensions of an indivisible theological unity.[17]

A Specific Theology in Dialogue with Other Traditions

Approaching the development of a theology in this way is not a call for exclusiveness, nor is it a complete rejection of the "universal" or "catholic" creeds and formulas. These creeds and formulas contain important, inescapable dimensions of the Western theological tradition. With Chalcedon, it is necessary to confess that Jesus is of God and of humanity. As is implied in the formula of the Trinity developed by the three Cappadocians, it is necessary to confess that the God of Abraham and Isaac and Jacob is the God who raised Jesus and the God who is immediately present to the children of God today through the Spirit. The catholic creeds and formulas are correct in making those points.

However, the foregoing discussion of nineteenth-century Mennonite and Amish writers reminds us what it means to take seriously that Jesus is of God. It means understanding that the ethical dimensions of being Christian belong inherently, integrally, and inseparably to the discussion of the work of Christ. For the most part, the theology of Western Christendom has rejected this assumption. Yet this assumption is the specific dimension of the Anabaptist-Mennonite tradition that should shape *how* we discuss the issues contained in the supposedly universal, catholic creeds.

In their linking of atonement and nonviolence, the nineteenth-century Mennonite writers demonstrated that their primal orientation was not that of Western orthodoxy. That orthodoxy used satisfaction atonement to save individual souls, but removed ethics and thus nonresistance (if any) to an entirely separate level of understanding.

The foregoing analysis shows that the modern development of a systematic theology for Mennonites should begin with the specific aspects of the Mennonite tradition, rather than with a more "universal" creed from another tradition. Such a stance does not call for a rejection of learnings from the Western creedal tradition. It means, rather, that Anabaptist-Mennonite assumptions about discipleship, community, peace, and nonviolence will shape the way Mennonites discuss the issues contained in the classic statements.

Such an approach will give those who make these assumptions a specifically peace-church theology. That theology can certainly dialogue with other traditions. After all, they will be discussing the same issues. But the dialogue needs to be in a way that makes clear the assumptions which have truly oriented the historic Anabaptist-Mennonite tradition.

Notes

Abbreviations

BCM	Bethel College Monthly (English ed. of MBC)
CBB	Christlicher Bundesbote
CGR	The Conrad Grebel Review
HdW	Der Herold der Wahrheit (German ed. of HT)
HT	The Herald of Truth (English ed. of HdW)
MBC	Monatsblätter aus Bethel College (German ed. of BCM)
MQR	The Mennonite Quarterly Review
SCJ	School and College Journal (Bethel College)

Chapter 1: Introduction

1. Harold S. Bender, "The Mennonites of the United States," MQR 11.1 (Jan. 1937): 79.

2. For references, see note 4, below.

3. Bender, "Mennonites of the United States," 80.

4. For examples of these perspectives on Anabaptist and Mennonite theologizing, see John Horsch, Mennonites in Europe (Scottdale, Pa.: Mennonite Publishing House, 1942), 293-380, esp. 370-380; Bender, "Mennonites of the United States," 79-80; "Walking in the Resurrection," MQR 35.2 (Apr. 1961): 102-103; Cornelius Krahn, "Prolegomena to an Anabaptist Theology," MQR 24.1 (Jan. 1950): 6; John C. Wenger, Glimpses of Mennonite History and Doctrine (Scottdale, Pa.: Herald Press, 1949), 145-46, 173. Affirming the priority of the practical is Robert Friedmann, "Anabaptism and Protestantism," MQR 24.1 (Jan. 1950): 12-24; and The Theology of Anabaptism: An Interpretation, Studies in Anabaptist and Mennonite History, no. 15 (Scottdale, Pa.: 1973), 1-35. Ronald J. Sider argued that, in essence, Mennonites should combine the issues of the two lists into a longer, single list. See his "Evangelicalism and the Mennonite Tradition," in Evangelicalism and Anabaptism, ed. C. Norman Kraus (Scottdale, Pa.: Herald Press, 1979), 149-168. Recent statements stressing the importance of Anabaptist agreement with the classic views are Walter Klaassen, "Sixteenth-Century Anabaptism: A Vision Valid for the Twentieth Century?" CGR 7.3 (Fall 1989): 245-246; and C. Arnold Snyder, "Beyond Polygenesis: Recovering the Unity and Diversity of Anabaptist Theology," in Essays in Anabaptist Theology, ed. H. Wayne Pipkin, Text Reader Series, no. 5 (Elkhart, Ind.: Institute of Mennonite Studies, 1994), 11-13; C. Arnold Snyder, Anabaptist History and Thought: An Introduction (Kitchener, Ont.: Pandora Press, 1995), 84-90.

5. Examples are Howard John Loewen, One Lord, One Church, One Hope, and

One God: Mennonite Confessions of Faith in North America (Elkhart, Ind.: Institute of Mennonite Studies, 1985); Howard J. Loewen, "One Lord, One Church, One Hope: Mennonite Confessions of Faith in America—An Introduction," *MQR* 57.3 (July 1983): 265-281; J. Denny Weaver, "The Work of Christ: On the Difficulty of Identifying an Anabaptist Perspective," *MQR* 59.2 (Apr. 1985): 107-129; J. Denny Weaver, "The Quickening of Soteriology: Atonement from Christian Burkholder to Daniel Kauffman," *MQR* 61.1 (Jan. 1987): 5-45; J. Denny Weaver, "Hubmaier Versus Hut on the Work of Christ: The Fifth Nicolsburg Article," *Archiv für Reformationsgeschichte* 82 (1991): 171-192; C. Norman Kraus, "Interpreting the Atonement in the Anabaptist-Mennonite Tradition," *MQR* 66.3 (July 1992): 291-311.

6. The assumption that there is a "mainstream" theology camouflages and bypasses another important question: What or who is the "mainstream"? In fact, there are different versions of what constitutes the so-called mainstream. I note an obvious example: both Roman Catholicism and the heirs of magisterial Protestantism carry the mantle of "mainstream," although their differences have kept them from uniting around their common assumption of trinitarian and Nicene-Chalcedonian orthodoxy. More germane for the peace-church tradition is the recognition that Mennonite theologians have disagreed about the nature of the "first list." For example, compare John Horsch's fundamentalist first list; the versions of an evangelical first list of Harold S. Bender, J. C. Wenger, and Ronald Sider; the classic-creeds list of A. James Reimer; and Thomas Finger's effort at a new synthesis combining redefined versions of material from both first and second lists. See John Horsch, *The Mennonite Church and Modernism* (Scottdale, Pa.: Mennonite Publishing House, 1924), esp. chaps. 1-7, 12; Bender, "The Mennonites of the United States," 79-80; "Walking in the Resurrection," 102-103; Wenger, *Glimpses of Mennonite History and Doctrine*, 137-162; Sider, "Evangelicalism and the Mennonite Tradition," 149-168; A. James Reimer, "Doctrines: What Are They, How Do They Function, and Why Do We Need Them?" *Conrad Grebel Review* 11.1 (Winter 1993): 21-36; "Trinitarian Orthodoxy, Constantinianism, and Theology from a Radical Protestant Perspective," in *Faith to Creed: Ecumenical Perspectives on the Affirmation of the Apostolic Faith in the Fourth Century*, ed. S. Mark Heim (Grand Rapids: Eerdmans, 1991), 129-161; Thomas N. Finger, *Christian Theology: An Eschatological Approach*, vol.1 (Nashville: Thomas Nelson, 1985; Scottdale, Pa.: Herald Press, 1987); vol. 2 (Herald Press, 1989); and "The Place to Begin Mennonite Theology," *Gospel Herald*, 30 July 1996, 1-3.

7. The idea that the Mennonite or peace-church tradition would have a "distinct" theology is already language that assumes a mainstream. "Distinct" assumes that truth depends on being different, which means that the other side—the assumed mainstream—is actually setting the terms, categories, and framework of the discussion. Thus, rather than describing a distinct theology for Mennonites and the peace church, I suggest using the term *specific* to indicate something that marks a particular species. Critique of the idea of a "mainstream" and recommendation for the use of the term *specific* as an alternative to *distinct* comes from John H. Yoder, in personal correspondence and in "A People in the World," chap. in his book *The Royal Priesthood: Essays Ecclesiological and Ecumenical*, ed. and introd. by Michael G. Cartwright, with a foreword by Richard J. Mouw (Grand Rapids: Eerdmans, 1994), 81, n. 19.

8. Historians and theologians may not be as different as is sometimes supposed. After all, historians do make value judgments. At the most universal level, it is a historian's assumptions about God and the nature of ultimate reality which determine how one talks about the direction of history. For example, I would suggest that a historian who believes that God's rule is personified in Jesus' rejection of violence will evaluate the wars of Western civilization differently from a historian who assumes that God's rule on earth is expressed through civil governments. Where one finds the rule and will of God in history is a confessional and theological matter rather than an empirical and historical question. For the beginning of that discussion with regard to American history, see James C.

Juhnke, "Manifesto for a Pacifist Reinterpretation of American History," *Fides et Historia* 24.3 (Fall 1993): 53-64, which also appears in Louise Hawkley and James C. Juhnke, eds., *Nonviolent America: History Through the Eyes of Peace*, Cornelius H. Wedel Historical Series, no. 5 (Bethel College: North Newton, Kan., 1993).

9. The figures of this study lived in the epoch covered by Theron F. Schlabach, *Peace, Faith, Nation: Mennonites and Amish in Nineteenth-Century America*, vol. 2 of *The Mennonite Experience in America* (Scottdale, Pa.: Herald Press, 1988); and James C. Juhnke, *Vision, Doctrine, War: Mennonite Identity and Organization in America, 1890-1930*, vol. 3 of *The Mennonite Experience in America* (Scottdale, Pa.: Herald Press, 1989).

10. Biographical data on all these individuals is found in *Mennonite Encyclopedia*, vols. 1-4 (Scottdale, Pa.: Mennonite Publishing House, 1955-59) and 5 (Scottdale, Pa.: Herald Press, 1990), and except for Gerhard Wiebe, in volumes 2 or 3 of *The Mennonite Experience in America* four-volume work (see note 7, above). Beyond these sources, additional bibliographical references for particular individuals are given where discussion of that individual begins.

11. Schlabach, *Peace, Faith, Nation*, 36.

Chapter 2: History of Atonement

1. Gustaf Aulén, *Christus Victor: An Historical Study of the Three Main Types of the Idea of Atonement*, trans. A. G. Hebert, with foreword by Jaroslav Pelikan (New York: Macmillan, 1969).

2. In addition to Aulén, *Christus Victor*, see also H. D. McDonald, *The Atonement of the Death of Christ in Faith, Revelation, and History* (Grand Rapids: Baker, 1985), 125-146; Thomas N. Finger, *Christian Theology: An Eschatological Approach*, vol. 1 (Nashville: Thomas Nelson, 1985; Scottdale, Pa.: Herald Press, 1987), 317-324; C. Norman Kraus, *Jesus Christ Our Lord: Christology from a Disciple's Perspective*, rev. ed. (Scottdale, Pa.: Herald Press, 1990), 154-160. Particularly useful for the analysis here and in the following section is James Wm. McClendon Jr., *Doctrine*, vol. 2 of *Systematic Theology* (Nashville: Abingdon, 1994), 199-213.

3. Aulén, *Christus Victor*, 7-12; Reinhold Seeberg, *Text-Book of the History of Doctrines*, trans. Charles E. Hay (Grand Rapids: Baker, 1961), 2:67-71; Jaroslav Pelikan, *The Growth of Medieval Theology (600-1300)*, vol. 3 of *The Christian Tradition: A History of the Development of Christian Thought* (Chicago: Univ. of Chicago, 1978), 136-139.

4. McClendon, *Doctrine*, 205-206.

5. See McClendon, *Doctrine*, 205; Pelikan, *Medieval Theology*, 3:141-144; Seeberg, *Text-Book*, 2:66-70; Wolfhart Pannenberg, *Jesus—God and Man*, trans. Lewis L. Wilkins and Duane A. Priebe (Philadelphia: Westminster, 1975), 42-43.

6. McClendon, *Doctrine*, 206-208; Kraus, *Jesus Christ*, 154-156; Pannenberg, *Jesus*, 278-280; H. D. McDonald, *Atonement*, 181-195.

7. McDonald, *Atonement*, 195, with reference to A. A. Hodge.

8. McClendon, *Doctrine*, 208; McDonald, *Atonement*, 203-207.

9. See Pelikan, *Medieval Theology*, 3:127-129; Finger, *Christian Theology*, 1:310-317; McDonald, *Atonement*, 174-180.

10. For more complete descriptions of the varying themes within the doctrine of atonement, see John H. Yoder, *Preface to Theology: Christology and Theological Method* (Elkhart, Ind.: Goshen Biblical Seminary, distributed by Co-Op Bookstore, n.d.), 206-243; and John Driver, *Understanding the Atonement for the Mission of the Church*, with a Foreword by C. René Padilla (Scottdale, Pa.: Herald Press, 1986). Yoder lists eleven themes and six different families of atonement theories. Driver's book deals with more than a dozen images of atonement in the New Testament.

11. See McClendon, *Doctrine*, 210-213; Finger, *Christian Theology*, 1:310-314; McDonald, *Atonement*, 299-302.

12. The list includes Gordon D. Kaufman, *Systematic Theology: A Historicist Perspective* (New York: Charles Scribner, 1968, 1978), 389-410; Yoder, *Preface to Theology*,

206-243; J. Denny Weaver, "Perspectives on a Mennonite Theology," *CGR* 2.3 (Fall 1984): 200-204; Finger, *Christian Theology*, 1:327-338; Driver, *Understanding the Atonement*, 71-82; Perry B. Yoder, *Shalom: The Bible's Word for Salvation, Justice, and Peace* (Newton, Kan.: Faith & Life, 1987), 60-69; Gayle Gerber Koontz, "The Liberation of Atonement," *MQR* 63.2 (Apr. 1989): 171-192.

13. "Atonement for the Non-Constantinian Church," *Modern Theology* 6.4 (July 1990): 307-323. See also my "Christus Victor, Ecclesiology, and Christology," *MQR* 68.3 (July 1994), 277-290; and "Some Theological Implications of Christus Victor," *MQR* 68.4 (Oct. 1994): 483-499. The following sketch borrows from these articles.

14. On the Constantinian shift, see John H. Yoder, "The Constantinian Sources of Western Social Ethics," in *The Priestly Kingdom: Social Ethics as Gospel* (Notre Dame: Univ. of Notre Dame, 1984), 135-147.

15. Josephus, *Jewish War* 2.184-203, in *The Jewish War, Books 1-3*, vol. 2 of *Josephus*, trans. H. St. J. Thackeray, Loeb Classical Library (Cambridge: Harvard Univ. Press, 1976), 395-403; Philo, *Embassy to Gaius* 197-348, in *The Embassy to Gaius*, vol. 10 of *Philo*, trans. F. H. Colson, Loeb Classical Library (Cambridge: Harvard Univ. Press, 1971), 101-175, also xii-xiv; Anthony A. Barrett, *Caligula: The Corruption of Power* (New Haven: Yale, 1990), 182-191; Emil Schürer, *The History of the Jewish People in the Age of Jesus Christ (175 B.C.-A.D. 135)*, vol. 1, rev. and ed. Geza Vermes and Fergus Millar (Edinburgh: T. & T. Clark, 1973), 388-392.

16. Josephus, *Jewish Antiquities* 20.101, in *Jewish Antiquities, Book 20*, vol. 10 of *Josephus*, trans. Louis H. Feldman, Loeb Classical Library (Cambridge: Harvard Univ. Press, 1981), 55; Tacitus, *Annals* 12.43, in Tacitus, *The Annals of Imperial Rome*, rev. ed., trans. and intro. Michael Grant (London: Penguin Books, 1988), 271; Suetonius, *Claudius* 18, in Suetonius, *The Twelve Caesars: Gaius Suetonius Tranquillus*, rev. ed., trans. Robert Graves (London: Penguin Books, 1989), 196-197; Hans Conzelmann, *Acts of the Apostles: A Commentary on the Acts of the Apostles*, trans. James Lindburg, A. Thomas Kraabel, and Donald H. Juel, ed. Eldon Jay Epp with Christopher R. Matthews (Philadelphia: Fortress, 1987), 90; Ernst Haenchen, *The Acts of the Apostles: A Commentary* (Philadelphia: Westminster, 1971), 374.

17. Suetonius, *Nero* 16.2, in *Twelve Caesars*, 221; Tacitus, *Annals* 15.44, in Tacitus, *The Annals*, 365-366.

This account corrects an error from my earlier discussion, which mistakenly related the "wild animals" of Rev. 6:8 to games in the Colosseum (Weaver, "Atonement," 312). If it is correct that seal 4 refers to Nero, then killing by wild animals cannot refer to spectacles in the Colosseum. The Colosseum did not yet exist in Nero's time. It was begun by Vespasian and inaugurated by Titus in A.D. 80.

18. Suetonius, *Nero* 39.1, in *Twelve Caesars*, 236.

19. While I have suggested a specific set of historical antecedents for the symbolism in Revelation, the more important point is to emphasize that Revelation is anchored in human history. I want to emphasize that my discussion of Christus Victor and Revelation does not depend on acceptance of my particular interpretation of the symbols and emperors. The fact that some biblical scholars may disagree on the specific first-century historical antecedents to the symbols of Revelation should not detract from my argument as a whole. Seeing the relationship of Christus Victor and Revelation does demand, however, that the antecedents of the symbols be situated somewhere within the framework and experience of first-century history, and that the antecedents to the symbols may not be located in later history or in the future, as a variety of popular apolypticists are increasingly wont to do as we near the year 2000.

Further, the biblical foundation of Christus Victor is not limited to a few remarks about the life of Jesus and to the book of Revelation. The theology of the cross in the Gospel of Mark, for example, could no doubt be developed with Christus Victor in mind, as can Paul's theology of the cross. A chapter on "Paul's Apocalyptic Theology" by J. Christiaan Beker "argues that Paul's thought is anchored in the apocalyptic world view and that the resurrection of Christ can only be understood in that setting. . . . The coherent center of Paul's gospel is constituted by the apocalyptic interpretation of the Christ-event." See Beker, *Paul the Apostle: The Triumph of God in Life and Thought* (Philadelphia: Fortress, 1980), 135. Also see Beker, *Paul's Apocalyptic Gospel: The Coming Triumph of God* (Philadelphia: Fortress, 1982); and Nancy J. Duff, *Humanization and the Politics of God: The Koinonia Ethics of Paul Lehmann* (Grand Rapids: Eerdmans, 1992), 117-152. Such discussions show that Christus Victor is more amenable than Anselmian atonement to the apocalyptic framework in which much of the New Testament was written.

20. According to James McClendon, *Doctrine*, 202, it was not that the Christus Victor imagery was emptied of content but that the identity of the victor had changed. Whereas previously the Christians and church triumphed over empire through the resurrection of Jesus, now the empire was assumed to represent the victorious kingdom of God.

21. This change in the character of the church took place over the course of several centuries, beginning in the second century. The fact that historians can cite any number of persons who are at some point between the "before and after" stances is not an unnecessary vilification of an epoch nor is it evidence that the shift was insignificant. Neither is my thesis undercut by the observation that Nicene Christology, eventually adopted as the church's official formulation, placed more restraint on the imperial office than did Arian Christology.

See George H. Williams, "Christology and Church-State Relations in the Fourth Century," *Church History* 20.3 (Sept. 1951): 3-31; 20.4 (Dec. 1951): 3-26; A. James Reimer, "Trinitarian Orthodoxy, Constantinianism, and Theology from a Radical Protestant Perspective," in *Faith to Creed: Ecumenical Perspectives on the Affirmation of the Apostolic Faith in the Fourth Century*, ed. S. Mark Heim (Grand Rapids: Eerdmans, 1991), 143.

When it suited their purposes, both Nicenes and Arians contended for the support and protection of the emperor, and approved when the emperor coerced their opponents. See Williams, "Christology and Church-State Relations," 10; R. P. C. Hanson, *The Search for the Christian Doctrine of God: The Arian Controversy 318-381* (Edinburgh: T. & T. Clark, 1988), 849-856. Hence, these are good observations about intermediate positions and degrees of christological restraint on the imperial role in the church; they supply evidence that the shift was of a gradual, evolutionary, and complex character.

While not arguing my thesis about the demise of Christus Victor, George H. Williams made a parallel argument: he linked the transition of atonement motifs to the shift from baptism to eucharist as the sacrament of incorporation into the body of Christ. Williams identified Christus Victor as a type of baptismal theory of atonement, related to a once-for-all concept of salvation and exorcism of the devil at a once-for-all baptism. Anselm's satisfaction theory developed in relation to the eucharist, a daily incorporation into the body of Christ, and penance took over some of the significance of baptism. The once-for-all sacrament of baptism, linked to Christus Victor, had "stressed the cosmic and decisive character of Christ's liberation of mankind from death and the demonic." Anselm then "dropped as inadequate a theory of God's ransom to or trickery toward the devil connected with ancient conceptions of testamentary believers' baptism and argued for a theory of redemption reflecting the enhanced significance of repetitive private penance and daily monastic and private masses." See George H. Williams, "The Sacramental Presuppositions of Anselm's *Cur Deus homo*," *Church History* 26.3 (Sept. 1957), 245-274; quotes from 247-248.

22. For the closely related discussion of the development of Christology in the Constantinian and post-Constantinian church, see my "Christology in Historical Perspective," in *Jesus Christ and the Mission of the Church: Contemporary Anabaptist Perspectives*, ed. Erland Waltner (Newton, Kan.: Faith & Life, 1990), 83-105; "Christus Victor, Ecclesiology, and Christology," *MQR* 68.3 (July 1994): 277-290; and "Some Theolog-

ical Implications of Christus Victor," *MQR* 68.4 (Oct. 1994): 483-499.

23. For a more detailed discussion of narrative Christology and atonement motifs, see J. Denny Weaver, "Narrative Theology in an Anabaptist-Mennonite Context," *CGR* 12.2 (Spring 1984): 171-188; and "Christus Victor, Ecclesiology, and Christology," *MQR* 68.3 (July 1994): 277-290.

24. See summary of Williams, "Sacramental Presuppositions," near the end of note 21, above.

25. The following description of nineteenth-century evangelicals follows the interpretations of Timothy L. Smith and Donald W. Dayton, along with the new social history of the 1960s and 1970s. In particular, see Dayton's *Discovering an Evangelical Heritage* (New York: Harper & Row, 1976); and Smith's *Revivalism and Social Reform: American Protestantism on the Eve of the Civil War* (Nashville: Abingdon, 1957), "Righteousness and Hope: Christian Holiness and the Millennial Vision in America, 1800-1900," *American Quarterly* 31.1 (Spring 1979), 21-45; Paul E. Johnson, *A Shopkeeper's Millennium: Society and Revivals in Rochester, New York, 1815-1837* (New York: Hill and Wang, 1978); Nathan O. Hatch, *The Democratization of American Christianity* (New Haven: Yale Univ., 1989); Jon Butler, *Awash in a Sea of Faith: Christianizing the American People* (Cambridge: Harvard Univ. Press, 1990; Robert T. Handy, *Undermined Establishment: Church-State Relations in America, 1880-1920* (Princeton, N.J.: Princeton Univ. Press, 1991).

26. Hatch, *Democratization*, 196.

27. Johnson, *A Shopkeeper's Millennium*.

28. This sketch of reasons for the demise of the reforming spirit follows Dayton, *Discovering*, ch. 10.

29. These observations are also supported by Hatch, *Democratization*, ch. 7.

30. Butler, *Awash*, ch. 9.

31. Butler, *Awash*, 257-288; Hatch, *Democratization*, 193-209; Handy, *Undermined Establishment*, 7-29.

32. This challenge is still in process. For the religious right of the late 1990s, abortion has become the issue which symbolizes unchristian America. The passion of the pro-life movement in its opposition to abortion and to Bill Clinton, a pro-choice president, is a current version of the promotion of a Christian society. For that view of the pro-life movement, see David M. Smolin, "Civil Religion and the Prolife Movement: The End of Christian Patriotism in America?" *SCLE Journal of Theology and Law* 1.1 (1996): forthcoming; and my response to Smolin's article in the same issue, " 'Civil Religion and the Prolife Movement': An Anabaptist Critique of the Concept of a Christian Nation."

33. Handy, *Undermined Establishment*, deals with the range of challenges to Christian America, although his principal focus follows the progressive side of the Protestant spectrum.

34. Quoted in Keith J. Hardman, *Charles Grandison Finney, 1792-1875: Revivalist and Reformer* (Syracuse, N.Y.: Syracuse Univ. Press, 1987), 152; see also 254-255, 374. For the millennial dimensions of Finney's 1830-31 campaign in Rochester, New York, see Johnson, *Shopkeeper's Millennium*, 109-115, with a similar quote, 109.

35. Marsden, *Fundamentalism and American Culture: The Shaping of Twentieth-Century Evangelicalism, 1870-1925* (New York: Oxford Univ. Press, 1980), 27-32; quote is from 31.

36. The following comparison of Finney and Princeton theology follows Dayton, *Discovering*, 128-133.

37. Schlabach, *Peace, Faith, Nation*, 166-170.

38. Parallel to the way evangelicals abandoned pacifism to support the Civil War, both fundamentalists and modernists, coming from different theological directions, each abandoned an inclination toward pacifism and allowed their respective social ethics to be shaped by the American nation's patriotic fervor of World War I. George Marsden describes this in *Fundamentalism and American Culture*, 141-153.

39. Charles G. Finney, *Lectures on Systematic Theology, Embracing Lectures on Moral Government Together with Atonement, Moral and Physical Depravity, Regeneration, Philosophical Theories, and Evidences of Regeneration* (Oberlin: James M. Fitch, 1846). A second volume appeared the following year.

40. Finney, *Lectures*, 1-2.

41. Finney, *Lectures*, 18-19.

42. Finney, *Lectures*, 29.

43. Finney, *Lectures*, 209.

44. Finney, *Lectures*, 292.

45. Finney, *Lectures*, 319-324.

46. Finney, *Lectures*, 386.

47. Finney, *Lectures*, 386.

48. Finney, *Lectures*, 386.

49. Finney, *Lectures*, 387.

50. Finney, *Lectures*, 387-388.

51. Finney, *Lectures*, 391.

52. Finney, *Lectures*, 398-399.

53. Finney, *Lectures*, 399.

54. Finney, *Lectures*, 403. Such comments by Finney, coupled with his rejection of Jesus' death as a full payment required by distributive justice, led Finney's biographer Keith Hardman to conclude that Finney had a moral influence theory of atonement; see Hardman, *Charles Grandison Finney*, 385-388. However, as the argument here has shown, Finney's whole understanding of atonement operated within a legal construct, and the object of the death of Christ was twofold—toward God and toward the law to uphold what Finney called public justice. Clearly Finney's approach to atonement falls within the family of satisfaction views, and within the general or governmental theory in particular. It is misleading for Hardman to characterize Finney's view as moral influence theory, merely because Finney described a moral influence component of atonement and because he did not espouse the most exclusive substitutionary view, as did B. B. Warfield, for example, who will be considered presently.

55. Finney, *Lectures*, 432.

56. Finney, *Lectures*, 439. In terms of recent classifications of kinds of support for war, Finney's view was not just war but that of crusade, the idea of an aggressive war in the name of a supposedly righteous cause. See Roland H. Bainton, *Christian Attitudes Toward War and Peace: A Historical Survey and Critical Re-evaluation* (Nashville: Abingdon, 1960), 101-121, 136-151; and John Howard Yoder, *When War Is Unjust: Being Honest in Just-War Thinking*, 2d ed. (Maryknoll, N.Y.: Orbis, 1996), 8-31.

57. Benjamin Breckinridge Warfield, " 'Redeemer' and 'Redemption,' " chap. in *The Person and Work of Christ*, ed. Samuel G. Craig (Philadelphia: Presbyterian and Reformed Publishing Co., 1950), 325-348; quotes are from 336, 347. This article appeared originally in *Princeton Theological Review* 14 (1916): 177-201.

58. Reprinted as "The Chief Theories of the Atonement," in *Person and Work of Christ*, 351-369; published originally in the *Schaff-Herzogg Encyclopedia of Religious Knowledge*.

59. Warfield, *Person and Work*, 353.

60. Warfield, *Person and Work*, 354.

61. Warfield, *Person and Work*, 354.

62. Warfield, *Person and Work*, 354.

63. Warfield, *Person and Work*, 356-368.

64. Warfield, *Person and Work*, 368. In this volume, see also "Modern Theories of Atonement," 373-387, which calls the "substitutive atonement" the "very heart of the gospel" and deals with other theories in popular fashion; and "Christ Our Sacrifice," 391-426, which argues that the New Testament writers used *sacrifice* to mean "an expiatory sacrifice," which thus means that Christianity is at heart a religion based on vicarious sacrifice.

65. Benjamin B. Warfield, *The Plan of Salvation*, rev. ed. (Grand Rapids: Eerdmans, 1966).

66. Warfield, *The Plan of Salvation*, 23. What Warfield here calls the universalistic approach, meaning that the death of Christ satisfies a condition for all sinners, corresponds to the governmental theory as held by Charles Finney.

67. Warfield, *The Plan of Salvation*, 26.

68. Warfield, *The Plan of Salvation*, 27.

69. Warfield, *The Plan of Salvation*, 28.

70. Warfield, *The Plan of Salvation*, 47-48, 60-61, 63-64.

71. Warfield, *The Plan of Salvation*, 87.

72. Warfield, *The Plan of Salvation*, 87.

73. Warfield, *The Plan of Salvation*, 95-96.

74. Warfield, *The Plan of Salvation*, 98.

75. Warfield, *The Plan of Salvation*, 100.

76. Warfield, *The Plan of Salvation*, 98.

77. Warfield, *The Plan of Salvation*, 104.

78. Timothy L. Smith, "Historical Fundamentalism," *Fides et Historia* 14.1 (Fall-Winter): 71.

79. See the citations of notes 62 and 64, above.

Chapter 3: Worldviews Surrounding Atonement Theory

1. The primary source for Jacob Stauffer's thought is his *Eine Chronik oder Geschicht-Büchlein von der sogenannten Mennonisten Gemeinde* (Lancaster, Pa.: Johann Bär und Sohn, 1855). A facsimile of the 1855 edition was printed in 1972 by Wilson Martin, New Holland, Pennsylvania. The facsimile carries no reprint date. For the various editions of *Eine Chronik*, see Amos B. Hoover, ed., *The Jonas Martin Era* (Denver, Pa.: Amos B. Hoover, 1982), 1078-1080.

2. Stauffer, *Chronik*, 317-318.

3. Stauffer, *Chronik*, 139-140.

4. Stauffer, *Chronik*, 164.

5. One should be clear, however, that Stauffer's perspective differed considerably from that which came to be identified with fundamentalism. Fundamentalism accepted the philosophical outlook of Scottish Realist or Commonsense philosophy, which defined truth propositionally and established unquestioned absolutes that then served to verify the truth of its religious claims. See George M. Marsden, *Fundamentalism and American Culture*, 14-15. In contrast, Stauffer's baseline for measuring truth began within the nonresistant Mennonite tradition, and most specifically within the Christian story of Jesus and the early church. Although neither Stauffer nor early fundamentalists would say it this way, Stauffer made the particular story of Jesus his assumed rational foundation for truth, whereas fundamentalism assumed a foundation in some universally accessible "absolutes" and used those to verify the truth it claimed to find in Jesus.

6. The three major primary sources from David Beiler are the following: "Memoirs of an Amish Bishop," trans. and ed. John S. Umble, *MQR* 22.2 (Apr. 1948): 94-115; also available as *Eine Vermanung oder Andenken* (Baltic, Ohio: Raber's Book Store, 1928, and reprints).

Das wahre Christenthum: Eine Christliche Betrachtung nach den Lehren der Heiligen Schrift (Lancaster, Pa.: Johann Bär's Söhnen, 1888). The manuscript of Isaac R. Horst's English translation of this work (not used here) is at Heritage Historical Library, Aylmer, Ont. Amos B. Hoover, Muddy Creek Farm Library, Denver, Pa., has obtained a hand-copied treatise by David Beiler on baptism which seems to be an early version of chapter 2 on the same subject in *Das wahre Christenthum.* The treatise is dated 1854, and it was copied in 1859 by Deacon Christian Brenneman of Iowa.

Eine Betrachtung über den Berg Predig Christi und über den Ebräer, das 11 Cap. (published by David Z. Esch Jr., Lancaster County, 1994; distributed from Aylmer, Ont., and LaGrange, Ind.: Pathway Publishers). The original manuscript of the latter work is in the Pequea Bruderschaft Library, Gordonville, Pa. The book's introduction by Amos B. Hoover explains how the manuscript recently came into the hands of David Z. Esch Jr., a sixth-generation descendant of David Beiler, and he printed it for the first time in 1994. The first 27 pages of the manuscript are a handbook of 1861 on such matters as how to baptize, how to receive members into the fellowship, and how to ordain new leaders; these 27 pages were not published in the 1994 edition but were published in a very limited edition as *Gemein Ordnungen* in 1945 by Benjamin F. Beiler of Lancaster County, Pa., a grandson of David Beiler. This latter material is apparently the same as David Beiler's 1861 letter of instructions for ministers, available in the Mennonite Historical Library, Goshen, Ind.

Two letters by David Beiler and one for which he was a co-writer are found in Paton Yoder, ed., *Tennessee John Stoltzfus: Amish Church-Related Documents and Family Letters*, trans. by Noah G. Good et al., Mennonite Sources and Documents, no. 1 (Lancaster, Pa.: Lancaster Mennonite Historical Society, 1987), 33-38, 46. For additional biographical data on Beiler, see Paton Yoder, *Tradition and Transition: Amish Mennonites and Old Order Amish, 1800-1900*, Studies in Anabaptist and Mennonite History, no. 31 (Scottdale, Pa.: Herald Press, 1991), pages listed after his name in the index.

7. Gerhard Wiebe left one written source, penned shortly before his death in 1900 and then copied and published by his son Diedrich. This small work is *Ursachen und Geschichte der Auswanderung der Mennoniten aus Russland nach Amerika* (Winnipeg: Druckerei des Nordwesten, [1900]). The English edition is *Causes and History of the Emigration of the Mennonites from Russia to America*, trans. Helen Janzen (Winnipeg: Manitoba Mennonite Historical Society, 1981). Except when noted, the following discussion uses Janzen's translation and supplies both German and English references. For biography of Wiebe, see Adolf Ens, "Wiebe, Gerhard," in *Dictionary of Canadian Biography*, vol. 12: *1891 to 1900*.

8. There is some discrepancy in the literature on when Wiebe ceased to function as bishop. Some assume that he did not resign until 1887: Henry J. Gerbrandt, *Adventure in Faith: The Background in Europe and the Development in Canada of the Bergthaler Mennonite Church of Manitoba* (Altona, Man.: D. W. Friesen, for the Bergthaler Mennonite Church of Manitoba, 1970), 80-81, 84; and Frank H. Epp, *Mennonites in Canada, 1786-1920: The History of a Separate People*, vol. 1 of *Mennonites in Canada* (Toronto: Macmillan, 1974), 294-295. Much more likely, the resignation came late in 1881 or early in 1882, just before David Stoesz succeeded Wiebe as bishop and leader: Dennis E. Stoesz, "A History of the Chortitzer Mennonite Church of Manitoba, 1874-1914" (M.A. thesis, Department of History, Univ. of Manitoba, Winnipeg, 1987), 192-193; William Schroeder, *The Bergthal Colony*, rev. ed. (Winnipeg: CMBC Publications, 1986), 130; Adolf Ens, "Wiebe, Gerhard." Stoesz in "History," 193-194, claims that the 1887 date likely came from the fact that after Wiebe had resigned the office, ministers and bishops continued to visit and consult with him. The precise nature of Wiebe's offense remains unclear, as well as whether it was his own scrupulousness or pressure from the church that forced the resignation. It is also unclear whether his church continued to hold Wiebe in high regard after the resignation, or if the later publication of the *Ursache* served to restore his image with the church. A lack of detailed information on these questions, however, does not materially affect the interpretation and understanding of Wiebe's theology for the purposes of this essay.

9. For history of the Mennonites in Russia and the immigration to North America, see James Urry, *None but Saints: The Transformation of Mennonite Life in Russia, 1789-1889* (Winnipeg: Windflower Communications, 1989); John Friesen, ed., *Mennonites in Russia 1788-1988: Essays in Honour of Gerhard Lohrenz* (Winnipeg: CMBC Publications, 1989); Epp, *Mennonites in Canada*, 1:159-206; Schlabach, *Peace, Faith, Nation*, 231-281. On the Bergthal Colony in Russia, see Gerbrandt, *Adventure in Faith*, 24-62; and Schroeder, *The Bergthal Colony*, 1-59. On the Bergthal Mennonites in southern

Manitoba in the time period of Gerhard Wiebe, see Adolf Ens, *Subjects or Citizens? The Mennonite Experience in Canada, 1870-1925*, Religions and Beliefs Series, no. 2 (Ottawa: Univ. of Ottawa, 1994), 11-170; Stoesz, "History"; Gerbrandt, *Adventure in Faith*, 63-126; Epp, *Mennonites in Canada*, 1:283-300.

10. On difficulties in Chortitza colony and the founding of Molotschna, see Urry, *None but Saints*, 64-82.

11. For particular claims of such divine protection, see incidents described in Wiebe, *Ursachen*, 31-33; *Causes*, 40-41.

12. Wiebe, *Ursachen*, 1-8, 46-49; *Causes*, 1-7, 59-63.

13. See esp. Wiebe, *Ursachen*, 49-58; references to end of world, 54, 58; *Causes*, 63-73; references to end of world, 68, 72-73.

14. Wiebe, *Ursachen*, 9; *Causes*, 9.

15. Wiebe, *Ursachen*, 8; *Causes*, 8-9.

16. Wiebe, *Ursachen*, 1; *Causes*, 1.

17. Wiebe, *Ursachen*, 10; *Causes*, 10. Constantine (emperor A.D. 306/312-337) symbolizes the evolution of the church from an illegal minority to a supporter of the institutions of society, that is, its development into the state church. One prominent characteristic of the shift is abandonment of pacifism as a normative position of the church. On the significance of the Constantinian shift, see John Howard Yoder, "The Constantinian Sources of Western Social Ethics," in *The Priestly Kingdom: Social Ethics as Gospel* (Notre Dame: Univ. of Notre Dame, 1984), 135-147; Stanley Hauerwas, *After Christendom? How the Church Is to Behave If Freedom, Justice, and a Christian Nation Are Bad Ideas* (Nashville: Abingdon, 1991), ch. 1.

18. Wiebe, *Ursachen*, 10; *Causes*, 10.

19. Wiebe, *Ursachen*, 10; see also 48-49; *Causes*, 10; see also 61-62.

20. Wiebe, *Ursachen*, 11; *Causes*, 12.

21. Wiebe, *Ursachen*, 13; *Causes*, 13-14.

22. Wiebe, *Ursachen*, 12; *Causes*, 13.

23. For additional passages linking the Constantinian shift and advanced education, see Wiebe, *Ursachen*, 48-49; *Causes*, 61-62.

24. Wiebe, *Ursachen*, 7; *Causes*, 7.

25. Wiebe, *Ursachen*, 9, 13; *Causes*, 9, 14. In order to assure and ensure that the preacher was not displaying his own arrogance or pushing new ideas, the conservative worship tradition of Gerhard Wiebe read sermons collected from earlier generations of ministers.

26. Wiebe, *Ursachen*, 19-20, 51-52; *Causes*, 23, 64-66.

27. Wiebe, *Ursachen*, 15-16; *Causes*, 16-17.

28. Wiebe, *Ursachen*, 22; see also 34-36; *Causes*, 26-27; see also 43-45.

29. Wiebe, *Ursachen*, 44-46; *Causes*, 57-58. Delbert Plett implies that Wiebe's expressions of personal humility and inferiority were not so much a lifelong outlook as a response to the death of his wife and three of his six children in 1876, and from reflections on the moral indiscretion which led to his resignation as elder. See Plett's "Ältester Gerhard Wiebe (1827-1900)—A Father of Manitoba," *Preservings* 6 (June 1995): 4.

30. Heinrich H. Ewert was born in Ober-Nassau on the Vistula in West Prussia in 1855. In 1874, he was part of the Mennonite immigration to central Kansas. He pursued education at several Normal schools, as well as more than two years of theological study at the Theological Seminary of the Evangelical Synod in Marthasville, Missouri, and courses from the School of Theology in Darmstadt, Illinois. When the Mennonite immigrants established a secondary school at Emmental, twelve miles from Newton, Kansas, in 1882, Ewert was the first teacher. When this school relocated in Halstead, Kansas, a year later and hired another teacher, Ewert became principal, the position he was fulfilling at the time of the call to Manitoba. See Gerhard J. Ens, *"Die Schule muss sein": A History of the Mennonite Collegiate Institute 1889-1989* (Gretna, Man.: Mennonite Collegiate Institute, 1990), 32-35; Epp, *Mennonites in Canada*, 1:340-341; Paul J. Schaefer,

Heinrich H. Ewert: Teacher, Educator and Minister of the Mennonites (Winnipeg: CMBC Publications, 1990).

31. Wiebe, *Ursachen*, 49; *Causes*, 63.

32. Wiebe, *Ursachen*, 49; *Causes*, 63.

33. Wiebe, *Ursachen*, 53; *Causes*, 67.

34. Wiebe, *Ursachen*, 52, 54; *Causes*, 66, 68.

35. Wiebe, *Ursachen*, 53; *Causes*, 67.

36. Wiebe's attack on the prideful education represented by Bethel College would encompass the views of C. H. Wedel, who became the institution's first president in 1893. Yet Wedel was likely not a particular object of Wiebe's suspicion. Wedel's first book appeared in 1899, while the remainder followed the writing of Wiebe's *Ursachen und Geschichte*.

37. Wiebe, *Ursachen*, 54.

38. Wiebe, *Ursachen*, 54; *Causes*, 68.

39. On Wedel and Holdeman, see following sections.

40. Wiebe, *Ursachen*, 11; *Causes*, 11.

41. Wiebe, *Ursachen*, 11; *Causes*, 11.

42. Wiebe's reference is to the church in Philadelphia, mentioned in Revelation 3:7-13.

43. Wiebe, *Ursachen*, 48-49; *Causes*, 61-62.

44. Wiebe, *Ursachen*, 7; *Causes*, 7.

45. Wiebe, *Ursachen*, 8; *Causes*, 8.

46. Epp, *Mennonites in Canada*, 1:290.

47. See Epp, *Mennonites in Canada*, 1:294-297; Gerbrandt, *Adventure in Faith*, 85-88, 103-107.

48. For biography of C. H. Wedel, see James C. Juhnke, *Dialogue with a Heritage: Cornelius H. Wedel and the Beginnings of Bethel College* (North Newton, Kan.: Bethel College, 1987). David C. Wedel gives a biographical sketch in *The Story of Alexanderwohl* (Goessel, Kan.: Goessel Centennial Committee, 1974), 148. Primary sources for Wedel include his numerous articles in the Bethel College periodicals, as completely listed in the Bibliography section for C. H. Wedel, as well as the books and manuscripts detailed in notes 49-50 and 78 in this chapter.

49. Six volumes published at Bethel College (Newton, Kan.) developed the synthesis from the beginning of the Old Testament through history to Wedel's own time: *Randzeichnungen zu den Geschichten des Alten Testaments* (1899). *Randzeichnungen zu den Geschichten des Neuen Testaments* (1900). *Die Geschichte ihrer Vorfahren bis zum Beginn des Täufertums im 16. Jahrhundert;* erster Teil, *Abriss der Geschichte der Mennoniten* (1900). *Die Geschichte des Täufertums in 16. Jahrhundert;* zweites Bändchen, *Abriss der Geschichte der Mennoniten* (1902). *Die Geschichte der niederländischen, preussischen und russischen Mennoniten;* drittes Bändchen, *Abriss der Geschichte der Mennoniten* (1901); *Die Geschichte der Täufer und Mennoniten in der Schweiz, in Mähren, in Süddeutschland, am Niederrhein und in Nordamerika;* viertes Bändchen, *Abriss der Geschichte der Mennoniten* (1904). The following discussion of Wedel's worldview draws liberally on Juhnke, *Dialogue;* James C. Juhnke, "*Gemeindechristentum* and Bible Doctrine: Two Mennonite Visions of the Early Twentieth Century," *MQR* 57.3 (July 1983): 206-221; and Juhnke, *Vision, Doctrine, War*, 101-105.

50. Wedel, *Meditationen zu den Fragen und Antworten unseres Katechismus* (Newton, Kan.: the author, 1910).

51. Wedel, *Meditationen*, 41.

52. Wedel, *Alten Testaments*, 4-5.

53. Wedel, *Alten Testaments*, 8-9. That sense of divine salvation in history appears several places throughout this volume, as in noting the new beginning of saving acts with Abraham (12) or identifying Palestine as the location of the preparations for salvation (30). *Neuen Testaments* again refers to the coming of Christ in the middle of history (3).

54. For a discussion of Keller, Brons, Seibert, and Gottfried Arnold as major influences on Wedel's thought, see Juhnke, *Dialogue*, 52-58.

55. As examples, see *Abriss*, 1:4; 2:117; 4:206-207. Wedel's treatment of atonement as depicted in chapter 5 of this study reveals the basis for his assessment.

56. For examples of Wedel's description of *Gemeindechristentum*, see *Neuen Testaments*, 60-63, 89-90; *Abriss*, 1:4-6, 14-16, 28-30; 2:149-158, 171-176.

57. On the Constantinian shift, see note 17.

58. Wedel's acceptance of the historical linking of these groups ought not discredit for modern people his attempt to understand an alternative theological continuity and an alternative church concept throughout Christian history. For additional discussion of an alternative church concept through history, see J. Denny Weaver, "Is the Anabaptist Vision Still Relevant?" *Pennsylvania Mennonite Heritage* 14.1 (Jan. 1991): 2-12; John H. Yoder, "The Believers' Church Conferences in Historical Perspective," *MQR* 65.1 (Jan. 1991): 5-19; and J. Denny Weaver, "Anabaptist Vision: A Historical or a Theological Future?" *CGR* 13.1 (Winter 1995): 69-86.

59. Wedel, "Aus der Reisemappe, V," *SCJ* 2.5 (May 1897): 37.

60. Wedel, "Nun aber ist Christus auferstanden," *MBC* 10.4 (Apr. 1905): 40-41.

61. Wedel, "Eine wesentliche Stütze des Kriegswesens," *MBC* 8.11 (Nov. 1903): 123-124.

62. Wedel, "Unter dem Kreuze Christi," *MBC* 9.4 (Apr. 1904): 37.

63. Wedel, "Ein Stündchen mit den Propheten," *MBC* 8.1 (Jan. 1903): 1-2; "Über die Auslegung der prophetischen Reden," *MBC* 8.2 (Feb. 1903): 13-15.

64. Wedel, "Über neutestamentliche Textkritik," *MBC* 9.5 (May 1904): 50-51; 9.6 (June 1904): 110-111; 9.7 (July 1904): 122-123; 9.8 (Aug. 1904): 134-135.

65. Wedel, "Aus der Sommerfrische," *MBC* 11.8 (Aug. 1906): 89. James C. Juhnke called Wedel's approach a "mediating position." For Juhnke's discussion, with some other examples, see Juhnke, *Dialogue*, 87-89.

66. "Über Hindernisse des Glaubens," *MBC* 10.7 (July 1904): 121-122.

67. C. H. Wedel, English trans. by David C. Wedel, "Ethik," 18-19; Heft 1:31-32 (German ms.). For data on "Ethik" and method of citation, see note 78 in this chapter.

68. C. H. Wedel, "Ethik," 100A; Heft 3:13.

69. Wedel, "Ethik," 120; Heft 3:43.

70. Wedel, "Ethik," 125; Heft 3:50.

71. Wedel, "Ethik," 126; Heft 3:50.

72. Wedel, "Ethik," 134-135; Heft 3:61-64.

73. Wedel, "Ethik," 127-128; Heft 3:51.

74. Wedel, "Dichtende Frauen," *MBC* 9.5 (May 1904): 49.

75. Wedel, "Dichtende Frauen," *MBC* 9.5 (May 1904): 49. Emphasis Wedel's.

76. Wedel, "Dichtende Frauen," *MBC* 9.5 (May 1904): 49-50.

77. See in particular, *Abriss*, 4:193-208. Juhnke has written that C. H. Wedel's "method was historical" and that "the centerpiece of his intellectual labors" was his six-volume history, which began with creation and ended with modern Mennonites. See Juhnke, "*Gemeindechristentum* and Bible Doctrine," 210. For full titles of the six volumes, see note 49, above. Juhnke's conclusion reflects work in Wedel's published works. I accept the unpublished "Glaubenslehre" and "Ethik" as integral parts of Wedel's complete works. They show that Wedel's worldview had a clear theological dimension, in addition to the evident historical dimension. (For "Glaubenslehre" and "Ethik," see note 78 in this chapter.) The theological affinity of the "Glaubenslehre" and the *Meditationen* underscores that conclusion. Their affinity shows that the *Meditationen*, a work of theology, was not an incidental item outside of Wedel's primarily historical work but rather a volume produced out of the theological work which occupied him until his death.

78. Wedel's unpublished "Glaubenslehre" is a comprehensive systematic theology, existing in four notebooks, with about 475 pages of handwritten Gothic script. This source material belongs to the C. C. Wedel collection of the Mennonite Library and Ar-

chives at Bethel College, North Newton, Kansas. The notebooks contain C. C. Wedel's copies of notes made by student William Unrau in C. H. Wedel's class in Christian doctrine at Bethel College. Unrau's originals have been lost.

Along with C. C. Wedel's copies, the Archives also possess an English translation of the first 353 pages made by David C. Wedel, son of C. C. Wedel, and a transcription in modern type prepared by Hilda Voth of the untranslated portion of "Glaubenslehre."

Several factors indicate that the German notebooks contain more than mere classroom lecture notes taken by a student. For one, the material is divided into short, numbered sections, in the same format as Wedel's six-volume synthesis of church history. More significant is the fact that the material reads coherently, better than one would expect from student notes made during a lecture. In conversation with me, David C. Wedel suggested that perhaps C. H. Wedel had either dictated his lectures to the class, to be recorded word for word, or that he made available his own manuscript for students to copy. Third, in "Glaubenslehre," beginning at Heft 4:159, are found the last seven sections of C. H. Wedel's "Ethik." The major portion of "Ethik" exists in three other notebooks copied by C. C. Wedel, also in the C. C. Wedel collection of the Mennonite Library and Archives at Bethel College. Placing the last parts of "Ethik" at the end of "Glaubenslehre" seems to indicate that these notebooks contain careful copies of complete lectures by C. H. Wedel.

Finally, on the inside of the front cover of "Glaubenslehre," Heft 1, is written in German script: " 'Glaubenslehre' bearbeitet von Prof. C. H. Wedel. Permission of copyright secured." No date accompanies that inscription. The notation could be read in at least two ways, either that C. H. Wedel himself had secured a copyright in preparation for publication, or that someone else had secured permission from C. H. Wedel to publish the materials. In a number of C. H. Wedel's published volumes, David Goerz is listed as the one who secured the copyright in the name of Bethel College. However, in response to my inquiry, I have a letter from the copyright office of the Library of Congress, dated 27 September 1989, stating that a search of their records disclosed no work identified as "Glaubenslehre" under any of these names. Apparently C. H. Wedel's premature death in 1910 halted plans to publish the "Glaubenslehre."

In any case, the comment inside the cover indicates that the notebooks contain a good statement of how C. H. Wedel organized his theology. In this essay, these materials are treated as a primary source equal to that of C. H. Wedel's published writings. For citations, David C. Wedel's English translation will be referenced as "Glaubenslehre," with page numbers; reference to the German handwritten notebooks will add notebook number and page number, for example, Heft 2:2.

The "Ethik," Wedel's comprehensive statement of ethics (about 238 pages), follows the same format of numbered paragraphs as do his other writings. After its introduction, the manuscript has long sections on personal ethics and ethics of marriage and family. Shorter sections deal with church and state and issues of church and culture. There is also a partial English translation of the "Ethik," made by David C. Wedel. For citations, David C. Wedel's English translation will be referenced as "Ethik," with page numbers; reference to the German handwritten notebooks will add notebook number and page numbers, for example, Heft 3:3. All translations in the current essay are my own but done in consultation with David C. Wedel's translation.

79. For particular examples of conservative and progressive appeals to Wedel, see Juhnke, *Dialogue*, 90-91.

80. Juhnke called Wedel's view a "mediating position," and commended the renewal possibilities which Wedel's vision poses for modern Mennonites. See Juhnke, *Dialogue*, 87-93.

81. Wedel, *Meditationen*, 320. David C. Wedel made this point both in personal conversation with me and in his dissertation: "The Contribution of C. H. Wedel to the Mennonite Church Through Education" (Th.D. diss., Iliff School of Theology, 1952), 160, 168.

82. Wedel, "Glaubenslehre," 7-24; Heft 1:16-48.

83. Wedel, "Ethik," 1-10; Heft 1:1-18.

84. I am indebted to James C. Juhnke for bringing this letter to my attention. It is in the P. H. Richert Collection, Box 3, Folder 20, in the Mennonite Library and Archives at Bethel College.

85. For additional bibliography on Johannes Moser, see the four obituaries: J. J. S., "Rev. John Moser Called Home," *The Pandora Times* 9.44 (16 July 1908): 1; J. J. S., "Laid to Rest," *The Bluffton News* 34.6 (16 July 1908): 1; "Gestorben: Prediger Johannes Moser," *CBB* 27.29 (23 July 1908): 6; [David G. Goerz], "Johannes Moser," *MBC* 13.9 (Sept 1908): 99-100.

86. Delbert Gratz's work and James O. Lehman's several congregational histories provide a wealth of historical data on the several congregations of nineteenth-century Swiss immigrants. However, they do not deal with the classical theological issues beyond chronicling questions discussed at conferences.

87. Johannes Moser wrote extensively for *Herold der Wahrheit* and *Christlicher Bundesbote*. I have identified 11 separate articles, several with multiple parts, appearing in 21 separate issues of *HdW*; and 38 titles in 43 issues of *CBB*. This totals 49 titles and 64 separate appearances in the Mennonite periodicals. For a complete list of these articles, see the Bibliography section for Johannes Moser. Apart from references to three articles on nonresistance, Moser's writing has not been dealt with in any modern study.

88. For references, see note 150 below.

89. Moser, "Menschen Sterblichkeit," *HdW* 15.9 (Sept. 1878): 146-147; "Erziehung der Jugend," *HdW* 16.3 (Mar. 1879): 41-44; "Gedanken über Spaltungen," *HdW* 21.9 (1 May 1884): 131-132; 21.10 (15 May 1884): 149-151; 21.11 (1 June 1884): 164-165; 21.12 (15 June 1884): 179-180; 21.13 (1 July 1884): 195-197; "Das Völligerwerden," *HdW* 21.19 (1 Oct. 1884): 292-293; "Siehe, ich komme bald," *HdW* 21.22 (15 Nov. 1884): 338-341; "Ein Vortrag über Nachbarschaft," *HdW* 22.4 (14 Feb. 1885): 49-51; 22.5 (1 Mar. 1885): 65-68; "Die Veranlassung und Beeinflussung zur Sünde," *CBB* 7.30 (2 Aug. 1888): 2-3; "Das Reizen zur Liebe und zu guten Werken," *CBB* 7.32 (16 Aug. 1888): 2; "Hindernisse der Mission," *CBB* 11.19 (12 May 1892): 1; "Festigkeit in Prüfungen," *CBB* 11.27 (14 July 1892): 2-3; "Keiner Wiederholung der Taufe," *CBB* 12.40 (12 Oct. 1893): 2; 12.41 (19 Oct. 1893): 2-3; "Göttlicher Natur teilhaftig werden," *CBB* 24.23 (8 June 1905): 1-2.

90. Moser, "Der Menschen Sterblichkeit," *HdW* 15.9 (Sept. 1878): 147. See also "Das Völligerwerden," *HdW* 21.19 (1 Oct. 1884): 292-293; "Keiner Wiederholung der Taufe," *CBB* 12.40 (12 Oct. 1893): 2; "Göttlicher Natur teilhaftig werden," *CBB* 24.23 (8 June 1905): 2.

91. Moser, "Vortrag über Nachbarschaft, II," *HdW* 22.5 (1 Mar. 1885): 65. Also, "Die Veranlasung und Beeinflussung zur Sünde," *CBB* 7.30 (2 Aug. 1889): 2.

92. Moser, "Vortrag über Nachbarschaft, II," *HdW* 22.5 (1 Mar. 1885): 67.

93. For major treatments, see Moser, "Gedanken über Missions- und Gemeinde-Verhältnisse," *CBB* 1.20 (15 Oct. 1882): 157-159; "Gedanken über Spaltungen." *HdW* 21.9 (1 May 1884): 131-132; 21.10 (15 May 1884): 149-151; 21.11 (1 June 1884): 164-165; 21.12 (15 June 1884): 179-180; 21.13 (1 July 1884): 195-197; "Ein Vortrag über Nachbarschaft," *HdW* 22.4 (14 Feb. 1885): 49-51; 22.5 (1 Mar. 1885): 65-68.

94. Moser, "Göttlicher Natur teilhaftig werden," *CBB* 24.23 (8 June 1905): 2.

95. Moser, "Keiner Wiederholung der Taufe," *CBB* 12.40 (12 Oct. 1893): 2; 12.41 (19 Oct. 1893): 2-3. On Heinrich Egly's practice of rebaptism, see his "Autobiography," 2-4. Data on Egly's "Autobiography" is in note 229, below.

96. Moser accepted the traditional Mennonite practice of placing women in a subordinate position. Inside the cover of his Bible, as part of a list of Scriptures on various themes, Moser wrote: "Die Weiber sollen schweigen in der Versammlung. 1 Cor 14:34. 1 Tim 2:12. 1 Pet 3:1-5." Johannes Moser's Bible is in the possession of his great-grandson John Moser of Bluffton, Ohio. See also note 140 below.

97. Moser, "Hindernisse der Mission," *CBB* 11.10 (12 May 1892): 1. Moser's pro-

test is illustrated in Jacob Steiner's obituary in *The Bluffton News* 24.34 (16 Feb. 1899): 2, which says, "[Steiner] and his wife were good members of the old congregation [Johannes Moser's congregation] for a number of years, when she was persuaded to join the New Mennonites.[Reformed Mennonite Church], he following a few years later."

Moser's lament also had a familial dimension. The death notice for his oldest sister, Mary Ann Steiner née Moser, stated that she was "born and raised in the Mennonite church, having been a member of her brother's congregation, when some years ago [as a widow] she joined the New Mennonites [Reformed Mennonites]. Her funeral was held from the New Mennonite church . . . and her remains laid by the side of her husband in the old churchyard." From *The Bluffton News* 28.50 (4 June 1903): 4.

The vehemence of Moser's opposition to the Reformed Mennonites is evident in his *Eine Verantwortung gegen Daniel Musser's Meidungs-Erklärung, welche er gemacht hat in seinem Buch, betitelt: 'Reformirte Mennoniten' "* (Lancaster, Pa.: Gedruckt von Samuel Ernst, 1876). The middle section of this 83-page book reproduced the letters of the Amish division in order to show that shunning as practiced by the Amish and by Musser and his followers "cannot find solid foundation in the holy scripture" (23). In the first and last sections, Moser made extended refutations of specific statements by Musser.

98. Moser, "Ein Vortrag über Nachbarschaft," *HdW* 22.5 (1 Mar. 1885): 68.

99. This summary of the division follows James O. Lehman, *Salem's First Century: Worship and Witness* (Kidron, Ohio: Salem Mennonite Church, 1986: 6-24.

100. See the discussion below on developing a constitution as an element of Moser's progressive agenda.

101. For a more detailed account of this conflict, see Roger Siebert, "Grace Mennonite Church—An Overview of the First 25 Years," in *Grace Mennonite Church, Pandora, Ohio, 1904-1979, 75th Anniversary*, 1-9 (a pictorial directory, available in Mennonite Historical Library, Bluffton College); and Don Schneck, ed., *St. John Mennonite Church, Pandora, Ohio, 1888-1988* (Pandora, Ohio: St. John Mennonite Centennial Committee, 1988), 30-33. Moser's resignation as elder with willingness to continue preaching follows E. J. Hirschler, *A Brief History of the Swiss Mennonite Churches of Putnam and Allen Counties, Ohio* (Bluffton, Ohio: Historical Committee, 1937), 26. An announcement of Moser's retirement and a worship service to celebrate fifty years of ministry appears in the column "German Settlement," in *Bluffton News* 29.17 (15 Oct. 1903), 1.

102. Moser, "Gedanken über Spaltungen," *HdW* 21.7 (1 Apr. 1884): 102-103; 21.8 (15 Apr. 1884): 117-119; 21.9 (1 May 1884): 131-132; 21.10 (15 May 1884): 149-151; 21.11 (1 June 1884): 164-165; 21.12 (15 June 1884): 179-180; 21.13 (1 July 1884): 195-197.

103. Moser, "Das Reizen zur Liebe und zu guten Werken," *CBB* 7.32 (16 Aug. 1888): 2.

104. According to John Moser, great-grandson of Johannes Moser, family tradition says that Johannes received a good deal of criticism from the congregation for taking the progressive act of writing a congregational constitution. For discussion of the constitution, see the context of note 140, below.

105. Moser, "Bekenntniss," *CBB* 11.16 (21 Apr. 1892): 5.

106. Moser, "Festigkeit in Prüfungen," *CBB* 11.27 (14 July 1892): 2-3.

107. Moser, "Konferenzgedanken," *CBB* 21.40 (9 Oct. 1902): 1-2.

108. Moser, "Gedanken über Missions- und Gemeinde-Verhältnisse," *CBB* 1.20 (15 Oct. 1882): 159.

109. "Die Veranlassung und Beeinflussung zur Sünde," *CBB* 7.30 (2 Aug. 1888): 2. See also "Gedanken über Spaltungen, Teil 7," *HdW* 21.13 (1 July 1884): 195-197; "Missbräuche," *CBB* 10.2 (8 Jan. 1891): 3.

110. Making women the brunt of the problem of pride and styles is particularly evident in "Erinnerung gegen Missbräuche, Ermahnung und Gebet, I, II," *CBB* 17.30 (4 Aug. 1898): 2; 17.31 (11 Aug. 1898): 2. From the modern standpoint, one cannot justify Moser's attitude toward women other than to say that his view was the typical one in that

era. John M. Brenneman, as shown in a following section, made remarks equally unacceptable by modern standards, identifying women primarily as the ones guilty of the sin of pride. See, for example, Brenneman's "Eine Wechstimme an die stoltzen Frauen," *HdW* 5.4 (Apr. 1868): 51-54; "Pride and Fashion," *HT* 10.5 (May 1873): 93; and the same article in German: "Hochmuth und Mode," *HdW* 10.5 (May 1873): 91.

111. Moser, "Eine Antwort," *HdW* 8.5 (May 1871): 70-71; "Gedanken über Spaltungen, *HdW* 21.12 (15 June 1884): 180; *CBB* 20.50 (19 Dec. 1901): 1-2.

112. Moser, "Bro. Joseph Steiner's Imprisonment," *HT* 28.7 (1 Apr. 1891): 101-102; "Br. Joseph Steiner's Gefangenschaft," *HdW* 28.7 (1 Apr. 1891): 102-103.

113. "Über die Wehrlosigkeit, II," *HdW* 16.2 (Feb. 1879): 21. Moser's comments on eschatology did not occur in a vacuum. Among the books from Moser's library, now in the possession of his great-grandson John Moser of Bluffton, Ohio, is a volume which attempts to situate the United States of the mid-nineteenth century in relation to predictions of the book of Revelation.

114. Moser, "Über die Wehrlosigkeit," *HdW* 16.2 (Feb. 1879): 21.

115. Moser, "Die Reizung zum Bösen," *CBB* 7.27 (12 July 1888): 2. In this particular article, Moser used the discussion about evil as the basis of an article on temperance. For additional statements of the argument that the existence of evil requires the existence of the devil in order to absolve God of authoring evil, see "Nachdenken über sich selbst," *CBB* 10.37 (17 Sept. 1891): 2. Moser argues for the existence of hell in a two-part article, "Eine Hölle," *CBB* 10.40 (8 Oct. 1891): 2; 10.41 (15 Oct. 1891): 2.

116. Moser, "Unglaube," *CBB* 10.39 (1 Oct. 1891): 2. This entire long, two-part article is devoted to opposing evolution, arguing for the existence of evil, and defending the truth of the Bible.

117. Moser, "Das Herrn Wort," *CBB* 20.38 (26 Sept. 1901): 1-2.

118. This is likely a reference to the forthcoming Chicago World's Fair, which opened 1 May 1893. Moser's remark is in "Die Menschen bedürfen Haus und Heim," *CBB* 11.32 (18 Aug. 1892): 2. Juhnke in *Vision, Doctrine, War*, 21-27, used a spectrum of Mennonite responses to the Chicago World's Fair to illustrate varying Mennonite stances vis-à-vis American society in the late nineteenth century. Moser fits near the center of that spectrum.

119. Moser, "Die Menschen bedürfen Haus und Heim," *CBB* 11.32 (18 Aug. 1892): 2. See also "Gedanken," *CBB* 13.6 (8 Feb. 1894): 2; and "Das Herrn Wort," *CBB* 20.38 (26 Sept. 1901): 1-2.

120. Moser's position on the existence of evil was also part of the specific context in which he discussed atonement. God needed to punish evil, and the coming of the Redeemer was the event which allowed the perpetual cycle of punishment to come to a halt. See the section on Moser in chapter 4.

121. Moser, "Gedanken über Missions- und Gemeinde-Verhältnisse," *CBB* 1.20 (15 Oct. 1882): 157-159.

122. Moser, "Mission," *CBB* 11.18 (5 May 1892): 1; "Hindernisse der Mission," *CBB* 11.19 (12 May 1892): 1; "Hindernisse der Mission in der Christenheid überhaupt," *CBB* 11.20 (19 May 1892): 1.

123. Moser, "Mission," *CBB* 11.18 (5 May 1892): 1.

124. Moser, "Das sind die Reisen der Kinder Israel," *CBB* 18.36 (14 Sept. 1899): 3.

125. Moser, "Gedanken über Missions- und Gemeinde-Verhältnisse," *CBB* 1.20 (15 Oct. 1882): 159; "Das sind die Reisen der Kinder Israel," *CBB* 18.36 (14 Sept. 1899): 3.

126. Moser, "Gedanken über Missions- und Gemeinde-Verhältnisse," *CBB* 1.20 (15 Oct. 1882): 157-159.

127. Moser, "Hindernisse der Mission," *CBB* 11.19 (12 May 1892): 1. It is not quite true that the Reformed Mennonites opposed all propagation of Christian faith. They believed that rather than forming new structures to carry out mission, it was personal testimony and the saved life of the believer that constituted the mission testimony. And since

there were unsaved persons right at home, there was no need to go to a foreign country to perform a Christian witness.

128. On progress defined in terms of new programs and structures, see Schlabach, *Peace, Faith, Nation*, 118, 201-203.

129. "Berichte," *CBB* 4.10 (15 Mar. 1885): 6.

130. A. Zurflüh, "Bericht der Verhandlungen der Sonntagschul-Convention, abgehalten in der Mennonitengemeinde bei Bluffton, . . ." *CBB* 4.22 (1 Nov. 1885): 6; 4.23 (1 Dec. 1885): 3. Moser's address to the 1889 convention in Putnam County was noted in *CBB* 8.43 (31 Oct. 1889): 2; and his opening of the 1893 convention in Putman County appeared in *CBB* 12.45 (16 Nov. 1893): 2.

131. Moser, "Das sind die Reisen der Kinder Israel. 4. Mose 33.1," *CBB* 18.36 (14 Sept. 1899): 3.

132. Moser, "Gedanken über Spaltungen," *HdW* 21.13 (1 July 1884): 196; "Korrespondenzen—Bluffton, O.," *CBB* 9.27 (10 July 1890): 5.

133. David Goerz, "Reise-Bericht," *CBB* 7.37 (20 Sept. 1888): 5. Moser also noted his support of Bethel College in his "Gedanken über Schulverhältnisse," *CBB* 17.50 (22 Dec. 1898): 3.

134. Moser may have been a late convert to the idea of higher education. At the 1879 conference of the Swiss Mennonite churches at Sonnenberg in Wayne County, Ohio, Moser functioned as moderator. With the majority, Moser signed the conference document which questioned progressive S. F. Sprunger's support of education and the Wadsworth Institute, and cautioned against worldly fashions in clothing. See James O. Lehman, *Sonnenberg: A Haven and a Heritage: A Sesquicentennial History of the Swiss Mennonite Community of Southeastern Wayne County, Ohio* (Kidron, Ohio: Kidron Community Council, 1969), 112-113. See also James O. Lehman, *Salem's First Century*, 7-8.

When Moser expressed solid support for Bethel College 10 years later, and then for Central Mennonite School in Bluffton, it might be that he had simply become more aware of the need for higher education. One can also conjecture that it was S. F. Sprunger and the apparent promotion of modish dress at Wadsworth which gave Moser a particular concern, but left him free to welcome an alternative school when that opportunity presented itself. For a description of the "unhumble" tone and deportment at the Wadsworth Institute, see Schlabach, *Peace, Faith, Nation*, 132-133. Johannes Moser's younger brother Abraham kept a diary while attending Wadsworth Institute; see Rachel W. Kreider and Anna Kreider Juhnke, eds., Nettie Hooley, trans., "The Abraham J. Moser Diary of Wadsworth Institute—1868," *Mennonite Life* 48.2 (June 1993): 4-12.

135. Moser, "Gedanken über Schulverhältnisse," *CBB* 17.50 (Dec. 1898): 2-3.

136. "Korrespondenzen," *CBB* 19.27 (12 July 1900): 5.

137. Moser, "Gedanken über Schulverhältnisse," *CBB* 17.50 (22 Dec. 1898): 3.

138. Moser, "Eine Hölle, II," *CBB* 10.41 (15 Oct. 1891): 2. See also "Haus Gottes," *CBB* 18.39 (5 Oct. 1899): 2; "Neujahrsgedanken," *CBB* 21.1 (2 Jan. 1902): 2.

139. On the contrast between traditional and modern versions of authority, see Schlabach, *Peace, Faith, Nation*, 123-124.

140. Moser, "Bekenntniss," *CBB* 11.16 (21 Apr. 1892): 5. This article advocated the need for a congregational confession (*Bekenntniss*), and included the kind of material that would commonly appear in a constitution. While the article said only that a constitution should deal with the indicated issues, the one Moser wrote for his congregation did clearly prohibit these items. Although the constitution did not have an article specifically forbidding women to preach, the section on the election of ministers spoke of selecting a *Bruder* and consistently used masculine pronouns. The constitution is *Gemeinde-Ordnung der Schweizer-Mennoniten Gemeinde bei Pandora und Bluffton, in Putnam und Allen County, Ohio*, Entworfen von dem Ältesten Johannes Moser (Lima, Ohio: Lima Courier, 1893). The only known original printing of this constitution is in the Mennonite Historical Library at Bluffton College.

141. Moser, "Bekenntniss," *CBB* 11.16 (21 Apr. 1892): 5.

142. "Korrespondenzen—Bluffton, O.," *CBB* 12.16 (12 Oct. 1893): 4.

143. Moser, "Missbräuche," *CBB* 10.2 (8 Jan. 1891): 3. See also "Die Veranlassung und Beeinflussung zur Sünde," *CBB* 7.30 (2 Aug. 1888): 3.

144. "Die Erziehung der Jugend," *HdW* 16.3 (Mar. 1979): 42; "Die Reizung zum Bösen," *CBB* 7.27 (12 July 1888): 2-3.

145. See note 134, above.

146. In May and June of 1868, this was one of the congregations in Missouri visited by John M. Brenneman, who participated in baptism and communion services. Brenneman noted their ardent desire to have a preacher. He concluded his report with many expressions of rejoicing for the love which had been manifested to him in Missouri. Brenneman also wrote, "I believe, it is fully as safe traveling in Missouri as in Ohio." See Brenneman, "A Journey to Missouri," *HT* 5.7 (July 1868): 105-106 = "Eine Reise nach Missouri," *HdW* 5.7 (July 1868): 105-106. Brenneman's visit is noted in *Souvenir Album: Fiftieth Anniversary of the Founding of the Bethel Mennonite Church in Morgan and Moniteau Counties near Fortuna, Missouri, Sunday, April 22, 1917* (Berne, Ind.: Berne Witness Co., [1917]), 18, 23. This booklet is bilingual. Page numbers cover both languages. A copy of the *Souvenir Album* is the Central District Conference Archives, at Bluffton College.

147. Fifty-one members remained at Bethel. Thirty-six formed the other, smaller group, which became Mt. Zion Mennonite Church.

148. *Souvenir Album of Bethel,* 11, 18, 23; *Mt. Zion Mennonite Church Centennial Program* (Versailles, Mo., 1971), 4-5; Abraham J. Moser, "Ansiedlung der Schweitzer und Amerikaner Mennoniten in Moniteau und Morgan Counties, Mo., Im Bethel gemeinde," manuscript in Central District Conference Archives, Bluffton College, 77-87; Lehman, *Salem's First Century,* 6-7. Foot washing is not mentioned as a specific issue in *Souvenir Album of Bethel.* However, both A. J. Moser and the *Mt. Zion Centennial Program* specify that the practice of foot washing was a key issue in the separation of Bethel and Mt. Zion. See A. J. Moser, "Ansiedlung," 77; *Mt. Zion Centennial Program,* 4. Several years later, in his "Johannes 13," *CBB* 6.12 (15 June 1887): 2-3, Johannes Moser explained why foot washing was not a ceremonial observance commanded by Christ.

149. See note 112 above.

150. S. F. Sprunger's congregation of Swiss at Berne, Indiana, had joined the General conference already in 1872, and Bethel in Missouri had joined in 1881. Noting those earlier decisions, James O. Lehman wrote, "Although the Bluffton Swiss church, under the conservative leadership of John Moser, waited until 1893 to join the General Conference, we may presume that there was no small debate as to whether Sonnenberg, the pioneer church of the Swiss migration, would also join their friends and relatives in the same conference." See Lehman, *Salem's First Century,* 11. S. F. Pannabecker characterized Moser as "tactful and ready to accept innovations but not the one to promote unpopular moves or risk division of the congregation." Pannabecker also noted the large conservative element in Bluffton that opposed the progressive leadership of S. F. Sprunger at Berne. Pannabecker did acknowledge that Moser moved in the same direction as Sprunger, but he noted that Moser lacked Sprunger's "training and aggressive quality." See Samuel Floyd Pannabecker, *Faith in Ferment: A History of the Central District Conference* (Newton, Kan.: Faith & Life, 1968), 55, 57.

151. For a description of events, see Lehman, *Salem's First Century,* 32. The appearance at the joint Salem-Sonnenberg worship service is reported in *CBB* 8.48 (5 Dec. 1889): 5.

152. Primary sources for John M. Brenneman include the booklet in German and English *Das Christenthum und der Krieg* (Lancaster, Pa.: Johann Bär's Söhnen, 1864) and *Christianity and War* (Elkhart, Ind.: John F. Funk, 1863), in several editions; and a long list of articles. I have identified 98 separate articles or letters or letter excerpts attributed to Brenneman in *HT* and *HdW.* The majority appeared in both English and German, though several titles occurred in one of the two languages but not both. Most but not all of the longer articles were reprinted. The largest collections of reprinted articles

were the books *Plain Teachings* or *Einfache Lehre* (both at Elkhart, Ind.: Mennonite Publishing Co., 1876). These books have a majority of reprinted titles in common, yet each has some titles not in the other. In addition, each of these two books contains two or three titles which I did not locate in earlier versions in *HT* or *HdW*. Other, smaller reprints include *Pride and Humility* (Elkhart, Ind.: John F. Funk, 1967, 1968, 1873) and *Hoffart und Demuth* (1968); *An Encouragement to Penitent Sinners and Joy over Their Conversion* and *Eine Aufmunterung der bussfertigen Sünder, und Freude über ihre Bekehrung* (both at Elkhart, Ind.: Mennonite Publishing Co., 1977); *Hope, Sanctification, and a Noble Determination* (both at Elkhart, Ind.: Mennonite Publishing Co., 1893).

Since the reprinted versions were sometimes expanded beyond the original articles, the following quotes the reprinted version where available. For a complete list of first appearances and languages for individual titles, see the Bibliography section for John M. Brenneman. For additional biography of John M. Brenneman, see Lehman, *Seedbed*, 12-22; and Grant M. Stoltzfus, *Mennonites of the Ohio and Eastern Conference from the Colonial Period in Pennsylvania to 1968*, Studies in Anabaptist and Mennonite History, no. 13 (Scottdale, Pa.: Herald Press, 1969), 138-139. John S. Umble, "The Allen County, Ohio, Mennonite Settlement," *MQR* 6.2 (April 1932): 81-109, gives biography of Brenneman, as well as a detailed history of the church community Brenneman served.

Brenneman appeared to use German and English virtually interchangeably. He wrote that the Sunday school at Elida was established in order to teach German (*HT* 6.1 [Jan. 1869]: 3-4 = *HdW* 6.1 [Jan. 1869]: 2-3). Hence, James O. Lehman suggested that Brenneman preferred the German language. See *Seedbed*, 19. Lehman's observation may be correct. However, since Brenneman's article on the Elida Sunday school was written to reassure conservatives that the new Sunday school posed no threat to traditional Mennonite values, his stress on German can reflect that intent as much as a preference for German. In fact, the pattern of Brenneman's articles in the *Herald* and *Herold* may suggest that he perhaps had a slight preference for English or may have developed the same. Since eight of Brenneman's last nine articles appeared only in English, written during his declining years when ill health rendered him generally inactive, it seems logical that in his weakened condition, he put all of his feeble energy into producing the one version that came most easily. See also comments in note 211 of chapter 3 and note 73 of chapter 5.

153. Brenneman, "Ought We to Have a Religious Paper?" *HT* 1.1 (Jan. 1864): 2-3 = "Sollten wir ein religiöses Blatt haben?" *HdW* 1.1 (Jan. 1864), 4. He expressed similar sentiment in "The Art of Writing a Great Privilege," *HT* 1.8 (Aug. 1864): 52 = "Die Schreibkunst, ein grosse Vorrecht," *HdW* 1.8 (Aug. 1864): 51.

154. Brenneman, "The True Foundation, and God's Building Considered," *Plain Teachings*, 5-28 = "Das wahre Fundament und Gottes Gebäude betrachtet," *Einfache Lehre*, 5-26; "Be Ye All of One Mind," *Plain Teachings*, 137-152 = "Seid allesammt gleich gesinnet," *Einfache Lehre*, 121-135.

155. Brenneman, "True Foundation and God's Building," *Plain Teachings*, 13 = *Einfache Lehre*, 12.

156. Virtually all of Brenneman's travel reports contained such comments. See the Brenneman section of the Bibliography for location of travel reports. For a summary of Brenneman's trips, see Lehman, *Seedbed*, 17-18.

157. Brenneman, "A Journey to Indiana," *HT* 4.3 (Mar. 1867): 41 = "Eine Reise nach Indiana," *HdW* 4.3 (Mar. 1867): 41-42; "Account of a Journey to Illinois, Iowa, and Missouri," *HT* 4.8 (Aug. 1867): 121-124 = "Bericht einer Besuchsreise nach Illinois, Iowa und Missouri," *HdW* 4.8 (Aug. 1867): 121-124; "A Visit to Pennsylvania," *HT* 6.7 (July 1869): 104-105 = "Ein Besuch nach Pennsylvanien," *HdW* 6.7 (July 1869): 104-105; "Account of a Journey," *HT* 8.7 (July 1871): 107-108 = "Reiseberichte," *HdW* 8.7 (July 1871): 107; "Antwort auf Obiges," *HdW* 8.10 (Oct. 1871): 158.

158. Brenneman, "Unity Among the Brethren," *HT* 3.3 (1866): 17 = "Die brüderliche Eintracht," *HdW* 3.3 (Mar. 1866): 17. By Swiss or *Schweizer Brüder,* Brenneman

meant the relatively recent Swiss immigrants who had settled in Holmes and Wayne counties in eastern Ohio, in Putnam and Allen counties in western Ohio (the congregation served by Bishop Johannes Moser), in Adams County in eastern Indiana, and in Morgan and Moniteau counties in Missouri. In the course of his travels, Brenneman visited and fellowshiped with several of these Swiss congregations.

Brenneman believed that two issues in particular could have been well handled by a general conference: the differing attitudes toward the Sunday school among Mennonites in East and West, and the conflicting opinions that the Virginia and Indiana conferences reached about remarriage after divorce. See Lehman, *Seedbed*, 18-19.

159. Brenneman, "Halte deine Zunge im Zaume! Jac 3.5," *HdW* 1.10 (Oct. 1864): 67; letter extract in *HT* 1.10 (Oct. 1864): 68.

160. Brenneman, "A Hint to Emigrants," *HT* 10.6 (June 1873): 109 = "Ein Wink an die Emigranten," *HdW* 10.6 (June 1873): 107.

161. Brenneman, "Menno Simons' Ansicht über den Gebrauch des Schwerts unter den Christen," *HdW* 14.9 (Sept. 1877): 141.

162. Brenneman's concern about Mennonite participation in war was based in part on firsthand experience. His travels on the frontiers put him in contact with many Mennonites whom he found little prepared for the threats posed by the Civil War. Further, neighbors in Fairfield County, Ohio, from where he had moved to Elida in 1855, received a great deal of pressure to enter military service. Many succumbed, while a number of the young men moved to Allen County, and some of his close acquaintances in Allen County were entering the war. See Lehman, *Seedbed*, 14-15.

163. Brenneman, *Christianity and War* (1868), 21; *Das Christentum und der Krieg* (1864), 25.

164. Brenneman, *Plain Teachings*, 54-74; *Einfache Lehre*, 46-66; "Aus dem Tod in das Leben," *HdW* 7.1 (Jan. 1870): 5.

165. Brenneman, "An Answer," *HT* 2.9 (Sept. 1865): 68-69 = "Eine Antwort," *HdW* 2.9 (Sept. 1865): 68-69.

166. Brenneman, "What Jesus Has Commanded, and Also What He Has Forbidden," *HT* 9.2 (Feb. 1872): 17-19 = "Was Jesus geboten, befohlen und auch verboten hat," *HdW* 9.2 (Feb. 1872): 17-19.

167. Brenneman, *Hope, Sanctification and a Noble Determination*, 15-16.

168. Brenneman, *Christianity and War*, 43-45, with quote from 45; *Das Christentum und der Krieg*, 53-55, with quote from 55.

169. Brenneman, *Christianity and War*, 42-43; *Das Christentum und der Krieg*, 50-52.

170. In August 1862, Brenneman drafted a petition in the name of Mennonites to President Lincoln, requesting that Mennonites receive exemption from military service in exchange for payment of a fine. This petition stressed the signers' loyalty and submission to Lincoln and the Union government, their willingness to pay the tax, and their commitment to suffer nonresistantly if the petition was not granted. It is not known whether the petition was actually sent to President Lincoln. See John M. Brenneman, "A Civil War Petition to President Lincoln," *Mennonite Historical Bulletin* 34.4 (Oct. 1973): 2-3. For additional discussion, see Lehman, *Seedbed*, 15.

171. Brenneman, "What Meanest Thou, O Sleeper? Arise and Call upon Thy God! (Jonah 1.16)," *HT* 1.3 (Mar. 1864): 9-10 = "Was schläfst du? Stehe auf, rufe deinen Gott an," *HdW* 1.3 (Mar. 1864): 9-10.

172. Brenneman, *Christianity and War*, 7; *Das Christentum und der Krieg*, 7.

173. Brenneman, "True Foundation and God's Building," *Plain Teachings*, 15; *Einfache Lehre*, 14.

174. Brenneman, "Das grüne und dürre Holz," *Einfache Lehre*, 189.

175. Brenneman, "Eine Neujahresstimme," *Einfache Lehre*, 175.

176. Brenneman, *Hope, Sanctification, and a Noble Determination*, 16.

177. In an article which described the various dimensions of humility and used

John M. Brenneman as the primary example, Joseph C. Liechty called humility "the foundation of Mennonites' religious outlook in the 1860s." Brenneman said nothing new in *Pride and Humility*. Yet Liechty wrote, "What he did was to say well and fully what his peers said fumblingly and partially." See Liechty, "Humility: the Foundation of Mennonite Religious Outlook in the 1860s," *MQR* 54.1 (Jan. 1980): 12-13.

178. Brenneman, *Pride and Humility* (1873), 6.

179. Brenneman, *Pride and Humility* (1873), 6.

180. Brenneman, *Pride and Humility* (1873), 31-35.

181. Brenneman, *Pride and Humility* (1873), 36-41.

182. Brenneman, *Pride and Humility* (1873), 41-44.

183. Brenneman, *Pride and Humility* (1973), 45.

184. Brenneman, "A Visit to Indiana," *HT* 2.12 (Dec. 1865): 101 = "Ein Besuch nach Indiana," *HdW* 2.12 (Dec. 1865): 101.

185. Liechty, "Humility," 16.

186. Brenneman, "I Beg Pardon," *HT* 5.7 (July 1868): 106 = "Ich halte um Geduld an," *HdW* 5.7 (July 1868): 106.

187. Brenneman, "A Caution," *HT* 23.7 (1 April 1886): 103.

188. Brenneman never allowed his picture to be taken, according to Lehman, *Seedbed*, 27.

189. Brenneman, *Pride and Humility* (1873), 11-12.

190. Brenneman, *Pride and Humility* (1873), 13.

191. Brenneman, *Pride and Humility* (1873), 13-14.

192. Brenneman, "A Visit to Pennsylvania," *HT* 6.7 (July 1869): 105 = "Ein Besuch nach Pennsylvanien," *HdW* 6.7 (July 1869): 105.

193. Brenneman, "How the World Lieth in Wickedness," *Plain Teachings*, 218-223.

194. Brenneman, *HdW* 5.4 (Apr. 1868): 51-54. This article was reprinted in *Hoffart und Demut* (1868) and as "An Alarm to the Proud," in *Pride and Humility* (1873).

195. Brenneman, "An Alarm to the Proud," in *Pride and Humility* (1873), 59.

196. Brenneman, "An Alarm to the Proud," in *Pride and Humility* (1873), 66.

197. Brenneman, *Einfache Lehre*, 190-193.

198. Brenneman, "Pride and Fashion," *HT* 10.5 (May 1873): 93 = "Hochmuth und Mode," *HdW* 10.5 (May 1873): 91. From a modern perspective, one cannot defend the way Brenneman singled out women for special warning, except to say that he reflected the prevailing outlook of his time. Brenneman's comments on women and dress seem to be echoed in later expressions by Johannes Moser and in milder form by C. H. Wedel; see above.

199. Brenneman, "Christians Ought Not Laugh Aloud," *Plain Teachings*, 242-243, and "Christen sollten nicht laut lachen," *Einfache Lehre*, 207-208. For Heinrich Egly's similar, if less strident, warning against laughing and frivolity, see the Egly section in chapter 4, the context of note 213.

200. Umble, "Allen County, Ohio, Mennonite Settlement," 103-104.

201. Lehman, *Seedbed*, 27; Andrew Shenk, "Bishop John M. Brenneman," *Gospel Herald* 22 (11 July 1929): 315.

202. Schlabach, *Peace, Faith, Nation*, 74.

203. Brenneman, *Plain Teachings*, 180, and *Einfache Lehre*, 160-161. Comments on idle talk appear in various articles and comprise the focus of two other articles, "Halte deine Zunge im Zaume! Jac 3.5," *HdW* 1.10 (Oct. 1864): 67; and "Sin Not with the Tongue," *HT* 7.12 (Dec. 1870): 188 = "Sündiget nicht mit der Zunge," *HdW* 7.12 (Dec. 1870): 189-190, directed toward children.

204. Brenneman, "Christus das Osterlamm," *Einfache Lehre*, 183-185, with paragraphs against transubstantiation added to the original article for this reprint; "Not Literal," *HT* 7.6 (June 1870): 87 = "Nicht buchstäblich," *HdW* 7.4 (Apr. 1870): 61; reprinted in *Plain Teachings*, 227-229.

205. Brenneman, "Baptism by Pouring Asserted," *HT* 22.11 (1 June 1885): 170 = "Die Taufe durch Begiessen," *HdW* 22.11 (1 June 1885): 169-170.

206. Brenneman, "Sanctification," *HT* 17.6 (June 1880): 101-103 = "Heiligung," *HdW* 17.6 (June 1880): 102-105; reprinted in *Hope, Sanctification, and A Noble Determination* (1893). Dimensions of this argument also appear in "An Encouragement to Penitent Sinners and Joy over Their Conversion," *HT* 13.4 (Apr. 1876): 65-70 = "Eine Aufmunterung der bussfertigen Sünder, und Freude über ihre Bekehrung," *HdW* 12.7 (July 1875): 97-101; and in "When and Where Was Paul Converted?" *HT* 20.21 (1 Nov. 1883): 321-322.

207. Brenneman, "Hope unto the End," *HT* 22.11 (1 June 1885): 161-162; reprinted in *Hope, Sanctification, and A Noble Determination*. Other articles with aspects of this argument include "Schaffet, dass ihr selig werdet, mit Furcht und Zittern," *HdW* 4.1 (Jan. 1867): 1-2; reprinted as "Eine Neujahrsstimme," *Einfache Lehre*, 173-178; "Worte des Trostes," *HdW* 7.8 (Aug. 1870): 113-114; and in *Einfache Lehre*, 203-207; "Of the Unpardonable Sin," *HT* 11.9 (Sept. 1874): 148-149.

208. For Egly on Moser, see the context of note 207 in chapter 4.

209. For a description of the organization and development of that Sunday school, see John S. Umble, *Ohio Mennonite Sunday Schools*, Studies in Anabaptist and Mennonite History, no. 5 (Goshen, Ind.: Mennonite Historical Society, 1941), 35-41, 166-167. On page 24 Umble gives 1863 as the date for the earliest Amish Mennonite Sunday school at South Union in Logan County, Ohio.

210. Lehman, *Seedbed*, 18; M. S. Steiner, *John S. Coffman, Mennonite Evangelist: His Life and Labors* (Spring Grove, Pa.: Mennonite Book and Tract Society, [1903]), 48.

211. Brenneman, "A Visit," *HT* 5.11 (Nov. 1868): 71-72 = "Ein Besuch," *HdW* 5.11 (Nov. 1868): 172. The Sunday school established by Brenneman did not long maintain the teaching of German.

212. Theron F. Schlabach, *Gospel Versus Gospel: Mission and the Mennonite Church, 1863-1944*, Studies in Anabaptist and Mennonite History, no. 21 (Scottdale, Pa.: Herald Press, 1980), 31.

213. Four books constitute the primary sources for John Holdeman. The first is *Der Alte Grund und Fundament aus Gottes Wort gefasst und geschrieben* (Lancaster, Pa.: Johann Bärs Söhnen, 1862). The next year he published his own English translation, *The Old Ground and Foundation* (Lancaster, Pa.: the author, 1863). Next came the history of the church and Holdeman's explanation for the necessity of founding a new church. This history appeared first as Johannes Holdeman, *Eine Geschichte der Gemeinde Gottes* (Lancaster, Pa.: Johannes Bars Söhnen, 1875). Holdeman then produced his own English edition of this work, *A History of the Church of God* (Lancaster, Pa.: Johannes Bärs Söhnen, 1876). He called it a translation, "but not strictly so," since he took the liberty to make some changes in the outline and to expand some sections and otherwise clarify his views. See Holdeman, *History*, 10.

This English translation, *History*, has been reprinted several times. Citations in this study refer to the most recent printing by Gospel Publishers of Moundridge, Kansas. Since Holdeman considered the 1876 English version more complete, it is used in this study, with references where useful to the earlier German text. For the same reason, this study also uses primarily Holdeman's English version of *Der Alte Grund*. The third book is *Spiegel der Wahrheit* (Lancaster, Pa.: Johann Bärs Söhnen, 1880). The English translation is a modern one, *A Mirror of Truth* (Moundridge, Kan.: Gospel Publishers, 1956; 5th printing, 1987). It should be used with some care, while comparing it with the German. The final book relevant for the discussion of Holdeman's view of atonement is *A Treatise on Redemption, Baptism, and the Passover and the Lord's Supper* (Jasper County, Mo.: the author, 1890). The first of this book's three parts outlines Holdeman's approach to atonement.

214. Holdeman, *On Redemption*, 57.

215. Holdeman, *History*, entire volume, esp. ch. 8; quote is from 136; *On Redemption*, 56-57.

216. For discussion of Wiebe and Wedel, see sections above, in this chapter.

217. George M. Marsden, *Fundamentalism and American Culture*, 14-16.

218. Holdeman, *Mirror*, 11,
219. Holdeman, *Mirror*, 11.
220. Holdeman, *Mirror*, 11.
221. Holdeman, *Mirror*, 11-16.
222. Holdeman, *Mirror*, 270-275.
223. Holdeman, *Mirror*, 270.
224. Holdeman, *Mirror*, 271-272.
225. Holdeman, *Mirror*, 273-275.
226. One might also include a statement such as the following, which comes from the preface to Holdeman's chapter on "The Kingdom of Christ on Earth": "If I write the truth, no one can overthrow it. The truth will be fulfilled in God's decreed providence, according to His revealed Word. . . . If I write falsehoods, they fall of themselves. . . . I shall endeavor to write that this presentation shall not be my own knowledge, but as God's unchangeable knowledge it resides in Him and is revealed to us." From Holdeman, *Mirror*, 326-327.
227. Clarence Hiebert, *The Holdeman People: A Study of the Church of God in Christ, Mennonite, 1859-1969* (South Pasadena, Calif.: William Carey Library, 1973), 379.
228. For additional biography on Egly, see the brief, laudatory work by his son-in-law and daughter, David N. and Kathryn E. Claudon, *Life of Bishop Henry Egly, 1824-1890* (n.p., [1947]); Harry F. Weber, *Centennial History of the Mennonites of Illinois, 1829-1929*, Studies in Anabaptist and Mennonite History, no. 3 (Goshen, Ind.: Mennonite Historical Society, 1931), 335-341; early sections of the history of Egly's denomination by Stan Nussbaum, *You Must Be Born Again: A History of the Evangelical Mennonite Church*, rev. ed. (Fort Wayne, Ind.: The Evangelical Mennonite Church, 1991); Willard H. Smith, *Mennonites in Illinois*, Studies in Anabaptist and Mennonite History, no. 24 (Scottdale, Pa.: Herald Press, 1983), 111-112; Yoder, *Tradition and Transition*, 184-186.
229. At present we have access to Egly's "Autobiography" only through an English translation, consisting of 25 single-spaced pages, done by Emma Steury of the Evangelical Mennonite Church, Berne, Indiana. Copies of that translation are in the Mennonite Historical Library, Bluffton College; Mennonite Church Archives, Goshen College; archives of the Evangelical Mennonite Church, Administrative Headquarters in Fort Wayne, Indiana; Egly Memorial Library of the EMC of Berne, Indiana. Sometime before Steury's death in 1980, Egly's original manuscript as well as a transcription were lost.

Egly published sixteen articles in *Herold der Wahrheit* and *Christlicher Bundesbote*. For a complete list, see the section of Bibliography for Egly. Five of these articles were reprinted posthumously along with three new ones, in Heinrich Egly, *Das Friedensreich Christi oder Auslegung der Offenbarung St. Johannes und noch etliche andere Artikel* (Geneva, Ind.: Jacob Schenbeck, 1895). Jacob Schenbeck, a son-in-law of Heinrich Egly, had the book printed by John F. Funk's publishing company in Elkhart, Indiana.

A letter of 22 April 1895 exists from Schenbeck to Funk concerning the publication. Schenbeck reported that he had just received the first three copies of the little book, and pronounced it very satisfactory, except for two small errors—*geben* for *gegen* on page 30, and *Josiah 61* for *Jesaia 61* on page 31. Schenbeck promised to remit payment when the rest of the books arrived. In a P.S. dated 25 April, Schenbeck stated that the books had arrived, and that he would send the money. This letter is in Hist Mss 1-1-2 John F. Funk Correspondance, Box 22, folder April 1895, in the Archives of the Mennonite Church, Goshen College, Goshen, Indiana. In what follows, references to reprinted articles will include both the original and the reprinted source. The undated tract of four pages by Heinrich Egly is "Vom Glauben und der Gewissheit," printed by C. R. Egle, Flanagan, Ill.
230. Egly, "Autobiography," 1.
231. Schlabach, *Peace, Faith, Nation*, 116. Similar comments appear in Yoder, *Tradition and Transition*, 185-186.

232. George M. Marsden, *Fundamentalism and American Culture*, 282, note 29. Marsden's source was a prepublication version of Nussbaum, *You Must Be Born Again*.

Chapter 4: Context for Atonement

1. Stauffer, *Chronik*, 22.
2. Stauffer, *Chronik*, 24.
3. Stauffer, *Chronik*, 24.
4. Stauffer, *Chronik*, 35.
5. Sandra Cronk has provided a good analysis of the function of *Ordnung* for the Old Order groups, with examples taken frequently from both Stauffer and David Beiler: "The Old Order way of life is structured by a series of rules and regulations called the *Ordnung*. These rules and regulations define how members live together. . . . The *Ordnung* orders all facets of life, from the furnishings of the house to the manner of earning a living. These regulations are the Old Order religious ritual. They are not ritual in the sense of some sacred, set-apart activity. . . . However, they are ritual in the sense of an activity which brings the participant into contract with the power of God. They provide the concrete ways in which members embody the goal of loving community. Amish and Mennonite ritual takes place in the ordinary spheres of everyday life. It incarnates the divine social order which the Old Order people believe God ordained for human beings." From "*Gelassenheit*: The Rites of the Redemptive Process in Old Order Amish and Old Order Mennonite Communities," *MQR* 55.1 (Jan. 1981): 6.
6. Stauffer, *Chronik*, 26.
7. Stauffer, *Chronik*, 27.
8. Stauffer, *Chronik*, 27-29.
9. Stauffer, *Chronik*, 27-30.
10. Stauffer, *Chronik*, 41.
11. Stauffer, *Chronik*, 44.
12. Stauffer, *Chronik*, 16. See also chapter 5, note 5.
13. Stauffer, *Chronik*, 44.
14. Most sections of Stauffer's *Chronik* return repeatedly to such themes.
15. Stauffer's chapter 5 is devoted to separation, in *Chronik*, 66-77.
16. Stauffer, *Chronik*, 123-124.
17. This summary follows Stauffer, *Chronik*, 126-127.
18. Stauffer's concerns about musical instruments and frivolous activities and talking of all kinds were echoed at some level by many Amish and Mennonites, including David Beiler, John Holdeman, John M. Brenneman, and Heinrich Egly. See Schlabach, *Peace, Faith, Nation*, 61-63.
19. Stauffer, *Chronik*, 85-87. For similar lists and descriptions, see 130-133; 266-269.
20. Schlabach, *Peace, Faith, Nation*, 58, 142.
21. Stauffer, *Chronik*, 27, 152.
22. Stauffer, *Chronik*, 237.
23. Stauffer, *Chronik*, 284-285.
24. Stauffer, *Chronik*, 22, 29, 50, 64; quote is from 402.
25. Stauffer, *Chronik*, 4-5, 12-14, 146-152.
26. Stauffer, *Chronik*, 153.
27. Stauffer, *Chronik*, 156.
28. Stauffer, *Chronik*, 156-157.
29. Stauffer, *Chronik*, 156.
30. Stauffer, *Chronik*, 80. This quote comes from the chapter which Stauffer summarized on 78: "How the weaponless and defenseless church of God, the truly reborn disciples of Jesus, are called through the gospel to walk without violence, revenge, or self-vindication."
31. Schlabach, *Peace, Faith, Nation*, 229.

32. In *Peace, Faith, Nation,* 212, Theron Schlabach described Beiler: "The earnest religion he called for was to be inner and subjective as well as outer, objective, and governed by *Ordnung.*" With reference to the theological analysis of Beiler, I do not disagree with Schlabach's assessment on the same page: "Beiler challenged his reader to recognize the divinity and saving work of Jesus, one's own sinfulness (almost but not quite innate depravity), and God's love and grace. He wrote earnestly of the need to repent truly, be born again, and walk a new path. Earnest, practical religion was built around the grace of God, the architect of salvation, and around the sacrificed Jesus. Salvation was Beiler's main point, not precisely *Ordnung.* But as the good bishop became practical, *Ordnung* moved very near the center. The new birth would show itself in a reformed life, and that life would show 'meekness, humility, patience in adversity,' and actual deeds of love for enemies. Persons who believed and took God's promises to heart, Beiler was sure, would 'well remain in the *Ordnung* of God and not sin against' it. The humble of heart let themselves be instructed in the *Ordnung* of Jesus Christ, for they were always concerned that out of weakness they might err."

33. Amish ministers follow a prescribed list of Scriptures on which they preach throughout the year. Beiler's *Wahre Christenthum* contains four such expositions of Scriptures. See Robert Friedmann, *Mennonite Piety Through the Centuries: Its Genius and Its Literature,* Studies in Anabaptist and Mennonite History, no. 7 (Goshen, Ind.: Mennonite Historical Society, 1949), 246-247; and John S. Umble, "Amish Service Manuals," *MQR* 15.1 (Jan. 1941): 26-32.

34. Since such biblically oriented comments permeate the sermon on John 3, it is virtually meaningless to quote page numbers. Beiler clearly typifies Paton Yoder's description of Amish soteriology in *Tradition and Transition,* 77: "The importance of the doctrine of the new birth is everywhere apparent in Amish religious literature of the nineteenth century."

35. Beiler, *Wahre Christenthum,* 239: "Wir können nicht in Geisteskraft von der Neugeburt und ihren Wirkungen und ihrer Frucht reden und sie Andere lehren, ohne dieselbige selbst erfahren zu haben, und dadurch zu einer wahren Umkehrung und Herzensbekehrung gekommen zu sein, also, dass wir in Wahrheit können mit Paulo sagen: 'Ich lebe nun nicht mehr, sondern Christus lebt in mir.' Wir müssen Christum theilhaftig werden durch den Glauben, und ihn in uns wirken lassen."

36. Beiler, *Wahre Christenthum,* 227-228. These quotes come from one long paragraph and show the development of thought in the passage.

37. Beiler, *Wahre Christenthum,* 208.

38. Beiler, *Wahre Christenthum,* 223-224.

39. Beiler, *Wahre Christenthum,* 226: "Darum müssen alle neugeborene Christen gesinnt sein, dem Befehl Jesu Christi in aller Gehorsamkeit nachzufolgen." Numerous similar references could be cited. This one is given because it leads to the next point.

Paton Yoder stated that Amish in the nineteenth-century generally asserted that Jesus was both example and Savior; that Jesus' substitutionary sacrifice "potentially" atoned for sins; and that pardon for sins was forthcoming, "*provided* the penitent would then walk consistently in obedience to God and his Word" [emphasis Yoder's]. See *Tradition and Transition,* 85, 88; quote is from 88.

40. Beiler, *Betrachtung über den Berg Predig,* 32, 49, 58, 90.

41. Beiler, *Betrachtung,* 14, 34, 57, 69, 86.

42. Beiler, *Betrachtung,* 12, 16, 106.

43. Beiler, *Betrachtung,* 12, 24, 27, 57, 70, 73-74, 78.

44. For example, Beiler, *Betrachtung,* 65.

45. Beiler, *Betrachtung,* 20-21, 28, 87, 91.

46. Beiler, *Betrachtung,* 46, 51-54, 73.

47. Beiler, *Betrachtung,* 104-109.

48. Beiler, *Betrachtung,* 62, 103, 105, 117-118.

49. *Wahre Christenthum,* 226: "Nicht nur allein seine Lehre annehmen mit dem

Mund, sondern mit vollem Herzen glauben, dass Jesus Christus die ewige Weisheit Gottes ist, in welchem die ganze Fülle der Gottheit leibhaftig wohnt, und welcher ist das Ebenbild des unsichtbaren Gottes."

50. That material occupies approximately pages 10-16 of Beiler's *Wahre Christenthum*. In the following discussion, notes indicate only direct quotes.

51. Beiler, *Wahre Christenthum*, 10: "gleiche Kraft und Herrlichkeit, ein Willen und Wesen von Ewigkeit her."

52. Beiler, *Wahre Christenthum*, 12.

53. Beiler, *Wahre Christenthum*, 12: "Denn er war nicht von Adams sündlichem Fleisch, wenn ihn schon die Schrift des Weibes Samen nennt." In Beiler, "Memoirs," 97, John S. Umble cited this christological paragraph as evidence that at times Beiler dealt with "theological or metaphysical themes."

54. Beiler, *Wahre Christenthum*, 12: "dass er vom Himmel gekommen ist."

55. Beiler, *Wahre Christenthum*, 245-246: "Ich glaube, wenn wir den Sinn und Grund seiner Reden verstehen wollen, so müssen wir es so fassen, dass Christus Jesus vom Himmel gekommen ist, und sein Leib oder Fleisch war nicht von der Erden, wie das unserige. Er war nicht von Adam's sündlicher Art, dem Tod und Verwesung unterworfen. Es war, wie Johannes anführt: 'Das Wort ward Fleisch.' "

56. Beiler, *Wahre Christenthum*, 155.

57. Paton Yoder in *Tradition and Transition*, 84, said that while "some Amish writers" reflected the influence of Menno Simons and Dirk Philips on this point of Christology, "the Amish were not united on this question."

58. Beiler, *Wahre Christenthum*, 14-15: "Der Vater, das Wort und der Heilige Geist. Und die drei sind eins. . . . Der Vater, Sohn und der Heilige Geist ein wahrhaftiger Gott ist von Ewigkeit her, wenn schon die Schrift ungleiche Wirkungen ihnen zuschreibt."

59. In *Mennonite Piety Through the Centuries*, 246-247, Robert Friedmann called Beiler's chapter (in *Wahre Christenthum*, 274-281) on the state of the soul after death "the only theological item in a book of prevailing practical character." This current summary and assessment of Beiler's understanding of atonement, Christology, and trinitarianism shows that Friedmann greatly underestimated the content of Beiler's theology.

60. Beiler, *Betrachtung*, 21-25.

61. Such points supplied the main themes of chapters in Beiler's *Wahre Christenthum*, while ideas such as humility and nonresistance, and the admonition to be obedient, occurred repeatedly throughout the book.

62. Beiler, *Betrachtung*, 22-23, 45, 124.

63. Beiler, *Betrachtung*, 42, 45, 46, 52-53, 59, 124.

64. Beiler, "Memoirs," 101-103.

65. See note 5 above, which describes the *Ordnung*. As already noted, Beiler was a leading voice in the wing of Amish that became known as the Old Order. For an in-depth discussion of the so-called Great Schism, which led to the emergence of the Old Order Amish, and Beiler's role in that process, see Paton Yoder, *Tradition and Transition*, chaps. 7-10. Also see pages 105-112 of the same book for a detailed description of shunning as practiced by nineteenth-century Amish.

66. See the context of note 32.

67. The victory motif, reflective of the classic theory, is more evident for "Tennessee" John Stoltzfus. Yet the theology of David Beiler also is paralleled in the sketches of theology which one can piece together for Stoltzfus, a liberal Amish counterpart to Beiler, of Pennsylvania. For example, in an 1885 letter, Stoltzfus wrote to his children about converts "who responded to the call of our Redeemer to all the weary and heavy laden 'to come to Him to accept His yoke, that is to say, the sweet heavenly doctrine in which blessed rest for souls is promised in obeying the commands of God."

In an undated tract, Stoltzfus stated, "The Son of God, turned into flesh and bone by the Virgin Mary at Bethlehem, . . . was sent by the Father to bring sinners to repentance, and out of bondage of Satan and sin, to everlasting life and rest in heaven.

. . . He had the strength of a lion, but let himself be nailed and handled to the cross as a lamb, to redeem us from the curse of the law. He was clean from all sin, and then to be nailed to the curse of the cross. Besides hanging in the nails, [driven] through the flesh, we may think of the great punishment he suffered, and what a great love to the world. [He] prayed, Father forgive them. . . . [He] died to give peace to the heavy laden, and shed his blood to wash away sins, and was buried. Also he went and preached unto the spirits in prison, and rose from the dead, was seen carried in a cloud to heaven, and then [was] set [at God's] right hand in the heavenly place." From Yoder, ed., *Tennessee John Stoltzfus*, 168-169, 173-174.

Enough theology is evident in the letters and papers of "liberal" Tennessee John Stoltzfus to demonstrate that for the theological questions on which this study focuses, there was essential agreement between the Amish factions in spite of schism. In other words, here is again evidence, if any more is necessary, that Amish (and Mennonite) divisions have overwhelmingly concerned theology as practice, "obeying the commands of God," rather than theology as mere words.

68. Theron Schlabach made similar comments about Beiler and Stauffer, in comparing them to Reformed Mennonites John Herr and Daniel Musser. See Schlabach, "Mennonites and Pietism in America, 1740-1880: Some Thoughts on the Friedmann Thesis," *MQR* 57.3 (July 1983): 234.

69. Wedel, *Meditationen*, 126; "Ethik," 51-54; Heft 1:71-72; 2:1-4.

70. Wedel, *Meditationen*, 131.

71. Wedel, *Meditationen*, 145.

72. Wedel, *Meditationen*, 162-163.

73. Wedel, *Meditationen*, 167.

74. Wedel, *Meditationen*, 168.

75. Wedel, "Glaubenslehre," 120; Heft 3:22.

76. Wedel, "Glaubenslehre," 127; Heft 3:35.

77. Wedel, "Glaubenslehre," 127-28; Heft 3:32-35.

78. Wedel, "Glaubenslehre," 128-131; Heft 3:36-40.

79. Wedel, "Glaubenslehre," 131-137; Heft 3:40-49.

80. Wedel, "Glaubenslehre," 138-139; Heft 3:49-51.

81. Wedel, "Glaubenslehre," 138-142; Heft 3:49-55.

82. Wedel, "Glaubenslehre," 144-148; Heft 3:58-64.

83. Wedel, "Glaubenslehre," 144-165; Heft 3:58-86.

84. Wedel, "Glaubenslehre," 161-162; Heft 3:82.

85. Wedel, "Glaubenslehre," 162-163; Heft 3:83-84. Of Menno, Wedel wrote, "This view contradicts the clear statement of the Scripture, throws us into Docetism, and robs us of our Lord as our brother, as a member of our race, and robs him of the jewel of his greatness as Savior, namely his full humanity." From "Glaubenslehre," 163; Heft 3:84.

86. Wedel, "Glaubenslehre," 165-182; Heft 3:86-95; 4:1-16.

87. Wedel, *Neuen Testaments*, 77: "Gott aber liess es zu, dass durch den Triumph menschlicher Bosheit die Erlösung der Menscheit ausgeführt wurde."

88. The stress on the inner, heartfelt nature of true religion occurs throughout the several volumes of Wedel's writings, in instances far too numerous to cite individually. The humorous dimension of one such remark merits its mention, even if it only partially illustrates the inner life. Wedel described Old Testament patriarch Isaac as a man of patience and submission (*Gedult und Gelassenheit*), in sum, "the 'Mennonite' of the Old Testament." From *Alten Testaments*, 15.

89. Wedel, *Meditationen*, 168-169.

90. Wedel, *Meditationen*, 179.

91. Wedel, *Meditationen*, 179.

92. Wedel, *Meditationen*, 177.

93. Wedel, *Meditationen*, 246.

94. Wedel, *Meditationen*, 247-255. While Wedel does not have traditional abso-

lutist positions on governmental service and nonswearing of oaths (see "Ethik," 69-70; Heft 2:32-35; "Glaubenslehre," Heft 4:160-166), the point in the current context is that he accepted the traditional Anabaptist categories as the appropriate external expression of the inner, spiritual faith.

95. Wedel, "Glaubenslehre," 206; Heft 4:44, including quotes.

96. Wedel, "Glaubenslehre," 206; Heft 4:45-46, including quotes.

97. Wedel, "Glaubenslehre," 207; Heft 4:47. On Wedel's summary of the history of the doctrine of predestination, see Heft 4:49-53.

98. Wedel, "Glaubenslehre," Heft 4:53.

99. Wedel, "Glaubenslehre," Heft 4:53-54.

100. Wedel, "Glaubenslehre," Heft 4:54-55.

101. Wedel, "Glaubenslehre," Heft 4:56.

102. Wedel, "Glaubenslehre," Heft 4:56-58.

103. Wedel, "Glaubenslehre," 205; Heft 4:42-43.

104. Wedel, "Glaubenslehre," Heft 4:59: "kann aber auch auf eine künstliche Weise gehoben und wohl auch erkünstelt werden, was man in den sog. Erweckungsversamlungen der Methodisten hat beobachten wollen."

105. Wedel, "Glaubenslehre," Heft 4:59.

106. Wedel, "Glaubenslehre," Heft 4:60-62.

107. Wedel, "Glaubenslehre," Heft 4:62-63.

108. Wedel, "Glaubenslehre," Heft 4:64-66.

109. Wedel, "Glaubenslehre," Heft 4:68-69.

110. Wedel, "Glaubenslehre," Heft 4:73-76.

111. Wedel, "Glaubenslehre," Heft 4:81-82. While the "Ethik" does not offer a specific critique of revivalist conversion, its discussion of the redeemed life clearly assumes the model of process and growth. See Wedel, "Ethik," 103-114; Heft 3:19-36.

112. Wedel, "Glaubenslehre," Heft 4:83-84.

113. Wedel, *Meditationen*, 11.

114. Wedel, "Glaubenslehre," Heft 4:83.

115. Wedel, "Glaubenslehre," Heft 4:85.

116. Wedel, *Meditationen*, 12.

117. Wedel, "Glaubenslehre," Heft 4:84-86.

118. See Juhnke, *Vision, Doctrine, War*, 82-83.

119. Wedel, "Glaubenslehre," Heft 4:105-110.

120. Wedel, "Glaubenslehre," Heft 4:91.

121. Wedel, "Glaubenslehre," Heft 4:91-94, with quote from 94. In *Meditationen*, 222, Wedel wrote: "It is thus quite natural that [the faithful], after reaching an independent decision, should join themselves to those who have tried their best to influence and to form them through lessons, wisdom, and example, so that together they might drink from the same health-giving stream."

122. In his own life, Wedel took the voice of the church quite seriously. His Alexanderwohl congregation provided a scholarship for seminary study at the German-language seminary at Bloomfield, New Jersey. In 1885, leaders of the new Halstead Seminary gave Wedel an invitation to teach. Wedel submitted the decision to the Alexanderwohl congregation, which debated whether he should accept the offer. After vigorous debate, they decided that he should turn down the job and continue his studies. See Juhnke, *Dialogue*, 6.

123. Juhnke, *Dialogue*, 88.

124. Wedel, "Ethik," 2; Heft 1:4-5.

125. As the section on Heinrich Egly in chapter 3 indicated, these observations concerning Wedel are somewhat parallel to the older Egly who apparently allowed ethics to come unhooked from atonement and salvation. For a discussion of ethics becoming detached from salvation in the context of the development of Mennonite missions, see Schlabach, *Gospel Versus Gospel*, 47-53.

126. See for example, Wedel, "Ethik," section 1-42, 47, 88-91; Heft 1:1-72, 2:1-15, 32-35; 3:70-72; "Glaubenslehre," Heft 4:159-165.

127. Wedel, *Meditationen*, 247-255.

128. Nonresistance headed a list of thirteen topics discussed at a conference of the Swiss Mennonite congregations on 15 October 1878 and reported by Moser in *HdW* 15 (Dec. 1878): 209. In the introduction to "Über die Wehrlosigkeit," *HdW* 16.1 (Jan. 1879): 1, Moser stated that the article constituted further thoughts on the conclusions reached by the Swiss Mennonite conference.

129. Moser, "Über die Wehrlosigkeit," *HdW* 16.1 (Jan. 1879): 1.

130. Moser, "Über die Wehrlosigkeit," 1-2.

131. Moser, "Über die Wehrlosigkeit," 2.

132. Moser, "Über die Wehrlosigkeit," 2: "In diesem Sinn hat der ganze Zusammenhang heiliger schrift Wehrlosigkeit gelehrt."

133. Moser, "Vertheidigung der Wehrlosigkeit, oder 'Nothwehr, nicht nach dem Geiste des Neuen Testaments,' " *HdW* 4.6 (June 1867): 86; 4.7 (July 1867): 97-100; 4.8 (Aug. 1867): 113-115.

134. James O. Lehman, *Sonnenberg*, 94, described the incident affecting Abraham Moser's Sonnenberg congregation in Wayne County, Ohio, which likely precipitated the question to his brother Johannes: "On May 26, 1865, thieves entered the home of Nicholas Gerber. Going upstairs they found Gerber's adopted son, Christian Zebinden, and stabbed him seven times. By this time the Gerbers were aroused downstairs. Upon the approach of one of the thieves, Nicholas stunned him with a blow in the stomach. His revolver fell and Gerber threw him down and began choking him until his wife had his hands and feet tied. They went upstairs to discover their dying son. No doubt this was the incident that caused a young man of the community, Abraham J. Moser, to have some questions on nonresistance before he could accept baptism." Lehman added that Johannes's letters to Abraham circulated among the young men of the community, and then they were sent to *Herold der Wahrheit* by Sonnenberg pastor Christian Schneck.

135. Moser, "Gedanken über Missions- und Gemeinde-Verhältnisse," *CBB* 1.20 (15 Oct. 1882): 157-159; "Unglaube," *CBB* 10.38 (24 Sept. 1891): 1-2; "Gedanken," *CBB* 13.6 (8 Feb. 1894): 2; "Das sind die Reisen der Kinder Israel. 4. Mose 33.1," *CBB* 18.36 (14 Sept. 1899): 2-3.

136. Moser, "Der Menschen Sterblichkeit," *HdW* 15.9 (Sept. 1878): 147; "Siehe, ich komme bald," *HdW* 21.22 (15 Nov. 1884): 341; "Die Veranlasung und Beinflussung zur Sunde," *CBB* 7.30 (2 Aug. 1888): 2; "Lasset uns halten am Hoffnungsbekenntniss," *CBB* 7.35 (6 Sept. 1888): 2; "Unglaube," *CBB* 10.38 (24 Sept. 1891): 1-2; and 10.39 (1 Oct. 1891): 1-2.

137. Moser, "Das geistliche Haus, I," *CBB* 12.13 (30 Mar. 1893): 2-3.

138. Moser, "Das geistliche Haus, I," 2.

139. Moser, "Das geistliche Haus, II," *CBB* 12.14 (6 Apr. 1893): 4. See also "Konferenzgedanken," *CBB* 21.40 (9 Oct. 1902): 2.

140. Moser, "Haus Gottes," *CBB* 18.39 (5 Oct. 1899): 1: "Gott ist der Stifter seiner Gemeinde (Kirche) und seine Verheissungen sind ihr gegeben. Unter besonderen Verhältnissen können zwar abgesonderte, vereinzelt stehende Personen, die durch wahre Busse und Glauben an Jesum Christum in Gottes Gemeinschaft getreten, in der Verheissung stehen (Luk. 23, 42). Wenn sich aber Gelegenheit bietet, so verpflichtet Christi Lehre und Vorbild sie, sich auch einer äusseren, sichtbaren christlichen Gemeinde anzuschliesen."

141. Moser, "Das Himmelfahrt Christi ist das Ende der leiblichen Lebensgeschichte Christi auf Erden," *CBB* 17.20 (19 May 1898): 2.

142. Brenneman, *Plain Teachings*, 34; also 38, 41.

143. Brenneman, *Plain Teachings*, 35.

144. Brenneman, *Plain Teachings*, 37.

145. Brenneman, *Plain Teachings*, 39.

146. Brenneman, *Plain Teachings*, 40.
147. Brenneman, *Plain Teachings*, 41-45.
148. Brenneman, *Plain Teachings*, 46-47.
149. Brenneman, "The Art of Writing a Great Privilege," *HT* 1.8 (Aug. 1864): 52 = "Die Schreibkunst, ein grosse Vorrecht," *HdW* 1.8 (Aug. 1864): 51.
150. Brenneman, "Halte deine Zunge im Zaume! Jac 3.5," *HdW* 1.10 (Oct. 1864): 67.
151. Brenneman, "The Signs and Miracles of Christ Sufficient for Believers," *HT* 11.2 (Feb. 1874): 34-36.
152. Brenneman, "What Jesus Has Commanded, and Also What He Has Forbidden," *HT* 9.2 (Feb. 1872): 17-19 = "Was Jesus geboten, befohlen und auch verboten hat," *HdW* 9.2 (Feb. 1872): 17-19; quote is from 17 in each.
153. Brenneman, "A Noble Determination After a Conflict," *HT* 19.7 (1 Apr. 1882): 97-99; quote is from 98. Reprinted in *Hope, Sanctification, and a Noble Determination*, with quote from 15.
154. Brenneman, *Encouragement*, 6.
155. Brenneman, *Encouragement*, 18-19.
156. Brenneman, *Encouragement*, 21.
157. Brenneman, *Encouragement*, 36.
158. Brenneman, "Christian Love," in *Plain Teachings*, 54-74.
159. Brenneman, *Pride and Humility*, and *Hoffart und Demuth*.
160. Brenneman, "Eine Wechstimme an die stoltzen Frauen," *HdW* 5.4 (Apr. 1868): 51-54.
161. For two such lists, see Brenneman, "What Jesus Has Commanded, and Also What He Has Forbidden," *HT* 9.2 (Feb. 1872): 17-19 = "Was Jesus geboten, befohlen und auch verboten hat," *HdW* 9.2 (Feb. 1872): 17-19; and *Hope, Sanctification and a Noble Determination*, 15-16.
162. For example, "What Jesus Has Commanded, and Also What He Has Forbidden," *HT* 9.2 (Feb. 1872): 19 = "Was Jesus geboten, befohlen und auch verboten hat," *HdW* 9.2 (Feb. 1872): 19.
163. Brenneman, "Affecting Incidents from Canada," *HT* 1.2 (Jan. 1864): 6 = "Wichtig von Canada," *HdW* 1.2 (Feb. 1864): 8; "A Visit," *HT* 5.11 (Nov. 1868): 171-72 = "Ein Besuch," *HdW* 5.11 (Nov. 1868): 172; "A Visit to Pennsylvania," *HT* 6.7 (July 1869): 104-105 = "Ein Besuch nach Pennsylvanien," *HdW* 6.7 (July 1869): 104-105; "Thou Shalt Die." *HT* 8.9 (Sept. 1871): 135; "Further Account of the Death of Henry A. Brenneman," *HT* 9.10 (Oct. 1872): 153-154 = "Ferneren Bericht von dem Tod des Heinrich A. Brenneman," *HdW* 9.10 (Oct. 1872): 153-154; "Man on Earth a Sojourner Only," in *Plain Teachings*, 239-241.
164. Holdeman, *Old Ground*, 1-7.
165. Holdeman, *Old Ground*, 5.
166. Holdeman, *Old Ground*, 7.
167. One such group in particular was that of Jacob Stauffer. Holdeman had some initial attraction for Stauffer's group. Holdeman and his father visited them, apparently hoping to find a church home with them, but could not unite. The problem appeared to be particular points of doctrine, which Holdeman did not specify when he wrote about Stauffer's group in *History*, 116: "This church reformed in church discipline to some extent, as well as in the avoidance, but did not in every point of doctrine accept the old ground." The fact that Stauffer gained few additional members, Holdeman added in *History*, 124, indicates that "the blessing of the Holy Spirit is not there to gather the children of God."
168. For example, Holdeman, *Old Ground*, 11, 22-23, 89-90.
169. There is a need for more research on the sources used by Holdeman and the kind of influence they might have exerted on his theological outlook. Although mentioning only a few titles, Clarence Hiebert in *Holdeman People*, 379, stated that Holdeman had accumulated a personal library of fifty to one hundred books.

170. Holdeman, *Spiegel,* 9: "Von der Erkenntniss des Dreieinigen Gottes, des Vaters, des Sohnes, und des Heiligen Geistes; und was sie uns lehrt." Holdeman's focus was changed a bit by the rendering of the title in *Mirror,* 17: "The Divine Trinity and What It Teaches Us."

171. Holdeman, *Spiegel,* 9: "Unwandelbare, allmachtige."

172. Holdeman, *Spiegel,* 11: "als Licht aus dem wahrhaftigen Lichte, Gott von dem wahrhaftigen Gotte, als ein ewiger Sohn Gottes geboren is worden, ehe er in diese Welt im Fleisch geboren worden ist."

173. Holdeman, *Spiegel,* 12: "Er auch zuvor muss gewesen sein."

174. Holdeman, *Mirror,* 20-37.

175. Holdeman, *Mirror,* 23-31.

176. Note the evolution in Holdeman's outline from *Old Ground,* through *History,* to *A Mirror of Truth.* This has some similarities to the development of outline and thought one generation later in Daniel Kauffman's three volumes of Bible doctrines. Chapter 6, below, recounts the changes in Kauffman's thought.

177. John C. Wenger, ed., *The Complete Writings of Menno Simons,* c. 1561. (Scottdale, Pa.: Herald Press, 1956), 489-498.

178. Holdeman, *On Redemption,* 12.

179. Holdeman, *On Redemption,* 14-15.

180. Holdeman, *On Redemption,* 13.

181. Holdeman, *On Redemption,* 20.

182. Holdeman, *On Redemption,* 20.

183. Holdeman, *On Redemption,* 23.

184. Holdeman, *On Redemption,* 23.

185. Holdeman, *On Redemption,* 26.

186. Holdeman, *On Redemption,* 23-50.

187. Holdeman, *On Redemption,* 26.

188. Holdeman, *History,* 63.

189. Holdeman, *History,* 121, 139.

190. Holdeman, *History,* 119-121.

191. On dreams and visions, see Holdeman, *History,* 147, 152-160; *Mirror,* 525-540. The church that Holdeman founded still maintains a stress on an experiential and emotional, revivalistic conversion and an intense personal piety. See Hiebert, *Holdeman People,* 278-279, 414-415, 618-620.

192. Egly, "Autobiography," 4, 10.

193. That is, the Amish church, which baptized unconverted persons and ordained unconverted ministers. See note 176, above.

194. Holdeman, *History,* 177.

195. At the close of his analysis of Christology in the opening chapter of *Mirror,* 37, Holdeman commended Menno's christological writings against Gellius Faber, John à Lasco, and Martin Micron as ones which "surpass all others in thoroughness, excepting the Holy Scriptures."

196. In the German, Holdeman wrote of the "Gottheit" of Jesus or of Christ. I would suggest that "deity" is a better rendering than "Godhead," frequently used by the translators of *A Mirror of Truth.* For example, see *Spiegel,* 12; *Mirror,* 22.

197. For example, see Holdeman, *Spiegel,* 12, 10: "dass er Gott ist."

198. Holdeman, *Spiegel,* 11, 21; *Mirror,* 22, 36.

199. Holdeman, *Spiegel,* 11; *Mirror,* 21.

200. William Keeney, "The Incarnation, A Central Theological Concept," in *A Legacy of Faith: The Heritage of Menno Simons,* ed. by Cornelius J. Dyck (Newton, Kan.: Faith & Life, 1962), 56.

201. Translation is mine, from Holdeman, *Spiegel,* 11: "Seine Menschwerdung wird eine Geburt geheissen; denn er ist von dem heiligen Geist in der reinen Jungfrau Maria empfangen, und aus ihr als Mensch geboren wborden, aber nicht zu einer geschaffenen Creatur, wie wir sind, sondern als Gott-Mensch; das Word oder Gott ward Fleisch; und

in diesem Fleisch hat er gelitten, und ist gestorben, und begraben, und auferstanden von den Todten."

202. Holdeman, *Spiegel*, 12; *Mirror*, 22.

203. My translation of Holdeman, *Spiegel*, 12: "Weil der Sohn Gottes sein Fleisch nicht von der Erde genommen hat, und nicht irdisch war, sondern der Herr selbst vom Himmel, darum konnte er die Verwesung nicht sehen, und ist, da er getödtet ward, wieder auferstanden von den Todten." The rendering of the passage in *Mirror*, 22, makes less obvious the celestial flesh Christology since it says that Christ was not a "carnal creature" and omits the mention of Christ's flesh not being earthly.

204. Holdeman, *Mirror*, 23-31.

205. Holdeman, *History*, 98-108; *Mirror*, 356-399.

206. Holdeman, *History*, 18; *Mirror* 356-357.

207. Note Holdeman's consideration of the relationship between old and new covenants and this treatment of the exercise of government and the sword. In general, it sounds somewhat like the different kinds of government and the distinction between Jews and Gentiles in dispensationalism. In contrast to dispensationalism, however, Holdeman considered the church to be the continuation of the people of Israel, and the church has a spiritual but not a secular government. See *Mirror*, 356-358.

208. See Holdeman, *Mirror*, 356-399.

209. See Holdeman, *Mirror*, 380.

210. Holdeman, *On Redemption*, 29-30.

211. See Holdeman, *Spiegel*, 285-305; *Mirror*, 326-355.

212. Paton Yoder in *Tradition and Transition*, 184, says, "Except for insisting on an experiential conversion, Egli was a typical Amish bishop."

213. J. Y. Schultz, "Besuchsreise nach Indiana und Ohio," *CBB* 6.16 (15 Aug. 1887): 6.

214. Most of Egly's articles have something to say to this point.

215. Egly, "Die Eingezogenheit der Christen," *HdW* 10.11 (Nov. 1873): 178. Similarly, he stated, "The teacher or explorer must first stand in this certainty of faith—that he is himself a participant in this love of God through faith in Jesus Christ, and his heart is circumcised with the living Word of God, that he loves God above all and his neighbor as himself, so that through his own experience of faith in God's promises he can say Yea and Amen to God's promises—in order to preach and proclaim what God will do and can do according to Jesus' will." See "Ein neu Gebot," *HdW* 15.2 (Feb. 1878), 19-20, and *Das Friedensreich Christi*, 14.

216. For Egly's account of the controversy and founding of his group, see "Autobiography," 1-2. See also Nussbaum, *Ye Must Be Born Again*, 2-3; Smith, *Mennonites in Illinois*, 111-112; Schlabach, *Peace, Faith, Nation*, 115-116; Yoder, *Tradition and Transition*, 184-186. Known first as the Egly Amish, they took the name Defenseless Mennonite Church, and became the Evangelical Mennonite Church in 1948. Nussbaum in *Ye Must Be Born Again*, 23, located the development of the name "Defenseless Mennonite" for the "Egly Amish" at 23 July 1898, when the Salem, Illinois, congregation put that name on a deed for church property.

However, something like that name was apparently in use some years before that date. In the *Herold der Wahrheit* issue for 1 September 1883, Egly issued an open invitation for interested persons to attend their conference which would convene the next month. Following a summary of the conference agenda, Egly added, "We wish to be better known on the basis of what we believe as Defenseless Christians or Mennonites (*wehrlose Christen oder Mennoniten*), and therefore issue a friendly invitation to visit us at that time and to attend the conference." See Egly, "Einladung," *HdW* 20.17 (1 Sept. 1883): 265. The self-designation in this invitation brings to mind the name "Taufs-Gesinnten oder Wehrlosen Christen," from the title of the German edition of *Martyrs Mirror*, which would have been familiar to Egly.

217. Egly, "Die Sanftmüthigen," *HdW* 16.5 (May 1879): 85.

218. Egly, "Die Pfingsten," *HdW* 16.6 (June 1879): 100; and *Das Friedensreich*

Christi, 21-23. In a somewhat similar way, a passage in Egly's "Autobiography," 16-17, reviews the Israelites' escape from Egypt, journey through the wilderness, and crossing the Jordan into the Promised Land. Then Egly compares it all with the spiritual journey which sinners make from the dark world, through the spiritual wilderness of temptation and testing, and finally into the state of forgiveness and joy in Jesus. Jesus underwent the same experience and overcame the devil after forty days of temptation.

219. Egly, "Autobiography," 11. See also note 100 in chapter 5, below.

220. Egly, "Autobiography," 14-15. For Egly's judgments about Oberholtzer and Gehman, see "Autobiography," 14-15. For details on that schism, see Schlabach, *Peace, Faith, Nation*, 117-127.

221. On sleeping preachers, see notes 225-227 for this chapter, and the context of note 96 in chapter 5, below.

222. For a time, Egly contemplated merger with Holdeman's group. That hope broke down, Egly wrote in "Autobiography," 4, because we "could not agree again about water baptism." For more detail, see discussion related to notes 180-182, above, in this chapter's section on Holdeman.

223. Egly, "Die Eingezogenheit der Christen," *HdW* 10.11 (Nov. 1873): 178.

224. Egly, "Vom Glauben und der Gewissheit" (Flanagan, Ill.: C. R. Egle, n.d.), a tract.

225. Egly, "Die Eingezogenheit der Christen," *HdW* 10.11 (Nov. 1873): 178.

226. For Brenneman, see chapter 3, above, in the context of notes 199-200.

227. Nussbaum, *Ye Must Be Born Again*, 8-9; Weber, *Mennonites of Illinois*, 340; Smith, *Mennonites in Illinois*, 112; Yoder, *Tradition and Transition*, 184-185.

228. Egly, "Autobiography," 23.

229. Egly, "Unser Bestreben nach oben," *HdW* 10.12 (Dec. 1873): 195-196.

230. Egly, "Essen und Trinken das Fleisch und Blut Christi," *HdW* 14.11 (Nov. 1877): 167-168.

231. Here are examples of Egly's articles stating that reborn sinners must love their enemies, or making nonresistance the supreme test of conversion and having received the Holy Spirit: "Vom Friedensreich Jesu Christi," *HdW* 14.12 (Dec. 1877): 183-185; and in *Das Friedensreich Christi*, 1-10; "Ein neu Gebot," *HdW* 15.2 (Feb. 1878): 19-20; "Säen und Ernten," *HdW* 15.12 (Dec. 1878): 201-202; "Die Sanftmüthigen," *HdW* 16.5 (May 1879): 85; "Suchet und forschet," *HdW* 20.14 (15 July 1883): 211-212; "Only One Gospel," in *Das Friedensreich Christi*, 31-32.

Articles noting the need to obey all commands of Christ, but without specifying the particular commands, include these: "Das Osterlamm," *HdW* 16.6 (June 1879): 102-103; and in *Das Friedensreich Christi*, 17-20; "Jesus der wahre Helfer," *HdW* 16.9 (Sept. 1879): 166; "Die seligmachende Glaube," *HdW* 27.11 (1 June 1890): 161-162; and in *Das Friedensreich Christi*, 24-25; "Etwas über die Wirkung des Satans," *CBB* 1.19 (1 Oct. 1882): 149-150.

232. Egly, "Vom Friedensreich Jesu Christi, welches seinen Anfang nahmen sollte sobald also Christus sein Opfer gethan hatte am Kreuze, nach allen prophetischen Schriften," *HdW* 14.12 (Dec. 1877): 183; and in *Das Friedensreich Christi*, 1.

233. Egly, "Vom Friedensreich Jesu Christi," *HdW* 14.12 (Dec. 1877): 183; and in *Das Friedensreich Christi*, 3.

234. "O, könnte das Sterben Jesu noch mehr an uns offenbar werden, so würde auch das Leben Jesu an uns sichtbar werden, also der Tod mächtig an den Vorgängern, aber das Leben an der Gemeine." From Egly, "Vom Friedensreich Jesu Christi," *HdW* 14.12 (Dec. 1877), 185; and in *Das Friedensreich Christi*, 10.

235. Egly, "Vom Friedensreich Jesu Christi," *HdW* 14.12 (Dec. 1877): 183-185; and in *Das Friedensreich Christi*, 1-10.

236. Nussbaum in *Ye Must Be Born Again*, 40, noted this sermon and Egly's rejection of premillennialism, in contrast to the adoption of premillennialism by the contemporary Evangelical Mennonite Church.

237. Noah Troyer and John D. Kauffman were the most famous of several Amish

ministers who acquired the nickname of "sleeping preachers" and gained fame in the 1870s and 1880s from their practice of preaching while in a trance. On sleeping preachers, see Schlabach, *Peace, Faith, Nation*, 220; *The Mennonite Encyclopedia*, "Kauffman, John D.," 3:158; and "Sleeping Preacher Churches," 4:543-544; and the discussion related to note 95 in chapter 5, below.

238. Egly, "Lasset euch Niemand verfühlen in keinerlei Weise," *CBB* 1.16 (15 Aug. 1882), 125-126. This article was Egly's extended response to the sleeping preachers.

239. See the supportive articles by John S. Coffman, "Noah Troyer," *HT* 17.10 (Oct. 1880): 180-181; "Noah Troyer," *HdW* 17.12 (Dec. 1880): 225; and by John F. Funk, "John D. Kauffman, the Sleeping Preacher," *HT* 19.6 (15 Mar. 1882): 81-83; "John D. Kauffman, der schlafende Prediger," *HdW* 19.6 (15 Mar. 1882): 85-87. In addition, Funk reprinted and sold copies of Troyer's sermons through his publishing company.

240. Egly, "Etwas über die Wirkung des Satans," *CBB* 1.19 (1 Oct. 1882): 150.

241. Egly, "Warum sind so wenige Christenbekenner glücklich und selig?" *CBB* 3.6 (15 Mar. 1884): 42.

242. Egly, "Vom lebendigen Glaube," *Das Friedensreich Christi*, 26.

Chapter 5: The Theory of Atonement

1. Stauffer, *Chronik*, 119-120.
2. Stauffer, *Chronik*, 257.
3. Stauffer, *Chronik*, 253.
4. Stauffer, *Chronik*, 13, referring to Heb. 6:6.
5. Stauffer, *Chronik*, 16.
6. Beiler, *Wahre Christenthum*, 11. See also Beiler, *Betrachtung über den Berg Predig*, 34, 57.
7. Beiler, *Wahre Christenthum*, 15-16. See also Beiler, *Betrachtung*, 57, 69, 86.
8. Beiler, *Wahre Christenthum*, 24.
9. Beiler, *Wahre Christenthum*, 33.
10. Beiler, *Wahre Christenthum*, 65. See Beiler, *Betrachtung*, 34, for a similar statement about God erasing "*die Handschrift*" or record of our transgressions, which was standing against us. This comes from Col. 2:14 in Luther's *Bibel*.
11. Beiler, *Wahre Christenthum*, 68.
12. Beiler, *Betrachtung*, 88: "Der Gerechte für die Ungerechten, der Reine für die Unreinen, der Unschuldige für die Schuldigen, der Sohn Gottes für die Menschen. Und die Ursach dass Christus gelitten hat eine solcher Schmach, und nicht weniger schmertzhaftiger Tod, war die Sünde Adam's und Eva's, und der ganzen Welt."
13. Beiler, *Wahre Christenthum*, 215-273.
14. Beiler, *Wahre Christenthum*, 227-228: "Und wie Gott alle Sünden, heimlich oder öffentlich begangen, hasst und strafen will mit ewiger Pein und Qual. Und auch, wie er seinen unschuldigen Sohn so viel hat leiden lassen, um die Sünde Adam's und Eva's und der ganzen Welt zu versöhnen."
15. Beiler, *Wahre Christenthum*, 233.
16. Wiebe, *Ursachen und Geschichte*, 35-36; *Causes*, 45.
17. Wiebe, *Ursachen und Geschichte*, 55-56; *Causes*, 69-70; quote is from 70.
18. Wiebe, *Ursachen und Geschichte*, 70. Translation is mine.
19. Wiebe, *Ursachen und Geschichte*, 56: his meaning here is ambiguous. The German sentence in question reads, ". . . Und jetzt nahm der Satan die Gelegenheit wahr, er dachte, jetzt ist er selbst von Gott verstossen, und wollte den Herrn mit all unseren Sünden erdrücken und töten, das war eine Angst, die kein Menschen beschreiben, viel weniger noch ertragen konnte."
Where the thought ends that Wiebe attributed to Satan is unclear. Also ambiguous is whether Wiebe intended to say that Satan or God wanted to crush Jesus, who was bearing "all our sins." If it is Satan who wants to do the crushing, the Christus Victor motif is more evident. If it is God who crushes Jesus bearing the sins of the world, then the penal,

substitutionary element is more consistent within Wiebe's theological outlook. Since Wiebe was far from a systematic thinker, it is perhaps best to allow the ambiguity to stand here, particularly since other elements of this passage indicate that he did assume substitutionary atonement.

20. Wiebe, *Ursachen und Geschichte*, 56; *Causes*, 70.

21. Written in Elbing, Prussia, in 1778, this catechism underwent a number of printings for the use of Mennonites in Prussia, Russia, and North America. At the time of the Russian Mennonite immigration to southern Manitoba, the Elbing Catechism was in use in North America by the Amish, the "old" Mennonite Church, and the General Conference Mennonite Church, as well as by all the immigrant groups in southern Manitoba, including the Bergthaler Mennonites, the Evangelical Mennonite Brethren, and the Kleine Gemeinde. See Stoesz, "History," 230-233; and Christian Neff and Harold S. Bender, "Catechism" in *Mennonite Encyclopedia*, 1:529-531.

22. Stoesz, "History," 84, 191, 229-230.

23. Elbing Catechism, ch 2, questions 10, 11, 12, 13, 16.

24. For example, Wiebe, *Ursachen und Geschichte*, 48; *Causes*, 61.

25. In discussing sin, Wedel dealt with the range of classic questions whose details need not occupy the current discussion. They include the Fall, the pre-Fall and post-Fall conditions of humanity, the fallenness of angels and the devil, the nature of sin in general, evil as a power in the world, theories concerning the origin of sin, and original sin. See "Glaubenslehre," 99-118; Heft 2:95-112; 3:1-9.

26. Wedel, *Meditationen*, 50.

27. Wedel, *Meditationen*, 67-88.

28. Wedel, "Glaubenslehre," 197-198; Heft 4:31-32.

29. Wedel, "Glaubenslehre," 198; Heft 4:32.

30. Wedel, *Meditationen*, 89-96.

31. The language of Lev. 7:1.

32. Wedel, *Meditationen*, 87.

33. Wedel, "Glaubenslehre," 120-182; Heft 3:22-95; 4:1-16. For extended analysis, see the discussion in chapter 4 (above) on the wider context of Wedel's theology of atonement.

34. Wedel, "Glaubenslehre," 174-177; Heft 3:90-95; 4:1-10.

35. Wedel, "Glaubenslehre," 177; Heft 4:10: "Als Hoherpriester seiligt sich der Herr selbst die Seinen in seinen hl. Leben, vollbringt sodann in seinen Leiden und Sterben das Werk der Versöhnung das Menschen mit Gott, und die Erlösung der selben von der Macht der Sünde. Seitdem vertritt er die Seinen vor Gott und seignet sie." On the priestly office of Christ, see "Glaubenslehre," 177-178; Heft 4:10-13.

36. In the one specific mention of atonement in his "Ethik," Wedel stated that Jesus' death satisfied the course of the law. Because Jesus' death satisfied the law, he can then be not only Redeemer but Teacher and example for sinners. See "Ethik," 51-54; Heft 1:71-72; 2:1-4.

37. Wedel, "Glaubenslehre," 184; Heft 4:18: ". . . so müsste die Sühnung der Sünde ein Tragen der Gesammtsünde der Menschen sein, damit die Sünde die ihr geburende [gebührende?] Strafe erhalte, Gottes Zorn sich in der Strafe auswerke, und auf diese Weise die Sünde kraftlos werden."

38. Wedel, "*Glaubenslehre*," 185-189; Heft 4:18-23.

39. Wedel, "*Glaubenslehre*," 189-193; Heft 4:23-27.

40. Wedel, *Meditationen*, 147. Wedel placed the death of Jesus in continuity with the Old Testament sacrifices. While it may fit well within the context of the satisfaction theory's legal structure, the Old Testament linking is not inherently necessary to it and does constitute a separate atonement motif. See Yoder, *Preface to Theology*, 210. Moser and Egly, as seen in what follows, built other kinds of links between the Old Testament and Jesus' death.

41. The three quotes are from Wedel, *Meditationen*, 157. For additional instances where Wedel noted the motif of Christ's death as an expression of divine love, or as origi-

nating in the love of God, see *Meditationen*, 92, 246. As following paragraphs note, "Glaubenslehre" also contains this combination of wrath and love.

42. Wedel, "Glaubenslehre," 198; Heft 4:32-33. Similar comments on the moral influence theory appear in the *Meditationen*, where Wedel called it the perspective of a "positive-thinking theologian." He characterized this theory as a statement that the life and death of Jesus are a rich and unfathomable testimony of Christ's love. While there is certainly much of value in this treasuring of the death of Christ, he wrote in *Meditationen*, 147, "it is nonetheless one-sided and cannot be reconciled with the words of Scripture."

43. Wedel, "Glaubenslehre," 193; Heft 4:27.

44. Wedel, "Glaubenslehre," 194; Heft 4:28: ". . . weil Christi unermassliches Opfer der Liebe die Schüld der Menschen aufgewogen hat, und unsere Sünde bezahlt hat."

45. Wedel, "Glaubenslehre," 194-195; Heft 4:28-29: "Es handelte sich ja nicht nur darum dass Gott anders zu dem Menschen stehen sollte als früher, d. h. anstatt zürnend, sollte er dem Menschen gnädig gegenüber stehen, sondern auch um ein neues Verhältnis der Menschen zu Gott."

46. Wedel, "Glaubenslehre," 195-196; Heft 4:29-30.

47. Wedel, "Glaubenslehre," 196; Heft 4:30: "Fassen wir zusammen: Christus sühnte unsre Sünde und hat damit unsre Versöhnung möglich gemacht, so dass es darauf hin schon heisst, Got ist versöhnt, durch sein Sühnopfer erlöste er uns aber von der Macht und Herschaft der Sünde. Als Sünder sehen wir in Gott einen zürnenden Gott, sobald wir jedes Christi Opfertod annehmen, sehen wir in ihm einen Gott der Liebe. Durch die Annahmen der Heils wird also die Versöhnung abgerundet."

48. Wedel, *Meditationen*, 93-94; parallel in "Glaubenslehre," 180-182; Heft 4:13-16. Wedel also noted Greek efforts to find salvation through knowledge in *Neuen Testaments*, 10.

49. Wedel, *Meditationen*, 147. See also "Glaubenslehre," 197; Heft 4:31: "Quite realistically Satan was presented as the jailer who had been conquered by Christ."

50. For comments on these several theories of atonement, see Wedel, *Meditationen*, 147. On "rationalistic" approach, see also "Glaubenslehre," 200-201; Heft 4:34-36.

51. Wedel, "Glaubenslehre," 199-202; Heft 4:33-37.

52. Moser, "Über die Wehrlosigkeit," *HDW* 16.1 (Jan. 1879): 1-4; 2 (Feb. 1879): 21-25.

53. Moser, "Über die Wehrlosigkeit," *HdW* 16.1 (Jan. 1879): 1.

54. Moser, "Über die Wehrlosigkeit," 2: "der unsere Sünden an unserer statt tragen sollte."

55. Moser, "Über die Wehrlosigkeit," 3: "An unserer Statt musste Er den Kampf wieder alle Macht des Todes und der Hölle aufnehmen; an unserer Statt musste Er die Schuld tragen und die Strafe der Sünde fühlen."

56. Moser, "Über die Wehrlosigkeit," 3.

57. Moser, "Nachdenken über sich selbst," *CBB* 10.37 (17 Sept. 1891): 2. The element of continuing retaliation as a preparation for Christ's gospel occurs finally in "Des Herrn Wort," *CBB* 20.38 (26 Sept. 1901): 1-2.

58. Moser, "Unglaube," *CBB* 10.38 (24 Sept. 1891): 1-2.

59. Moser, "Lasset uns halten am Hoffnungsbekenntniss," *CBB* 7.35 (6 Sept. 1888): 2.

60. Moser, "Johannes 13," *CBB* 6.2 (15 June 1887): 33. See also "Die Himmelfahrt Christi ist das Ende der leiblichen Lebensgeschichte Christi auf Erden," *CBB* 17.20 (19 May 1898): 2.

61. Moser, "Über die Wehrlosigkeit," *HdW* 16.1 (Jan. 1879): 3. Similar statements of victory and love occur throughout Moser's articles. For example, "Lasset uns halten am Hoffnungsbekenntniss," *CBB* 7.35 (6 Sept. 1888): 10.

62. Brenneman was actually one of the individuals who sensed the need for a

church periodical and urged the young John F. Funk to try his hand at producing it. See Lehman, *Seedbed*, 16; Schlabach, *Peace, Faith, Nation*, 139.

63. Brenneman, "Peace Be with You All That Are in Christ Jesus," *HdW* 1.1 (Jan. 1864): 3; *Plain Teachings*, 213-214.

64. Brenneman, *Plain Teaching*, 104-136; *Einfache Lehre*, 92-120.

65. Brenneman, *Plain Teachings*, 104; *Einfache Lehre*, 92.

66. Brenneman, *Plain Teachings*, 109, 124; *Einfache Lehre*, 96, 109-110.

67. Brenneman, *Plain Teachings*, 110. *Einfache Lehre*, 97.

68. Brenneman, *Plain Teachings*, 112. *Einfache Lehre*, 99.

69. Brenneman, *Plain Teachings*, 114. *Einfache Lehre*, 100-101.

70. Brenneman, *Plain Teachings*, 116. *Einfache Lehre*, 102.

71. Brenneman, *Encouragement to Penitent Sinners*, 35.

72. Brenneman, *Aufmunterung der Bussfertigen Sünder*, 31; *Einfache Lehre*, 39.

73. While that pattern of expanding explanations shows that the German edition was probably written first, it does not necessarily contradict the earlier conclusion that Brenneman preferred the English language or came to have a slight preference for it. (See note 152 in chap. 3.) Perhaps he started with the most difficult language and then added expansive comment in the edition with which he felt most comfortable.

74. Brenneman, *Plain Teachings*, 208-209.

75. Brenneman, *Plain Teachings*, 122.

76. Brenneman, *Plain Teachings*, 124.

77. See the numerous reports of trips and journeys in the Brenneman section of the Bibliography.

78. Brenneman, "Das Osterlamm," *HdW* 2.5 (May 1865): 33; appeared as "Christus das Osterlamm," in *Einfache Lehre*, 180-184.

79. Brenneman, *Einfache Lehre*, 180. As a following section shows, Heinrich Egly also made use of Passover as an atonement type.

80. The following summary comes from Holdeman, *History*, 13-20.

81. In German, Holdeman used such terms as *Figur* (type), *bezahlen*, *versöhnen*, *Versöhnung*, and *Opfer*. For example, see *Geschichte*, 13.

82. Quotes are from Holdeman, *History*, 18. See *Geschichte*, 14: "Unserer Sünden Strafe ward auf ihn gelegt." "So musste Jesus Christus die Schuld auf sich nehmen . . . und von unserer Schuld zu befreien, und in dieser Freisprechung von unserer sünden Strafe. . . ." These examples, as well as those in note 80, above, show that Holdeman's German usage was the traditional language of the satisfaction theory of atonement, which he shared with his Mennonite and Amish brethren.

83. Holdeman, *History*, 18.

84. Holdeman, *History*, 18.

85. Representative passages in Holdeman include *Mirror of Truth*, 25, 30-31, 39, 51-52, 57, 182-187, 191-192; *Spiegel der Wahrheit*, 13-14, 17, 32-33, 24-25, 28, 178-183, 185-186.

86. Holdeman, *A Treatise on redemption*, 7-9.

87. Holdeman, *On Redemption*, 7-8.

88. Egly, "Unsere Bestreben nach oben," *HdW* 10.12 (Dec. 1873): 195.

89. Egly, "Essen und Trinken das Fleisch und Blut Christi," *HdW* 14.11 (Nov. 1877): 167.

90. Egly, "Vom Friedensreich Jesu Christi," *HdW* 14.12 (Dec. 1877): 183-185; reprinted in *HdW* 32.8 (15 Apr. 1895): 116-118, perhaps in conjunction with its appearances as the chapter which supplied the title for *Das Friedensreich Christi*. An English version appeared as "The Kingdom of Peace of Jesus Christ," *The Evangelical Mennonite*, 15 August 1965, 8-10.

91. Egly, "Vom Friedensreich Jesu Christi," *HdW* 14.12 (Dec. 1877): 184; *Das Friedensreich Christi*, 8.

92. Egly, "Die Sanftmüthigen," *HdW* 16.5 (May 1879): 85.

93. Egly, "Die Pfingsten," *HdW* 16.6 (June 1879): 101; *Das Friedensreich Christi*, 22-23.

94. For quote, see Egly, "Osterlamm," *HdW* 16.6 (June 1879): 102; also see 103; *Das Friedensreich Christi*, 18 for quote, 19. Note additional mentions of *Versöhnung*, of one who is "versöhnt durch das Opfer Jesu," and of one becoming worthy "allein durch das verdienst Jesu am Kreuze," in "Osterlamm," 103; *Das Friedensreich Christi*, 19-20.

95. Egly, "Der Seligmachende Glaube," *HdW* 27.11 (1 June 1890): 161; *Das Friedensreich Christi*, 24. Similar comment in *Das Friedensreich Christi*, 29: "Gott will die Sünde an das Licht bringen."

96. On the sleeping preachers, see context and liberature of notes 225-227 in chapter 4.

97. Egly, "Lasset euch Niemand verfühlen in keinerlei Weise," *CBB* 1.16 (15 Aug. 1882): 125.

98. Egly, "Etwas vom lebendigen Glaube," in *Das Friedensreich Christi*, 28.

99. Heinrich Egly's "Autobiography" consists of reminiscences he penned between 27 April 1887 and 20 May 1890. He died 23 June 1890. Given the nature of the "Autobiography," any theological comments in it likely represent Egly's final or fixed opinions more than his thought at the times of the events he discussed.

100. Egly, "Autobiography," 7. Egly summarized more briefly similar deliberations at the conference of October of the following year (1883), meeting in Adams County, Indiana, in "Autobiography," 9: "We had open meetings and everything went in order, in peace unanimous, all one mind and having the same opinion as we can read in God's Word. We rehearsed about the fall of man through Adam, then what Jesus Christ did for our sins (died on the cross and was raised again the third day), and if we believe on Him and repent our sins are forgiven and we are made righteous by Him." Corroboration of that summary is contained in an English translation of the proceedings, lodged in the archives of the Evangelical Mennonite Church, Berne, Indiana. The descriptions of questions 1 (why people are sinners) and 2 (how to be made right before God) follow closely Egly's description of the issues from the previous year as well as the summary of the conference of October 1883.

101. Such unrest doubtlessly forms part of the context in which Johannes Moser wrote "Gedanken über Spaltungen," *HdW* 21.7-13 (1 April—1 July, 1884): 102-103; 117-119; 131-132; 149-151; 164-165; 179-180; 195-197. Egly noted having been in Allen County several times before the meetings of October 1884, which resulted in the eighteen baptisms. There must have been considerable friction between Egly and the Swiss Mennonite community. Describing meetings in Putnam County the following February, Egly in "Autobiography," 11, reported that while God blessed the journey and five were added to the church, "the old serpent was very much against us[;] one preacher in the Swiss Mennonite church, John Moser was one of the instruments through which he worked against us, but had no assurance of his salvation in his heart." See also note 207 in chapter 4, above.

102. Egly, "Autobiography," 10. On another occasion, Egly in "Autobiography," 18, said that "35 souls found peace and found their redemption in the blood of the Lamb and the forgiveness of sins."

103. Similar language occurred in Egly's description of a tension-filled visit of 1 April 1885 with Chris Zimmerman, pastor of the Apostolic Church. Egly noted his own efforts to leave the old church and build a new church "on the foundation of the Apostles and the Prophets, the redemption through Jesus Christ, the forgiveness of sins through His blood, and obeying His command to baptize those that believe on Him, etc." A part of a description of another extended preaching trip included the words, from "Autobiography," 11-12: "Jesus Christ died on the Cross for our sins and was raised again and made redemption for our sins."

104. Egly, "Autobiography," 17. Reference to redemption and forgiveness in the blood of Jesus was a recurrent formula in Egly's description of the results of his preaching trips. See also "Autobiography," 18, 23.

105. See note 1 in chapter 1, above.

Chapter 6: The Separation of Atonement and Ethics

1. Coffman, "The Atonement," *HT* 23 (1886): 6; cited in J. Denny Weaver, "The Quickening of Soteriology," *MQR* 61.1 (Jan. 1987): 33. This summary of Coffman is based on "Quickening," 31-34.

2. Coffman, "Foot Washing," *HT* 25.15 (1 Aug. 1888), 229: "The Scriptures enjoin upon us not to avenge ourselves against evil, not to swear by heaven or any other oath, not to be conformed to the world, not to go to law before the unbelievers. These are duties in one sense, but more properly restrictions." See also Coffman's diagram and explanation in John S. Coffman, Comp., *Outlines and Notes Used at the Bible Conference Held at Johnstown, Pennsylvania, from Dec. 27, 1897, to Jan. 7, 1898* (Elkhart, Ind.: Mennonite Publishing Co., 1898), 36-39.

3. See Theron F. Schlabach, "Reveille for *Die Stillen im Lande*: A Stir Among Mennonites in the Late Nineteenth Century," *MQR* 51 (1977): 224-225; Schlabach, *Gospel Versus Gospel*, 51-52; Weaver, "Quickening," 34.

4. The following summary of Kauffman is based on Weaver, "Quickening," *MQR* 61.1 (Jan. 1987): 34-42. See also Schlabach, "Reveille," *MQR* 51.3 (1977): 225. The three volumes of Kauffman are his *Manual of Bible Doctrines, Setting Forth the General Principles of the Plan of Salvation* (Elkhart, Ind.: Mennonite Publishing House, 1898); Kauffman, ed., *Bible Doctrine: A Treatise on the Great Doctrines of the Bible Pertaining to God, Angels, Satan, and the Salvation, Duties and Destiny of Man* (Scottdale, Pa.: Mennonite Publishing House, 1914); Kauffman, ed., *Doctrines of the Bible: A Brief Discussion of the Teachings of God's Word* (Scottdale, Pa.: Mennonite Publishing House, 1928).

5. Kauffman, *Manual*, 205.

6. Kauffman, *Bible Doctrine*, 457.

7. *Doctrines of the Bible*, 442.

Chapter 7: Conclusion

1. Eschatology and the acceptance or rejection of premillennialism and dispensationalism became a controversial topic among Mennonites at the turn to the twentieth century. The few references to eschatology in this study are only the beginning of that argument. A significant project for further research is to develop an extended analysis of this argument about eschatology. Specifically, the analysis should explore the extent to which the argument was fueled by commitment to a nonresistant or nonviolent theology. Was Daniel Kauffman's amillennialism, for example, based on nonresistance, even though he had relegated nonresistance to the category of a "restriction"?

2. Friedmann, *Mennonite Piety Through the Centuries*, 9-13, 72-88, 146; quotes are from 12, 146.

3. Ernst Crous, "Mennonitentum und Pietismus: Ein Versuch," *Theologische Zeitschrift* 8.4 (July/August 1952): 279-281; and "Anabaptism, Pietism, Rationalism and German Mennonites," in *Recovery of the Anabaptist Vision*, ed. Guy F. Hershberger (Scottdale, Pa.: Herald Press, 1957; 3d printing, 1972), 237-241.

4. See Brown's summary comments at the end of chapters on ecclesiology, exegesis, ethics, experience, and eschatology, as well as his own perspective in the final chapter of *Understanding Pietism* (Grand Rapids: Eerdmans, 1978), as well as Dale Brown, *Anabaptism and Pietism: I. Points of Convergence and Divergence; II. Living the Anabaptist and Pietist Dialectic*, Two Public Lectures Presented at the Young Center of the Study of Anabaptist and Pietist Groups (Elizabethtown, Pa.: Elizabethtown College, 1990). A more implicit rehabilitation of Pietism for Anabaptists by a Church of the Brethren scholar is Donald F. Durnbaugh, *New Understandings of Anabaptism and Pietism* (Elizabethtown, Pa.: Elizabethtown College, 1987).

5. Martin H. Schrag, "The Impact of Pietism upon the Mennonites in Early American Christianity," in *Continental Pietism and Early American Christianity*, ed. F. Ernest Stoeffler (Grand Rapids: Eerdmans, 1976), 74-122.

6. Carl F. Bowman, *Brethren Society: The Cultural Transformation of a "Peculiar People"* (Baltimore: Johns Hopkins, 1995), 47.

7. Richard K. MacMaster, *Land, Piety, Peoplehood: The Establishment of Mennonite Communities in America 1683-1790*, Mennonite Experience in America, 1 (Scottdale, Pa.: Herald Press, 1985), chaps. 5, 6, 10.

8. Schlabach, *Peace, Faith, Nation*, 88-95; quote is from 95; see also Schlabach, "Mennonites and Pietism in America, 222-240.

9. Bowman, *Brethren Society*, 47-48.

10. Bowman, *Brethren Society*, 46.

11. George A. Lindbeck, *The Nature of Doctrine: Religion and Theology in a Post-liberal Age* (Philadelphia: Westminster, 1984), 32-41, esp. 32-34; "Barth and Textuality," *Theology Today* 43.3 (Oct. 1986): 361-376; "Confession and Community: An Israel-like View of the Church," *Christian Century* 107.16 (9 May 1990): 492-496.

12. Stanley Hauerwas, "The Testament of Friends," *Christian Century* 107.7 (28 Feb. 1990): 213.

13. Stanley Hauerwas, *The Peaceable Kingdom: A Primer in Christian Ethics* (Notre Dame: Univ. of Notre Dame, 1983), 55.

14. James Wm. McClendon Jr., *Ethics*, vol. 1 of *Systematic Theology* (Nashville: Abingdon, 1986), 17.

15. McClendon, *Ethics*, 45.

16. Ronald J. Sider, "Evangelicalism and the Mennonite Tradition," in *Evangelicalism and Anabaptism*, ed. C. Norman Kraus (Scottdale, Pa.: Herald Press, 1979), 159-168; A. James Reimer, "The Nature and Possibility of a Mennonite Theology, *CGR* 1.1 (Winter 1983): 33-55; A. James Reimer, "Trinitarian Orthodoxy, Constantinianism, and Theology from a Radical Protestant Perspective," in *Faith to Creed: Ecumenical Perspectives on the Affirmation of the Apostolic Faith in the Fourth Century*, ed. S. Mark Heim (Grand Rapids: Eerdmans, 1991), 129-161; A. James Reimer, "Doctrines: What Are They, How Do They Function, and Why Do We Need them?" *CGR* 11.1 (Winter 1993): 21-36. In apparent support of the call to base a theology for Mennonites on the classic formulas or creeds are the assertions of Walter Klaassen and Arnold Snyder that most sixteenth-century Anabaptists affirmed the classic creeds (chap. 1, note 4). See comments in Klaassen, "Sixteenth-Century Anabaptism," 245-246; and Snyder, "Beyond Polygenesis," 11-13; Snyder, *Anabaptist History and Thought*, 84-90.

17. For my own initial and ongoing discussion of the reformulation of Christology and atonement from within the narrative of Jesus, see Weaver, "Mennonites: Theology, Peace, and Identity," *CGR* 6.2 (Spring 1988): 119-145; "Christology in Historical Perspective," in *Jesus Christ and the Mission of the Church: Contemporary Anabaptist Perspectives*, ed. Erland Waltner (Newton, Kan.: Faith & Life, 1990), 83-105; "Atonement for the Non-Constantinian Church," *Modern Theology* 6.4 (July 1990): 307-323; "The Search for a Mennonite Theology," in *Mennonite World Handbook*, ed. Diether Götz Lichdi (Carol Stream, Ill.: Mennonite World Conference, 1990), 143-152; "Christus Victor, Ecclesiology, and Christology," *MQR* 68.3 (July 1994): 277-290; "Some Theological Implications of Christus Victor," *MQR* 60.4 (Oct. 1994): 483-499.

For a fine effort to formulate theology on the basis of Mennonite presuppositions, in conversation primarily with neo-orthodoxy, see C. Norman Kraus, *Jesus Christ Our Lord: Christology from a Disciples's Perspective*, rev. ed. (Scottdale, Pa.: Herald Press, 1990); and *God Our Savior: Theology in a Christological Mode* (Scottdale, Pa.: Herald Press, 1991).

Bibliography

Abbreviations

BCM	Bethel College Monthly (English ed. of MBC)
CBB	Christlicher Bundesbote
CGR	The Conrad Grebel Review
HdW	Der Herold der Wahrheit (German ed. of HT)
HT	The Herald of Truth (English ed. of HdW)
MBC	Monatsblätter aus Bethel College (German ed. of BCM)
MQR	The Mennonite Quarterly Review
SCJ	School and College Journal (Bethel College)

General

Amstutz, P. B. *Geschichtliche Ereignisse der Mennoniten-Ansiedlung in Allen und Putnam County, Ohio, nebst einem Bericht von Gesehenem und Erfahrenem der Orientreise vom Verfasser im Jahr 1914.* Bluffton, Ohio: the author, 1925.

_____. *Historical Events of the Mennonite Settlement in Allen and Putnam Counties, Ohio.* Trans. Anne Konrad Dyck. Bluffton, Ohio: Swiss Community Historical Society, 1978.

Aulén, Gustaf. *Christus Victor: An Historical Study of the Three Main Types of the Idea of Atonement.* Trans. A. G. Hebert. Foreword by Jaroslav Pelikan. New York: Macmillan, 1969.

Bainton, Roland H. *Christian Attitudes Toward War and Peace: A Historical Survey and Critical Re-evaluation.* Nashville: Abingdon, 1960.

Barrett, Anthony A. *Caligula: The Corruption of Power.* New Haven: Yale, 1990.

Beker, J. Christiaan. *Paul the Apostle: The Triumph of God in Life and Thought.* Philadelphia: Fortress, 1980.

_____. Christiaan. *Paul's Apocalyptic Gospel: The Coming Triumph of God.* Philadelphia: Fortress, 1982.

Bender, Harold S. "The Mennonites of the United States." *MQR* 11.1 (Jan. 1937): 79-80.

_____. "Walking in the Resurrection." *MQR* 35.2 (Apr. 1961): 102-103.

"Berichte." *CBB* 4.10 (15 Mar. 1885): 6.

Bowman, Carl F. *Brethren Society: The Cultural Transformation of a "Peculiar People."* Baltimore: Johns Hopkins, 1995.

Brown, Dale. *Anabaptism and Pietism: I. Points of Convergence and Divergence; II. Living the Anabaptist and Pietist Dialectic.* Two Public Lectures Presented at the Young Center of the Study of Anabaptist and Pietist Groups. Elizabethtown, Pa.: Elizabethtown College, 1990.

_____. *Understanding Pietism.* Grand Rapids: Eerdmans, 1978.

Butler, Jon. *Awash in a Sea of Faith: Christianizing the American People.* Cambridge: Harvard Univ. Press, 1990.

Claudon, David N. and Kathryn E. *Life of Bishop Henry Egly, 1824-1890.* N.p., [1947].

Conzelmann, Hans. *Acts of the Apostles: A Commentary on the Acts of the Apostles.* Trans. James Lindburg, A. Thomas Kraabel, and Donald H. Juel. Ed. Eldon Jay Epp with Christopher R. Matthews. Philadelphia: Fortress, 1987.

Cronk, Sandra. *"Gelassenheit:* The Rites of the Redemptive Process in Old Order Amish and Old Order Mennonite Communities." *MQR* 55.1 (Jan. 1981): 6.

Crous, Ernst. "Mennonitentum und Pietismus: Ein Versuch." *Theologische Zeitschrift* 8.4 (July/Aug. 1952): 279-281.

Dayton, Donald. *Discovering an Evangelical Heritage.* New York: Harper & Row, 1976.

Dictionary of Canadian Biography. Vol. 12, *1891 to 1900.* Toronto: Univ. of Toronto Press, 1990.

Driver, John. *Understanding the Atonement for the Mission of the Church.* Foreword by C. René Padilla. Scottdale, Pa.: Herald Press, 1986.

Duff, Nancy J. *Humanization and the Politics of God: The Koinonia Ethics of Paul Lehmann.* Grand Rapids: Eerdmans, 1992.

Durnbaugh, Donald F. *New Understandings of Anabaptism and Pietism.* Elizabethtown, Pa.: Elizabethtown College, 1987.

Dyck, Cornelius J., ed. *A Legacy of Faith: The Heritage of Menno Simons.* Newton, Kan.: Faith & Life, 1962.

Egly, Albert and Anna S., comp. *Egly Family Record: Chronology of the Descendents of Henry Egly, 1824 to 1958.* Fort Wayne, Ind.: the authors, [1958].

Ens, Adolf. *Subjects or Citizens? The Mennonite Experience in Canada, 1870-1925.* Religions and Beliefs Series, no. 2. Ottawa: Univ. of Ottawa Press, 1994.

Ens, Gerhard, J. *"Die Schule muss sein": A History of the Mennonite Collegiate*

Institute, 1889-1989. Gretna, Man.: Mennonite Collegiate Institute, 1990.

Epp, Frank H. *Mennonites in Canada, 1786-1920: The History of a Separate People.* Vol. 1 of *Mennonites in Canada.* Toronto: Macmillan, 1974.

Erland, Waltner, ed. *Jesus Christ and the Mission of the Church: Contemporary Anabaptist Perspectives.* Newton, Kan.: Faith & Life, 1990.

Finger, Thomas N. *Christian Theology: An Eschatological Approach.* Vol. 1. Nashville: Thomas Nelson, 1985; reprinted Scottdale, Pa.: Herald Press, 1987. Vol. 2. Scottdale, Pa.: Herald Press, 1989.

————————. "The Place to Begin Mennonite Theology." *Gospel Herald,* 30 July 1996, 1-3.

Finney, Charles G. *Lectures on Systematic Theology, Embracing Lectures on Moral Government Together with Atonement, Moral and Physical Depravity, Regeneration, Philosophical Theories, and Evidences of Regeneration.* Oberlin: James M. Fitch, 1846.

Friedmann, Robert. "Anabaptism and Protestantism." *MQR* 24.1 (Jan. 1950): 12-24.

————————. *Mennonite Piety Through the Centuries: Its Genius and Its Literature.* Studies in Anabaptist and Mennonite History, no. 7. Goshen, Ind.: Mennonite Historical Society, 1949.

————————. *The Theology of Anabaptism: An Interpretation.* Studies in Anabaptist and Mennonite History, no. 15. Scottdale, Pa.: 1973.

Friesen, John, ed. *Mennonites in Russia, 1788-1988: Essays in Honour of Gerhard Lohrenz.* Winnipeg: CMBC Publications, 1989.

Funk, John. F. "John D. Kauffman, der schlafende Prediger." *HdW* 19.6 (15 Mar. 1882): 85-87.

————————. "John D. Kauffman, the Sleeping Preacher." *HT* 19.6 (15 Mar. 1882): 81-83.

Gerbrandt, Henry J. *Adventure in Faith: The Background in Europe and the Development in Canada of the Bergthaler Mennonite Church of Manitoba.* Altona, Man.: D. W. Friesen, for the Bergthaler Mennonite Church of Manitoba, 1970.

"German Settlement." *The Bluffton News* 24.34 (16 Feb. 1899): 2; 29.17 (15 Oct. 1903), 1.

"Gestorben: Prediger Johannes Moser." *CBB* 27.29 (23 July 1908): 6.

Goeters, Gerhard. "Ludwig Haetzer, a Marginal Anabaptist." *MQR* 29.4 (Oct. 1955): 251-262.

[Goerz, David G]. "Johannes Moser." *MBC* 13.9 (Sept. 1908): 99-100.

Gratz, Delbert. L. *Bernese Anabaptists and Their American Descendants.* Studies in Anabaptist and Mennonite History, no. 8. Goshen, Ind.: Mennonite Historical Society, 1953.

Grieser, Orland R., and Ervin Beck Jr. *Out of the Wilderness.* Grand Rapids: The Dean-Hicks Co., 1960.

Handy, Robert T. *Undermined Establishment: Church-State Relations in America, 1880-1920.* Princeton, N.J.: Princeton Univ. Press, 1991.

Hanson, R. P. C. *The Search for the Christian Doctrine of God: The Arian Controversy, 318-381.* Edinburgh, T. & T. Clark, 1988.

Hardman, Keith J. *Charles Grandison Finney, 1792-1875: Revivalist and Reformer.* Syracuse: Syracuse Univ. Press, 1987.

Hatch, Nathan O. *The Democratization of American Christianity.* New Haven: Yale Univ. Press, 1989.

Hauerwas, Stanley. *After Christendom? How the Church Is to Behave If Freedom, Justice, and a Christian Nation Are Bad Ideas.* Nashville: Abingdon, 1991.

_____. *The Peaceable Kingdom: A Primer in Christian Ethics.* Notre Dame: Univ. of Notre Dame Press, 1983.

_____. "The Testament of Friends." *Christian Century* 107.7 (28 Feb. 1990): 212-216.

Hawkley, Louise, and James C. Juhnke, eds. *Nonviolent America: History Through the Eyes of Peace.* Cornelius H. Wedel Historical Series, no. 5. Bethel College: North Newton, Kan., 1993.

Heim, S. Mark, ed. *Faith to Creed: Ecumenical Perspectives on the Affirmation of the Apostolic Faith in the Fourth Century.* Grand Rapids: Eerdmans, 1991.

Hershberger, Guy F., ed. *Recovery of the Anabaptist Vision.* Scottdale, Pa.: Herald Press, 1957; 3d printing, 1972.

Hiebert, Clarence. *The Holdeman People: The Church of God in Christ, Mennonite, 1859-1969.* South Pasadena, Calif.: William Carey Library, 1973.

Hirschler, E. J. *A Brief History of the Swiss Mennonite Churches of Putnam and Allen Counties, Ohio.* Bluffton, Ohio: Historical Committee, 1937.

Hoover, Amos. B. *The Jonas Martin Era.* Denver, Pa.: Amos B. Hoover, 1982.

Horsch, John. *The Mennonite Church and Modernism.* Scottdale, Pa.: Mennonite Publishing House, 1924.

_____. *Mennonites in Europe.* Scottdale, Pa.: Mennonite Publishing House, 1942.

Johnson, Paul E. *A Shopkeeper's Millennium: Society and Revivals in Rochester, New York, 1815-1837.* New York: Hill and Wang, 1978.

Josephus. *Jewish Antiquities, Book 20.* Vol. 10 of *Josephus.* Trans. by Louis H. Feldman. Loeb Classical Library. Cambridge: Harvard Univ. Press, 1981.

_____. *The Jewish War, Books 1-3.* Vol. 2 of *Josephus.* Trans. by H. St. J. Thackeray. Loeb Classical Library. Cambridge: Harvard Univ. Press, 1976.

Juhnke, James C. *Dialogue with a Heritage: Cornelius H. Wedel and the Beginnings of Bethel College.* North Newton, Kan.: Bethel College, 1987.

_____. "Gemeindechristentum and Bible Doctrine: Two Mennonite Visions of the Early Twentieth Century." *MQR* 57.3 (July 1983): 206-221.

_____. "Manifesto for a Pacifist Reinterpretation of American History." *Fides et Historia* 24.3 (Fall 1993): 53-64.

_____. *Vision, Doctrine, War: Mennonite Identity and Organization in America, 1890-1930*. Vol. 3 of *The Mennonite Experience in America*. Scottdale, Pa.: Herald Press, 1989.

Kaufman, Gordon D. *Systematic Theology: A Historicist Perspective*. New York: Charles Scribner, 1968, 1978.

Klaassen, Walter. "Sixteenth-Century Anabaptism: A Vision Valid for the Twentieth Century?" *CGR* 7.3 (Fall 1989): 245-246.

Koontz, Gayle Gerber. "The Liberation of Atonement." *MQR* 63.2 (Apr. 1989): 171-192.

"Korrespondenzen." *CBB* 19.27 (12 July 1900): 5.

"Korrespondenzen—Bluffton, O." *CBB* 12.16 (12 Oct. 1893): 4.

Krahn, Cornelius. "Prolegomena to an Anabaptist Theology." *MQR* 24.1 (Jan. 1950): 6.

Kraus, C. Norman, ed. *Evangelicalism and Anabaptism*. Scottdale, Pa.: Herald Press, 1979.

_____. *Community of the Spirit: How the Church Is in the World*. Rev. ed. Scottdale, Pa.: Herald Press, 1993.

_____. *Dispensationalism in America: Its Rise and Development*. Richmond, Va.: John Knox, 1958.

_____. *God Our Savior: Theology in a Christological Mode*. Scottdale, Pa.: Herald Press, 1991.

_____. "Interpreting the Atonement in the Anabaptist-Mennonite Tradition." *MQR* 66.3 (July 1992): 291-311.

_____. *Jesus Christ Our Lord: Christology from a Disciples's Perspective*. Rev. ed. Scottdale, Pa.: Herald Press, 1990.

Lehman, James O. *Salem's First Century: Worship and Witness*. Kidron, Ohio: Salem Mennonite Church, 1986.

_____. *Seedbed for Leadership: A Centennial History of the Pike Mennonite Church*. Elida, Ohio: Pike Mennonite Church, 1974.

_____. *Sonnenberg: A Haven and a Heritage: A Sesquicentennial History of the Swiss Mennonite Community of Southeastern Wayne County, Ohio*. Kidron, Ohio: Kidron Community Council, 1969.

Lichdi, Diether Götz, ed. *Mennonite World Handbook*. Carol Stream, Ill.: Mennonite World Conference, 1990.

Lindbeck, George A. "Barth and Textuality." *Theology Today* 43.3 (Oct. 1986): 361-376.

_____. "Confession and Community: An Israel-like View of the Church." *Christian Century* 107.16 (9 May 1990): 492-496.

_____. *The Nature of Doctrine: Religion and Theology in a Postliberal Age*. Philadelphia: Westminster, 1984.

Loewen, Howard John. *One Lord, One Church, One Hope, and One God: Mennonite Confessions of Faith in North America, An Introduction*. Elkhart, Ind.: Institute of Mennonite Studies, 1985.

_____. "One Lord, One Church, One Hope: Mennonite Confessions of Faith in America—An Introduction." *MQR* 57.3 (July 1983): 265-281.

MacMaster, Richard K. *Land, Piety, Peoplehood: The Establishment of Mennonite Communities in America, 1683-1790.* Vol. 1 of *The Mennonite Experience in America.* Scottdale, Pa.: Herald Press, 1988.

Marsden, George. M. *Fundamentalism and American Culture: The Shaping of Twentieth-Century Evangelicalism, 1870-1925.* New York: Oxford Univ. Press, 1980.

Marshall, Bruce D. "The Church in the Gospel." *Pro Ecclesia* 1.1 (Fall 1992): 27-41.

McClendon, James Wm. Jr. *Ethics*, vol. 1 of *Systematic Theology. Doctrine*, vol. 2 of *Systematic Theology.* Nashville: Abingdon, 1986-94.

McDonald, H. D. *The Atonement of the Death of Christ in Faith, Revelation, and History.* Grand Rapids: Baker, 1985.

Mennonite Encyclopedia, The. Vols. 1-4, ed. H. S. Bender, C. Krahn, et al.; Scottdale, Pa.: Mennonite Publishing House, 1955-59. Vol. 5, ed. C. J. Dyck et al.; Scottdale, Pa.: Herald Press, 1990.

Mennonite Experience in America, The. See Juhnke; MacMaster; Schlabach.

Moser, Abraham J. "Ansiedlung der Schweitzer und Amerikaner Mennoniten in Moniteau und Morgan Counties, Mo., Im Bethel gemeinde." In manuscript in Central District Conference Archives, Bluffton College, 77-87.

Mt. Zion Mennonite Church Centennial Program. Versailles, Mo., 1971.

Nussbaum, Stan. *You Must Be Born Again: A History of the Evangelical Mennonite Church.* Rev. ed. Fort Wayne, Ind.: The Evangelical Mennonite Church, 1988.

Pannabecker, Floyd Samuel. *Faith in Ferment: A History of the Central District Conference.* Newton, Kan.: Faith & Life, 1968.

Pannenberg, Wolfhart. *Jesus—God and Man.* Trans. Lewis L. Wilkins and Duane A. Priebe. Philadelphia: Westminster, 1975.

Pelikan, Jaroslav. *The Growth of Medieval Theology (600-1300).* Vol. 3 of *The Christian Tradition: A History of the Development of Christian Thought.* Chicago: Univ. of Chicago Press, 1978.

Philo. *The Embassy to Gaius.* Vol. 10 of *Philo.* Trans. H. Colson. Loeb Classical Library. Cambridge, Mass.: Harvard Univ. Press, 1971.

Pipkin, H. Wayne, ed. *Essays in Anabaptist Theology.* Text Reader Series, no. 5. Elkhart, Ind.: Institute of Mennonite Studies, 1994.

Plett, Delbert. "Ältester Gerhard Wiebe (1827-1900)—A Father of Manitoba." *Preservings* 6 (June 1995): 1-5.

Raid, Howard. *The First Seventy-Five Years.* Bluffton, Ohio: First Mennonite Church, 1986.

Reimer, A. James. "Doctrines: What Are They, How Do They Function, and Why Do We Need Them?" *CGR* 11.1 (Winter 1993): 21-36.

_____. "The Nature and Possibility of a Mennonite Theology." *CGR* 1.1 (Winter 1983): 33-55.

S., J. J. "Rev. John Moser Called Home." *The Pandora Times* 9.44 (16 July 1908): 1.

——————. "Laid to Rest." *The Bluffton News* 34.6 (16 July 1908): 1.

Schaefer, Paul. J. *Heinrich H. Ewert: Teacher, Educator and Minister of the Mennonites.* Winnipeg: CMBC Publications, 1990.

Schlabach, Theron F. *Gospel Versus Gospel: Mission and the Mennonite Church, 1863-1944.* Studies in Anabaptist and Mennonite History, no. 21. Scottdale, Pa.: Herald Press, 1980.

——————. "Mennonites and Pietism in America, 1740-1880: Some Thoughts on the Friedmann Thesis." *MQR* 57.3 (July 1983): 222-240.

——————. *Peace, Faith, Nation: Mennonites and Amish in Nineteenth-Century America.* Vol. 2 of *The Mennonite Experience in America.* Scottdale, Pa.: Herald Press, 1988.

——————. "Reveille for *Die Stillen im Lande*: A Stir Among Mennonites in the Late Nineteenth Century." *MQR* 51.3 (1977): 213-226.

Schneck, Don, ed. *St. John Mennonite Church, Pandora, Ohio, 1888-1988.* Pandora, Ohio: St. John Mennonite Centennial Committee, 1988.

Schroeder, William. *The Bergthal Colony.* Rev. ed. Winnipeg: CMBC Publications, 1986.

Schultz, J.Y. "Besuchsreise nach Indiana und Ohio." *CBB* 6.16 (15 Aug 1887): 6.

Schürer, Emil. *The History of the Jewish People in the Age of Jesus Christ (175 B.C.-A.D. 135).* Vol. 1. Rev. and ed. Geza Vermes and Fergus Millar. Edinburgh: T & T Clark, 1973.

Seeberg, Reinhold. *Text-Book of the History of Doctrines.* Trans. Charles E. Hay. Grand Rapids: Baker, 1961.

Siebert, Roger. "Grace Mennonite Church—An Overview of the First 25 Years." In *Grace Mennonite Church, Pandora, Ohio 1904-1979, 75th Anniversary.*

Smith, Timothy L. "Historical Fundamentalism." *Fides et Historia* 14.1 (Fall-Winter): 71.

——————. *Revivalism and Social Reform: American Protestantism on the Eve of the Civil War.* Nashville: Abingdon, 1957.

——————. "Righteousness and Hope: Christian Holiness and the Millennial Vision in America, 1800-1900." *American Quarterly* 31.1 (Spring 1979): 21-45.

Smith, Willard H. *Mennonites in Illinois.* Studies in Anabaptist and Mennonite History, no. 24. Scottdale, Pa.: Herald Press, 1983.

Smolin, David M. "Civil Religion and the Prolife Movement: The End of Christian Patriotism in America?" *SCLE Journal of Theology and Law* 1.1 (1996). Forthcoming.

Snyder, C. Arnold. *Anabaptist History and Thought: An Introduction.* Kitchener, Ont.: Pandora Press, 1995.

Souvenir Album: Fiftieth Anniversary of the Founding of the Bethel Mennonite

Church in Morgan and Moniteau Counties near Fortuna, Missouri, Sunday, April 22, 1917. Berne, Ind.: Berne Witness Co., [1917].

Steiner, Menno Simons. John S. Coffman, Mennonite Evangelist: His Life and Labors. Spring Grove, Pa.: Mennonite Book and Tract Society, [1903].

Stoeffler, F. Ernest, ed. Continental Pietism and Early American Christianity. Grand Rapids: Eerdmans, 1976.

Stoesz, Dennis. E. "A History of the Chortitzer Mennonite Church of Manitoba, 1874-1914." M.A. thesis, Department of History, Univ. of Manitoba, Winnipeg, 1987.

Stoltzfus, Grant M. Mennonites of the Ohio and Eastern Conference from the Colonial Period in Pennsylvania to 1968. Studies in Anabaptist and Mennonite History, no. 13. Scottdale, Pa.: Herald Press, 1969.

Suetonius. The Twelve Caesars: Gaius Suetonius Tranquillus. Rev. ed. Trans. Robert Graves. Rev., intro. Michael Grant. London: Penguin Books, 1989.

Tacitus. The Annals of Imperial Rome. Rev. ed. Trans., intro. Michael Grant. London: Penguin Books, 1988.

Umble, John S. "Amish Service Manuals." MQR 15.1 (Jan. 1941): 26-32.

_____. "The Allen County, Ohio, Mennonite Settlement." MQR 6.2 Apr. 1932): 81-109.

_____. Ohio Mennonite Sunday Schools. Studies in Anabaptist and Mennonite History, no. 5. Goshen, Ind.: Mennonnite Historical Society, 1941.

Urry, James. None but Saints: The Transformation of Mennonite Life in Russia, 1789-1889. Winnipeg: Windflower Communications, 1989.

Warfield, Benjamin B. The Person and Work of Christ. Ed. Samuel G. Craig. Philadelphia: Presbyterian and Reformed Publishing Co., 1950.

_____. The Plan of Salvation. Rev. ed. Grand Rapids: Eerdmans, 1966.

Weaver, J. Denny. "Anabaptist Vision: A Historical or a Theological Future?" CGR 13.1 (Winter 1995): 69-86.

_____. "Atonement for the Non-Constantinian Church." Modern Theology 6.4 (July 1990): 307-323.

_____. "Christus Victor, Ecclesiology, and Christology." MQR 68.3 (July 1994): 277-290.

_____. " 'Civil Religion and the Prolife Movement': An Anabaptist Critique of the Concept of a Christian Nation." SCLE Journal of Theology and Law 1.1 (1996). Forthcoming.

_____. "Hubmaier Versus Hut on the Work of Christ: The Fifth Nicolsburg Article." Archiv für Reformationsgeschichte 82 (1991): 171-192.

_____. "Is the Anabaptist Vision Still Relevant?" Pennsylvania Mennonite Heritage 14.1 (Jan. 1991): 2-12.

_____. "Mennonites: Theology, Peace, and Identity." CGR 6.2 (Spring 1988): 119-145.

_____. "Narrative Theology in an Anabaptist-Mennonite Context." *CGR* 12.2 (Spring 1994): 171-188.

_____. "Perspectives on a Mennonite Theology." *CGR* 2.3 (Fall 1984): 189-210.

_____. "The Quickening of Soteriology: Atonement from Christian Burkholder to Daniel Kauffman." *MQR* 61.1 (Jan. 1987): 5-45.

_____. "Some Theological Implications of Christus Victor." *MQR* 60.4 (Oct. 1994): 483-499.

_____. "The Work of Christ: On the Difficulty of Identifying an Anabaptist Perspective." *MQR* 59.2 (Apr. 1985): 107-129.

Weber, Harry. F. *Centennial History of the Mennonites of Illinois, 1829-1929.* Studies in Anabaptist and Mennonite History, no. 3. Goshen, Ind.: Mennonite Historical Society, 1931.

Wedel, David C. *The Story of Alexanderwohl.* Goessel, Kan.: Goessel Centennial Committee, 1974.

Wenger, John C., ed. *The Complete Writings of Menno Simons, c. 1496-1561.* Scottdale, Pa.: Herald Press, 1956.

Wenger, John C. *Glimpses of Mennonite History and Doctrine.* Scottdale, Pa.: Herald Press, 1949.

Williams, George H. "Christology and Church-State Relations in the Fourth Century." *Church History* 20.3 (Sept. 1951): 3-31; 20.4 (Dec. 1951): 3-26.

_____. "The Sacramental Presuppositions of Anselm's *Cur Deus Homo.*" *Church History* 26.3 (Sept. 1957): 245-274.

Yoder, John H. "The Believers' Church Conferences in Historical Perspective." *MQR* 65.1 (Jan. 1991): 5-19.

_____. *Preface to Theology: Christology and Theological Method.* Elkhart, Ind.: Goshen Biblical Seminary, Co-Op Bookstore, n.d.

_____. *The Priestly Kingdom: Social Ethics as Gospel.* Notre Dame, Ind.: Univ. of Notre Dame Press, 1984.

_____. *The Royal Priesthood: Essays Ecclesiological and Ecumenical.* Ed. Michael G. Cartwright. Foreword by Richard J. Mouw. Grand Rapids: Eerdmans, 1994.

_____. *When War Is Unjust: Being Honest in Just-War Thinking.* 2d ed. Maryknoll, N.Y.: Orbis, 1996.

Yoder, Paton, ed. *Tennessee John Stoltzfus: Amish Church-Related Documents and Family Letters.* Trans. Noah G. Good et al. Mennonite Sources and Documents, no. 1. Lancaster, Pa.: Lancaster Mennonite Historical Society, 1987.

_____. *Tradition and Transition: Amish Mennonites and Old Order Amish, 1800-1900.* Studies in Anabaptist and Mennonite History, no. 31. Scottdale, Pa.: Herald Press, 1991.

Yoder, Perry B. *Shalom: The Bible's Word for Salvation, Justice, and Peace.* Newton, Kan.: Faith & Life, 1987.

Zurflüh, A. "Bericht der Verhandlungen der Sonntagschul-Convention, abge-

halten in der Mennonitengemeinde bei Bluffton, Allen Co., O., Freitag
und Samstag, den 16. und 17. Oktober 1885," *CBB* 4.22 (15 Nov. 1885): 6;
4.23 (1 Dec. 1885): 3.

In following sections, chronological publication order prevails for
discrete items and the first item in a series, which then follows its
own sequence. Undated items are at the end of a section.

Jacob Stauffer

*Eine Chronik oder Geschicht-Büchlein von der sogenannten Mennonisten
Gemeinde.* Lancaster, Pa.: Johann Bär und Sohn, 1855.

David Beiler

*Das wahre Christenthum: Eine Christliche Betrachtung nach den Lehren der
Heiligen Schrift.* Lancaster, Pa.: Johann Bär's Söhnen, 1888. Reprinted by
Pathway Publishers, Aylmer, Ont., and LaGrange, Ind. Manuscript of Isaac
R. Horst's English trans. at Heritage Historical Library, Aylmer, Ont.
"Anzug aus David Beilers hinterlassenen Schriften." *HdW* 31.4 (15 Feb. 1894):
52-53; 31.5 (1 Mar. 1894): 66-67. Excerpts from *Das wahre Christenthum.*
Eine Vermahnung oder Andenken von David Beiler. Baltic, Ohio: Raber's Book
Store, 1928 (and reprints). Trans. as "Memoirs."
Gemein Ordnungen. Title page: *Wahres Christenthum und Ermahnung für die
Diener und die Gemein und auch Formen u. s. w.* Published by Benjamin F.
Beiler, Lancaster County, Pa., 1945. Minister's manual of 1861, with writ-
ings. Similar to *Das wahre Christenthum.*
"Memoirs of an Amish Bishop." Trans. and ed. John S. Umble. *MQR* 22.2 (Apr.
1948): 94-115. English translation of *Vermahnung oder Andenken.*
"Letters" of Oct. 14, 1851; Mar. 21, 1859; and the "Report" of a June 7, 1853,
meeting of David Beiler with two other bishops. In Paton Yoder, *Tennessee
John Stoltzfus: Amish Church-Related Documents and Family Letters,* 33-
38, 46. Trans. Noah G. Good et al. Mennonite Sources and Documents,
no. 1. Lancaster, Pa.: Lancaster Mennonite Historical Society, 1987.
Eine Betrachtung über den Berg Predig Christi und über Ebräer, das 11 Cap.
Published by David Z. Esch Jr., Lancaster County, Pa., 1994. Distributed
by Pathway Publishers, Aylmer, Ont., and LaGrange, Ind. The longer 1861
manuscript is at Pequea Bruderschaft Library, Gordonville, Pa.

Unpublished
"Treatise on Baptism." German manuscript of 1854, copied by hand in 1859 by Christian Brenneman of Iowa. Preserved by Amos B. Hoover, Muddy Creek Farm Library, Denver, Pa.
"Letter from Bishop David Beiler, Bird-in-Hand, Lancaster County, Pa., July 3, 1861, to Jacob Schwartzendruber." Typescript copy, 71-75, by Elmer G. Swartzendruber. At Mennonite Historical Library, Goshen, Ind. Listed by John Umble as item XV in "Catalog of an Amish Bishop's Library," *MQR* 20 (July 1946): 230-239. Instructions for ministers, as in *Das wahre Christenthum.*

Gerhard Wiebe
Ursachen und Geschichte der Auswanderung der Mennoniten aus Russland nach Amerika. Winnipeg: Druckerei des Nordwesten, [1900].
Causes and History of the Emigration of the Mennonites from Russia to America. Trans. Helen Janzen. Winnipeg: Manitoba Mennonite Historical Society, 1981. English ed. of *Ursachen.*

Cornelius H. Wedel
Books
Randzeichnungen zu den Geschichten des Alten Testaments. Newton, Kan.: Bethel College, 1899.
Randzeichnungen zu den Geschichten des Neuen Testaments. Newton, Kan.: Bethel College, 1900.
Die Geschichte ihrer Vorfahren bis zum Beginn des Täufertums im 16. Jahrhundert. Erster Teil, *Abriss der Geschichte der Mennoniten.* Newton, Kan.: Bethel College, 1900.
Die Geschichte des Täufertums in 16. Jahrhundert. Zweites Bändchen, *Abriss der Geschichte der Mennoniten.* Newton, Kan.: Bethel College, 1902.
Die Geschichte der niederländischen, preussischen und russischen Mennoniten. Drittes Bändchen, *Abriss der Geschichte der Mennoniten.* Newton, Kan.: Bethel College, 1901.
Die Geschichte der Täufer und Mennoniten in der Schweiz, in Mähren, in Süddeutschland, am Niederrhein und in Nordamerika. Viertes Bändchen, *Abriss der Geschichte der Mennoniten.* Newton, Kan.: Bethel College, 1904.
Bilder aus der Kirchengeschichte für mennonitische Gemeindeschulen. Newton, Kan.: Bethel College, 1899; 2d enlarged ed., 1904; 3d ed., 1915; 4th ed., 1930; 5th ed., 1937; 6th ed., 1937; 7th ed., rev. by C. H. Krahn, 1951.
Sketches from Church History for Mennonite Schools. Trans. Gustav A. Haury. Newton, Kan.: Western District Conference, 1920; rev. ed., 1925, 1932. English ed. of *Bilder.*

Geleitworte an junge Christen zunächst in unsern mennonitischen Kreisen. Newton, Kan.: Bethel College, 1903; 2d ed., 1912; 3d ed., 1931.

Words to Young Christians, Particularly to Those of the Mennonite Church. Trans. Theodore O. Wedel. Berne, Ind.: Mennonite Book Concern, 1926; repr. ca. 1955. English ed. of *Geleitworte.*

Kurzgefasste Kirchengeschichte für Schulen und Familien. Newton, Kan.: Bethel College, 1905.

Briefliche Blätter an einen Lernenden über Bildung, Gesellschafts- und Heiratsfragen. Newton, Kan.: Bethel College, 1906.

Meditationen zu den Fragen und Antworten unseres Katechismus. Newton, Kan.: the author, 1910.

Unpublished
"Ethik." Manuscript trans. David C. Wedel, from three German handwritten notebooks, Hefte 1-3 (about 229 pages): in the C. C. Wedel collection of the Mennonite Library and Archives at Bethel College, North Newton, Kan. The last 13 pages of "Ethik" are at the end of Heft 4 of "Glaubenslehre." See note 78 for chapter 3, above.

"Glaubenslehre." Manuscript in four German handwritten notebooks, Hefte 1-4 (about 475 pages): in the C. C. Wedel collection of the Mennonite Library and Archives at Bethel College, North Newton, Kan. See note 78 for chapter 3, above.

Articles in *Christlicher Bundesbote* (*CBB*)
"Die Unterrichtsmethode in den mittleren Klassen der Sonntagschule." *CBB* 4.14 (15 July 1885): 2-3.

"Drei Tage mit den Mormonen." *CBB* 7.28 (19 July 1888): 2-3; 7.29 (26 July 1888): 3.

"Pater Damian—eine Heldengestalt in der neuesten Missionsgeschichte." *CBB* 8.25 (20 June 1889): 1; 8.26 (27 June 1889): 1.

"Genesis 14." *CBB* 11.1 (7 Jan. 1892): 2; 11.2 (14 Jan. 1892): 3.

"In was für einem Verhältnis sollten Gemeinde und Jugendverein zu einander stehen?" *CBB* 13.34 (30 Aug. 1894): 2.

"Eine neue Bibel und doch unsere alte." *CBB* 14.6 (7 Feb. 1895): 2-3; 14.7 (14 Feb. 1895): 2-3.

"Neuerungen." *CBB* 15.5 (30 Jan. 1896): 2-3.

"Kirchliche und wirtschaftliche Verhältnisse in Russland." *CBB* 16.32 (19 Aug. 1897): 4-5.

"Allgemeines über weibliche Gemeindediakonie nach Sinn und Eigenart unserer Gemeinschaft." *CBB* 22.38 (24 Sept. 1903): 2-3.

Articles in Bethel College Periodicals
School and College Journal (*SCJ*), the first Bethel College periodical, had material in English and German. Vol. 1, no. 1 is dated Jan. 1896. *SCJ* was suc-

ceeded by two periodicals, *Bethel College Monthly* (*BCM*) in English, and *Monatsblätter aus Bethel College* (*MBC*) in German. Volume numbers for both successors continue from *SCJ*. In the following, usually it is certain but sometimes assumed that C. H. Wedel authored the indicated article.

"Bemerkungen über den Lehrplan." = "Remarks on the Course of Study," in "Fourth Catalogue of Bethel College." *SCJ* 1.6 (June 1896) and 1.7 (June 1896): 47-48, 50-51, 55-56. ("Catalogue" in both German and English.)

"Eröffnungsrede des Principals von Bethel-College, beim Beginn des Schuljahres 1895-'96." *SCJ* 1.11 (Nov. 1896): 83-86.

"Aus der Reisemappe, I-XV." *SCJ* 2.1 (Jan. 1897): 4-8; 2.2 (Feb. 1897): 12-14; 2.3 (Mar. 1897): 21-24; 2.4 (Apr. 1897): 30-32; 2.5 (May 1897): 37-39; 2.6 (June 1897): 46-48; 2.7 (July 1897): 54-56; 2.8 (Aug. 1897): 61-64; 2.9 (Sept. 1897): 68-71; 2.10 (Oct. 1897): 78-80; 2.11 (Nov. 1897): 86-88; 2.12 (Dec. 1897): 94-96; 3.4 (Apr. 1898): 29-32; 3.5 (May 1898): 37-39; 3.6 (June 1898): 46-48.

"Am Büchertisch." *SCJ* 2.4 (Apr. 1897): 29.

"Die Mennonitenschulen in Südrussland." *SCJ* 2.6 (June 1897): 44-46; 2.10 (Oct. 1897): 76-78.

"Missionar P. H. Wedel: Ein schlichtes Erinnerungsblatt an denselben." *SCJ* 3.1 (Jan. 1898): 4-7; 3.2 (Feb. 1898): 12-14; 3.3 (Mar. 1898): 21-22.

"Eine Anklage." *SCJ* 3.4 (Apr. 1898): 28-29.

"Reiseskizzen und Randglossen, I-XII." *SCJ* 4.1 (Jan. 1899): 4-7; 4.2 (Feb. 1899): 13-15; 4.3 (Mar. 1899): 22-24; 4.4 (Apr. 1899): 29-31; 4.5 (May 1899): 38-40; 4.6 (June 1899): 45-47; 4.7 (July 1899): 54-56; 4.8 (Aug. 1899): 62-64; 4.9 (Sept. 1899): 69-71; 4.10 (Oct. 1899): 77-78; 4.11 (Nov. 1899): 87-88; 4.12 (Dec. 1899): 94-96.

Wedel with H. O. Kruse. "Aus dem Bericht der Bethel College-Fakultät." *SCJ* 4.4 (Apr. 1899): 28-29.

"Ältst. C. P. Wedel." *SCJ* 5.3 (Mar. 1900): 20-22.

"Mit verbindlichem Danke." *SCJ* 5.10 (Oct. 1900): 80.

"Berichte der Professoren u. Lehrer." *SCJ* 6.5 (May 1901): 36-37.

"Einladung." *SCJ* 7.9 (Sept. 1902): 68.

"Zum Neuen Jahre." *MBC* 8.1 (Jan. 1903): 1.

"Ein Stündchen mit den Propheten." *MBC* 8.1 (Jan. 1903): 1-2.

"Die russichen Mennoniten im Roman, 1-2." *MBC* 8.1 (Jan. 1903): 3-4; 8.2 (Feb. 1903): 16-17.

"Zwei deutsche Theologen." *MBC* 8.1 (Jan. 1903): 4-5.

"Ein geschichtlicher Überblick." *MBC* 8.2 (Feb. 1903): 13.

"Über die Auslegung der prophetischen Reden." *MBC* 8.2 (Feb. 1903): 13-15.

"Das Neueste über Menno Simons." *MBC* 8.2 (Feb. 1903): 15-16.

"Ruckblick und Ausblick." *MBC* 8.3 (Mar. 1903): 25. (Comment appended to poem.)

"Das Bibelstudium des heiligen Bernhard." *MBC* 8.3 (Mar. 1903): 25-26.

"Das Neueste über die Mennoniten, 1-2." *MBC* 8.3 (Mar. 1903): 27-28; 8.4 (Apr. 1903): 39-40.
"Ein Abend mit Charles M. Sheldon." *MBC* 8.3 (Mar. 1903): 28-29.
"Das Kreuz ist unser Heilspanier." *MBC* 8.4 (Apr. 1903): 37.
"Im heiligen Lande in den Ostertagen." *MBC* 8.4 (Apr. 1903): 38-39.
"Die südrussichen Kolonisten." *MBC* 8.4 (Apr. 1903): 40-41.
"Fromme Wünsche." *MBC* 8.5 (May 1903): 49.
"Ein vorzüglicher Kommentar zur heiligen Schrift." *MBC* 8.5 (May 1903): 49-51.
"Über gewisse Schwächen der Reformatoren." *MBC* 8.5 (May 1903): 51-52.
"Die preussischen Mennoniten im Roman." *MBC* 8.5 (May 1903): 52-53.
"Christus in uns." *MBC* 8.6 (June 1903): 61.
"Biblische Persönlichkeiten." *MBC* 8.6 (June 1903): 61-63.
"Die Friedensidee auf sozial-politischen Gebiet." *MBC* 8.6 (June 1903): 63-64.
"Eine Karrikatur der mennonitischen Indianermission." *MBC* 8.6 (June 1903): 64-65.
"Zur Sommerzweit." *MBC* 8.7 (July 1903): 73.
"Die Kirche als Trägerin des Friedens." *MBC* 8.7 (July 1903): 74-75.
"Über soziales Christentum." *MBC* 8.7 (July 1903): 75-76.
"Schuster, bleib bei deinem Leisten!" *MBC* 8.7 (July 1903): 76-77.
"Abendlied." *MBC* 8.8 (Aug. 1903): 85.
"Einige Randglossen und fragezeichen." *MBC* 8.8 (Aug. 1903): 85-86.
"Die Grundidee des 'Quitt.' *MBC* 8.8 (Aug. 1903): 87-88.
"Peter Nosegger." *MBC* 8.8 (Aug. 1903): 88-89.
"Die Sterbesakrament der römischen Kirche." *MBC* 8.8 (Aug. 1903): 89.
"Colligite Animas!" *MBC* 8.9 (Sept. 1903): 97.
"Über wahre Bildung." *MBC* 8.9 (Sept. 1903): 97-99.
"Amerikanisches Schulwesen." *MBC* 8.9 (Sept. 1903): 99-100.
"Wunderblumen eigener Art." *MBC* 8.9 (Sept. 1903): 101.
"Ein Märtyrerlieb." *MBC* 8.10 (Sept. 1903): 109.
"Eine Reformationsbetrachtung." *MBC* 8.10 (Sept. 1903): 109-112.
"Eine passende Lektüre in diesen Tagen." *MBC* 8.10 (Sept. 1903): 112-113.
"Ein ergreifendes Bild." *MBC* 8.10 (Sept. 1903): 113.
"Ein Wort über Auszeichnungen." *MBC* 8.11 (Nov. 1903): 121.
"Unsere Brüder an der Molotschna." *MBC* 8.11 (Nov. 1903): 121-123.
"Eine wesentliche Stütze des Kriegswesens." *MBC* 8.11 (Nov. 1903): 123-124.
"Peter Noseggers jüngstes Werk." *MBC* 8.11 (Nov. 1903): 125.
"The Largest Organ." *BCM* 8.12 (Dec. 1903): 46-47.
"Vom Himmel hoch, da komm ich her." *MBC* 8.12 (Dec. 1903): 133.
"Etwas über die Waldenser neuerer Zeit." *MBC* 8.12 (Dec. 1903): 133-135.
"Eine enfache Frömmigkeit." *MBC* 8.12 (Dec. 1903): 135-136.
"Eine verunglückte Schulgeschichte." *MBC* 8.12 (Dec. 1903): 136-137.
"Zur Jahreswende." *MBC* 9.1 (Jan. 1904): 1.
"Die letzte Schrift des Neuen Testaments." *MBC* 9.1 (Jan. 1904): 1-3.

"Im Ellerwald vor hundert Jahren." *MBC* 9.1 (Jan. 1904): 3-4.
"Goethe unser Ideal?" *MBC* 9.1 (Jan. 1904): 4-5.
"Eine gesunde Selbstständigkeit." *MBC* 9.2 (Feb. 1904): 13-14.
"Der erste Thessalonicherbrief." *MBC* 9.2 (Feb. 1904): 14-15.
"Im Ellerwald vor hundert Jahren." *MBC* 9.2 (Feb. 1904): 15-17.
"Herbert Spencer." *MBC* 9.2 (Feb. 1904): 17.
"Über Jesu Jugendzeit." *MBC* 9.3 (Mar. 1904): 25.
"Die erste paulinische Sendschreiben." *MBC* 9.3 (Mar. 1904): 26-28.
"Im Ellerwald vor hundert Jahren." *MBC* 9.3 (Mar. 1904): 28-29.
"Zörn Uhl." *MBC* 9.3 (Mar. 1904): 29.
"Unter dem Kreuze Christi." *MBC* 9.4 (Apr. 1904): 37-38.
"Ein Blick in den zweiten Thessalonischerbrief." *MBC* 9.4 (Apr. 1904): 38-39.
"Im Ellerwald vor hundert Jahren." *MBC* 9.4 (Apr. 1904): 39-41.
"Noch etwas über Jörn Uhl." *MBC* 9.4 (Apr. 1904): 41.
"Dichtende Frauen." *MBC* 9.5 (May 1904): 49-50.
"Über neutestamentliche Textkritik, 1-4." *MBC* 9.5 (May 1904): 50-51; 9.6 (June 1904): 110-111; 9.7 (July 1904): 122-123; 9.8 (Aug. 1904): 134-135.
"Unsere Weltanstellung in St. Louis." *MBC* 9.5 (May 1904): 51-53.
"Kansas in einem deutschen Roman." *MBC* 9.5 (May 1904): 53.
"Aus der neueren deutschen Lyrik." *MBC* 9.6 (June 1904): 109-110.
"Ein mennonitischer Gelehrter ersten Ranges." *MBC* 9.6 (June 1904): 111-113.
"Über die Stellung eines deutschamerikanischen Pastors." *MBC* 9.6 (June 1904): 113.
"Über Hindernisse des Glaubens." *MBC* 9.7 (July 1904): 121-122.
"Ein unchristlicher Heroismus." *MBC* 9.7 (July 1904): 123-124.
"Frau Anna Brons." *MBC* 9.7 (July 1904): 124-125.
"Hindernisse des Glaubens." *MBC* 9.8 (Aug. 1904): 133.
"Die Protestationskirche in Speier." *MBC* 9.8 (Aug. 1904): 135-137.
"Aus der Landesschule zu Pforta." *MBC* 9.8 (Aug. 1904): 137.
"Carpe diem." *MBC* 9.9 (Sept. 1904): 145-146.
"Schwierige Bibelstellen." *MBC* 9.9 (Sept. 1904): 146-147.
"Tillie, A Mennonite Maid, 1-2." *MBC* 9.9 (Sept. 1904): 147-148; 9.10 (Oct. 1904): 160-161.
"Ein pädagogische Grundsätze des berühmten Flattich." *MBC* 9.9 (Sept. 1904): 148-149.
"Eine Reformationsbetrachtung." *MBC* 9.10 (Oct. 1904): 157-159.
"Unter den letzten Märtyrern in den Niederlanden." *MBC* 9.10 (Oct. 1904): 159-160.
"Toren drängen sich, wo Engel leisen treten." *MBC* 9.11 (Nov. 1904): 169.
"Eine wehmütige Ferienlektüre." *MBC* 9.11 (Nov. 1904): 169-172.
"Ein gefährlicher Spaziergang." *MBC* 9.11 (Nov. 1904): 172-173.
"Weihnachtsgedanken." *MBC* 9.12 (Dec. 1904): 181.
"Eine kirchliche Grösse ersten Ranges." *MBC* 9.12 (Dec. 1904): 181-183.

"Über das Geheimnis der Menschwerdung Christi." *MBC* 9.12 (Dec. 1904): 183-185.

"Aufbauende Kräfte." *MBC* 9.12 (Dec. 1904): 185.

"Über die Bedeutung der christlichen Predigt." *MBC* 10.1 (Jan. 1905): 1-3.

"Die 'Doopsgesinde Bijdragen' des Jahres 1904." *MBC* 10.1 (Jan. 1905): 3-4.

"Wie sich das Evangelium packend predigen lässt." *MBC* 10.2 (Feb. 1905): 13-15.

"Ein Brief aus Emden." *MBC* 10.2 (Feb. 1905): 15-16.

"Wie lässt sich das Evangelium anziehend predigen?" *MBC* 10.3 (Mar. 1905): 25-27.

"Über den Brief aus Emden." *MBC* 10.3 (Mar. 1905): 27-29.

"Unsere Kanzel." *MBC* 10.4 (Apr. 1905): 37-40.

"Nun aber ist Christus auferstanden." *MBC* 10.4 (Apr. 1905): 40-41.

"Über die den Zuhörer bereichernde Predigt des Evangeliums." *MBC* 10.5 (May 1905): 49-51.

"Zur Schillerfeier." *MBC* 10.5 (May 1905): 51-53.

"Über friede und Wissenschaft." *MBC* 10.6 (June 1905): 61-63.

"Zur Schillerfeier." *MBC* 10.6 (June 1905): 64-65.

"Über Friede und Wissenschaft." *MBC* 10.7 (July 1905): 73-75.

"Göthes 'Iphigenie.' " *MBC* 10.7 (July 1905): 75-77.

"Das deutsche Schulwesen in der Belletristik." *MBC* 10.8 (Aug. 1905): 85-87.

"Noch einige Gedanken über Göthes 'Iphigenie.' " *MBC* 10.8 (Aug. 1905): 87-89.

"Im Schatten der Unversöhnlichkeit." *MBC* 10.9 (Sept. 1905): 97-99.

"Personen, nicht Persönlichkeiten." *MBC* 10.9 (Sept. 1905): 99-101.

"Eine Reformationsbetrachtung." *MBC* 10.10 (Oct. 1905): 109-112.

"Drei Grundschäden der Kirche des Mittelalters." *MBC* 10.10 (Oct. 1905): 112-113.

"Wie ein römischer Theologe über die Reformation denkt." *MBC* 10.11 (Oct. 1905): 122-123.

"Die süddeutschen Täufer in der Belletristik, 1-3." *MBC* 10.11 (Oct. 1905): 123-125; 10.12 (Dec. 1905): 133-135; 11.1 (Jan. 1906): 3-5.

"Ein edler Judenmissionar." *MBC* 10.11 (Oct. 1905): 125.

"Über höheres kirchliches Schulwesen." *MBC* 10.12 (Dec. 1905): 136-137.

"Zum neuen Jahre." *MBC* 11.1 (Jan. 1906): 1-3.

"Über die Stimmen der Weissagung in der Heidenwelt." *MBC* 11.1 (Jan. 1906): 5.

"Über die Dreieinigkeit Gottes, 1-4." *MBC* 11.2 (Feb. 1906): 13-15; 11.3 (Mar. 1906): 25-27; 11.4 (Apr. 1906): 37-38; 11.5 (May 1906): 49-50.

"Das Ende des Reichsprofosen Aichelin." *MBC* 11.2 (Feb. 1906): 15-16.

"Eine gewinnreiche Unterhaltungsschrift für Mädchen." *MBC* 11.2 (Feb. 1906): 17.

"Sabina, A Story of the Amish, 1-4." *MBC* 11.3 (Mar. 1906): 27-28; 11.4 (Apr. 1906): 38-40; 11.5 (May 1906): 52-53; 11.6 (June 1906): 62-64.

"Aus schönen Jugendtagen." *MBC* 11.4 (Apr. 1906): 40-41.

"Es giebt ein ewiges Leben." *MBC* 11.5 (May 1906): 50-52.

"Was soll denn aus ihm werden? 1-4." *MBC* 11.6 (June 1906): 61-62; 11.7 (July 1906): 73-75; 11.8 (Aug. 1906): 85-87; 11.9 (Sept. 1906): 98-100.

"Über das Schicksal russischer Landgeistlichen, 1-2." *MBC* 11.6 (June 1906): 64-65; 11.7 (July 1906): 75-76.

"Professor Rauschenbusch über die Mennoniten." *MBC* 11.7 (July 1906): 76-77.

"Ein Missionsjubiläum." *MBC* 11.8 (Aug. 1906): 87-88.

"Aus der Sommerfrische, 1-5." *MBC* 11.8 (Aug. 1906): 89; 11.9 (Sept. 1906): 100-101; 11.10 (Oct. 1906): 113; 11.11 (Nov. 1906): 124-125; 11.12 (Dec. 1906): 136-137.

"Über kirchliche Hochschulen." *MBC* 11.9 (Sept. 1906): 97-98.

"Über die Heiligkeit des Alten Testaments, 1-3." *MBC* 11.10 (Oct. 1906): 109-111; 11.11 (Nov. 1906): 121-122; 11.12 (Dec. 1906): 133-135.

"Aus dem fernen Indien, 1-2." *MBC* 11.10 (Oct. 1906): 111-113; 11.11 (Nov. 1906): 123-124.

"Aus Elias schrenks Jugendzeit." *MBC* 11.12 (Dec. 1906): 135-136.

"Zum neuen Jahre." *MBC* 12.1 (Jan. 1907): 1-2.

"Die Lieder der Wiedertäufer." *MBC* 12.1 (Jan. 1907): 2-3.

"Aus der Fürstenschule zu Grimma." *MBC* 12.1 (Jan. 1907): 4-5.

"Über unsere Negerfrage." *MBC* 12.1 (Jan. 1907): 5.

"Die ältesten Lieder der Täufer, 2." *MBC* 12.1 (Feb. 1907): 13-14.

"Wie der treue Herr junge Leute hält, sucht, findet." *MBC* 12.1 (Feb. 1907): 15-17.

"So nebenbei, 1-4." *MBC* 12.2 (Feb. 1907): 17; 12.3 (Mar. 1907): 29; 12.4 (Apr. 1907): 41; 12.5 (May 1907): 53.

"Das älteste Gesangbuch der Täufer." *MBC* 12.3 (Mar. 1907): 25-27.

"Vicisti Galilaee! 1-4." *MBC* 12.3 (Mar. 1907): 27-29; 12.4 (Apr. 1907): 39-41; 12.5 (May 1907): 51-53; 12.6 (June 1907): 63-65.

"Über die Lieder der niederländischen Täufer." *MBC* 12.4 (Apr. 1907): 37-39.

"Die ersten Lieder der deutschen Mennoniten." *MBC* 12.5 (May 1907): 49-51.

"Etwas Weiteres über den 'Ausbundt.' " *MBC* 12.6 (June 1907): 61-63.

"Die Behandlung kindischen Eigensinns." *MBC* 12.6 (June 1907): 65.

"Über die Lieder der Hutterschen Brüder." *MBC* 12.7 (July 1907): 73-75.

"Aus glücklichen Kindertagen." *MBC* 12.7 (July 1907): 75-77.

"Eine Friedensgarantie denkwürdigster Art." *MBC* 12.7 (July 1907): 77.

"Ein Blick in die Zukunft." *MBC* 12.8 (Aug. 1907): 85-86.

"Eine Schulzeit voller Leben und Sterben." *MBC* 12.8 (Aug. 1907): 86-88.

"Wie sich die moderne Theologie gibt." *MBC* 12.8 (Aug. 1907): 88-89.

"Eine Jugendschrift voll anregender Gedanken." *MBC* 12.9 (Sept. 1907): 97.

"Eine schöne Universitätszeit." *MBC* 12.9 (Sept. 1907): 97-100.

"Das neueste Werk Frenssens." *MBC* 12.9 (Sept. 1907): 100-101.

"Schöne Universitätsjahre." *MBC* 12.10 (Sept. 1907): 109-111.

"Wie es in höhern Anstalten zugehen kann." *MBC* 12.10 (Sept. 1907): 111-113.
"Meine erste Ohrenbeichte." *MBC* 12.11 (Nov. 1907): 121-122.
"Aus St. Petersburg in der zweiten Hälfte des 19. Jahrhunderts." *MBC* 12.11 (Nov. 1907): 122-124.
"Über den geistlichen Hunger des russischen Volks." *MBC* 12.11 (Nov. 1907): 124-125.
"Die Fülle der Zeit." *MBC* 12.12 (Dec. 1907): 133-134.
"Über das Gift des Unglaubens." *MBC* 12.12 (Dec. 1907): 134-136.
"Noch etwas aus dem 'Mentor.'" *MBC* 12.12 (Dec. 1907): 136-137.
"Beim Jahreswechsel." *MBC* 13.1 (Jan. 1908): 1.
"Über jüdischen Fanatismus." *MBC* 13.1 (Jan. 1908): 1-3.
"Über Frauenarbeit und Frauenwert." *MBC* 13.1 (Jan. 1908): 3-4.
"Kennst du das Land?" *MBC* 13.2 (Feb. 1908): 13-14.
"Ein Stündchen mit dem vierten Evangelium, 1-3." *MBC* 13.2 (Feb. 1908): 14-16; 13.3 (Mar. 1908): 25-26; 13.4 (Apr. 1908): 38-40.
"Über das syrische Waisenhaus in Jerusalem." *MBC* 13.3 (Mar. 1908): 26-27.
"Modernes Gottsuchen." *MBC* 13.4 (Apr. 1908): 37-38.
"Über die Authentie des vierten Evangeliums." *MBC* 13.5 (May 1908): 50-52.
"Über den Heimgang unseres früheren Direktors Bernhard Warkentin." *MBC* 13.5 (May 1908): 54-57.

Johannes Moser

Books

Eine Verantwortung gegen Daniel Musser's Meidungs-Erklärung, welche er gemacht hat in seinem Buch, betitelt: 'Reformirte Mennoniten.'" Lancaster, Pa.: Gedruckt von Samuel Ernst, 1876.

Gemeinde-Ordnung der Schweizer-Mennoniten Gemeinde bei Pandora und Bluffton, in Putnam und Allen County, Ohio. Lima, Ohio: Lima Courier, 1893.

Articles

"Vertheidigung der Wehrlosigkeit." *HdW* 4.6 (June 1867): 86; 4.7 (July 1867): 97-100; 4.8 (Aug. 1867): 113-115.
"Eine Antwort." *HdW* 8.5 (May 1871): 70-71.
"Die Menschen Sterblichkeit." *HdW* 15.9 (Sept. 1878): 146-147.
"Dienerversammlung der Schweizer Mennoniten." *HdW* 15.12 (Dec. 1878): 209.
"Über die Wehrlosigkeit." *HdW* 16.1 (Jan. 1879): 1-4; 16.2 (Feb. 1879): 21-25.
"Die Erziehung der Jugend." *HdW* 16.3 (Mar. 1879): 41-44.
"Gedanken über Missions- und Gemeinde-Verhältnisse." *CBB* 1.20 (15 Oct. 1882): 157-159.
"Gedanken über Spaltungen." *HdW* 21.7 (1 Apr. 1884): 102-103; 21.8 (15 Apr.

1884): 117-119; 21.9 (1 May 1884): 131-132; 21.10 (15 May 1884): 149-151; 21.11 (1 June 1884): 164-165; 21.12 (15 June 1884): 179-180; 21.13 (1 July 1884): 195-197.

"Das Völligerwerden." *HdW* 21.19 (1 Oct. 1884): 292-293.

"Siehe, ich komme bald." *HdW* 21.22 (15 Nov. 1884): 338-341.

"Ein Vortrag über Nachbarschaft." *HdW* 22.4 (14 Feb. 1885): 49-51; 22.5 (1 Mar. 1885): 65-68.

"Johannes 13." *CBB* 6.12 (15 June 1887): 2-3.

"Die Reizung zum Bösen." *CBB* 7.27 (12 July 1888): 2-3.

"Die Veranlassung und Beeinflussung zur Sünde." *CBB* 7.30 (2 Aug. 1888): 2-3.

"Der Lebens-Compass: Was die Presse darüber sagt." *CBB* 7.31 (9 Aug. 1888): 4-5.

"Das Reizen zur Liebe und zu guten Werken." *CBB* 7.32 (16 Aug. 1888): 2.

"Lasset uns halten am Hoffnungsbekenntniss." *CBB* 7.35 (6 Sept. 1888): 2.

"Korrespondenzen—Bluffton, O." *CBB* 9.49 (11 Dec. 1890): 4.

"Missbräuche." *CBB* 10.2 (8 Jan. 1891): 3.

Johannes Moser and Peter Schumacher. "Eine Bittschrift." *HdW* 28.7 (1 Apr. 1891): 102-103. (also *HT*, same date)

"Nachdenken über sich selbst." *CBB* 10.37 (17 Sept. 1891): 2.

"Unglaube." *CBB* 10.38 (24 Sept. 1891): 1-2; 10.39 (1 Oct. 1891): 1-2.

"Eine Hölle." *CBB* 10.40 (8 Oct. 1891): 2; 10.41 (15 Oct. 1891): 2.

"Bekenntniss." *CBB* 11.16 (21 Apr. 1892): 4-5.

"Mission." *CBB* 11.18 (5 May 1892): 1.

"Hindernisse der Mission." *CBB* 11.19 (12 May 1892): 1.

"Hindernisse der Mission in der Christenheit überhaupt." *CBB* 11.20 (19 May 1892): 1.

"Festigkeit in Prüfungen." *CBB* 11.27 (14 July 1892): 2-3.

"Die Menschen bedürfen Haus und Heim." *CBB* 11.32 (18 Aug. 1892): 2.

"Der Alten Heim und ihre Erinnerungen." *CBB* 11.33 (25 Aug. 1892): 2.

"Das geistliche Haus, I, II." *CBB* 12.13 (30 Mar. 1893): 2-3; 12.14 (6 Apr. 1893): 4-5.

"Keiner Wiederholung der Taufe." *CBB* 12.40 (12 Oct. 1893): 2; 12.41 (19 Oct. 1893): 2-3.

"Zum Jahreswechsel—Nachdenken über Zeit." *CBB* 13.1 (4 Jan. 1894): 2.

"Gedanken." *CBB* 13.6 (8 Feb. 1894): 2.

"Nachdenken." *CBB* 13.7 (15 Feb. 1894): 5.

"Die Himmelfahrt Christi ist das Ende der leiblichen Lebensgeschichte Christi auf Erden." *CBB* 17.20 (19 May 1898): 2.

"Was soll ich denn machen mit Jesu?" *CBB* 17.24 (16 June 1898): 1-2.

"Erinnerung gegen Missbräuche, Ermahnung und Gebet." *CBB* 17.3 (11 Aug. 1898): 2.

"Gedanken über Schulverhältnisse." *CBB* 17.50 (22 Dec. 1898): 2-3.

"Das sind die Reisen der Kinder Israel. 4. Mose 33.1." *CBB* 18.36 (14 Sept. 1899): 2-3.

"Haus-Gottes." *CBB* 18.39 (5 Oct. 1899): 1-2.
"Der ewig Unveränderliche zum neuen Jahre." *CBB* 19.2 (11 Jan. 1900): 3.
"Eine Dürre." *CBB* 20.32 (15 Aug. 1901): 2.
"Des Herrn Wort." *CBB* 20.38 (26 Sept. 1901): 1-2.
"Gemeindezucht." *CBB* 20.50 (19 Dec. 1901): 1-2.
"Neujahrsgedanken." *CBB* 21.1 (2 Jan. 1902): 1-2.
"Konferenzgedanken." *CBB* 21.40 (9 Oct. 1902): 1-2.
"Advents-Gedanken." *CBB* 21.47 (27 Nov. 1902): 2.
"Göttlicher Natur teilhaftig werden." *CBB* 24.23 (8 June 1905): 1-2.

John M. Brenneman

Books

J. M. Brenneman with D. Brenneman, John Brenneman, and M. Brenneman. *Invitation to Sinners.* Mountain Valley, Va.: Joseph Funk & Sons, 1858.

Das Christenthum und der Krieg: eine Predigt, die Leiden der Christen darstellend. Lancaster, Pa.: Johann Bär's Söhnen, 1864.

Christianity and War: A Sermon Setting Forth the Sufferings of Christians. Elkhart, Ind.: John F. Funk, 1868. English ed. of *Das Christenthum.*

Pride and Humility: Discourse, Setting Forth the Characteristics of the Proud and the Humble. Also an Alarm to the Proud. Elkhart, Ind.: John F. Funk, 1873. 1st ed., 1867, and 2nd ed., 1868, lack "Alarm."

Hoffart und Demuth, einander gegenüber gestellt; nebst einer Weckstimme an die stolzen Frauen. Elkhart, Ind.: John F. Funk, 1868. German ed. of *Pride.*

Einfache Lehre, oder deutliche Erklärungen und Ermahnungen über gewisse Schrifstellen. Elkhart, Ind.: Mennonite Publishing Co., 1876.

Plain Teachings or Simple Illustrations and Exhortations from the Word of God. Elkhart, Ind.: Mennonite Publishing Co., 1876. English ed. of *Einfache.*

Eine Aufmunterung der bussfertigen Sünder, und Freude über ihre Bekehrung. Elkhart, Ind.: Mennonite Publishing Co., 1877.

An Encouragement to Penitent Sinners and Joy over Their Conversion. Elkhart, Ind.: Mennonite Publishing Co., 1877. English ed. of *Eine Aufmunterung.*

Hope, Sanctification, and a Noble Determination. Elkhart, Ind.: Mennonite Publishing Co., 1893.

Articles

"A Civil War Petition to President Lincoln [letter of Aug. 19, 1862]." *Mennonite Historical Bulletin* 34.4 (Oct. 1973): 2-3.

"Ought We to Have a Religious Paper?" *HT* 1.1 (Jan. 1864): 2-3. = "Sollten wir ein religiöses Blatt haben?" *HdW* 1.1 (Jan. 1864): 4.

"Peace Be with You All That Are in Christ Jesus." *HT* 1.1 (Jan. 1864): 3-4. = "Friede sei mit euch Allen, die in Christo Jesu sind," *HdW* 1.1 (Jan. 1864): 3-4. *Plain Teachings*, 212-217.

"Affecting Incidents from Canada." *HT* 1.2 (Jan. 1864): 6. = "Wichtig von Canada." *HdW* 1.2 (Feb. 1864): 8.

"What Meanest Thou, O Sleeper? Arise and Call upon Thy God! (Jonah 1.16)," *HT* 1.3 (Mar. 1864): 9-10. = "Was schläfst du? Stehe auf, rufe deinen Gott an." *HdW* 1.3 (Mar. 1864): 9-10.

"Be Ye All of One Mind." *HT* 1.5 (May 1864): 21-22. = "Seid allesammt Gleich gesinnet." *HdW* 1.5 (May 1864): 21-22. *Plain Teachings*, 137-152. *Einfache Lehre*, 121-135.

"A Visit." *HT* 1.5 (May 1864): 25. = "Ein Besuch." *HdW* 1.5 (May 1864): 26-27.

"Extracts from Letter, &c." *HT* 1.6 (June 1864): 34. = "Auszüge aus Briefen, u." *HdW* 1.6 (June 1864): 34.

"Repentance." *HT* 1.7 (July 1864): 37-39. = "Busse." *HdW* 1.7 (July 1864): 37-39. *Plain Teachings*, 28-53.

"The Art of Writing a Great Privilege." *HT* 1.8 (Aug. 1864): 52. = "Die Schreibkunst, ein grosse Vorrecht." *HdW* 1.8 (Aug. 1864): 51.

"A Journey to Indiana." *HT* 1.9 (Sept. 1864): 55-56. = "Eine Reise nach Indiana." *HdW* 1.9 (Sept. 1864): 57-58.

"A Hint to Our Ministers." *HT* 1.9 (Sept. 1864): 56. = "Ein Wink an unsere Prediger." *HdW* 1.9 (Sept. 1864): 59.

"A Warning to Parents." *HT* 1.10 (Oct. 1864): 66. = "Eine Warnung für Eltern." *HdW* 1.10 (Oct. 1864): 66.

"Halte deine Zunge im Zaume! Jac 3.5." *HdW* 1.10 (Oct. 1864): 67; plus letter extract of *HT* 1.10 (Oct. 1864): 68.

Letter extract. *HT* 1.10 (Oct. 1864): 68.

"A Visit to Erie Co., N.Y. and Canada." *HT* 2.1 (Jan. 1865): 3. = "Ein Besuch in Erie Co. N.Y. und Canada." *HdW* 2.1 (Jan. 1865): 3.

"A Visit to Illinois." *HT* 2.1 (Jan. 1865): 3. = "Ein Besuch in Illinois." *HdW* 2.1 (Jan. 1865): 3.

"Not Wholly Endorsed." *HT* 2.3 (Mar. 1865): 22. = "Damit nicht ganz einstimmig." *HdW* 2.3 (Mar. 1865): 22.

"Christian Love." *HT* 2.4 (Apr. 1865): 26-28. = "Die christliche Liebe." *HdW* 2.4 (Apr. 1865): 26-29. *Plain Teachings*, 54-74. *Einfache Lehre*, 46-66.

"Das Osterlamm." *HdW* 2.5 (May 1865): 33. Reprinted as "Christus das Osterlamm" in *Einfache Lehre*, 180-184.

"The Fear of God." *HT* 2.6 (June 1865): 41-42. = "Die Furcht Gottes." *HdW* 2.6 (June 1865): 41-42.

"A Visit." *HT* 2.7 (July 1865): 54. = "Ein Besuch." *HdW* 2.7 (July 1865): 54-55.

"Christ the True Foundation, and God's Building." *HT* 2.9 (Sept. 1865): 73-75. = "Christus das wahre Fundament, und Gottes Gebäude betrachtet." *HdW* 2.9 [Sept. 1865]: 73-75. *Plain Teachings*, 5-28. *Einfache Lehre*, 5-26. Sequel to previous item, "A Visit" = "Ein Besuch."

"An Answer." *HT* 2.9 (Sept. 1865): 68-69. = "Eine Antwort." *HdW* 2.9 (Sept. 1865): 68-69.

"A Visit to Indiana." *HT* 2.12 (Dec. 1865): 101. = "Ein Besuch nach Indiana." *HdW* 2.12 (Dec. 1865): 101.

"An Appeal to the Readers of the Herald." *HT* 3.1 (Jan. 1866): 5. = "Ein Aufruf an die Leser des Herolds." *HdW* 3.1 (Jan. 1866): 6-7.

" 'How Readest Thou?' (Luke 10:26)." *HT* 3.2 (Feb. 1866): 9. Reprinted in *HT* 7.2 (Feb. 1870): 21.

"Unity Among the Brethren." *HT* 3.3 (Mar. 1866): 17. = "Die brüderliche Eintracht." *HdW* 3.3 (Mar. 1866): 17.

"Answer." *HT* 3.3 (Mar. 1866): 21. = "Antwort." *HdW* 3.3 (Mar. 1866): 21.

Letter excerpt. *HT* 3.4 (Apr. 1866): 35. = Letter excerpt. *HdW* 3.4 (Apr. 1866): 35.

"The Ever Living Soul." *HT* 3.5 (May 1866): 38-39. = "Die unsterbliche Seele." *HdW* 3.6 (June 1866): 49-50. *Plain Teachings*, 197-205. *Einfache Lehre*, 196-203.

"Pride and Humility." *HT* 3.6 (June 1866): 45-46; 3.7 (July 1866): 53-54; 3.8 (Aug. 1866): 61-62. = "Hoffart und Demuth einander gegenübergestellt." *HdW* 3.6 (June 1866): 45-46; 3.7 (June 1866): 53-54; 3.8 (Aug. 1866): 61-62. Reprinted as tracts: *Pride and Humility*, and *Hoffart und Demuth*.

John M. Brenneman with J. F. Funk. "A Journey from Chicago to Columbiana, Ohio." *HT* 3.6 (June 1866): 50; 3.7 (July 1866): 56. = "Eine Reise von Chicago nach Columbiana, Ohio." *HdW* 3.6 (June 1866): 50; 3.7 (July 1866): 56.

"A Visit to Indiana and Michigan." *HT* 3.6 (June 1866): 50-51. = "Ein Besuch in Indiana und Michigan." *HdW* 3.6 (June 1866): 50-51.

"From Allen Co., Ohio." *HT* 3.12 (Dec. 1866): 96. = "Aus Allen County, Ohio." *HdW* 3.12 (Dec. 1866): 96-97.

"Schaffet, dass ihr selig werdet, mit Furcht und Zittern." *HdW* 4.1 (Jan. 1867): 1-2. Reprinted as "Eine Neujahrsstimme" in *Einfache Lehre*, 173-178, with long poem added, 178-180.

"Contrast Between the Righteous and the Wicked." *HT* 4.3 (Mar. 1867): 33-36; 4.4 (Apr. 1867): 49-52. = "Unterschied zwischen dem Gerechten und Gottlosen." *HdW* 4.3 (Mar. 1867): 33-36; 4.4 (Apr. 1867): 49-52. *Plain Teachings*, 75-104. *Einfache Lehre*, 66-92.

"A Journey to Indiana." *HT* 4.3 (Mar. 1867): 41. = "Eine Reise nach Indiana." *HdW* 4.3 (Mar. 1867): 41-42.

"Account of a Journey to Illinois, Iowa, and Missouri." *HT* 4.8 (Aug. 1867): 121-124. = "Bericht einer Besuchsreise nach Illinois, Iowa und Missouri." *HdW* 4.8 (Aug. 1867): 121-124.

"A Visit." *HT* 4.10 (Oct. 1867): 152-153. = "Ein Besuch." *HdW* 4.10 (Oct. 1867): 152.

"A Journey to Virginia and Pennsylvania." *HT* 4.11 (Nov. 1867): 169-170. = "Besuchsreise nach Virginien und Pennsylvanien." *HdW* 4.11 (Nov. 1867): 170-171.

"Visit to Michigan." *HT* 4.12 (Dec. 1867): 186-187. = "Besuchreise nach Michigan." *HdW* 4.12 (Dec. 1867): 187-188.

"Matthew 19:9." *HT* 5.2 (Feb. 1868): 26-28. = "Eine Frage über Matth. 19.9 beantwortet." *HdW* 5.2 (Feb. 1868): 27-28.

"Eine Wechstimme an die stolzen Frauen." *HdW* 5.4 (Apr. 1868): 51-54. In *Hoffart und Demut* (1868), 46-69. As "An Alarm to the Proud," in *Pride and Humility* (1873 edition), 50-73.

"A Journey to Missouri." *HT* 5.7 (July 1868): 105-106. = "Eine Reise nach Missouri." *HdW* 5.7 (July 1868): 105-106.

"I Beg Pardon." *HT* 5.7 (July 1868): 106. = "Ich halte um Geduld an." *HdW* 5.7 (July 1868): 106.

"Visit to Seneca County, O." *HT* 5.8 (Aug. 1868): 121. = "Ein Besuch nach Seneca County, O." *HdW* 5.8 (Aug. 1868): 121.

"A Visit." *HT* 5.11 (Nov. 1868): 171-72. = "Ein Besuch." *HdW* 5.11 (Nov. 1868): 172.

"Report of the Sunday School in Allen County, Ohio." *HT* 6.1 (Jan. 1869): 3-4. = "Ein Bericht von der Sonntag-Schule in Allen County, Ohio." *HdW* 6.1 (Jan. 1869): 2-3.

"From Allen Co., Ohio." *HT* 6.4 (Apr. 1869): 57. = "Aus Allen Co., Ohio." *HdW* 6.4 (Apr. 1869): 57.

"Der äusserliche Schmuck verboten." *HdW* 6.7 (July 1869): 98. *Einfache Lehre*, 190-193.

"A Visit to Pennsylvania." *HT* 6.7 (July 1869): 104-105. = "Ein Besuch nach Pennsylvanien." *HdW* 6.7 (July 1869): 104-105.

"Be Serious When You Write for the 'Herald.'" *HT* 6.7 (July 1869): 107. = "Seid ernsthaft, wenn ihr für den Herold schreibet." *HdW* 6.7 (July 1869): 101.

"Das grüne und dürre Holz." *HdW* 6.9 (Sept. 1869): 131-132. *Einfache Lehre*, 185-190.

"Aus dem Tod in das Leben." *HdW* 7.1 (Jan. 1870): 5.

"Leprosy." *HT* 7.1 (Jan. 1870): 10-11. = "Der Aussatz." *HdW* 7.1 (Jan. 1870): 10-11.

"Water Baptism Not the New Birth." *HT* 7.3 (Mar. 1870): 33-35. = "Die äusserliche Wassertaufe nicht die neue Geburt." *HdW* 7.3 (Mar. 1870): 33-35. *Plain Teachings*, 153-167. *Einfache Lehre*, 135-147.

"Not Literal." *HT* 7.6 (June 1870): 87. = "Nicht buchstäblich." *HdW* 7.4 (Apr. 1870): 61. *Plain Teachings*, 227-229.

"Apollo hat begossen." *HdW* 7.6 (June 1870): 83-84.

"Worte des Trostes." *HdW* 7.8 (Aug. 1870): 113-114. *Einfache Lehre*, 203-207.

"Auszug eines Briefes." *HdW* 7.8 (Aug. 1870): 123-124.

"Sin Not with the Tongue." *HT* 7.12 (Dec. 1870): 188. = "Sündiget nicht mit der Zunge." *HdW* 7.12 (Dec. 1870): 189-190.

"Das Neue Jahr." *HdW* 8.1 (Jan. 1871): 1.

"Serious Reflections." *HT* 8.1 (Jan. 1871): 11. = "Bedeutungsvolle Betrachtungen." *HdW* 8.1 (Jan. 1871): 4.

"Account of a Journey." *HT* 8.7 (July 1871): 107-108. = "Reiseberichte." *HdW* 8.7 (July 1871): 107.

"How the World Lieth in Wickedness." *HT* 8.8 (Aug. 1871): 115-116. = "Wie

die Welt in Argen liegt." *HdW* 8.8 (Aug. 1871): 113-114. *Plain Teachings*, 218-223.
"Thou Shalt Die." *HT* 8.9 (Sept. 1871): 135.
"Antwort auf Obiges." *HdW* 8.10 (Oct. 1871): 158.
"What Jesus Has Commanded, and Also What He Has Forbidden." *HT* 9.2 (Feb. 1872): 17-19. = "Was Jesus geboten, befohlen und auch verboten hat." *HdW* 9.2 (Feb. 1872): 17-19.
"The Unanswerable Question of the Great Salvation." *HT* 9.6 (June 1872): 81-83; 9.7 (July 1872): 97-99; 9.8 (Aug. 1872): 113-115. = "Die unbeantwortliche Frage von der grossen Seligkeit." *HdW* 9.6 (June 1872): 81-83; 9.7 (July 1872): 97-99; 9.8 (Aug. 1872): 113-115. *Plain Teachings*, 104-136. *Einfache Lehre*, 92-121.
"A Visit to Indiana." *HT* 9.7 (July 1872): 105. = "Ein Besuch in Indiana." *HdW* 9.7 (July 1872): 105.
"Further Account of the Death of Henry A. Brenneman." *HT* 9.10 (Oct. 1872): 153-154. = "Ferneren Bericht von dem Tod des Heinrich A. Brenneman." *HdW* 9.10 (Oct. 1872): 153-154.
"Shall the Saints Know Each Other in Heaven?" *HT* 10.5 (May 1873): 81-82. = "Werden die Heiligen im Himmel einander kennen?" *HdW* 10.6 (June 1873): 97-98. *Plain Teachings*, 229-236.
"Pride and Fashion." *HT* 10.5 (May 1873): 93. = "Hochmuth und Mode." *HdW* 10.5 (May 1873): 91.
"A Hint to Emigrants." *HT* 10.6 (June 1873): 108-109. = "Ein Wink an die Emigranten." *HdW* 10.6 (June 1873): 106-107.
"Idolatry." *HT* 10.7 (July 1873): 113-115. = "Abgötterei." *HdW* 10.6 (June 1873): 99-101. *Plain Teachings*, 168-177. *Einfache Lehre*, 164-173.
"Be Diligent." *HT* 10.7 (July 1873): 119. = "Wir sollen fleissig sein." *HdW* 10.7 (July 1873): 117-118. *Plain Teachings*, 237-239.
"Our Duty Towards the Russian Brethren." *HT* 10.10 (Oct. 1873): 165-166. = "Unsere Pflicht gegen unsere Russischen Brüdern." *HdW* 10.10 (Oct. 1873): 165.
"Warning Voice." *HT* 11.1 (Jan. 1874): 4-5.
"Let Us Have Compassion on the Poor." *HT* 11.2 (Feb. 1874): 22-23. = "Habt doch Mitleiden für die Armen." *HdW* 11.2 (Feb. 1874): 22-23.
"The Signs and Miracles of Christ Sufficient for Believers." *HT* 11.2 (Feb. 1874): 34-36.
"An Encouragement to Earnest Prayer." *HT* 11.9 ((Sept. 1874): 145-147. = "Eine Aufmunterung zum ernstlichen Gebet." *HdW* 11.9 (Sept. 1874): 146-48. *Plain Teachings*, 185-197. *Einfache Lehre*, 147-157. Also reprinted as booklets.
"Of the Unpardonable Sin." *HT* 11.9 (Sept. 1874): 148-149.
"The Better Way Recommended." *HT* 12.6 (June 1875): 83-84. = "Es ist besser, in das Klaghaus gehen, denn in das Trinkhaus." *HdW* 4.5 (May 1867): 67-68. *Plain Teachings*, 178-184. = *Einfache Lehre*, 158-164.

"Eine Aufmunterung der bussfertigen Sünder, und Freude über ihre Bekehrung." *HdW* 12.7 (July 1875): 97-101. = "An Encouragement to Penitent Sinners and Joy over Their Conversion." *HT* 13.4 (Apr. 1876): 65-70. Reprinted as booklets: German, ca. 1877; English, 1877.
"A Question Answered." *HT* 12.11 (Nov. 1875): 186-187. Reprinted as "Mammon of Unrighteousness" in *Plain Teachings*, 224-226.
"Put Not Your Trust in Riches." *HT* 13.5 (May 1876): 86-87.
"A Mistake Corrected." *HT* 13.8 (Aug. 1876): 135.
"The Right Way to Be Saved." *HT* 13.11 (Nov. 1876): 178. *Plain Teachings*, 244-248.
"Menno Simon's Ansicht über den Gebrauch des Schwerts unter den Christen." *HdW* 14.9 (Sept. 1877): 140-141.
"The Two Spirits." *HT* 15.2 (Feb. 1878): 32.
"Answer to Question in March Herald." *HT* 16.4 (Apr. 1879): 73.
"An Alarming Voice for the New Year." *HT* 17.1 (Jan. 1880): 4-5.
"Sanctification." *HT* 17.6 (June 1880): 101-103. = "Heiligung." *HdW* 17.6 (June 1880): 102-105. Reprinted in *Hope, Sanctification, and a Noble Determination* (1893), 5-12.
"A Noble Determination After a Conflict." *HT* 19.7 (1 Apr. 1882): 97-99. Reprinted in *Hope, Sanctification, and a Noble Determination* (1893), 13-20.
"When and Where Was Paul Converted?" *HT* 20.21 (1 Nov. 1883): 321-322.
"Hope unto the End." *HT* 22.11 (1 June 1885): 161-162. Reprinted in *Hope, Sanctification, and a Noble Determination* (1893), 1-4.
"Baptism by Pouring Asserted." *HT* 22.11 (1 June 1885): 170. = "Die Taufe durch Begiessen." *HdW* 22.11 (1 June 1885): 169-170.
"A Caution." *HT* 23.7 (1 Apr. 1886): 103.

Titles in *Plain Teachings* Not Identified in *HT*
"A Good Advice to the Young," 205-211.
"Christians Ought Not Laugh Aloud," 242-243.
"Man on Earth a Sojourner Only," 239-241.

Titles in *Einfache Lehre* Not Identified in *HdW*.
"Christen sollten nicht laut lachen," 207-208.
"Wer wollte nicht gerne ewig reich sein?" 193-196.

John Holdeman
Der alte Grund und Fundament aus Gottes Wort gefasst und geschrieben. Lancaster, Pa.: Johann Bär's Söhnen, 1862.
The Old Ground and Foundation. Lancaster, Pa.: John Baer's Sons, 1863. English ed. of *Der alte Grund.*
Eine Geschichte der Gemeinde Gottes. Lancaster, Pa.: Johann Bär's Söhnen, 1875.

A History of the Church of God. Lancaster, Pa.: John Baer's Sons, 1876. English ed. of *Eine Geschichte*.

Spiegel der Wahrheit. Lancaster, Pa.: Johann Bär's Söhnen, 1880.

A Mirror of Truth. Moundridge, Kan.: Gospel Publishers, 1956. 5th printing, 1987. English ed. of *Spiegel*.

A Treatise on Redemption, Baptism, and the Passover and the Lord's Supper (Jasper County, Mo.: the author, 1890).

Heinrich Egly

Book

Das Friedensreich Christi oder Auslegung der Offenbarung St. Johannes und noch etliche andere Artikel. Edited by Jacob Schenbeck. Adams County, Ind.: 1895.

Articles

"Die Eingezogenheit der Christen." *HdW* 10.11 (Nov. 1873): 178.

"Unser Bestreben nach oben." *HdW* 10.12 (Dec. 1873): 195-196.

"Essen und Trinken das Fleisch und Blut Christi." *HdW* 14.11 (Nov. 1877): 167-168.

"Vom Friedensreich Jesu Christi." *HdW* 14.12 (Dec. 1877): 183-185; reprinted in *HdW* 32.8 (15 Apr. 1895): 116-118; and in *Das Friedensreich Christi*, 1-10. English trans., "The Kingdom of Peace of Jesus Christ," in *The Evangelical Mennonite*, 15 August 1965, 8-10.

"Ein neu Gebot." *HdW* 15.2 (Feb. 1878): 19-20. In *Das Friedensreich Christi*, 11-16.

"Säen und Ernten." *HdW* 15.12 (Dec. 1878): 201-202.

"Die Sanftmüthigen." *HdW* 16.5 (May 1879): 85.

"Die Pfingsten." *HdW* 16.6 (June 1879): 101. In *Das Friedensreich Christi*, 21-23.

"Das Osterlamm." *HdW* 16.6 (June 1879): 102-103. In *Das Friedensreich Christi*, 17-20.

"Jesus der wahre Helfer." *HdW* 16.9 (Sept. 1879): 166.

"Suchet und forschet." *HdW* 20.14 (15 July 1883): 211-212.

"Einladung." *HdW* 20.17 (1 Sept. 1883): 265.

"Die seligmachende Glaube." *HdW* 27.11 (1 June 1890): 161-162. In *Das Friedensreich Christi*, 24-25.

"Lasset euch Niemand verführen in keinerlei Weise." *CBB* 1.16 (15 Aug. 1882): 125-126. Responses in *CBB* 1.17 (1 Sept. 1882): 133-134.

"Etwas über die Wirkung des Satans." *CBB* 1.19 (1 Oct. 1882): 149-150.

"Warum sind so wenige Christenbekenner glücklich und selig?" *CBB* 3.6 (15 Mar. 1884): 42.

"Etwas vom lebendigen Glaube." In *Das Friedensreich Christi*, 26-28.

"Gott will die Sünde an das Licht bringen." In *Das Friedensreich Christi*, 29-30.

"Only One Gospel." In *Das Friedensreich Christi*, 31-32.
"Vom Glauben und der Gewissheit." Flanagan, Ill.: C. R. Egle, n.d. A tract.

Unpublished
"Autobiography." Adams County, Ind., 1887. Trans. Emma Steury. In Mennonite Historical Library, Bluffton College; Mennonite Church Archives, Goshen College; Archives of the Evangelical Mennonite Church, Administrative Headquarters in Fort Wayne, Ind.; Egly Memorial Library of the Evangelical Mennonite Church of Berne, Ind.

John S. Coffman and Daniel Kauffman

Articles
Coffman, John S. "Noah Troyer." HT 17.10 (Oct. 1880): 180-181.
Coffman, John S. "Noah Troyer." *HdW* 17.12 (Dec. 1880): 225.
Coffman, John S. "Foot Washing." *HT* 25.15 (1 Aug. 1888): 229.
Coffman, John S. "The Atonement." *HT* 23 (1886): 6.

Books
Coffman, John S., Comp. *Outlines and Notes Used at the Bible Conference Held at Johnstown, Pennsylvania, from Dec. 27, 1897, to Jan. 7, 1898*. Elkhart, Ind.: Mennonite Publishing Co., 1898.
Kauffman, Daniel. *Manual of Bible Doctrines, Setting Forth the General Principles of the Plan of Salvation*. Elkhart, Ind.: Mennonite Publishing Co., 1898.
Kauffman, Daniel, ed. *Bible Doctrine: A Treatise on the Great Doctrines of the Bible Pertaining to God, Angels, Satan, and the Salvation, Duties and Destiny of Man*. Scottdale, Pa.: Mennonite Publishing House, 1914.
Kauffman, Daniel, ed. *Doctrines of the Bible: A Brief Discussion of the Teachings of God's Word*. Scottdale, Pa.: Mennonite Publishing House, 1928.

Index

The Author

J. Denny Weaver is Professor of Religion and chair of the Department of Religion, History, Political Science, and Philosophy at Bluffton (Ohio) College. He teaches courses in Christian theology and ethics, Mennonite history and thought, Protestant history and thought, Catholic history and thought, and sacred and civil religion in America.

Weaver was born in 1941 to Alvin and Velma Weaver, of Kansas City, Kansas. With his family he attended the local Argentine Mennonite Church, where he became a member. After two years at Hesston (Kan.) College and two at Goshen (Ind.) College, he graduated in 1963 with a major in mathematics. Then he studied for two years at Associated Mennonite Biblical Seminaries (now Seminary; AMBS, Elkhart, Ind.), focusing on Old Testament studies.

While the Vietnam War was widening, Weaver volunteered with Mennonite Central Committee for a term of alternative service as a conscientious objector. He and his wife spent a year in French language study and then served during 1966-68 in Algeria under the MCC Teachers Abroad Program (TAP). Weaver taught English in an Algerian public school, using French as the language of instruction.

Weaver tried to understand events and attitudes in the newly liberated Algeria as well as in France, formerly its colonial ruler. As a result, he became more aware of the need to know history for interpreting the current situation. This reoriented his academic interests toward historical studies. After the MCC assignment, Weaver focused on church history for a year at Kirchliche Hochschule Bethel, in Germany, and continued that emphasis in his final year at AMBS. At Duke University, his doctoral studies were in church history, with a specialty in sixteenth-century Anabaptism.

After teaching at Goshen College for a year, Weaver joined the Bluffton faculty. For two decades he has been refining historical perspectives that shape his work in theology. His goal is to develop systematic theology that reflects an Anabaptist-Mennonite and peace-church historical tradition and incorporates his belief that rejecting violence is intrinsic to the gospel of Jesus Christ.

Weaver is a frequent participant in conferences on Mennonite and believers church theology and has written widely on aspects of Mennonite history and thought. His *Becoming Anabaptist* (Herald Press, 1987) is the first book to synthesize the account of Anabaptist origins from the perspective of polygenesis historiography. It stresses the relevance of that story for the contemporary peace church.

His many articles and essays have appeared in books and dictionaries, and in academic and church periodicals, such as *Mennonite Quarterly Review, Conrad Grebel Review, Journal of Mennonite Studies, Modern Theology, Archiv für Reformationsgeschichte, Fides et Historia, Christian Scholar's Review, Mennonite Life, Pennsylvania Mennonite Heritage, Gospel Herald,* and *The Mennonite.* Subjects include Anabaptist and Mennonite theology from the sixteenth century to the present, use of a peace church perspective to analyze the classic statements of Christology and atonement from the early and medieval church, and the development of statements of Christology, atonement, and other issues for the contemporary peace churches.

Weaver is a member of the executive committee of the Mennonite Historical Society. He also belongs to the American Academy of Religion, the American Society of Church History, and the Conference on Faith and History.

He is a member of the First Mennonite Church of Bluffton, where he has served as deacon, chair of the pastoral search committee, and teacher of Sunday school classes. He served on the Peace, Service, and Justice Committee of Central District Conference of the General Conference Mennonite Church, and on three Christian Peacemaker Team delegations to Haiti. In 1990-91, he was visiting professor of theology at Canadian Mennonite Bible College (Winnipeg).

In 1965 Denny married Mary Lois Wenger (a daughter of J. C. Wenger, author of SAMH, no. 10). They have three grandchildren and three adult daughters, Sonia Katharina, Lisa Denise, and Michelle Therese.